Philosophical Writings of Etienne Bonnot, Abbé de Condillac

Philosophical Writings of Etienne Bonnot, Abbé de Condillac

Translated by Franklin Philip
with the collaboration of Harlan Lane

LEA

LAWRENCE ERLBAUM ASSOCIATES, PUBLISHERS

1982 Hillsdale, New Jersey   London

Lawrence Erlbaum Associates, Inc. Publishers
365 Broadway
Hillsdale, New Jersey 07642

Library of Congress Cataloging in Publication Data

Condillac, Etienne Bonnot, de, 1714-1780.
    The Philosophical writings of Etienne
Bonnot de Condillac.

    1. Thought and thinking—Addresses, essays,
lectures.   2. Senses and sensation—Addresses,
essays, lectures.   I. Title.
B1982.E5   1982   194   81-12462
ISBN 0-89859-181-3   AACR2

Printed in the United States of America

Contents

Preface

**BOOK I:
A TREATISE ON SYSTEMS**

BOOK II:
A TREATISE ON THE SENSATIONS

Part One: On Senses That By Themselves
Do Not Judge External Objects

**BOOK III:
LOGIC, OR THE FIRST DEVELOPMENTS OF THE
ART OF THINKING**

**Part One: How Nature Itself Teaches Us To Analyze; And How
        With This Method We Explain The Origin And
        Development Of Either Ideas Or The Faculties Of The Mind**

**Part Two: Analysis Considered In Its Means And Effects,
    Or The Art Of Reasoning Reduced To A Well-Formed Language**

Preface

In the course of the eighteenth century, two near contemporaries—David Hume (1711-1776), writing in English, and Etienne Bonnot, abbé of Condillac (1715-1780), in French—argued independently that the only available medium for constructing a rational understanding of reality is the individual person's successive instants in the having of sensations.

Within subsequent philosophy, the brilliant Scotsman has enjoyed a fame that almost totally eclipses the memory of the dogged Frenchman. This translation of three of the philosophical works of Condillac is being published in the hope of redressing the balance between the two.

Hume was skeptical about the reasonableness of certain common-sense assumptions, and the tensions created by his practically intolerable but seemingly irrefutable skepticism have helped to keep Humean metaphysics alive. Condillac, despite his official status as metaphysician for the acute critics of the French Enlightenment, was himself mostly not skeptical. The absence of tension between his sensationalism and common sense may, together with his compatriots' characteristic impatience with empirical ideas, account for Condillac's comparative obscurity even in French philosophy.

Condillac has had a continuing influence, however, on Western thought, for his constructive ideas have been incorporated into the behavioral sciences. From the first psychiatrist Philippe Pinel's use of *observation* of the mentally infirm to the application of Maria Montessori's *sensory* training of the child, the social sciences have explicitly relied on Condillac's genetic theory of mental operations.

Of the three books included in this volume, the first, the *Treatise on Systems* (1746), contrasts Condillac's philosophic system with rationalistic systems that end in contemplation rather than observation. The *Treatise on Sensations* (1754) details the development of knowing, desiring, and acting, beginning with a single impression in one sense modality and ending with the full reconstitution of the external and mental worlds of the individual. Finally, the posthumously published *Logic* (1792) elaborates Condillac's universal method for acquiring knowledge by a child, an adult, or a discipline—the method of analysis.

Condillac came from a family belonging to the minor aristocracy of Grenoble. After receiving holy orders in the Catholic church, he dressed in a cassock but did not otherwise pursue the priestly vocation. Most of his adult life was spent in Paris, where he became acquainted with the leading intellectual figures of the time, including Voltaire, and often dined with Rousseau and Diderot. Accounts of salon life suggest that he was socially unassertive. He died at his estate in the Loire valley at the age of sixty-five.

These books have been translated from the French edition of Condillac's works edited by Georges Le Roy, *Oeuvres Philosophiques de Condillac.* Paris: Presses Universitaires de France, 1948.

This publication was made possible by grant number RL 28904-77-1364 from the Translation Program, Division of Research Grants and by grant number RP-2038-80 from the Publications Support Program of the National Endowment for the Humanities.

Franklin Philip
Harlan Lane

Philosophical Writings of Etienne Bonnot, Abbé de Condillac

BOOK I:

A TREATISE ON SYSTEMS

1 Three Sorts of Systems Should be Distinguished

A system is nothing other than the arrangement of different parts of an art or science in an order in which they all lend each other support and in which the last ones are explained by the first ones. Parts that explain other parts are called principles, and the fewer principles a system has the more perfect it is. It is even desirable to reduce all principles to a single one.

In the works of philosophers we can observe three sorts of principles from which three sorts of systems are formed.

The principles I put in the first class, as the most fashionable ones, are general or abstract maxims. They must be so evident or so well-proven that we cannot cast doubt on them. In fact, if they were uncertain, we could not be certain of the conclusions we draw from them. The author of the *Art of Thinking* is speaking about these principles when he says:[1]

> Everyone agrees that it is important to have in mind several axioms and principles that, being clear and indubitable, can serve us as a basis for understanding the most hidden things. But those that are generally given are so rarely useful that it is quite pointless to know them. For what they call the first principle of knowledge, "it is impossible for the same thing to be and not to be," is perfectly clear and certain; but I find no occasion where it can ever serve to give us any knowledge. I thus believe that the following can be more useful.

He then gives us a first principle: "Everything included in the clear and distinct idea of a thing can be truly affirmed of it." As a second principle: "The

---

[1]Part 4, Chapter 7.

idea of everything that we conceive clearly and distinctly includes at least possible existence"; as a third principle: "Nothing cannot be the cause of anything." But it would be needless to relate the other principles; the ones just mentioned are sufficient to serve as examples.

Philosophers ascribe such great virtue to these sorts of principles that they naturally have tried to increase their number. Metaphysicians particularly distinguished themselves in this way. Descartes, Malebranche, Liebniz, and others outdid each other in lavishing them on us, and we have no one else to blame now but ourselves if we do not penetrate as far as "the most hidden things."

Principles of the second kind are suppositions formulated to explain things that we could not otherwise give an account of. If these suppositions do not appear impossible and if they provide some explanation of known phenomena, philosophers do not doubt that they have discovered the true guiding principles of nature. Would it be possible, they say, for a false supposition to yield an appropriate outcome? Whence arises the opinion that the explanation of phenomena proves the truth of a supposition, and that we should judge a system less by its principles than by the way it explains things. Suppositions that are at first arbitrary are considered to become indisputable through the skill with which they are employed.

The metaphysicians were as inventive with this second kind of principle as with the first. And because of their work, metaphysics no longer encountered anything that could be a mystery for it. In their language, metaphysics means the science of first truths, the first principles of things. But it must be agreed that we do not find this science in their works.

Abstract ideas are merely ideas constructed out of what several particular ideas have in common. An example is the idea of animal. It is extracted from what belongs alike to the ideas of man, horse, monkey, and so on. In this way, an abstract idea can appear to explain what we observe in particular objects. For example, if we ask why the horse walks, drinks, or eats, someone will give a highly philosophical answer stating that it is merely because the horse is an animal. When we analyze this answer, however, it merely means that the horse walks, drinks, and eats because in fact it walks, drinks, and eats. But people are rarely dissatisfied with an initial answer. It seems that their curiosity leads them less to learn about one thing than to raise questions about many things. The philosopher's confident manner obliges them to do this. They would fear appearing stupid if they insisted too much on the same point. It is enough for the oracular pronouncement to be composed of familiar expressions, and they will be ashamed of not understanding it. Or if they cannot close their eyes to its obscurity, a single look from their teacher would appear to clear it up. Can we doubt matters when he in whom we place all our confidence does not doubt them himself? Thus we have nothing to be surprised at if abstract principles have proliferated and have always been regarded as the source of our knowledge.

Abstract ideas are absolutely necessary to put order in our knowledge because they indicate the class of each idea. This is their sole proper use. But to suppose that abstract ideas are formed so as to lead us to some knowledge of particulars is all the more unenlightened as they themselves are made up only of that knowledge. When I criticize abstract principles, then, do not suspect me of demanding that we relinquish all abstract ideas. That would be ridiculous. I am merely claiming that we ought never to take them for principles appropriate for leading to discoveries.

As for suppositions, they are such a handy expedient for ignorance, imagination makes them up with so much pleasure and so little pain. It is from our beds that we create, we govern the universe. All this costs no more than a dream, and philosophers dream readily.

It is less easy to consult experience and to assemble facts with discrimination. That is why we rarely take only well-established facts for principles, although perhaps we have many more of them than we think. For want of the habit of using them, however, we do not know how to apply them. To all indications, we have the explanation of many phenomena already close at hand but we look for it afar. The gravity of bodies, for example, has always been a well-established fact, but it is only in our own day that it has been recognized as a principle.

True systems, the only ones that merit the name, are based on principles of this last kind. For it is only by means of these principles that we can explain the things whose mainsprings we are permitted to discover. I shall call abstract systems those based only on abstract principles, and hypotheses those based only on suppositions. By mixing these different sorts of principles we could form still other sorts of systems. However, as they would always be more or less related to one of the three I have just mentioned, there is no need to make up new classes of them.

The only proper scientific principles are established facts. How then could others have been imagined? This is what we are going to find out.

Systems are older than philosophers. Nature creates them, and there were no inadequate systems when nature was man's only teacher. For then a system was and could only be the result of observation. It had not yet been suggested that everything could be explained. Man had needs, and he sought only the means for satisfying them.

Only observation could reveal these means. And man observed because he was forced to. Ignorant of what has since been called a principle, man at least had the advantage of steering clear of many errors, for a start in knowledge is required to go astray, and it often seems that philosophers had only this start.

Therefore, man observed, that is, he noticed facts related to his needs.

Because he had few needs, he had few observations to make. Because his needs were primary, he was rarely mistaken or at least his errors could be only short-lived: he was soon alerted to these errors since the needs went unsatisfied.

Since observation as yet took place only through trial and error, a man would not always make sure of a fact as soon as he thought he had discerned it. He suspected it, he assumed it, and for lack of anything better, a supposition took the place of discovery, which a new observation either confirmed or disproved.

This is the way that nature guided man and the way he taught himself without noticing that he was going from one bit of knowledge to another by a series of carefully observed facts.

When he had made discoveries related to his needs, it is obvious that to make discoveries of another kind, he had only to keep to the same behavior. A first observation, which would have been only some tentative trial, would have given him hints. These hints would have indicated other observations to make, and these observations would have confirmed or disproved the supposed facts.

Once men had a sufficient number of facts to explain the phenomena they sought the reason for, the systems would have completed themselves, as it were, because the facts would have arranged themselves in an order in which they successively explained each other. Then men would have perceived that every system has a first fact that is its beginning and that for this reason would have been called a "principle," for "principle" and "beginning" are two words that normally mean the same thing.

Suppositions are strictly mere suspicions, and if we need to make them, it is because we are reduced to groping.

As soon as suppositions are mere suspicions, they are not observed facts. Thus they cannot be the principle or beginning of a system. For an entire system would then reduce to a suspicion.

But if they are not the principle or beginning of a system, they are the principle or beginning of our means for discovering one. Now because they are the principle of these means, it has been believed that they are also the principle of the system. Thus two very different things have been confounded.

As we acquire bits of knowledge, we are obliged to assign them to different classes. We have no other way to put them in order. The least general classes are comprised of individuals and are called species in relation to more general classes called genera. Classes that are genera in relation to subordinate classes become themselves species in relation to other more general classes. Thus we go from class to class up to a genus that comprises all of them.

When this distribution has been performed, we have a highly abbreviated way for giving an account of our knowledge. It is to begin with the most general classes. For the highest genus is properly an abbreviated expression that includes all the subordinate classes and that lets us take them all in a glance. When I say "being," for example, I understand "substance" and "modification," "body" and "mind," "quality" and "property." In short, I understand all the divisions and subdivisions included between being and individuals. Thus I should begin with a general class when I want to represent quickly a multiplicity of things. Then it can be said that this general class is a beginning or principle. This is what people were vaguely perceiving when they said: "general ideas and general maxims are the principles of the sciences."

So I repeat that only carefully established facts can be the true principles of the sciences. And if suppositions and general maxims have been taken as the principle of a system, it is because without realizing what they were seeing, people realized that general suppositions and maxims are the principle or beginning of something.

2 On the Uselessness of Abstract Systems

Philosophers who believe in abstract principles will tell you: "Consider attentively the ideas that come closest to the universality of first principles, make propositions out of them, and you will have less general truths; then consider ideas whose universality brings them closest to the discoveries that you have just made and make new propositions out of them; continue in this way, not forgetting to apply your first principles to each proposition that you discover, and you will descend by degrees from general principles to the most specific knowledge."

According to these philosophers, in creating our souls, God is satisfied with engraving certain general principles thereon, and the knowledge that we acquire later consists merely of our deductions from these innate principles. We know that our body is larger than our head only because we apply the principle that a whole is greater than a part to the ideas of body and head. But so that we are not surprised to find we apply this principle without our perceiving it, we are told that it is done by a secret operation, and that our habit of often repeating the same judgments prevents us from observing their true source. According to these philosophers abstract principles are thus so surely the origin of our knowledge that if these principles are taken away from us, it cannot be imagined how any of the most obvious truths could be within our grasp. But these philosophers reverse the order in which our ideas develop.

It is the role of easier ideas to prepare the intellect for more difficult ideas. Now our own experience shows us that ideas are easier as they are less abstract and closer to the senses, and that on the other hand they are harder as they are further from the senses and become more abstract. The reason for this experience is that all our knowledge comes from the senses. An abstract idea must be explained by a less abstract idea, and so on successively until we reach a particular sensory idea.

Moreover, a philosopher's main purpose should be to specify his ideas exactly. Particular ideas and only particular ideas are specified strictly by themselves. On the other hand, abstract notions are naturally vague and have nothing fixed about them, being specified by other ideas. But are these ideas even more abstract? Doubtless not, for such ideas would have even more need of specification. Thus we must resort to particular ideas. Indeed, nothing explains an idea better than the one that gave rise to it. Consequently it is quite wrong to contend that our knowledge has its source in abstract principles.[2]

Besides, what would these principles be? Would they be maxims so universally accepted no one dares dispute them? "It is impossible for a thing to be and not to be at the same time." "Everything that is, is." And other similar ones. It would take a long time to find a philosopher who had derived some knowledge from these maxims. In speculating, they all agree, in truth, that first principles are those that are universally adopted. Their method even has something beguiling about it in the way it is first presented. But to follow them in practice it is curious to see how they soon go their separate ways and with what scorn some of them reject others' principles. It seems to me that one cannot begin such an inquiry without realizing that these sorts of propositions are inadequate to lead to knowledge.

If abstract principles are general propositions, true in every possible case, they are not knowledge so much as an abbreviated way of presenting several bits of particular knowledge acquired before principles had even been thought of. "A whole is greater than any of its parts" means "my body is larger than my arm; my arm is larger than my hand; my hand is larger than my finger," and so on. In short, this axiom involves only particular propositions of this kind. And the truths that we imagine it leads to were known before it was itself.

This method would thus be utterly barren if it were based only on such maxims as these. Thus there are two ways to make it appear fruitful. The first one begins with propositions that, being true in many respects—especially the most salient respects—make it reasonable to suppose that they are true in every case. Indeed, if we understood them and drew only precise conclusions from them, it is obvious that they would be like the principles we have just

---

[2]Locke knew that abstract maxims are not the source of our knowledge. He gives reasons I will not cite since his work is readily available. See the *Essay on Human Understanding*, Book 4, Chapter 7, Sections 9 and 10. But at the end of Section 11 of the same chapter, the authority of the mathematicians has sway over him and he agrees that abstract principles are used as preliminaries to reveal known truths. I believe I have shown the uselessness and the excesses of proceeding in this way. See the *Logic* and the *Art of Thinking*.

discussed. But this is to be thoroughly avoided; on the contrary, they are taken to be true in many respects in which they are completely false. Whereupon they are applied to quite inappropriate things, and conclusions are drawn that seem all the more novel for not being contained in the original proposition. One example is the Cartesian principle: "We can affirm of a thing everything that is included in our clear idea of it." For I will show that this is not always true.[3]

This way of giving a kind of fertility to an abstract system is the most adroit one; the second is rather crude but it is employed just as widely. It consists in imagining something unknown in accordance with something whose ideas are more familiar. When in this way a number of abstract relations and frivolous definitions are formulated, one reasons about the unknown as he would reason about the known. Thus it is that many philosophers employ the language used for physical objects to explain what happens in the mind. They need only imagine some relations between these two substances. We shall see examples of this.

There are thus three sorts of abstract principles commonly used. The first are general propositions true in evey case. The second are propositions that are true in the most salient respects, and for that reason are supposed true in every respect. The last are vague relations imagined between completely different things.

This analysis is sufficient to show that some of these principles lead nowhere, and that others lead only to error. However, there you have the whole art of abstract systems.

If the foregoing reflections are not enough to convince us of the uselessness of these principles, let us give someone the principles of a science that he does not know and ask if he can carry it much further with such feeble help? Let him meditate on these maxims: "The whole is equal to all its parts; add equal magnitudes to equal magnitudes and the wholes will be equal; add unequals to them and they will be unequal." Will he then have what it takes to become a profound geometer?

But to make this clearer, I would rather like to snatch out of his study or school one of those philosophers who see such great fruitfulness in general principles, and offer him the command of an army or government. If he did himself justice, he would probably excuse himself by saying he understood neither war nor politics. But this would be the feeblest possible excuse. Soldiery and politics have their general principles, like all the other sciences. If we teach them to him—which will only take a few minutes—why could he not discover all of their implications, and after a few hours of meditation become a Condé, a Turenne, a Richelieu, or a Colbert? What would stop him

---

[3]Chapter 6, Article 2.

from choosing from among these great men? We can sense how absurd this supposition is because to enjoy the reputation of a good statesmen or general—like that of a good philosopher—it is not enough to lose oneself in vain speculations. But is it less requisite for a philosopher to reason well than for a general or statesman to act well? The general or statesman would have to master or at least carefully study the details of all subordinate tasks whereas a philosopher suddenly becomes a sage, a man for whom nature holds no secrets, and that through the magic of two or three propositions!

Another consideration well-suited to showing the inadequacy of abstract systems is that it is impossible with them to take into account every aspect of a question. For since the notions making up these principles are merely partial ideas, we cannot use them without disregarding many essential considerations. This is why somewhat complicated subjects with a thousand possible angles of approach give rise to a great many abstract systems. For example, it is asked what the origin of evil is. Bayle bases his answer on the principles of the goodness, holiness, and omnipotence of God. Malebranche prefers the principles of order and wisdom. Liebniz believes that only the sufficient reason of God explains everything. Theologians use the principles of freedom, universal providence, and the fall of Adam.[4] The Socinians reject divine prescience. The Origenists assert that our difficulties are not everlasting. Spinoza admits only a blind and fatal necessity. Finally, the Manicheans have always piled up principles on top of principles, absurdities on top of absurdities. I will not discuss the pagan philosophers who, by reasoning from different principles, have stumbled into some of these systems or into others such as metempsychosis.

This example shows us the impossibility of using abstract principles to erect a system embracing all aspects of a question. Nevertheless, philosophers show no hesitation. In these sorts of cases each philosopher has his favorite system which he wants all the others to yield to. Reason plays little part in their choice; usually the passions decide everything on their own. A naturally sweet-tempered and benevolent mind will adopt the principles derived from the goodness of God because he finds nothing greater or more beautiful than to do good. Thus this ought to be the chief trait of divinity to which everything should be referred. Someone else with a powerful imagina-

---

[4]The principles employed by Bayle, Malebranche, Liebniz, and the theologians are truths. That is their one advantage over those of the Socinians, Origenists, and others. But none of these truths is fertile enough for us to explain everything. Bayle is not incorrect in saying that God is holy, good, and omnipotent. He is incorrect in believing these facts are sufficient to create a system. I would say the same about the others. The few truths that our reason can discover and those revealed to us make up part of a system proper for resolving all possible problems, but they are not destined to make it understandable to us, and the church does not approve of the theologians who undertake to explain everything.

tion and high-minded ideas will prefer the principles taken from order and wisdom because nothing pleases him more than in infinite chain of causes and an admirable combination of all the parts of the universe, even of the unhappiness of all creatures is a necessary consequence. Finally a person who is somber, melancholy, misanthropic, and odious to himself and others will have a taste for the words "destiny," "fatality," "necessity," and "chance" because, anxious and discontented with himself and eveything else around him, he is obliged to regard himself as an object of scorn and horror, or to convince himself that there is neither good nor evil, neither order nor disorder. Can he hesitate? Wisdom, honor, virtue, probity—these are vain sounds. Destiny, fatality, chance, necessity—this is his system.

It would be too presumptuous to think that everyone could be straightened out on this subject. When curiosity is combined with a little imagination, we immediately try to extend our sight further, to embrace everything, to know everything. This intention makes us neglect details, the things within our reach. We travel through unknown territory and construct systems. It remains true, however, that to acquire a general and encompassing point of view that is fixed and certain we must begin by familiarizing ourselves with particular truths. Perhaps the early thinkers were mediocre only because they neglected this study. Perhaps one of them would have earned the praise due the greatest men if he had taken greater care to acquire the smallest details of the knowledge necessary for the tasks he set himself. Wise conduct would increase his talents and develop his genius.

Today some physical scientists, particularly chemists, stick simply to collecting phenomena because they recognize that they should take in the effects of nature and discover their interdependence before formulating explanatory principles. The example of their predecessors has served as a lesson. They at least try to avoid the errors that the craze for systems led to. If only other philosophers imitated them!

But in general thinkers have merely tried to increase the number of abstract principles. Descartes, Malebranche, Liebniz, and many others saw a richness in many maxims that no one before them had noticed. Who knows whether some day new philosophers will not give birth to new principles? How many systems have we not created? How many more will we not create? If only we found one system that was nearly universally accepted by all its partisans! But what foundations could anyone have built with systems that undergo a thousand changes in passing through a thousand different hands; that appear and disappear in a twinkling like a jack-in-a-box that are so inconsistent we can often use them to defend both the pro and the con?

Imagine people waking from a deep sleep and, seeing themselves in the middle of a labyrinth, proposing general principles for discovering the way out. What could be more ridiculous? Nevertheless this is how philosophers behave. We are born in the middle of a labyrinth where a thousand turns are laid out for the sole purpose of leading us into error. If there is a way leading to truth, it is not at first apparent. Often it is the one that appears to least warrant our confidence. Thus we cannot be too cautious. Let us proceed slowly, examine carefully all the places we go through, and acquaint ourselves with them so thoroughly that we are able to retrace our steps. It is more important to find ourselves merely where we were at first than to believe prematurely that we are out the labyrinth. This will be proven in the following chapters.

3 On the Misuses of Abstract Systems

If I wanted to systematize some subject all of whose details I had thoroughly studied, I would merely have to observe the relations among its different parts, and to single out those where the parts are so interrelated that the first ones known would be sufficient to explain the others. Thereupon, I would have principles whose applications were so well specified that it would be impossible to restrict them or extend them to cases of a different nature. But when we try to erect a system about some topic whose details are completely unknown, how can we establish the scope of the principles? And when the principles are vague, how can the expressions have any precision? If, however, convinced that I could acquire knowledge only in this way, I devote myself to it completely, if I pile up principles on principles, if I draw conclusion after conclusion, soon foisting them upon myself, I will admire the fruitfulness of this method; I will congratulate myself on my alleged discoveries, and will not doubt the solidity of my system for an instant. Its principles will seem to me natural, its expressions simple, clear, and precise, and the conclusions perfectly derived. Thus the first misuse of systems, which is the source of many others, is that we believe we are acquiring true knowledge when our thoughts only involve words with no definite meaning.

Even more, it is that we are encouraged by the ease and richness of this method and we do not think of doubting the principles on which we have reasoned. On the contrary, persuaded that they are the source of all our knowledge, the more we use them, the less careful we are. If we dared to doubt them, what truth could we lay claim to? This is what has sanctioned the singular maxim that "principles should not be called into question"—a maxim whose misuse is all the greater as there is no error that it cannot lure us into.

Once this axion is adopted, however unreasonable it may be, it is natural to think that we should no longer judge a system other than by the way it explains phenomena. Although it may be based on the clearest ideas and the most certain facts, if it is lacking in this respect, it must be rejected. And we should adopt an absurd system when it explains everything. Such is the excessive blindness people have fallen prey to. As an example I will cite what Bayle wrote about Manicheanism.[5]

> The *clearest*[6] and most *certain* ideas of order teach us that a being that exists by itself, that is necessary and eternal, must be unique, infinite, omnipotent, and endowed with every sort of perfection. Thus, in consulting these ideas, we find nothing *more absurd* than the hypothesis of two eternal and independent principles one of which had no goodness and could thwart the intention of the other. These are what I call *a priori* reasons. They necessarily lead us to reject this hypothesis and to admit only one principle for all things. If only that were required for the goodness of a system, the case would be settled to the confusion of Zoroaster and all of his followers. But to be good, every system needs these two things: one, that its ideas be distinct, and the other, that it can explain phenomena.

These two things are indeed both essential. If clear and certain ideas are insufficient to explain phenomena, we would not know how to construct a system out of them. We should confine ourselves to regarding them as truths belonging to a science that we know only a small part of. Nothing would be less reasonable than to take absurd ideas for principles. That would be trying to explain things that we do not understand by others whose falsity we are well aware of. From which we would have to conclude that, supposing the system of the unity of principle is insufficient to explain phenomena, there is still no reason for admitting the Manichean system as true. An essential condition is missing.

But Bayle reasons very differently. For the purpose of concluding that we must appeal to revelation to destroy the Manichean system, as if revelation were necessary to overturn an opinion admittedly contrary to the clearest and most certain ideas, he invents an argument between Melissus and Zoroaster, and makes the latter say:

> You outdo me in the beauty of your ideas and a priori reasons, and I outdo you in explanations of phenomena and in a posteriori reasons. And since the chief characteristic of a good system is its capacity to explain experiences, and the

---

[5]The Manicheans.

[6]I have italicized the expressions that should be particularly noted.

inability to explain them is by itself a proof that a hypothesis is not good, however beautiful it otherwise seems, agree that, by admitting two principles, I strike home and you do not, you who admit only of a single one.

In supposing that the main feature of a system is to explain phenomena, Bayle adopts one of the most widely received prejudices, which is a consequence of the principle that "principles should not be called into question." It is easy to provide Melissus with a more reasonable answer than Zoroaster's argument.

If the a priori reasons of two systems [I would have him say] are both good, we should prefer the one that explained the phenomena. But if the one system is based on clear and certain ideas and the other on absurd ideas, we should not take account of the latter's seeming to explain phenomena. It does not and cannot explain them, because the true cannot be explained by the false. The absurdity of principles is thus a proof that a hypothesis is not good. It is thus proven that you have not struck home.

As for what you say about a supposition being bad solely because it is inadequate to explain phenomena, I make the following distinctions: the hypothesis is bad if this inadequacy stems from the very foundation of the supposition itself so that its nature makes it unable to explain phenomena. But if this inadequacy comes from the limits of our mind and from the fact that we have not yet acquired enough knowledge to use it to explain everything, it is false that the hypothesis is a bad one. For example, I recognize only a single first principle because by your own admission it is the clearest and most certain idea. But I am unable to grasp the ways of this supreme being, my intelligence is insufficient to explain his works. I limit myself to gathering the different truths that come within my ken and I do not undertake to connect them and to make them into a system explaining all the contradictions that you imagine you see in the universe. In fact, for the truth of the system that God has prescribed, where is the necessity that I be able to understand it? Therefore, agree that the fact that I cannot explain phenomena with a single principle does not warrant your concluding that there are two of them.

You would have to be very prejudiced not to realize how much sounder than Zoroaster's is this reasoning of Melissus.

Physicists have contributed more than a little to giving currency to the principle that "it is enough for a system to explain phenomena." They needed it, especially when they tried to explain how God created and preserved the universe. But if to construct a system we can propose all sorts of principles, take the most absurd ones as the most evident, and entangle various causes without reason, what merit can there be in books of this kind? Would they even be worth refuting if they were not defended by famous authors?

Nevertheless, however clear this abuse, you need only be versed in philosophers' writings to be convinced of how little care they take to avoid it.

Here is the behavior of those who want to create a system—and who does not want to do so? Prejudiced in favor of an idea, often without knowing why, they first take all the words that appear to be related to it. He who tries to work on metaphysics, for example, seizes on the following: "being, substance, essence, nature, attribute, property, mode, cause, effect, freedom, eternity," and the like. Then, on the pretext that we are free to attach to terms any idea we wish, he defines them according to his whims. The one precaution he takes is to choose the definitions most convenient for his purpose. However odd these definitions, he can always find relations among them. This is what gives him the right to draw conclusions and to reason as far as the eye can see. If he goes back over the chain of propositions he has forged in this way, he will find it hard to believe that definitions of words could have led him so far. Moreover, he would scarcely suspect that he had reasoned wholly in vain. He thus concludes that the definitions of words have become definitions of things, and he admires the profundity of his supposed discoveries. As Locke observed about such cases, however, he resembles people who, without money or knowledge of legal tender, would count large sums with tokens that they would call louis, pound, or crown. Whatever calculations they made, their sums would always be mere tokens. Whatever reasoning a philosopher such as the one I am speaking of conducts, his conclusions would never amount to anything more than words.

And that's the story with most, or rather all, abstract systems that involve mere sounds. The same terms are usually found in all, but because each author believes himself justified in defining them in his own way, we outdo each other in drawing very different conclusions, and we seem to suppose that truth depends on the vagaries of our language.

For instance: let *man* be that concerning which you would by these first principles demonstrate anything, and we shall see, that, so far as demonstration is by these principles, it is only verbal and gives us no certain, universal, true proposition or knowledge of any being existing without us. First, a child having framed the *idea* of a *man*, it is probable that his *idea* is just like that picture which the painter makes of the visible appearances joined together; and such a complication of *ideas* together in his understanding makes up the single complex *idea* which he calls man. Whereof white or flesh-colour in *England* being one, the child can demonstrate to you that *a negro is not a man*, because white colour was one of the constant simple *ideas* of the complex *idea* he calls *man*; and therefore he can demontrate, by the principle, *It is impossible for the same thing to be and not to be*, that *a negro is not a man*; the foundation of his certainty being not that universal proposition, which perhaps he never heard nor thought of, but the clear, distinct perception he hath of his own simple *ideas* of black and white, which he cannot be persuaded to take nor can ever mistake one for another, whether he knows that maxim or no; and to this child or anyone who hath such an *idea* which he calls *man*, can you never demonstrate that a *man* hath a soul, because his *idea* of man includes no such notion or *idea* in it. And therefore, to him, the principle of *What is, is* proves not this matter; but it depends upon collection and observation, by which he is to make his complex *idea* called *man*.

Secondly, another that hath gone further in framing and collecting the *idea* he calls *man*, and to the outward shape adds *laughter* and *rational discourse*, may demonstrate that infants and changelings are no men, by this maxim, *It is impossible for the same thing to be and not to be*; and I have discoursed with very rational men who have actually denied that they are *men*.

Thirdly, perhaps another makes up the complex *idea* which he calls *man*, only out of the *ideas* of body in general and the powers of language and reason, and leaves out the shape wholly;[7] this man is able to demonstrate that a man may have no hands but be *quadrupes*, neither of those being included in his *idea* of *man*: and in whatever body or shape he found *speech* and *reason* joined, that was a *man*; because, having a clear knowledge of such a complex *idea*, it is certain that *What is, is*.[8]

I have cited Locke's example at some length because it shows clearly how absurd the use of abstract principles is. Here it is easy to be persuaded of this fact because the principles are applied to familiar things. But when we are dealing with abstract metaphysical ideas, with the indefinite expressions that fill this science, how many contradictions and absurdities will these principles lead to?

The method I am criticizing is too widely accredited not to remain an obstacle to the art of reasoning. Suitable for proving all sorts of opinions at will, it gratifies all the passions as well. It dazzles the imagination by the boldness of the conclusions it leads to. It beguiles the mind because we do not reflect when imagination and passion oppose reflection; and as a necessary consequence, it gives rise to and nourishes a commitment to the most monstrous errors, a love of dispute, and the bitterness with which it is maintained, a disinterest in the truth or insincerity in seeking it. Finally, if the philosopher is in a critical frame of mind, he begins to perceive the uncertainties to which this method leads. Then, convinced that there can be no better method, he no longer adopts any system, he goes to another extreme, and he affirms that there is no knowledge to which we can lay claim.

---

[7]"I can well imagine a man without hands, without feet; I could even imagine him without a head if experience had not taught me that it is there that he thinks. It is thus thought that creates the essential being of man and without which man is inconceivable." *Pensées* of Pascal, Chapter 23, Number 1.

[8]Locke, *Essay on Human Understanding*, Book 4, Chapter 7, Sections 16, 17, 18. We see that Locke was aware of one of the main abuses of abstract principles. Everything he says on this topic comes down to that. It would have been desirable for him to undertake an analysis of the techniques of systems that bear on these kinds of principles.

If philosophers were concerned only with purely speculative matters, we could be spared the trouble of criticizing their performance. It is the least we can do to allow people to speak nonsense when their errors are inconsequential. But we should not expect them to be any wiser in their thinking about practical subjects. Abstract principles are a rich source of paradoxes, and the paradoxes are all the more fascinating as they concern everyday affairs. Consequently, what abuses this method must have led to into morality and politics!

Few philosophers study morality, which may be a blessing. Politics is the prey of a greater number of minds, because it either flatters their ambition or their imagination finds more pleasure in the greater issues that are its object. Moreover, there are few citizens who do not take some interest in government. Unfortunately for the people, this science must thus have more abstract principles than any other.

Experience teaches only too well how political maxims that are true only in certain circumstances become dangerous when taken as a general rule of conduct. And everyone knows that the plans of those in power are defective only because they are based on principles that are only partially understood. History teaches us about the misuses of these systems. Abstract principles are strictly mere jargon. We can already see this and it will be even clearer in the following chapters. This is a confirmation of a great truth that I have proven[9], "that the art of reasoning reduces to a well-formed language."

---

[9]*Logic.*

4 First and Second Examples of the Misuse of Abstract Systems

Philosophers owe their reputations to the importance of the subjects they treat rather than to the way in which they handle them. Few people would be justified in scorning the blindness that so frequently makes philosophers attempt things beyond their abilities; and the common run of men believe them great because they apply themselves to great subjects. With this prejudice we cast aside all possible suspicions about their enlightenment. Against all reason we suppose that some knowledge lies beyond the grasp of any intelligent mind. And we attribute the obscurity of writings that we do not understand to the profundity of the subjects. Indeed, so much attention is required to guard against a vague notion, a meaningless word, or some ambiguity, that we have admired rather than criticized these writings. Thus the more difficult the questions raised by philosophers, the more secure their reputation. They themselves sense this and without understanding it too well, they are led, as if by instinct, to delve into things that nature tries to hide from us. But let us draw them away for some moments from these depths, where they can only get lost. Let us apply their way of reasoning to familiar objects, and the flaws in their procedure will become clear. With this in view, I have chosen for this chapter two examples whose absurdity will immediately be clear to everyone's eyes. The most everyday beliefs will provide me with examples for what follows. In another chapter I will describe errors that common people and philosophers seem to disagree about. Finally, I shall set forth beliefs that, although held only by philosophers, are no less false or absurd. My purpose here is to show that the philosopher and the common man are led astray for the same reasons. This will confirm what I have already proven elsewhere.[10] I shall cite a great number of examples because nothing seems to me to be more important than to get rid of our predilection for abstract systems.

Someone born blind, after much questioning and thinking about colors, concluded that he perceived the idea of scarlet in the sound of a trumpet. No doubt he needed only to be given eyes to make him realize how ill-founded his certainty was.

If we want to investigate his way of reasoning, we will recognize that of philosophers. I suppose that someone told him that scarlet was a brilliant, vivid color, and he reasoned like this: I have the idea of something brilliant and vivid in the sound of a trumpet; scarlet is a brilliant and vivid thing; thus I have the idea of scarlet in the sound of a trumpet.

With this principle the blind man could equally well form ideas of all other colors and lay down the basis of a system in which he proves: (1) that melodies could be played with colors, as they are with sounds; (2) that a concert could be performed with differently colored objects as it is with musical instruments; (3) that melodies could be seen, just as they can be heard; (4) that a deaf person can dance in tempo and perhaps a thousand other things each more novel and curious than the next.

The blind man would surely exploit the potential advantages of his system; he would exaggerate the drawbacks of a hearing loss in professional dancers and singers. He would overlook no platitude on this topic and he would teach us how we could use our eyes to compensate for our ears. What would he not say about the way to mix these two harmonies, about the art of measuring the relation between colors and sounds, and on the marvelous effects that music coming to the mind from two senses at a time would produce? With what cleverness would he not conjecture that we will probably find some music that will reach the mind through an even greater number of senses? And with what modesty would he not leave the result of this discovery to those shrewder than he? He would no doubt be in wonder that it was given only to him to discover things that escaped all sighted people. He would find his principles confirmed by considering the conclusions he would have drawn from them, and would certainly be regarded as a genius by those who were similarly handicapped, but his triumph would be only among blind people.

There is a harmony among colors; that is, our visual sensations have certain relations and pleasant proportions. For this reason, the sensations of touch, smell, and taste also have a certain harmony. But whoever wants to

---

[10]*The Art of Thinking*, Part 2, Ch. 1. Also see the *Logic*.

create melodies for each of these senses reveals that he is more attached to the sound of a word than to its meaning.

In truth, the establishment of such a system would scarcely be surprising. We have always been led to suppose true music in every case where we could use the word "harmony". Was it not on this basis that people believed that the movement of the stars formed a perfect concert? They could even find reasons for this conception if they wanted at all to apply their imagination to discovering relations among musical elements and parts of this world. I am going to do this, and thereby derive my second example.

It is obvious, I remark first, that if there are seven tones in music, there are also seven planets. Second, I can suppose that experts on the sizes of these planets, their distances, or other properties would find proportions similar to those among seven sonorous objects in the diatonic order. That being so (for we can suppose everything that is not impossible; and who, for that matter, could prove the opposite?), nothing would prevent us from recognizing that celestial bodies form a perfect concert.

We should be all the more inclined to accept this as a true proposition as it becomes a rich and fertile principle leading us to discoveries that we would never have dared aspire to without its help.

Everyone agrees that the fixed stars are just so many suns. I take care not to suggest anything arguable. Now it would doubtless be interesting to know how many planets each star illuminates. Everyone will admit that no astronomer or physicist has hitherto been able to resolve this question, but in my system the issue is explained quite simply and naturally. For if the celestial bodies are in perfect harmony and if music has only seven fundamental tones, each star must be encircled by seven basic planets.

If some uneasy mind, unaccustomed to grasping and savoring these sorts of truths, thought there could be more planets, I reply that what he takes for basic planets are merely satelites.

Moreover, whom would this music be for? I note here that there are creatures very much larger than we. No doubt, those destined to enjoy this celestial harmony have ears suited to these concerts and hence ears larger than our own, larger in fact than any philosopher's. Oh, what a happy discovery! But further, their ears are proportional to their other bodily organs. The size of these creatures thus surpasses ours in the same measure as the heavens surpass our concert halls. How immense they must be! This is where "the imagination stands amazed; this is where it gets lost—a convincing proof it has no part in the discoveries I have just made. They are the work of pure understanding, they are wholly spiritual truths."[11]

---

[11]Here I add a famous man's conjectures about the inhabitants of the planets. These conjectures prove that there is nothing exaggerated about the absurdity of the systems I have imagined here.

Jesting aside, for I do not know whether the reader will excuse this playfulness in such a serious work, people should be cautious in using metaphorical expressions. We soon forget that they are merely metaphors. We take them literally, and we fall into absurd errors.

In general, nothing is more ambiguous than the language we use to talk about our sensations. The word *doux* ("sweet"), for example, contains nothing precise. A thing can be *doux* in many respects—to sight, taste, smell, hearing, touch, to the mind, the heart, or the imagination. It has such a different sense in every case that we cannot judge one by the other. It is the same way with the word *harmonie* and many others.

Analogy leads us to judge that life exists on the planets. We know how gracefully this argument unfolds in the *Plurality of worlds*. But M. de Fontenelle is too philosophical to draw unwarranted conclusions from a principle. Huyghens and Wolf were not as wise. According to them, the stars are peopled with men like us, and Wolf further believed he had good reasons to specify even the size of these extraterrestrials. "In my opinion" (*Elements of astronomy*, Geneva: 1735, Part 2) "it is almost beyond doubt that the inhabitants of Jupiter are much taller than those of the earth; they must be giants. In fact, the pupils dilate or contract as the light is stronger or weaker. Now the light on Jupiter is, at the same height of the sun, weaker than the light on the Earth, for Jupiter is much farther from the sun. Consequently, the Jupiterians must have larger pupils than earthlings. Now experience clearly shows that the pupil is proportional to the eye, and the eye to the rest of the body, so that animals with larger pupils have larger eyes and, having larger eyes, they have a larger body. The Jupiterians are thus taller than we. I even have reasons to prove that they are the same size as Og, the king of Bazan, whose bed, according to Moses, was nine cubits long and four cubits wide. For Jupiter's distance from the sun is to the earth's distance from the sun as 26 is to 5. The amount of sunlight on Jupiter thus is to the amount of sunlight on the earth as 5 times 5 is to 26 times 26. But experience teaches us that the pupil dilates less in proportion as the amount of light decreases; otherwise a distant object and a nearer one could appear to have the same illumination. The distant one, however, appears to be much less illuminated. Thus the pupils of the Jupiterians, when either maximally contracted or maximally dilated, must be smaller relative to those of earthlings than the proportion of 26 times 26 relative to 5 times 5." (Here I am extending Wolf's reasoning somewhat, for it did not seem to be sufficiently explicit.) "Hence it follows that the diameter of the pupil of the Jupiterians will be smaller in relation to that of the pupil of earthlings than 26 is to 5, for the sizes of the pupils are like the squares of the diameters."

"Let us then suppose that the ratio of the two diameters is 10 to 26, or 5 to 13; that being so, the size of the earth's inhabitants being usually five Parisian feet 7/32, or 7515 particles, of which the Parisian foot contains 1440 (I myself am of that height), we see that the normal Jupiterian height must be 19,539 particles or 13 feet 819/1440. Now according to M. Eisenschmid, the Hebrew cubit contains 2389 particles of a Parisian foot: the length of the bed mentioned by Moses is then some 21,456 particles. Let us subtract one foot, or 1,440 particles, and the height of Og is 20,016 or 13 feet 1296/1440. We can see how close this measurement is to the height of the Jupiterians, since it is 13 feet 819/1440.

5 Third Example: On the Origin and Development of Divination

The mind of the common man is systematic like that of the philosopher, but the principles that lead it astray are less easy to identify. Its errors accumulate in such great numbers, and sustain themselves by analogies that are at times so subtle, that the man himself is not capable of recognizing his own work in the systems he has fashioned. The history of divination offers us a very clear example of this phenomenon. I am going to reveal the train of ideas from which so many superstitions have arisen.

If the life of man were only one continuous sensation of pleasure or pain, in the one case happy with no idea of unhappiness, in the other unhappy with no idea of happiness, he would enjoy his happiness or suffer his unhappiness without casting around to discover if some being watched out for his survival or worked to do him harm. The alternation between these states leads him to reflect that he is never so unhappy that his nature does not allow him to be occasionally happy and also that he is never so happy that he cannot become unhappy. Whence arise his hope of seeing an end to the evils he suffers, and his fear of losing some good he enjoys. The more aware he becomes of this alternation, the more he sees that its causes are out of his control. Each circumstance teaches him his dependence on all that surrounds him. And when he knows how to guide his reflection to trace effects back to their true underlying cause, everything will indicate or prove to him the existence of the first being.

Among the evils we are heir to, for some the causes are evident, while for others, we do not know what to attribute them to. The latter evils were a source of conjectures for people who thought they were examining nature when they were merely consulting their own imaginations. This way of satisfying one's curiosity, still so common today, was the only one for people unenlightened by experience. This, then, was the first intelectual undertaking. As long as the evils affected only a few individuals, none of these conjectures gained enough ground to become generally held beliefs. But are they more widespread? Is it the plague, for example, that devastates the earth? Then, this phenomenom holds everyone's attention and men with imagination succeed in getting their systems adopted. Now to what cause can still-primitive minds attribute the evils assaulting us if not to beings who find pleasure in inflicting misery on mankind?

Nevertheless, it would have been terrible always to be afraid. Thus, hope was not long in coming to modify this system. It led men to imagine more benevolent beings who could offset the power of the evil ones. People believed themselves loved by these beings as they believed they were hated by the others.

These two kinds of beings were multiplied according to circumstances. Airy spirits and genies of every kind filled the air. Houses were opened to them; they were the household gods. Finally they were dispersed to the woods, the waters, everywhere, because fear and hope accompany people everywhere.

But it was not enough to people the earth with friendly or hostile beings. The sun's influence on all existing things was too great to go unnoticed. No doubt this star was early on assigned to the benevolent stars. Nor did people take long to imagine that the moon had an influence; these influences were gradually given all the clearly observable stars. Then the imagination freely imputed a good or malign character to this influence, and ever since the heavens appeared to conduce to the happiness or unhappiness of mankind. Nothing could happen there without being significant. People studied the stars and attributed their different influences to their different positions. People did not fail to attribute the most important events—famines, wars, the death of kings, and the like—to the rarest and most extraordinary phenomoma such as eclipses and comets; imagination easily supposes some relation between these things.

If people could have thought that everything in the universe is connected, and that what we take for the action of a single part is the result of the combined actions of all its parts—from the largest bodies down to the tiniest atoms—they would never have thought of regarding a planet or constellation as a basic cause of what happened to them. They would have realized how unreasonable it was in explaining an event to take account only of the smallest part of its contributing causes. But fear, the first principle of this prejudice, does not allow for reflection; it shows the danger, magnifies it, and we are only too happy to be able to ascribe that danger to any cause whatever. It gives us a kind of relief from the evils we suffer.

So people recognized the influence of the stars, and the only question remaining was to divide up among them the allocation of goods and evils. Here is the basis for this division.

Familiar with the language of articulate sounds, people judged that nothing was more natural than to give things the names that had been given them from the first. They thought this way because these names seemed natural to them; they had no other reason and that is what led them astray; moreover, this opinion doubtless had a basis in reason. In fact, it is certain that when people tried to name things, the need to make themselves understood forced them to choose words with the greatest analogy either to their ideas or to the language of action that presided over the formation of languages.[12] But people imagined that these names recalled what objects were in themselves, and consequently they judged that only the gods could teach these names to men. For their part, philosophers, who were too biased or too conceited to suspect the limits of the human mind, did not doubt that the first inventors of languages understood the nature of beings. The study of names must thus have seemed a highly appropriate means for discovering the essence of things; and confirming this opinion was the fact that among the names peoples saw many that still clearly indicated the properties or character of objects. As this prejudice was still generally received, it was not difficult to determine the influence that could be attributed to each planet.

Men who achieved fame were ranked with the gods and after their deification were ascribed the same earthly character. Either because their names were given to stars during their lifetime out of flattery or because this was done only after their death to mark the place that would receive them, divinities and stars had the same names in common.

Thus, one only had to refer to the character of each god to guess the influence of each planet. Thus Jupiter signified high rank, great care, justice, and so on; Mars, strength, courage, vengeance, rashness, and the like; Venus, beauty, grace, sensuality, hedonism, and similar qualities. In short, each planet was judged by the idea of its divine namesake. As for the signs of the zodiac, they owed their virtue to the animals who were their namesakes.

People did not stop there. Once some power had been attributed to the stars, there was no further reason for restricting their influence. If some planet produced a particular effect, why should it not produce another closely related one? As astrologers' imaginations proceeded in this way from one analogy to another, it is no longer possible to discover the different connections of ideas on which their systems were constructed. The same planet had in the end to produce entirely different effects, and the most opposed planets to produce very similar ones. Thus everything will be

---

[12]*Grammar*, Part 1.

confounded by the same way of reasoning that first dispensed a particular power to each star.

This influence could not be accorded indifferently to every part of the heavens. It was natural to believe that those parts with no observed variation had no influence or if they did have some, they tended to keep things always in the same state. That is why astrologers, limiting everything to the revolutions of the zodiac, usually attributed influence only to the twelve signs and the planets that course through them.

Since in this system each planet had its own particular power, it was natural to infer that they mutually modified their action according to their location in the sky as well as their interrelations.

It should thereby have been concluded that a planet's power changes at every instant. But it would have been impossible to determine this power, and astrology would have become impracticable.

This was not the account given by astrologers who had a stake in taking unfair advantage of people's simplicity, nor that given by those who, acting in good faith, were the first to be deceived. To judge the influence of the planets, then, it was established that they did not have to be observed at all the points of the zodiac, and people confined themselves to the twelve principal positions of the signs.

Another difficulty was circumvented in the same way. It was not enough to have determined the constellation in which each star should be observed. It still had to be decided whether we should take account of our location on earth. On what basis would it have been supposed that a planet has similar effects on a Chinese and a Frenchman, since the direction of the sun's rays is not the same for both? But such precision would have made the calculations too involved. In view of its distance from the heavens, the earth was considered as a point, and it was decided that the different direction of the rays was so negligible that it should be not taken into account.

But what could trouble astrologers most was that in their system the stars had to influence an animal at every instant, from the moment of conception to the end of life. Astrologers saw no reasons for suspending this action up to a certain time after conception, nor for stopping it entirely before the moment of death.

Now the planets, alternating between a state in which they exercise all this power and a state in which they can do nothing, would thus have successively cancelled each other out. We would have experienced all the vicissitudes inevitably produced by this conflict, and the series of events would have been about the same for every person. If there had been some difference, it would have been only insofar as the stars whose influence was experienced first made impressions so deep as never to be entirely eliminated. Then, to determine this difference, we would have had to ascertain the exact moment of conception; we would even have had to go further back in time. For why would it not have been said that the action of the stars prepared the seed long before the animal was conceived?

We cannot guess how the astrologers would have overcome these difficulties if a certain prejudice did not come to their aid. Happily for them, people had always been convinced that throughout the course of life we are only what we are born. Consequently, astrologers laid down the principle that it was sufficient to observe the stars relevant to the moment of birth. We can sense how much this maxim eased their minds.

Nevertheless it was still very difficult to determine exactly what a person's moment of birth was. Even if the most precise astronomer had observed it, we could not be certain that there was no error. Now an error of a minute, a second, or even less, is enough for the influence to be different. But astrologers were far from pursuing such precision which would have made their art impracticable. People who were curious to hear about their future and consulted them were satisfied provided that something had been predicted. So astrologers usually confined themselves to the day and hour of birth, as if events had to be the same for all persons born the same day and hour. If some astrologers seemed to pride themselves on greater precision, the purpose was to cause their charlatanery to be believed.

As this astrological system took shape, predictions were made. Among the many, some were confirmed by events, and astrologers took advantage of them, while others were not a blow to the system at all. Instead, people put the blame on astrologers who were held to be uninformed; or if they were considered skilled, they were excused by attributing to some calculation error what was due to a defect in the whole art; more often yet, people paid no attention to incorrect predictions. Once people indulge in superstition, they simply stray from one error to another. Of a thousand observations, 999 could have saved them from error; they make only one, and that is the one they latch onto.

There is a stratagem that has often succeeded for astrologers, which is to deliver their prophecies obscurely and ambiguously, and to leave to events the trouble of clearing them up. But they do not always need to be this clever, and sometimes they expect their prophecies to be fulfilled only in the imagination of the people concerned. Prophecies threatening some misfortune are more commonly fulfilled than others because fear has much greater power over us than hope. The examples of this are legion.

For believers in astrology, there is thus some danger in having one's horoscope drawn. I add that it can even be imprudent for an unbeliever. If unpleasant things are predicted for me that are connected with the various circumstances that my way of life leads me naturally to encounter, each of these circumstances will remind me of them despite myself. These sad images will trouble me the more vividly I remember them. The impression will be strong, especially if I believed in astrology as a child. For imagination retains the power over me now that I am rational that it had when I was not. In vain will I tell myself that there is madness in worrying: philosophical enough to know how ill-founded my anxiety is, I will not be sufficiently so to dispel it.

I have read somewhere that a young man destined by birth and talent to take part in the government of the republic began to enjoy some favorable regard there. To be agreeable, he accompanied two or three friends on a visit to an oracle. They urged him to take his turn at having his horoscope drawn, but he refused. As convinced as anyone could be of the futility of this art, he answered only by ridiculing the sibyl. "You may joke, you may joke," replied this woman, annoyed, "but I tell you that you will lose your head on the scaffold." At the time the young man did not think that this utterance made the slightest impression on him. He laughed at it and, without being troubled, took his leave. Nevertheless his imagination had been struck, and he was amazed that at every opportunity the soothsayer's threat came to mind and tormented him as though he believed it. He fought this madness for a long time but the slightest disturbance in the republic evoked it and made all his efforts useless. Finally, he found no other remedy than to give up public affairs and to go into exile from his country to live under a more peaceful government.

We could conclude from this that philosophy involves making us distrust ourselves enough to avoid situations that can haunt us, rather than flattering us that we can always master the anxiety imagination can arouse.

When the astrologers could cite a few predictions confirmed by events, they boasted that a long series of observations testified in their favor.

I shall not pause here to refute such a claim; its falsity is evident. It is undeniable that the precision of astrological observations depends on knowledge acquired in astronomy. Modern progress in astronomy thus clearly shows how for many centuries astrologers were ignorant of many things required for their art.

Nevertheless they did not hesitate to create systems. The Chaldeans and Egyptians each had their principles. The Greeks who inherited this ridiculous art from them made some changes in it, as they did with everything they borrowed from abroad. The Arabs in turn took similar liberties with Greek astrology and transmitted systems to the moderns which all of them add to and subtract from according to their pleasure. Astrologers agree only on one point, which is that there is an art of knowing the future by the inspection of the stars. As for the laws to follow, every astrologer prescribes a set peculiar to him, and condemns those of the other astrologers.

Nevertheless, the common man, who did not see how little intelligence prevailed among the astrologers, believed that all the tales told him were truths confirmed by extensive experience. He did not doubt, for example, that the planets divided up the days, nights, countries, plants, trees, minerals, and that since each thing was under the domination of some star, the sky was a book in which could be read everything that had to happen to empires, kingdoms, provinces, cities, and individuals. We can see from astrological works that the only basis for this division was some imaginary relation between the character given the stars and the things people wanted to put under the star's protection.

Merely to have provided in this way for the regulation of the world was a lot, but there still remained one drawback, a considerable one no doubt, to astrologers' eyes, which is that the benevolent stars sometimes encountered obstacles to making us feel the effects of their influence. Remedies were sought; and as people believed that the stars were gods, or at least that they were controlled by intelligences to which the care of world had been entrusted, they imagined that we had only to call these spirits down to earth. This is what was called "evocation."

It was suggested that the stars were happier in those locations from which they had a stronger influence, and that they had a particular propensity for the objects under their protection. Consequently people invoked the stars in the name of these things; and, to pray with more hope, people procured a stick with which they sketched the shapes of these everyday objects—in the air, on the ground, and on the walls. This was, I think, the origin of magic. As this superstition probably arose while the language of action was very familiar, it was natural for a person to attach magical power to certain movements.

More was done. People believed that if it were important to be able to summon these beings, it was even more important always to carry on oneself something continually assuring their protection. People reasoned according to the same principles as before, and concluded that it was sufficient to engrave the same shapes that were sketched customarily to evoke the spirits and the prayers offered them. No one doubted that this device would succeed, provided that one took the precaution of choosing the stone and metal appropriate to the planet whose assistance was desired, engraved them with the day and hour assigned to the planet, and above all chose the moment when it was in the celestial position where it enjoyed its full powers. This is the origin of abracadabra and talismans.

Another cause contributed a great deal to maintaining and spreading these prejudices.

Since the establishment of alphabets made people completely forget the meanings of hieroglyphics, it was easy for priests to make these characters pass in peoples' eyes for sacred things concealing the deepest mysteries. The priests thus ascribed with such power as pleased them to these characters, and they were all the more readily believed as it was not doubted that the gods were the authors of the science of hieroglyphics, that is, a science that was to include everything for the sole reason that what it included was unknown. All the hieroglyphic characters thus gradually passed into magic, and this system became all the more fecund.

This magic, combined with the mysterious science of hieroglyphics, gave rise to other superstitions.

Hieroglyphics incorporated all kinds of lines. Every line therefore became a sign. Thus instead of consulting the heavens, magicians had merely to examine people's hands and they could promise them good or bad fortune depending on the nature of the lines on their palms. But because their principles did not allow any happening without the influence of the stars, each line was assigned to one of the planets. This was enough for the magicians to attribute the same portents to it, and the practice of this art became all the easier. It was given the name "palmistry."

On the one hand, in hieroglyphic writing, the sun, moon, and stars represented nations, empires, kings, and great men; the eclipse and extinction of these luminous bodies signalled earthly disasters; fire and flood meant a devastation by war or famine; a snake indicated some illness; a viper, money; frogs, imposters; partridges, impious persons; a swallow, afflictions or death—in short there was no known object that did not serve to foretell the future.

On the other hand, in sleep the human imagination never acts without making new combinations of known elements. Thus it cannot fail to remind people of the same objects used in hieroglyphic writing. But people did not yet suspect that dreams were the work of imagination. As far as actions engaged with knowledge and reflection were concerned, it was said that "they are the effects of our will," and that was thought to explain everything. But involuntary acts seemed to happen within us but without our aid. To whom could they be attributed, then, if not to a god? Thus the gods were the authors of both hieroglyphics and dreams. And it could not be doubted that during sleep the gods tried to make their will known to us when they used the same language they had established for writing. This is the origin of oneiromancy or divination by dreams.[13]

Once this prejudice was accepted—that the gods are the source of all our

---

[13]M. Warburton attributes this art to the same origins. *Essay on hieroglyphics*, sec. 43.

involuntary acts—we see how readily people would find in themselves reasons for fear and hope. An accidental gesture, one foot inadvertently brought forward in front of the other, a sneeze—for them everything became a good or a bad omen.[14]

Among the hieroglyphic shapes there were birds flying toward different parts of the world or that appeared to be singing. In the beginning, hieroglyphic writing was used to refer to completely natural things, such as the changes of the seasons, the winds, and so forth. But when hieroglyphics became sacred, people believed they contained some mystery. And it is probably owing to this prejudice that soothsayers imagined they could discover the future by the flight and song of birds.

Although the gods were always busy instructing people about the future, they must have been especially so during sacrifices. It was even natural to think that they struck the victim, and left marks of anger or of favor on his breast. Thus people could not be uninterested in observing all the details of sacrifices and, above all, in inspecting the entrails of the sacrificial animals. These were the foundations of the art of the haruspices.

Although people did not question any of these ways of knowing the future, they were too curious not to have occasionally a sense of its inadequacy. They wished for something more precise, and the wish was fulfilled by conditions that gave rise to oracles. Some words escaping unintentionally from the mouth of the person presiding at the sacrifice had some chance relation to the reason for invoking the gods. These utterances were taken as inspired. This success was conducive to more than one slip of this kind. And because the less control the person seemed to have over his movements, the more directly they seemed to come from a god, it was believed that oracles should be pronounced only after a trance had been entered. That is why people could be counted on to build temples in those places where fumes arising from the earth could unhinge the mind. Elsewhere people used other means to inspire the trance. Finally, people became more and more superstitious and required fewer preparations. And prophecies made calmly and deliberately became very common.[15]

It only remained to make the statues of the gods move and speak. In this, the imposture of the priests satisfied people's superstition. The statues became oracles.[16]

---

[14]This is perhaps the origin of the practice of acknowledging a sneeze. People wanted to ally themselves with a good sign or implore the gods to ward off the evils that a bad sign portended. This is an explanation I saw somewhere.

[15]The oracles owed their origin to different causes depending on the various countries. Here is a conjecture on this topic equally natural and philosophical. "There was a hole on Parnassus from which fumes issued that made the goats dance and went to people's heads. Perhaps someone who was intoxicated by it began to speak without knowing what he was saying and

Imagination moves quickly when it goes astray, because nothing is so fertile as a false principle. There are gods everywhere; everything is due to them; thus anything can reveal the destiny awaiting us. By this reasoning, the most common things as well as the rarest all became, depending on circumstances, good or bad omens. The objects that inspired veneration, thereby having some connection with the idea of divinity, seemed the most appropriate for satisfying man's curiosity. It was in this way, for example, that a high regard for Homer made people believe they could find prophecies in his works.

Some of these prejudices were nourished by the opinions of philosophers. According to them, our mind was just a portion of the mind of the world. Enveloped in matter, it no longer partook of the divinity of the substance from which it had been separated. But in dreams, in a trance, and in all unreflective actions, the mind's intercourse with its body was interrupted. So it went back to the bosom of divinity and the future manifested itself to it.

Magicians also knew how to take advantage of knowledge obtained in medicine. They profited from superstition, which always attributes to supernatural causes the things that our ignorance prevents us from understanding.

Finally, politics also promoted priestly divination. For nothing of consequence was undertaken without consulting omens, haruspices, or oracles.

Thus everything coincided to feed these gross errors. They were so widespread that the light of religion did not prevent them from gaining ground, at least in part, among the Jews and Christians. Among them people were seen to use ceremonies invoking the devil and the dead, ceremonies rather similar to those used by pagans conjuring stars and demons. People were seen searching holy scripture for discoveries in physics and everything else that could satisfy their curiosity or greed.

Such is the system of divination of astrologers, magicians, interpreters of

---

spoke some truth. Thereupon there had to be something divine in these fumes, they contained the science of the future, people began to approach the hole with respect and ceremonies gradually formed. Thus, apparently, the oracle at Delphi was born. And as he owed his origin to fumes that went to his head, it was absolutely necessary that Pythius enter into a trance in order to be able to prophecize. For most of the other oracles, the trance was unnecessary. Once one had been established, you can well imagine that a thousand were. If the gods speak clearly there, why would they not speak here at all? Struck by the wonder of it all and eager to profit by it, people wanted nothing better than to see oracles come forth everywhere, and then these oracles who accorded them everything on earth acquired seniority." *History of oracles.* Dissertation 1, Ch. 2. I am only touching lightly on this part of divination because M. de Fontenelle has perfectly described everything about it.

[16]This is also explained by saying that the demons made the pronouncement themselves. But this cause is supernatural and it is up to theologians to expand on it. The philosopher sticks to natural causes; but, while passing over the others in silence, he does not reject them.

dreams, and omens, haruspices, and the like. If we could follow all the writers who tried to establish these follies, we would see all of them take the same starting point, and each one go astray, depending on how he was guided by his imagination. We would even see them stray so far and by paths so bizarre that we would have considerable difficulty identifying the first occasion for their divagations. But it is enough to show how naturally people acquired these prejudices, and nevertheless how ridiculous it was to believe in them.

6 Fourth Example: On the Origin and Consequences of the Preconception of Innate Ideas

I do not know who is more responsible, the common people or philosophers, for the system of innate ideas, but I cannot doubt that they have created formidable obstacles to the development of the art of reasoning. It can be seen if I am correct, from the slightest consideration of the origin and consequences of this error.

First Article: On the origin of the preconception of innate ideas

At the birth of philosophy, the more impatient people were to acquire knowledge, the less they observed. Observation seemed too slow, and the best minds thought they could understand nature through divination. They could begin, however, only with the primitive knowledge that they shared with the rest of mankind. This comprised, to speak the language of geometers, all their givens. They could achieve distinction only by their adroitness in using these givens. They did not examine them closely and they were satisfied with the vaguest ideas. Experience had not yet taught them the danger of beginning badly; indeed we are scarcely knowledgeable about this nowadays. Were philosophers trying to explain something? They looked for the thing's possible relations to common ideas, made a comparison, seized on some metaphorical expression, and erected systems. They observed, for example, that objects were reflected in waters, and they imagined the mind as a polished surface on which were traced images of all the things that we are capable of knowing.

Mirror images represent objects exactly. Nothing more was required to

believe that the images in our minds also conformed to external objects. It
was concluded that we could judge objects confidently from the way they
were represented by images. These images were given the names "ideas,"
"notions," "archetypes," and several others suitable for self deception and
for giving the impression of superior knowledge on the subject. Eventually
names were regarded as realities that betoken, so to speak, external beings.
How indeed could one hesitate? Was this not well-grounded in basic
principles? Ideas illuminate the mind, they are more or less extensive, one
can compare them, consider them in different respects, and find relations of
every kind among them. Now can nothing have so many properties?[17] No end
of reasons for reifying even the most abstract ideas! But where is the source of
these many ideas enjoyed by the mind? To realize that they come from the
senses, we would have to go back to their origin by explicating their
development, and grasp by what transformations the most concrete ideas
become spiritual, as it were. But that required a degree of insight and wisdom
that people could not yet have. Even today how many philosophers are there
who cannot understand this truth! Moreover, there are abstract ideas that
seem so remote from their origin that it was impossible then to guess what has
now been proven to be the case. Finally, since ideas are realities, according
to the received assumption, how could the senses have contributed to
increasing the reality of the mind? Thus it was said, as many people still
persist in saying, that ideas are innate and they were regarded as realities that
are part of each mental substance. Indeed, since people were unable to
explain how ideas would have been acquired, it was natural for them to think
that we have always had them. One could not waver on this, especially when
one paid attention to those ideas that were known before the age of reason
and hence do not allow us to identify the period when we first had them.

Images reflected in water appear only when objects are present; they
cannot be the model for our imagination of those ideas that are supposed to
be born with our mind and preserved independently of the action of objects.
So it was necessary to appeal to a new comparison (comparisons are a great
resource for many philosophers.) The mind was represented as a stone on
which different shapes were engraved and people believed they were explaining themselves clearly by speaking of ideas or images engraved, imprinted, or
stamped on the mind. Because air and time alter the best engravings, it was
imagined that passions and prejudices also change our ideas. Although there
exist engravings so lightly etched or made on such soft stones that time
completely effaces them, it seems that people did not want to push the
comparison that far and thought our ideas were not imprinted superficially

---

[17]This is the way even the Cartesians reasoned on this subject.

enough, or that our minds were not soft enough, for the impressions God made on them to be completely effaceable.

To see how unreasonable some opinions are, we do not always have to go into great detail; it is sufficient to observe how we arrived at them. We would see how little it costs to pass oneself off as a philosopher, since it is often enough to imagine any old resemblence between mental and material things; and if we recognized that common people speak only by assuming this resemblance, we would discover in the most commonly held preconceptions the foundation of many philosophical systems.

When we are talking about the mind, its ideas, thoughts, and everything it experiences, we use and can only use figurative language. I have shown elsewhere how mental operations were named following the very names given to sensory operations.[18] Now both philosophers and the common people were deceived by this language, and that is why they thought they could explain everything with words.

As innate ideas were established on such foundations, the only issue remaining was to determine how many such ideas there were.

Some people had no difficulty admitting an infinite number of innate ideas and saying that all our ideas are born with us, not imagining how we could otherwise perceive each particular object. But people who were too far-sighted to be hindered by such a small obstacle found a happy solution in some fashionable systems. Having observed that everything depends on certain fertile principles, they said that nothing was innate except these principles, that we see particular truths in general ideas, and that we understand the finite itself only through the idea of the infinite.

But what are these general ideas that alone are imprinted on our minds? Let philosophers address themselves to an engraver and ask him to engrave a man-in-general. That would not be asking for the impossible, since according to them there is such close correspondence between our ideas and the images imprinted on objects, since they imagine so well how the image of a man-in-general is imprinted in us. Let them merely tell the engraver that if he did not know how to engrave a man-in-general, he would never engrave a man-in-particular because he understands the latter only through his idea of the former. If despite the conclusiveness of this argument, the engraver avers his inability, they would doubtless by justified in treating him like someone ignorant even of the first principles of things and to conclude that a person cannot be a good engraver without being a good philosopher.

But let us make every effort to discover in their language the knowledge they think they have. We will see only engraved, imprinted, and stamped

---

[18]*Grammar*. Part 1.

stamped images that change and are effaced—expressions with a clear and precise sense when we are speaking of bodies but that, when applied to the mind and its ideas, are merely metaphors, imprecise terms which lead the mind astray in vain imaginings.

Locke did great honor to the doctrine of innate ideas through the number and soundness of his arguments against it. More than were needed to destroy such a useless phantasm.[19] If I invented a system proving that the world contains beings I cannot explain, it would be much more natural to advise me to formulate ideas of the things that I want to contend than to undertake seriously to refute me. This is precisely our situation with respect to all abstract systems. We refute them better with a few good questions rather than with long arguments. Ask a philosopher what he means by such and such a principle. If you press him, you will soon discover the weak spot. There you will see that his system merely turns on certain metaphors or far-fetched comparisons, and so it will be as easy for you to overturn him as to attack him.

Second article on the consequences of the partiality to innate ideas

If some philosophers have tried to deprive particular ideas of the privilege of being innate, it is because it was easy to observe which sense transmitted them to the mind. The difficulty of making the same observation about abstract notions prevented these philosophers from making the same judgment about them. For every abstract term invented, everyone believed a new innate idea had been discovered, that is, an idea that, engraved in us by a being who cannot deceive us, is clear, distinct, and completely conformable to the essence of things. The more philosophers imbued with this approach searched for a knowledge of nature in ideas remote from the senses, the more certain they were that their efforts would be successful. They multiplied vague definitions and abstract principles ad infinitum; and thanks to the terms "being", "substance", "essence", "property," and the like, they did not encounter anything that they thought they could not explain.

What made them fall still further into this abuse of abstract terms is the success with which they are used in geometry. As this language is adequate for determining the essence of *abstract* magnitudes, they thought that it was

---

[19]Locke devoted the whole of the first book of his *Essay On Human Understanding* to attacking this opinion. For the most part, his reasons appear to me to be valid. But it seems to me that he does not take the most direct route to dispel this error. For myself, I believed I ought to confine myself to showing its origin. If I had wanted to attack it with other weapons, I would have been able to find them nearly exclusively in Locke. I prefer to refer the reader to Locke himself.

also adequate for determining the magnitudes of substances. My conjecture is all the more probable since when they try to explain their essences, perplexed to take examples from metaphysics, they borrow them from geometry. But I advise them to compare their ideas with those of geometers. This comparison alone will show them that they are as far from knowing the essence of substances as we are close to knowing that of shapes.

Their stubborn attachment to their method prevents them from taking this advice, and saddles them with a language in which they themselves no longer understand each other. It finally reaches the point where philosophers talk about ideas but do not know what they are. Certainly, they have no criteria for recognizing one. They do not know where to find rules and principles. These are three traps they cannot avoid falling into. Here is the proof.

According to the doctrine that all our knowledge comes from the senses, nothing is easier than to form a precise notion of ideas. For sensations are perceptible ideas if we think of them in the objects to which we refer them, and they are abstract ideas, if we think of them separately from objects.[20] Thus, by starting with what we sense, we begin with something determinate. So the same precision can be given to all the notions to be analyzed. But, in the doctrine of innate ideas we can only begin with something vague. Consequently it is impossible to determine exactly what we should understand by "idea." Thus a famous Cartesian took the position that "idea" is one of a group of ideas so clear they cannot be explained by others[21]; and as if he wanted to illustrate forthwith that there are no words to explicate the sense of "idea," he adds an explanation that is, at best, unintelligible.[22] Descartes makes a major effort, but nothing is more awkward or sometimes more absurd than what he imagines. As for Malebranche, we know what fantasies he spun on this subject.

Since certainty is based on ideas, we clearly see that we cannot know what is certain as long as we do not know what ideas are themselves. The proof of this lies in philosophers' attempts to identify some sign for recognizing certainty. They have only vague advice to give. Descartes says to avoid prejudice and overhastiness and always make your judgments clear and distinct. Says Malebranche, consult your internal teacher and give your

---

[20]See the Preliminary lessons in the *Course of study*.

[21]Logic of Port-Royal.

[22]"I do not give this name," he says (Part 1) "to fancifully painted images but to everything that is in our mind when we can truthfully say that we conceive a thing, in whatever way we conceive it." Also see what he says in the same place where, comparing truth to light, he assures us that we can recognize it by the clarity that surrounds it. See further (Part 2, Ch. 1) how vague the criteria are by which he wants us to recognize certainty.

assent only when you cannot reject him without feeling some internal pain and the secret criticisms of your consciousness, for this is how this teacher answers you.

The same reasons preventing them from recognizing certainty make philosophers unable to devise rules with any practical utility. Indeed, arguments are made up of propositions; propositions of words; and words are the signs of our ideas. Ideas are thus the pivot of the whole art of reasoning. And insofar as we have not worked out what ideas are all about, there is no use for the rules invented by logicians to formulate propositions, syllogisms, and arguments.

Here a host of examples offer themselves, but I will confine myself to examining the principle regarded as paramount. It is one of Descartes', and I do not know any more widely received. Indeed, there is something very beguiling about it. Here it is.

"Everything included in the clear and distinct idea of a thing can be correctly affirmed of it."

In the first place, philosophers like the Cartesians, not knowing what an idea is, know no better what makes it clear and distinct. Their language seems to make an idea clear and distinct merely because we see distinctly and clearly that it conforms to its object. Their principle thus reduces to saying that "we can affirm of a thing everything that we clearly and distinctly see conforms to it." In this case, it is true. But what will its utility be?

In the second place, I say that this principle is dangerous in practice.

We have many ideas that are only partial, either because things often include a thousand properties that we are ignorant of or because the properties we are acquainted with are too numerous to embrace all at once, and we divide them into different ideas that we consider separately. Later, familiar with these partial ideas, we take them for as many complete ideas, and we suppose there are in nature an equal number of objects that perfectly correspond to them and that include nothing more than what they represent. If on these occasions we use the Cartesian principle, it will merely confirm us in this error. Seeing that several partial ideas are clear and distinct, and not realizing that they belong only to a single thing, we think we are justified in proliferating existences according to the numbers of our ideas. I will give an example of this that the Cartesians cannot dispute.

Philosophers who admit the possibility of a vacuum base their opinion on the Cartesian principle. We have, they say, the idea of some extension that is divisible, mobile, and impenetrable. We have further the idea of an extension that is indivisible, immobile, and penetrable. Now it is clearly and distinctly included in these ideas that the one is not the other. Thus we can state that outside of us there are two quite different extensions, one a vacuum and the other a property of physical objects.

Although this argument is not very difficult to overturn, I do not see that the Cartesians have yet met it, or could meet it, with a valid counter-argument. Those who are somewhat versed in philosophy, especially metaphysics, can easily observe how many chimeras arise from this principle: "Everything included in the clear and distinct idea of a thing can be correctly affirmed of it."

It is true that when Descartes first uses this principle, he makes it as clear as we could wish because he applies it to a particular case where we must know what a clear and distinct idea is. Attempting to doubt everything, Descartes recognizes as a first truth that he is a thing that thinks. Seeking his reason for holding to this proposition, he finds himself in a clear and distinct perception of his existence and his thought, and he thereby infers that he can establish as a general rule that everything he perceives clearly and distinctly is true.

Here the idea or the clear and distinct perception is merely the consciousness of our existence and our thought—a consciousness known so intimately to us that nothing is more evident. Thus every time we try to use the rule, we should examine whether our certainty is equal to our certainty of our existence and thought. This rule cannot be extended to cases different from the example that gave rise to it.

If the Cartesians had not exceeded these limits, we could not object to the clarity of their principle. But their applications of it soon make it obscure, and their clear and distinct ideas are no more than an I-know-not-what that they cannot define.

Let us conclude that, by starting with the assumption of innate ideas, philosophers have made a beginning too inadequate for achieving genuine knowledge. Their principles, applied to vague expressions, can engender only opinions that are absurd and defensible against criticism only by the obscurity that must envelop them.

7 Fifth Example: Taken From Malebranche

We can conclude from the preceding chapters that to construct a system, we merely need a word whose vague meaning lends itself to anything and everything. If we have more than one word, the system will be more extensive and worthier of those philosophers who think that nothing lies beyond the reach of their minds. Such foundations are not very solid, but their edifice is bolder, more extraordinary, and thereby more likely to please the imagination.

Perhaps I will be suspected of trying to make these philosophers appear absurd. But their own arguments will show whether I have exaggerated the faults of their method. I shall begin with Malebranche because he is a metaphysician whose intellectual brilliance has made him among the most famous. Let us see how he formulates ideas of the understanding, will, freedom, and inclinations. These things are entirely in the domain of metaphysics and they very much warranted discussion, as did many others.

"The human mind," says this philosopher, "being neither material nor extended, is doubtless a simple and completely uncompounded substance. But we customarily distinguish two faculties in it, to wit, the understanding and the will, which must be explained first in order to attach a precise notion to those two words. For it appears that our notions or ideas of these two faculties are not sufficiently clear or distinct."[23]

It appears that if Cartesians are prepared to notice the imprecision of the ideas of others, they are less successful in making their own ideas precise. Malebranche will be proof of this.

---

[23]*Inquiry into truth*. Book 1, Ch. 1.

But because these ideas are highly abstract and fall outside the province of the imagination, it seems appropriate to express them in relation to properties characteristic of matter, which being readily imaginable, will make the notions that it is good to attach to the words "understanding" and "will" more distinct and even more familiar.

"More familiar," that is true. More "distinct,"—the following will show that Malebranche is wrong. Thus he missed the most essential point. Philosophy already contains far too many notions that are merely familiar, for it is difficult to get people used to precise ideas when they have acquired the habit of using words without troubling themselves to determine their meaning other than by some rather haphazard comparisons. Thus nowhere do preconceptions put out deeper roots than in the head of a philosopher.

We need only be mindful of the fact that these relations between mind and matter are not entirely correct, and that we are comparing these two things only in order to make the mind more attentive and to lead others to get some sense of what we mean.

What! At the very moment Malebranche is concerned that these ideas are not sufficiently clear or distinct and proposes to make them precise, he uses a means that, by his own admission, instead of giving exact notions of what he means, will make it only somewhat sensed! Comparisons give no ideas of things, they are fit only for familiarizing us with the ideas we already have.

But it is rather common to take merely familiar notions for precise ones. Malebranche let himself be deceived on this point. In fact, he promises clear and distinct ideas but he is merely attempting to make us familiar with his vague ideas about the understanding and will. He scarcely completes his comparison of mind and matter than he thinks he has done everything he promised. And we see him use the words "will" and "understanding" with the same assurance as if he had perfectly worked out everything concerning the nature of these faculties. We see that the failing of this philosopher is the one I generally condemn in all those who construct abstract systems. He wants to formulate an idea of a thing according to the idea of something else of a completely different nature. That is one of the things that, as I have said,[24] contributes to the fecundity of these sorts of systems.

Matter or extension includes two properties or faculties. The first faculty is that of having different shapes; the second is the capacity to be moved. Similarly, the human mind involves two faculties: the first, the understanding, is that of having several ideas, that is, of apprehending several things; the second, the will, is that of having several inclinations or of wanting various things.

---

[24]Ch. 2.

Does this beginning thus offer such clear and distinct ideas? Can we explain what we see when we represent the mind's faculty of having different ideas and inclinations by matter's property of having different shapes and movements? But the following seems to me even more unintelligible. Malebranche is going to explain first the relations he finds between the faculty of having different ideas and the faculty of having different shapes.

Extension is capable of having two sorts of shapes. Some are only external, like the roundess in a glob of wax. Others are internal, like those belonging to all the tiny parts of which wax is composed. For unquestionably the tiny parts making up a glob of wax have very different shapes from the parts making up a piece of iron. Thus, I simply call external shape, "shape," and I call "configuation" the shape that is internal and necessary to all the parts of which wax is composed so that it is what it is.

Similarly, we can say that the mind's perceptions of ideas are of two sorts. The first kind, called pure perceptions, are so to speak, superficial to the mind. They do not penetrate it nor modify it appreciably. The second kind, called sensory perceptions, penetrate it more or less acutely. Examples are pleasure and pain, light and colors, tastes, smells, and so forth. For I shall show in what follows that sensations are nothing other than the mind's ways of being, and it is for that reason that I call them modifications of the mind.

In the first editions of the *Inquiry into truth*, Malebranche expresses the relation between ideas and shapes in a different way. Distinguishing two sorts of shapes, one of which is internal and belongs to all the tiny parts making up an object and the other external, he observes that the mind's ideas are of two sorts. The first kind represents something outside us, such as a quarry, a house, or the like. The second kind represents what happens in us, such as our sensations, pain, and pleasure.[25]

No doubt Malebranche subsequently felt some uneasiness and feared that he had not given sufficiently precise ideas. Indeed, what relation is there between the external shape of an object and an idea that represents what is outside of us: between the internal shapes belonging to the tiny parts of an object and the ideas that represent what happens in ourselves? So he preferred to indicate this relation by thinking of ideas as being, so to speak, superficial to the mind, and sensations as penetrating it more keenly. But in truth what on earth are ideas and sensations when they are imagined this way!

Malebranche endeavors to make a sharper distinction between ideas and sensations than actually exists. He is far from thinking that ideas are modifications of the mind, as if the same sensations modifying the mind did not give an adequate representation of external things. The obstinacy of

---

[25]This is how Malebranche still expresses himself in the fourth edition.

Cartesians on this subject stems from their ignorance of the origin of ideas, and it is incredible how much they have contributed to muddling up all metaphysics.

The first and chief correspondence between matter's faculty of having different shapes or configurations and the mind's faculty of having different ideas or modifications is that in the same way that the body's faculty of having different shapes or configurations is utterly passive and includes no action, so too the faculty of having different ideas and modifications in the mind is utterly passive and includes no action. I call this faculty or capacity of the mind for having all these things "understanding."

Thus, the mind forms no ideas by itself. They come to it ready-made. These are the conclusions we adopt when we reason only according to comparisons. But when we try to consult experience, we see that the understanding is passive only as regards ideas that ome directly from the senses, and that the others are all its product. This . be.ieve I have proven elsewhere.[26]

"The other correspondence between the mind's passive faculty and that of matter is that, as matter is not truly changed by a change in shape . . . the mind is not appreciably changed by the diversity of its ideas . . ."

This is probably because it undergoes merely superficial change. But would this be to say that Malebranche's mind, once he had learned everything that he put into his *Inquiry into truth*, was much the same as before?

"Moreover, as we can say that matter undergoes considerable change when wax loses the configuration proper to its parts to take on that belonging to fire and smoke . . . thus we can say that the mind undergoes very considerable changes when it changes its modifications and suffers pain after having felt pleasure."

In the transition from complete ignorance to genuine science the mind changes as much as in that from pleasure to pain.

"We must conclude that pure perceptions are to the mind rather like what shapes are to matter, and that configurations are to matter rather like what sensations are to the mind."

In the final editions he adds: "But it should not be imagined that the comparison is exact . . . " It is rather extraordinary that, having criticized others for not giving a sufficiently clear or distinct idea of the understanding, he undertakes to make up for it merely by a comparison that he warns us not to take as precise. Only the imagination can represent ideas by shapes and sensations by configurations. If we try to conceive things clearly, we all realize that this method does not provide the means for doing so. Neverthe-

---

[26]Preliminary lessons, *Grammar; Treatise on the sensations.*

less, Malebranche sees nothing to add to what he has said and he goes on to the second faculty of the mind in order to compare it with the second faculty of matter.

"In the same way that the author of nature is the universal cause of all the movements of matter, He is also the general cause of all the natural mental inclinations. And in the same way that all movements follow a straight line [*ligne droite*] if they do not encounter some external and particular causes that affect them and produce a curved course by their opposition, so too all our inclinations from God are right [*droites*] and they could have no other end than to possess the good and the true if there were not an external cause that affected nature's impulsion and directed it toward bad ends".

What would Malebranche have done if the metaphorical expression "*des inclinations droites*" had not existed in French? His comparison would no doubt have lost a great deal. The movement of objects in a straight line is certainly a very clear and palpable image of the right inclinations of minds. Thus this philosopher is going to substitute the word "movement" for that of "inclination" apparently for greater precision.

There is a considerable difference between the impulsion or movement that the author of nature produces in matter and the impulsion or movement toward the good-in-general that the same author continually imposes on the mind. For matter is utterly passive. It has no power to stop its movement and turn it to one side rather than another. It always moves, as I just said, in a straight line. And when it is prevented from continuing in this way, it describes a circular line, the largest one possible and consequently the closest to a straight line, because it is God who impels its movement and who controls its course. But it is not the same with the will. We can say that in a sense the will is acting because our mind can variously affect the inclination and the impulsion that God gives it. For, although the will cannot stop this impulsion, it can in a sense deflect it to the side that it pleases and thus cause all the disorder to be found in its inclinations, and all the miseries that are the necessary and certain consequences of sin.

God alone controls the movement of matter because matter is powerless and passive. On the other hand, minds themselves control the movements with which they are endowed. They thus have power and action. But, we may ask Malebranche, what is this power and action? Is it not only the movement that comes from God? Then, the mind no more acts than does matter, and movement remains as God Himself determines it. Or is it something different from this movement? Then the mind has a power and action that do not come from God.

In following these comparisons of Malebranche, it is impossible to explain why the mind, rather than matter, has the power to determine the character that God gives it. He appeals in vain to internal sentience and to faith[27] in order to make this claim persuasive. The more he tries to prove thereby that we control the forces that shape us, the more he reveals that his principles are defective if instead of explaining the matter, they lead to absurdities. Let us examine Malebranche's explanations.

When the mind controls the movement that it receives from God, it is not, according to Malebranche, actually doing something. It stops, rests, and does not follow the whole pattern of this movement. There is an act in it, but it is of a highly peculiar nature. "It is an immanent act that does not produce anything physical in our substance—an act that in this case does not even require of the true cause that some physical effect occur in us, or some idea, or new sensation—in short, an act that does nothing and that does not make the general cause as such[28] do anything."

Who would have thought that there were acts that consisted of resting and doing nothing? But when the mind is taken up with its inaction, when it acts without doing anything, does the movement given it by God decrease? Not at all. God always pushes it toward Himself with the same force, and that leads to the discovery of a marvelous difference between the movement of the mind and that of matter. The *movement of* the mind *does not cease, even when we are at rest, in seeking to possess the good, whereas the movement of the body does cease in rest.*[29]

"I admit, that we have no clear idea or even an internal feeling of this constancy of impulsion or natural movement toward the good." He must be very biased in favor of his principles to maintain something that by his own admission he has no idea of and that he is not even conscious of. But everyone who makes up astract systems is reduced to this.

In matter, everything happens through movement. The idea of movement is thus one of the most familiar ones. So it was natural for Malebranche to use it in explaining what happens in the mind. But his difficulties in doing so reveal how imprecise his ideas are.

Movement in matter is, in relation to us, nothing other than an object's going from one place to another. Will Malebranche give a similar definition of the movement that he ascribes to the mind? Doubtlessly not. What idea will he give of it then?[30] The mind senses the needs of its body and the

---

[27]*Clarification.*

[28]*Clarification.*

[29]*Clarification.*

[30]Nowhere does he define what he means by the "movement of the mind."

movement that leads the body toward objects suited to its survival. It thereby comes about that movement in the body never occurs without sensations in the mind. This is why the two have been confused under the same name. But the word "movement" is very far from revealing the nature of these sensations.

To pass on to different inclinations, to the will and freedom, here are the principles that Malebranche establishes.[31]

God can have no other chief end than Himself. His lesser ends are creatures; he wants their survival and loves them, but for His own sake, and He cannot strictly speaking have any love other than the love of Himself. As the natural inclinations of minds are certainly continual impulsions of the will of him who has created and preserves them, it seems to me necessary, says Malebranche, that these inclinations be completely similar to those of their creator and preserver. From this principle, where there is an "it seems to me," he concludes positively that God endows us with only one love which is the love of the good-in-general. But why substitute the love of the good-in-general for the love of God? It seems to me that for his conclusion to be precise, he should have said that God endows us with the love only of himself. No doubt Malebranche preferred to be inconsistent rather than to contradict exprience too obviously.

According to Malebranche, this movement toward the good-in-general is the mainspring of all our inclinations, passions, and loves.[32] To understand it, you need only imagine that the mind directs this movement toward particular objects. From this Malebranche derives his ideas of the will and freedom.

By the word "*will*" I mean the impulsion or natural movement that leads us toward toward the indeterminate good-in-general, and by "*freedom*" I understand the *mind's power to direct this impulsion toward objects that please us and thus make our natural inclinations terminate in some particular object.* These inclinations were previously vague and indeterminate toward the general or universal good, that is, toward God, who is the only good-in-general because He alone includes all good things.[33]

First, is it reasonable, on the pretext that God includes all good things, to confound him with something so vague, indeterminate, and abstract as the good-in-general?

Second, what idea can we form of the will if we understand by this word a movement that directs the mind toward some indeterminate good? It would have been desirable for Malebranche to have found some object moved toward a point-in-general. This philosopher does not understand that we

[31]Book 4, Ch. 1.

[32]Book 4, Ch. 1.

[33]Book 1, Ch. 1.

could have particular loves without being moved toward the good-in-general. It seems to me, on the contrary, that all our loves are confined to highly determinate objects. What we call love of the good-in-general is strictly not a love, but merely an abstract way of thinking of our particular loves. Biased in favor of abstract principles which he regarded as the source of our know-ledge, Malebranche believed that our loves had to originate in some abstract love. But here we see clearly how unsound this way of reasoning is.

Such is the system that Malebranche conceived for explaining the nature of the understanding and will. Its foundation reduces to the principle that "ideas and inclinations are to the mind what shapes and movement are to matter"— a principle that he owes to a comparison of two completely different substances. We should thus not be surprised that he failed to formulate precise ideas. These notions were highly influential in many places in his work, but it would take too long to examine them along with all their implications. To show clearly where they can lead, I shall limit myself to using them as principles for a proposition obviously false but for which I shall give a geometric proof, as the metaphysicians do.

THEOREM

Or Proposition to be Proved

Love and hate are the same thing.

DEFINITION 1

Love is a movement that leads us toward an object.

DEFINITION 2

Hate is a movement that leads us away from an object.

AXIOM 1

Whatever is led toward a point is by the same movement led away
from a diametrically opposed point.

AXIOM 2

The object of love and that of hate are diametrically opposed,
for the object of love is the good or being, and that of hate is evil or nothing.

Proof of the Theorem

Hate is the movement that leads us away from an object (by the second definition), and (by the first definition) love is the movement that leads us toward an object. Now we move away from an object only as we are led by this same movement toward some diametrically opposed object (by the first axiom). And the objects of love and hate are diametrically opposed (by the second axiom). Thus, it is by a single movement that we love and hate. Thus, love and hate are one and the same movement, and therefore one and the same thing.

Malebranche himself[34] says that "the movement of hate is the same as that of love. But," he adds, "the emotion of hate is quite different from that of love . . . Movements are acts of the will. Emotions are modifications of the mind." There you have love and hate as the same acts of the will, that is, strictly one and the same thing, for it never occurred to us to think of love and hate other than as acts of the will. One could thus love and hate independently of this emotion that comes to affect our minds. And if Malebranche recognized some difference in the sentiment of these two passions, it was only because he was obliged to do so by his own experience which taught him that he was not doing the same thing when he hated as when he loved.

As an example of an abstract system I could have given Malebranche's views on ideas, but it would have been too long to spell out. Besides it has few supporters, and the imprecision of the principles that I have just criticized is perhaps not as generally recognized.

Malebranche was one of the finest minds of the last century. Unfortunately, however, he was too much influenced by his imagination. He saw only through his imagination and believed he heard the answers of the all-wise, of universal reason, of the Word. Admittedly, when Malebranche gets hold of the truth, no one compares to him. How clever he was in identifying the errors of the senses, the imagination, the mind and heart! He has a nice touch in his illustrations of the different characters of people who are misled in the search for truth. Is he himself mistaken? He has such a beguiling manner that he seems clear even when he is incomprehensible.

He was well acquainted with mankind. But he understood man less philosophical than humanistic. His ignorance in this respect was due to two principles. First, that we see everything in God; second, that we do not love anything except through our love of God or the good-in-general. Indeed, with principles like these it was impossible to go back to the source of human knowledge and passions, or to follow their complete evolution.

Malebranche and Locke are usually compared, probably because they both wrote about human understanding. In fact, they could not be more unalike. Locke had none of Malebranche's shrewdness, methodicalness, or style. But neither did he have any of Malebranche's faults. He understood the origin of our knowledge, but he does not follow its evolution in sufficiently extensive or clear detail. Locke is on the way to truth like a man obliged to

---

[34]Book 5, Ch. 3.

beat a path for the first time. He finds obstacles and does not always overcome them, takes detours, staggers, falls, and makes many attempts to regain his way. The path he opens up is often so steep that it proves as hard to reach the truth by following his steps as it is not to go astray in following those of Malebranche. Locke argues very soundly. Often, he makes very subtle observations about the most ordinary things, but he seems to succeed less well in difficult matters. More philosophical than humanistic, he is more instructive in his *Essay on Human Understanding* than Malebranche is in his *Inquiry Into Truth.*

8 Sixth Example: Monads

Leibniz sets forth only a very summary account of his system. For the key to it, we must examine several of his works to see that nothing is omitted that can shed light on his thought. Sometimes he seems to aim for obscurity and, fearing that he will offend received opinion, he approximates ordinary ways of speaking and gives us to understand the opposite of what he means. Perhaps it is also true that in discussing the different parts of his system several times over, he was forced to alter his language as he developed his ideas. He says, for example, that fully occupied space can have no more reality than a vacuum—it is merely a phenomenon, an appearance. Nevertheless, to judge from his manner of speaking about it, we would think that however little it accords with his principles, he takes it for something real.

As for Wolf, his most famous disciple, apart from the fact that he did not adopt all Leibniz's ideas, his method is so abstract and tedious that we would have to be extremely curious about the system of monads to have the determination to learn about it by reading his works.[35] As for me, since I want to set it forth with all the clarity permitted by a subject that cannot always be stated clearly, I shall present the sequence of ideas by which I imagine it developed in Liebniz's mind. To be brief, I shall make him speak, but I will not make him say anything that he did not say or that he would not have said if he had had to explain his system in its full extent and without detours. This is the subject of the first part of this chapter; in the second I will present counterarguments.

---

[35]I am speaking only of those he wrote in Latin, for they are the only ones with which I am acquainted.

PART ONE:
DISCUSSION OF THE SYSTEM OF MONADS

Article 1: On the Existence of Monads

There are compounds. Thus there are simple entities, for nothing exists without sufficient reason. Now the reason for a thing's compoundedness cannot be found in other compound things because it could still be asked where their compoundedness came from. Thus, the reason lies elsewhere, and consequently it can only be found in simple things.

In fact, every existing thing is either a unit or a collection of units. Thus a unit is not itself a collection. Otherwise there would be collections of units even though there were no units, which is a manifest self-contradiction. Now strictly speaking, unity—namely, that which is not a collection—cannot apply to a compound thing, namely a collection. Thus there are simple entities, units. For this reason I will call them "monads."

At one time I adopted atoms but I later perceived that the principle of true unity could not be found in them, for the unalterable attachment of their parts, some separate from others, does not lessen their diversity. I thus saw that only formal atoms, that is, true units absolutely devoid of parts, could be the principles of the compoundedness of things.

Being simple, monads have no parts. Without parts, they are without extension. Without extension, they are without shape, cannot occupy space, or be in a place. Not occupying space, they cannot move.

Genuinely extended things can be distinguished by differences in location. Monads are different. To be distinguished, they must have completely different properties. If two monads were similar in every respect, they would be two by supposition and in truth would be only one.

If extension, shape, location, and movement do not apply to any monad in particular, no more do they apply to an assemblage of monads. A collection of unextended things could not constitute extension. We must reason the same way about location, shape, and movement. The universe, or the assemblage of all the monads, thus does not occupy a space that is more real than a single simple thing and this assemblage properly has no extension, shape, or movement. In short, there is nothing of what is commonly understood by body. Thus we should not think of these things as so many realities. They are merely phenomena or appearances such as colors and sounds. This is what I must warn the reader so he avoids the mistakes that my language could occasion when I am obliged to use the words "extension," "shape," "movement," and "body."

Article II: On Extension and Movement

If we could penetrate the nature of things to the point of clearly distinguishing all their contents, we would see them as they are. Thus appearances come only from the imperfect way we see things. And we need only consider how we perceive objects for us to discover the artifice that produces phenomena.

We perceive ourselves and we have perceptions that yield for us the appearances of many things that we distinguish from ourselves and from each other. But our perceptions can make us distinguish things in this way only as they represent them as existing separately from ourselves and each other. And our perceptions cannot reveal them to us under this appearance without our immediately thinking we see extension.[36] Thus, extension does not presuppose that there are entities genuinely separate from each other and genuinely extended. It presupposes only that we have perceptions representing a multiplicity of distinct entities.

Once our perceptions have produced the phenomenon of extension, they can produce the phenomena that depend on it. We see different parts in extension. We observe all sorts of shapes in it. Some of them will appear near, others far away, and so on.

The things that our perceptions represent as separate from each other can always be represented in the same order, or our perceptions can change this order so that something that has appeared immediately adjacent to another will appear to be separated from it by a second thing, then by a third, and so on successively. The first case is an instance of the phenomenon of rest; the second, movement.

Nothing exists without a sufficient reason. Consequently, the order in which our perceptions represent things has its reason in the order of the things themselves. Thus the reality of things will provide the seeker after it with the most detailed explanation of the development of each phenomenon. But our ignorance in this matter obliges us to take a different route. Instead of explaining phenomena by the reality of things, we will judge reailty by phenomena, and imagine in things something analogous to the appearances produced by perceptions. Consequently, this is how I reason.

Phenomena represent compounds or wholes whose parts are more closely related to each other than to anything else. Simple things thus combine in such a way that several closely related things constitute something analogous to compounds. This is what I call collections or aggregates of monads.

Phenomena reveal to us compounds that are touching and form a continuum, as well as other compounds that are remote. Thus relations exist

---

[36]Even that is not enough. Distinct entities are properly separate from each other. To produce the phenomenon of extension, they must while appearing contiguous, also seem to form a continuum.

among aggregates suited to yielding these appearances. For example, let aggregate A have an immediate relation with B, B with C, and C with D. A, B, C, and D will produce the phenomenon of a continuum of which A and D will appear to be distant points.

Finally, by considering how our perceptions perserve the same order among things or change it, we will judge that the aggregates of monads really do possess an order that varies or stays the same. This is where we find the first reason for the phenomena of movement and rest.

In reality, extension is merely the order among monads and aggregates which makes our perceptions represent them as existing outside each other.[37] Rest is the order preserved without alteration; movement is the change that happens to it.

When the relations among several aggregates change, the reason for it can be found in a single aggregate or in all of them. If it is found in only one of them, the aggregate alone will appear to move. If the reason is found in all the aggregates, they will all appear to move. The phenomenon of movement thus has its reason in the aggregate in which the change of relation has its source. When I am walking, for example, it is my body that moves and not the place I am going through because it is my body that contains the reason for its changes of relation to this place.

Moreover, we can notice movement only when our perceptions represent the changes of relations so well that we can exactly distinguish them from each other. But if our perceptions represent these changes so confusedly that we cannot distinguish them, they become nothing for us and the phenomenon of rest continues. Thus when we notice movement, it must be that in reality things change their relations. And when we do not observe movement, it must be that, if the relations do not stay the same, our perceptions at least represent the changes only in a very confused way.

Article III: On Space and Objects

It is impossible to perceive changes without imagining something fixed to which they are related. For example, we can represent some extension that moves only if we represent some extension that that does not move at all. We then consider movable and immovable extensions as two different things, the former giving us the idea of object and the latter, the idea of space. These ideas have even been so sharply contrasted that it has been asked whether empty space exists—extension without an object—or whether everything is

---

[37]This is what Leibniz means then he says that extension is merely the order of coexisting things.

full. But there is properly neither a vacuum nor a plenum, since extension itself is merely a phenomenon.

Objects seem to move in an extension that we judge to be immovable. We take this extension to be penetrable. Thus space implies the idea of penetrability as well as immobility. Space seems to receive objects and thereby becomes the place for each of them.

Objects, on the other hand, must seem to us impenetrable. Being movable, objects are readily imagined to succeed each other in the same space. But as portions of extension, objects are necessarily represented as separate from each other and consequently as unable to occupy the same space at the same time, that is, to penetrate each other.

Notice that when we say objects are impenetrable, we are comparing some objects with other objects. In relation to the space they move in, they are penetrable, for since they penetrate it, they are penetrated by it—the relation is reciprocal. We also imagine the parts of space as necessarily outside each other, and consequently as mutually impenetrable. But when we think of the parts of space as the place in which objects move, we judge those parts as penetrable.

Thus objects and space are properly just extension, that it, aggregates of simple things considered as separate from each other. But taken as immovable and penetrable, extension is space. Taken as movable and impenetrable, it is an object.

An object is thus not an extended substance made up of an infinity of extended substances. Strictly speaking, there are no other substances than simple things, and an object is merely an aggregate, a collection of substances. When I call it a substance, I do so only to comply with custom. The expression should not be taken literally.

With these principles it is easy to resolve the question whether objects exist. There are none, if, taking this word in the vulgar sense, we understand by object something genuinely extended. There are objects if we mean something that is merely apparently extended, that is, if we take an object to be a collection of simple things that, because of the way we perceive them, produce the subjective phenomenon of extension.

Being merely aggregates of monads, objects have different essences depending on the simple things that make them up and the combinations made of them. Now each monad is essentially different from every other one. Thus there are no two physical objects perfectly alike. We shall see further on how all objects are constituted, how each object has a dominant monad to which all other monads are subordinate, and finally how everything occurring in the object is in harmony with what happens to the dominant monad, and vice-versa.

Article IV: How Every Monad Has Perceptions and the Power to Produce Them

I have posited relations among monads because in fact several things cannot exist without having such relations. Moreover there are relations among objects; hence there are relations among monads: because objects are merely aggregates, the reason for their properties must lie in their simple constituent entities. In short, we must suppose that there are relations and changes in relations among monads, just as there are among phenomena, and that everything occurs in the same proportions for both.

Up to this point we know what monads are not, but that is insufficient to form an idea of the relations among them. If we could be sure of nothing else than that they are not extended, shaped, or movable, and so forth, it would follow that for us they are nothing. The absence of properties makes for nothing and, to exist, a thing must have something positive.

Monads are simple substances. The notion of a mind can thus serve as a model for the idea that we should form of a monad. All we have to imagine in each monad is something analogous to having sensations, and to what is generally called perception. This is what is positive in it. The monad undergoes changes when it has different perceptions.

But what is the source of these perceptions? On the one hand, we cannot conceive that a monad can be changed or experience within its substance changes caused by the actions of another entity. For as it is simple, nothing can escape its substance to act externally, and nothing can enter its substance to make it suffer. Thus monads do not interact, nor is there any reciprocal action or passion among them and, consequently, the changes in them do not have any external source.

On the other hand, if we consult the essence of monads, we shall still not find the reason for the changes happening to them. The essence of a thing determines merely what belongs to it constantly. For example, it determines the possibility of changes. But when a change is possible, it is not actual. We must thus identify in every substance another reason how and why that particular change rather than any other becomes actual. Now I call this reason power. Thus every monad contains a power that is the source of all the changes happening to it or of all its perceptions, and we can define substance as that which has in itself the source of its changes.

Although the notion of power falls within the scope of metaphysics, it is not any the less intelligible. For everyone can notice in himself a continual effort every time he tries to act. For example, if I want to write and someone stays my hand, I continually make an effort and, when my hand is freed, this effort produces the action so that, as long as this effort lasts, I continue to write, and as soon as it stops, I stop writing. Power thus consists in a continual effort to act.

Thus when I speak of the power of monads, I mean that an effort exists in them, a continual tendency toward action, that is, to produce a change in them by producing a new perception. For because their changes of state are perceptions, the power that tends to change their state tends to produce new perceptions.[38]

But since each simple thing is unitary, so is its power. Its power thus encounters nothing that resists its continual effort to act. Consequently, the power must continually produce new changes. Thus the state of monads changes continually. Thus they endlessly experience new perceptions.

Article V: On pre-established harmony

To us phenomena represent the connection among all the parts of the universe. Thus some phenomena include the simple entities making up the universe. If these entities interacted, this would be sufficient to enable us to imagine the connection between them. But that is not enough. Each person has his own particular power, and this power produces a sequence of changes in him that is completely independent of the sequences occurring in others. In this system monads thus seem like so many isolated entities with no interconnections. Consequently, objects do not have any interconnections nor are they connected with the dominant monads with which I shall show they are united.

Nevertheless, nothing prevents the sequences of change from being interrelated or from combining with each other to tend toward some common end in the same order as if the entities really did interact. Hence, we imagine a harmony among all the parts of the universe that creates all their interconnection.

For example, my mind or the monad dominating my body successively experiences different perceptions, and it would experience them as well and in the same order if it were not united with any body. My body, without being in any way influenced by perceptions, also continually changes its state, and its changes are merely the effects of its mechanism. In short everything mental takes place as if there were no body, and everything bodily takes place as if there were no mind. But there is a harmony between these two substances because their changes correspond to each other as precisely as if they watched out for their mutual preservation by interacting.

God alone is the cause of this harmony because He pre-established it. Not that He himself determined the changes in one of these two substances so as

---

[38]This power, this tendency toward action, Leibniz also calls appetite.

to make them accord with what had to happen in the other, but He consulted what had to happen to each possible substance by virtue of its own particular power; and He united the substances in which this accord had to be found. Imagine a skilled mechanic who, anticipating your orders to your valet tomorrow, builds a robot who will carry out these orders to the letter. The same thing happens in the system of pre-established harmony. When God chooses the body for the mind, the body, owing to its mechanism, carries out orders exactly. When the mind is chosen for the body, it seems in turn to obey, although it merely goes through the changes produced in it by its particular power.

We can imagine the harmony of the whole universe if we represent the correspondence among all it parts as the same as the correspondence between my body and my mind. But to clarify matters, let us follow the Cartesians in reifying the phenomenon of the plenum. According to this hypothesis, the slightest movement should be transmitted at all distances; and some object's stimulation of a sense organ cannot be limited to just an impression of the object, but must further be an impression of all the objects in the universe. All the parts of the world thereby coexist and succeed each other in such a way that the modifications of each object are determined by the whole world, that is, every body has a certain shape and a certain amount of movement because there is a sufficient reason for it in the present state of the universe. If this were not so, this body would not be connected with other bodies and would not be part of this world.

Now the phenomenon of the plenum is perfectly analogous to the reality of things; it is their shape. Thus everything is connected in reality as everything seems to be connected in the plenum.

But we should recall that this connection does not presuppose a genuine interdependence of substances. It merely presupposes an ideal interdependence and we can say that substances are interdependent only in the ordinary sense and only following appearances. Hence it is in this way that we say with the common people "the sun rises and sets" although we agree with Copernicus in believing that the earth turns.

Monads, being independent of each other, actually exist one by one. Thus in reality there is nothing that is compound, nor consequently is there anything that merits the names "whole" or "part." What we call "whole" and "part" are phenomena included in the notion of body and that result uniquely from the pre-established harmony among monads.

Go to a concert and consider the sounds as diffused in the air and existing independently of each other, and you will not think of any connection among them. Then consider them in relation to your sense organs and you will immediately perceive them as connected and forming harmonies. It is the same way with all the phenomena of the universe.

Article VI: On the nature of things

I call the power peculiar to a simple thing the nature of this thing. All the changes happening to a thing are thus a consequence of its nature. Thus an aggregate of several monads gives rise to the phenomenon of the body, and from the combined powers of these same monads results another phenomenon, motor force. This force is thus the nature of the body, that is, the source of all the changes occurring in the phenomenon of movable and impenetrable extension.

This force always stays the same in every object and even inactivity cannot change it. For an object cannot exist for an instant without combining all the powers of the simple entities of which it is an aggregate. Thus the universe always contains the same quantity of power.

Although the powers of all objects tend toward the same end, they do not all do so equally. They appear to create obstacles for each other and thereby produce the phenomenon of inertia or resistance.

Thus to round out the notion of a physical object, we must add to the ideas of extension, mobility, and impenetrability, the ideas of motor and inertial force. Thus, a physical object is an aggregate of simple entities that, through the order preserved among themselves, produce the phenomena of extension, mobility, impenetrability, motor force, and inertial force.

If we make an abstraction from motor force, we have the idea of matter, that is, a substance that is extended, movable, impenetrable, and endowed with inertial force.

Finally, let us consider the combination of all motor forces, and we have universal nature, namely, the source of all the phenomena of the universe.

The Cartesian system is unphilosophical. Instead of explaining things by natural causes, they appeal to a deus ex machina and every effect seems to be the result of a miracle. In the Liebnizian system God sticks to creating and preserving simple entities and leaves the rest to nature. In every monad, every object and in the whole universe, nature is the source of everything. Nature is like a laborer working on matter that he finds ready created. God unceasingly gives reality to simple entities, and nature unceasingly produces extension, movement, and all other phenomena.

Article VII: How every monad represents the universe

The current state of one monad is related to the current state of all the others. This is what sustains the harmony of the whole universe. Every state of a monad expresses and thus represents the relations between it and the rest of the monads. And since each monad constantly changes, it constantly goes through new representative states. Now a monad's successive perceptions and the different states it goes through are one and the same thing. Thus every perception is representative, and because it is an effect of the monad's power, we can best define it by saying that a monad is an act in which a substance represents something.

But since everything is connected, there is no reason to set limits to this representation. Thus it embraces everything and tends toward the infinite. So every perception represents the current state of the whole universe. And because this state is connected with the past of which it is the effect, and with the future with which it is pregnant,[39] the same perception represents the past, present, and future. Consequently, we would have the most exact and detailed idea of the universe if we had a complete knowledge of the current state of a single monad.[40]

Nevertheless, not all monads represent the universe in the same way. Each monad represents the universe according to its relation to all other entities, and consequently from a different point of view. It does not represent directly things that are only distantly related to it. A highly complex object is for example not directly represented in a simple entity, but the object is represented in a less complex object, the less complex object in still another even less complex object, and so on. So that as the representation passes from one entity to another by the smallest gradations, it gets closer and closer to the smallest possible objects and terminates in a simple entity.

It must be this way because of the principle of sufficient reason. For if the representation passed from one object to another that did not have the closest relation to it there would be a kind of unaccountable "jump." Thus we must conclude that every portion of matter contains an infinity of objects, each smaller than the next, which decrease by infinitely small differences down to one most directly related to the simple entity. This is the only hypothesis without abrupt transitions. Thus a monad can represent the universe only when it is united with an infinitely small object, and because it is in the nature of each monad to represent the universe forever, it is also in its nature to be forever inseparable from that object.

Article VIII: On different sorts of perceptions and how each one includes an infinity of others

It may be asked how a substance can have perceptions, that is, to act and to produce internal changes that represent something without being conscious of its perceptions or of what it represents. I would reply that it is because its perceptions are totally obscure. Make some of them clear and it will immediately be conscious of them. Make others clear and its consciousness

---

[39]"The present is pregnant with the future." This is Leibniz's expression.

[40]This is what led Leibniz to say that every substance, every monad, is a living mirror, a concentration of the universe.

will be even further extended, and so on as more of them become clearer.

When I hear the sound of the ocean, for example, I also hear the sound of each wave. But my perception of the overall noise is clear and conscious, and my perception of the sound of one particular wave is obscure and gets confused in the totality. I cannot distinguish it and have no consciousness of it.

If I hear the sound of a single wave, my perception will not be confused with any other. It will be clear and conscious. But the sound of this wave is itself composed of the sound made by each particle of water. Thus this is a perception resulting from many others of which I am unaware. If all our perceptions are decomposed this way, it is not true that they are resolved into several others that, because of our inability to discriminate them, are confounded into a single one.

The total perception resulting from the confusion of several others I call confused. Thus perception can be clear and confused at the same time. My consciousness of it is clear. It is confused because I do not discriminate the particular perceptions that cause it. Finally, it becomes distinct as I distinguish more particular perceptions in it. The perception of a tree, for example, is distinct because I can identify a trunk, branches, leaves, and so on.

But however we try to decompose our perceptions, we never arrive at an absolutely simple one. Each perception is like a point in which an infinity of other points comes to be joined and confounded. A sensation of color, for example, can represent a colored object only by creating obscure perceptions that represent the movements and shapes that are the physical causes of this color. These obscure perceptions can represent these movements and shapes only to the extent that the perceptions result from the obscure perceptions representing the determinations that are the sources of movements and shapes; and so on down to the first determinations of monads. Consequently, a sensation of color is the result of an infinitude of perceptions confounded into a single one. If we could discriminate them successively, first the color would disappear and we would see only certain parts of extension variously shaped and moved. Soon afterward, the phenomena of shape and movement would in turn disappear and only the different determinations of simple entities would remain. Thus a color disappears when the microscope allows us see the colors forming the mixture.[41]

We see that in this system perceptions do and do not represent the real state of objects. They represent it by this infinite multitude of things of which we are unaware. But as regards just what is discriminated in them, they do not represent it, they are mere phenomena or appearances.

---

[41]Mix two very fine colored powders together and the result will be a third color. But a microscope will make the first two colors reappear.

Article IX: Of different sorts of monads depending on the different sorts of perceptions they are capable of

According to the preceding article, our perceptions can be confounded or distinguished ad infinitum, depending on our powers of discrimination. If they are confounded to the point of indiscriminability, they are totally obscure and we are not conscious of any one of them. This is what happens to us in sleep. If, on the other hand, they are so sharply distinguished that we notice each one in particular, then we discern them all and thus are conscious of them all. An entity with just these sorts of perceptions sees distinctly everything that exists.

This state belongs only to God. There is no thing infinitely distant from Him. Our sensations represent only confusedly. And if we sometimes say that sensations are distinct, this should not be understood strictly, as if we discriminated everything included in them; it merely means that we distinguish a part of them.

From the state in which all perceptions are totally obscure to the state in which each of them is clear and distinct, we can imagine a continuum representing all possible states of monads. They proceed beyond the first state only as their perceptions develop and become clearer and more distinct. And that is what everything does that differentiates them. Thus the different sorts of perceptions determine the different classes of entities. In some of them perceptions are totally obscure, and I call then entelechies. In others, perceptions begin to have some degree of clarity and to be accompanied by consciousness. These are minds. In addition, they develop sufficiently to raise monads to a knowledge of necessary truths. They create reasoning minds. Finally they become even more distinct and make reasoning minds rise to a state superior to their present one.

Article X: On the transformations of animals

An organized object is one whose parts are so harmoniously attuned that they all converge to the same end and in an order in which they appear to work together. The human body, for example, is organized because everything in it is properly proportioned for transmitting to the mind perceptions that are sometimes obscure and confused, sometimes fairly clear and distinct. Now every monad is united with a body by which it represents the universe. Therefore every monad has an organized body; the monad has an aggregate of simple entities all of which are subordinate to it. For this reason, I call it the dominant entelechy.

We can thereby suppose that nothing in nature is dead. Everything is sentient and animate, and every portion of matter is a world of created beings, minds, entelechies, and infinite species of animals. Among so many living beings, few are called to appear in this great theater where we play so many different roles. But the stage is the same. They are born, multiply, and perish, as we do.

Nevertheless, nowhere is there, properly speaking, either birth or death. Since it is in the nature of a monad to represent the universe, each monad has been united with a body and remains forever inseparable from it. Conception, development, and destruction are merely metamorphoses and transformations of animals from one species to another. This is the way a caterpillar becomes a butterfly. Consequently a natural machine is never destroyed, although the loss of its large parts reduces it to a smallness no more detectible by the senses than the size of the animal before its so-called birth. Through different transformations the machine sometimes strips itself of one of its parts and at other times it acquires new ones. It thereby appears sometimes extended, sometimes contracted, and as concentrated when believed lost. But it always continues to be an organized object. Every monad thus remains united with the object of which it is the dominant entelechy. In this way animals like minds continue to exist and like them are indestructible.

In these transformations everything tends toward perfection, not only the universe in general but also every particular thing. Thus bodies evolve only to transmit clearer and more distinct perceptions to dominant entelechies and to make them go from one class to a higher one.

Thus it is not at the moment of conception that our minds are created. They were created with the world and became rational when their bodies were sufficiently developed to transmit perceptions to them with a certain degree of clarity. Nor are they destroyed at death, but as each one continues to be united with its first body, each preserves its personality and passes on to a more perfect state than the one it leaves. Other monads that are still only pure entelechies will in turn go through the same transformations,[42] and these metamorphoses will continue for all eternity.

This is the system of monads. There is nothing it does not explain, and difficulties insoluble in every other system are explained here in the most intelligible way.[43] We must thus regard it as something better than a hypothesis.

---

[42]Gottlieb Hanschius reports in a commentary on Liebniz's principles that the philosopher said to him while drinking coffee that perhaps his cup contained a monad that would some day become a reasoning mind.

[43]Among the reasons on which Leibniz based his system, he relies heavily on the fact that any other hypothesis leaves phenomena inexplicable.

PART TWO:
REFUTATION OF THE SYSTEM OF MONADS

I thought I should explicate the whole system of monads, either because it is curious enough to warrant publication or because it was an appropriate way to ensure that I myself understood it. If I tried to confine myself to just the principles that I propose to criticize, I would not have combined the different parts of the system as much as I have and I would have often digressed from Leibniz's thought. This is what usually happens to those who undertake to refute the beliefs of others. M. Justi[44] is a good example of this. He sets forth the basic principles of Leibniz's entire system but because he did not take the precaution of following Leibniz's use of them, he attributes ideas to Leibniz that Leibniz never had, and his critique is irrelevant to the system of monads.[45]

Article I: On the critical principles of this system

There are two drawbacks to avoid in a system. The first is to assume the phenomena that one is trying to explain. The second is to explain them with principles that can be understood no better than the phenomena themselves. Cartesians fall into the former trap when they say that a substance is extended because it is made up of extended substances. But the Leibnizians fall into the second trap if, when they say that a substance is extended because it is an aggregate of several unextended substances, they do not conceive of an unextended substance any better than they do a substance supposed to be genuinely extended. In fact would we be better off to agree with them that the phenomenon of extension occurs because the primary elements of things are unextended than to agree with the Cartesians that there is extension because the primary elements of things are extended?

I agree that the compound, always compounded down to its smallest parts or rather down to the infinitely small, is a thing that makes the mind boggle. The more we analyze this idea, the more contradictory it seems. Shall we thus go back to simple entities? But how shall we conceive of them? Will it be

---

[44]Justi, *Dissertation, qui a remporté le Prix proposé par l'Académie royale (de Berlin) sur le Système des Monades, avec les Pièces qui ont concourut*, Berlin, 1748

[45]Here is an example: Observing correctly (§ 5) that simple entities cannot take up space, he has Leibniz say that there must be a sufficient reason for a simple entity to be in one place rather than another; that each simple entity (§ 14) occupies a point in space and that several of them together thereby fill up space, and produce extension.

by denying of them everything we know about the compound? In this case we obviously conceive of simple entities no better than the compound ones. If we cannot conceive of what a body is, we cannot conceive any better an entity about which we can say nothing except that it has no bodily quality. So to conceive of monads, we must know not only what they are not, we must also know what they are. Leibniz felt strongly that he had an obligation to fulfill this twofold purpose so he made every effort to acquaint us with the positive qualities of monads. He believed he had discovered two things in them; a power and perceptions whose nature was to represent the universe. If he can give us an idea of this power and these perceptions, he will show us how to conceive of his monads and he will be justified in using them to explain phenomena. But is this power and these perceptions are empty words, his system becomes completely silly. It reduces to saying that extension exists because something unextended exists and that bodies exist because something that is not a body exists, and so forth. I shall thus confine myself to an examination of what the Leibnizians say to establish the power and perceptions of simple entities.

Article II: That we cannot form an idea of what Leibniz calls the "power" of monads

To judge whether we have the idea of a thing, often all we have to do is check with our names for it. The name of a known cause directly designates the thing: examples are the words "pendulum," "wheel," and so forth. But when

---

A simple entity does not occupy space, he then says (§ 49), *but several of them together do occupy space. Can one more manifestly contradict oneself?* He takes up several paragraphs to prove that this is contradictory. Does he think that Leibniz could fall into such an obvious absurdity? One should be very sure of one's facts before attributing such mistakes to somebody of such intelligence and who in every respect earned great honor for Germany. As for me, the more I study the system of monads, the more interconnections I find. Leibniz does err but not in the places indicated by M. Justi. My explication of Leibniz is sufficient to resolve all the contradictions that Justi thought he spotted. He does not seem to have been careful enough to grasp always Leibniz's thought. And when he does grasp it, his counterarguments seem to be unclear and unsound.

For example, to refute the principle that "there are compound things, thus there are simple entities," he argues (§ 22, 23, 24) as follows. The simple is a geometric idea, the compound is a metaphysical one. Now the subject of geometry is imaginary, that of metaphysics is real. Thus, Leibniz's conclusion jumbles up something imaginary with something real. Thus, it is false. "By carefully considering the explanation of the compound," he says, (§ 25) we can think of nothing that could lead us to the idea of the simple. Compound entities are those that have parts. The first conclusion thus can only be that where there are compounds, there also are parts. Now the idea of a part does not yet lead us to the idea of the simple. Simple entities are those that have no parts. Thus to proceed further, we would have to conclude that where there are parts, there are no parts—which would be manifest contradiction.

a cause is unknown, our name for the thing indicates only some cause or other with some relation to the effect produced, and it is always made up of names that refer to the effect. This is how the terms "centrifugal force," "centripetal force," "alive," "dead," "gravity," "attraction," "impulsion," and the like were invented. These words are highly convenient, but to see how inappropriate they are for giving us an adequate idea of the causes we are looking for, we have only to compare them with the names of known causes.

If I said, "The sufficient reason for the potentiality of a watch hand's movement lies in the essence of the hand; but when this movement is merely potential, it is not actually moving. Thus the watch has to have a reason for its actuality. Now I call this reason *wheel, pendulum*, and so on." If I explained myself in this way, would I be giving an idea of the springs that make the watch hand move?

A substance changes. Thus it has a reason for its changes. I agree. I further consent to giving this reason the name power, provided that this expression gives me an idea of power.

I have some sort of idea of my own power when I act. I know it at least consciously. But when I use the word power to explain the changes in other substances, it is merely a name that I give to the unknown cause of a known effect. This language shows us the essence of things when my imperfect idea of *wheels, pendulums*, and so on, form clocks.

If our mind occasionally acted without the body, perhaps we would get some idea of a monad's power. But as simple as it is, the monad depends so much on the body that its action is as it were confounded with bodily action. We do not observe the power that we feel in ourselves as belonging to a simple entity; we feel it as suffused throughout a compound whole. Thus it cannot serve as a model representing the power we attribute to each monad.

But often it is sufficient to give something whose name we do not know the name of something we do know to make us think we know them both. Nothing is more familiar than the power that we feel in ourselves. That is why the Leibnizians thought they were forming an idea of the source of the changes in each substance by giving it the name power. Thus we should not be surprised if they ran into more and more difficulties as they tried to gain

---

"The essence of the compound," he says further (§ 30), "necessarily consists in compoundedness. When we reflect about a thing, what comes to mind first and what makes it what it is, is its essence. When we consider compounds, the first thing that comes to mind is compoundedness and it is only compoundedness that makes them into compounds. Thus the essence of compounds coasists in compoundedness." It is from arguments such as this that M. Justi infers that we can explain compounds without reference to simple entities. Moreover, I believe I ought to alert the reader to the fact that Justi was writing in German, and that I can judge his discussion only by the translation that the Academy of Berlin later published."

further insight into the nature of this power. They say, on the one hand, that it is an effort and, on the other, that it encounters no obstacles. But because of our idea of what is called effort and obstacle, effort is useless when there is no obstacle to overcome. Consequently, if there is no resistance in simple entities, there is no power, or if there is a power, there is also some resistance.

We must conclude from all this that Leibniz is no better off in recognizing a power in simple entities than if he had confined himself to saying that they have a reason in them for the changes in them, whatever this reason might be. For either the word power implies the idea of some reason whatever, or if we try to make it mean something more, it is by an obvious misuse of terms and we cannot make clear the ideas that we attach to it. Here we see the usual defects in abstract systems—vague notions and things not known explained by others understood no better.

Article III: That Leibnez does not prove that monads have perceptions

Our mind has perceptions, that is, it experiences something when objects make an impression on the senses. That is what we feel. But we have such an inadequate understanding of the nature of the mind and what it experiences when it has perceptions that we cannot discover what makes us capable of perceptions. How then could our inadequate idea of the mind explain how other beings have perceptions just as it does. To explain the nature of monads by the notion of mind, would we have to find in this notion the very nature of this substance?

Monads and minds are simple entities. In this respect they are similar, that is, they have in common that they both exclude extension and its dependent qualities such as shape, divisibility, and so forth. But from the fact that entities are similar in not having certain qualities, does it follow that they must be similar in having the same qualities in other respects? And would this conclusion be correct? Monads are like our minds in that they are neither extended nor divisible. Thus monads, like minds, are perceptions.

Let us conclude that to decide what qualities minds and monads have in common, it is not enough for us to conceive of these substances as extended, we must further conceive of the nature of both. So Leibniz's explanations in this regard are still inadequate.

Article IV: That Leibniz gives no idea of the perceptions he attributes to each monad

What is a perception? As I have just stated, it is what the mind experiences when an impression is made on the senses. This is vague and does not reveal its nature, I agree. And after this confession, there are no more questions to ask me. But should I attribute perceptions to some entity different from our mind? I will be told that to have an idea of these perceptions, it is not enough to recall what we experience, and that they should further be explained in themselves. In fact, as long as we know these perceptions only through our consciousness of them, we cannot be justified in attributing them to other beings except those that we can assume are conscious of them.

Thus if I agreed with Leibniz that perceptions are the different states that monads go through, it would be objected that the word "state" is still too vague. If, to make its meaning specific, I added that these states represent something and that the monads are therefore like mirrors that endlessly reflect new images, one would persist in further questioning. I will be asked what in their strict sense do the words "represent," "mirror," and "images" mean? Shapes, such as those traced in painting and sculpture. But a simple entity can contain nothing of the kind. Consequently, it will be added, you are not taking these words in their strict sense when you talk about monads. But if you take away the original idea that you have made them mean, what is the idea that you claim should take its place?

In fact, in changing from the literal sense to the figurative one, these terms are only vaguely related to their original meaning. They mean that simple entities are representative but the representations are completely different from the ones we know, that is, we have no idea of them. To say that perceptions are representative states is thus to say nothing.

What in fact does the state of a monad represent? The state of other monads. Thus the state of monad A represents the states of monads B, C, D, and so on. But I have no more idea of states B, C, D, and so on, than I do of A. Consequently to say that state A represents states B, C, D, and so on, is to say that something I do not know represents others that I know no better.

These things are properly the absolute qualities of entities that make them what they are. The relations we see in them do not really belong to them. These relations are merely ideas that we form when we compare their qualities. Thus entities must first be described with their absolute qualities. To take them otherwise is tacitly to admit that we have no idea of them. There will be talk about the relations assumed to exist among entities, but the talk will be extremely vague. We could thus claim to give the idea of several pictures by saying that they reciprocally represent each other. Now Leibniz does not explain monads by the absolute character of their contents. All his efforts culminate in imagining relations among them that he can specify only with the help of vague and figurative terms such as mirror or "representation." Thus he has no idea of them.

In this case, Leibniz's error was to ignore the fact that terms with a precise literal meaning evoke only very vague notions when they are used figuratively. He thought he was explaining phenomena when he was using only the rather unphilosophical language of metaphors, and he did not realize that the necessity for these sorts of expressions proves that we have no idea of what we are talking about. These mistakes are common among those who create abstract systems.

Article V: We do not understand how there could be an infinity of perceptions in each monad or how they represent the universe

The more Leibniz tried to explain what he meant by the word "perception," the more perplexing his idea of it becomes.

The relatedness of all things in the universe leads him to judge that there is no reason to set limits to the representations occurring in monads. According to him, every representation tends toward the infinite and each of our perceptions includes an infinity of other perceptions. So a monad contains an infinite number of different orders. In A there is an infinity of perceptions representing the perceptions of B; in B, another infinity representing those of C, and so on ad infinitum. A in turn is represented in B, C, and so on, and in the same way that this monad represents all the others, it is represented in every other one, so that every piece of matter represents the monad an infinite number of times and provides it with an infinity of perceptions. We thereby see in how many infinities of ways perceptions are combined in each entity.

A great deal could be said about the infinite. To be brief I shall confine myself to saying that it is a name given to an idea that we do not have but that we judge different from an idea that we do have. It thus contains nothing positive and merely serves to render Leibniz's system even more unintelligible.

Leibniz relied in vain on the relatedness of all things in the universe. We will never understand how they are all concentrated in each one or how the whole is so perfectly represented in each part that someone who wanted to know the present state of a monad would see a distinct and detailed image of the universe's present, past, and future. If this representation took place, it would be merely by virtue of the power that Leibniz attributes to each monad. But this power can produce nothing of the kind.

Either the monads interact reciprocally, so that there are reciprocal actions and passions among them (suppositions that some Leibnizians do not reject),[46] or they merely appear to act this way.

In the first case, we see in a monad all its active power and everything that this power can produce, supposing that it does not encounter any obstacle. We see further all its resistance to any action coming from some external

---

[46]M. Wolf among others.

source. But we cannot see in it the state or connection of all entities. These states and this connection consist in the relations of action and of passion. A monad's power does not produce externally all its possible effects. It only produces an effect proportional to the resistance it encounters. The perception of a monad does not suffice for finding out how its action connects it with the rest of the universe; we must further perceive all other substances as well. Thus in a single moment we cannot see the state and connection of all the monads, supposing that they act or suffer reciprocally.

Nor can we see more if, as Leibniz thinks, the actions and passions are merely apparent. According to this supposition, a monad depends on nothing else. By itself and through an effect of its own power, it is everything that it is and it includes in itself the source of all its changes. He who saw only one of them would not guess that there was anything else.

But, Leibniz says, it is a result of pre-established harmony that every monad is related to everything that exists. I agree. Thus its present state expresses and represents these relations. Thus every monad represents the whole universe. I deny this conclusion.

If I said, "One side of a triangle is related to the other two sides and to the three angles; therefore this side represents the length of the other two and the degree of each angle in particular," the falsity of this conclusion would be obvious. Everyone knows that you have to know more than one side to be able to represent a triangle. I also say that the knowledge of a single monad cannot include the representation of the whole universe. In vain is the state of this monad related to the state of all the others; even the supreme intelligence, if it knew only itself, could discover nothing further. Knowing one side, we must also know the two angles if we wanted to have an idea of all the facts about a triangle. In the same way, to be able to discover the current state of each particular entity, we must add the knowledge of a monad to a knowledge of the general harmony of the universe. Thus a monad does not properly represent the whole world but we could, by comparing its state with the universal harmony, judge the state of everything that exists.

God wanted to create such a world. Consequently, all entities were subordinated to this purpose, and the state of each particular one was determined. It is the same if I intend to write a number—123489, for example—and the choice and placement of the numerals are immediately determined. So God had reasons for arranging the elements, as I do for arranging my numbers. My reasons are subordinated to my intention to write this number. And someone ignorant of my plan who saw only the number 2 would not know any of the other numerals. God's reasons are subordinate to His plan of creating this world, and someone ignorant of this decree could never, even with a complete knowledge of a substance, discover with certainty I do not say the state of the whole world but even the least of its parts.

Wolf did not judge it appropriate to ascribe perceptions to all monads. He admits them only in minds. But everything in Leibniz's system is so closely connected that we must either accept everything or reject everything.

On the one hand, the disciple agrees with his teacher that the mind's perceptions are just different states it goes through, that these states are representative of external objects because we can explain the states of the mind by the states of the objects. On the other hand, he admits in each substance a series of changes each of which can be explained by the state of external objects. Why then does he not also recognize that these changes are representative? Why does he refuse to give them the name perception? He is all the more incorrect as the mind's perceptions and the changes in the other entities come from the same source—the power he believes proper to each substance. If in some entities this power can produce changes that are not perceptions, on what basis can he be as certain as he is that the mind always has perceptions?

Leibniz, who is more consistent, admits perceptions even in the body. He says the body has as-it-were perceptions. The "as-it-were" added to soften the conclusion means nothing. Either the body's motor force produces changes in it representing the universe, or it does not. In the former case, it has perceptions. In the latter case, it does not.

But for this representation to be transmitted without any gap, the difference between one body and another must be infinitesimal; each organized body must be composed of organized bodies; the tiniest bits of matter right down to the most infinitesimal must be true machines; and finally each body must have a dominant entelechy and each monad a body.

Leibniz's reasoning seems untenable here. In particular, I do not understand how every monad has a body. How can monads giving rise to the least compound bodies have bodies? I can conceive of this only by using the same monad in two ways, to form compounds and to animate them. But Leibniz never said anything of the kind.

Leibniz gives us no idea of the power of monads. Nor does he give us any better an idea of their perceptions. On these topics he uses mere metaphors. Finally, he gets lost in the infinite. Thus he does not make clear the elements of things. He does not explain anything properly, and it is as if he confined himself to saying that there is extension because there is something not extended, that there are bodies because there is something not a body, and so forth.

It is in this way that by trying to reason about objects lying beyond our grasp, we find ourselves after many detours at the original starting point. Because I have refuted Leibniz's system, some Leibnizians said that I did not understand it. If that is so, the system of monads as I have explained it is thus my own. I do not disavow it, but it nonetheless proves to be an abuse of abstract systems.

9

Seventh Example: Taken from a Work Entitled "Of Physical Pre-Motion or the Action of God on Creatures"[47]

It is not enough to appeal to matter to form an idea of the mind, or to the mind to form an idea of matter. That could be enough for Malebranche or Leibniz, but here is a philosopher who takes an easier way. With a view to explaining the source and development of our knowledge and our loves, he lays down three principles. In the first one, he claims that all our knowledge and loves consist of so many distinct entities. In the second one, he suggests that we acquire new knowledge and form new loves only insofar as God creates them and adds them to our minds. And in the third (invented to maintain the mental activity that the two others seem to preclude) he tries to show that in creating new entities of knowledge or love, God uses our initial mental being, making it contribute to this creation.

I shall not pursue all the conclusions he draws from these principles. I shall merely discuss whether they do not have the usual faults common to all abstract principles. The author gives the following argument to establish the first principle.

Matter, he says, acquires new modalities without acquiring new degrees of being. My fingers make this ball of wax triangular or square. But these shapes are not different beings of the parts of the wax, they are merely its parts in a different arrangement. Variety is thus found simply in the location of the parts, and the beings are always the same and equal in number.

But I ought not to reason the same way about my mind, which is simple and without parts. Thus its different modalities and actions are not due so much to the different arrangement of its parts as to the different modalities of the body. Consequently the modalities of the mind must be different degrees of being, that is, that God, who preserves the mind only because He creates it at every instant, sometimes produces it with a certain degree of being, sometimes with another; and that, when without stripping the mind of what it had, He adds new modalities to it which are new degrees of being.

This writer further says that when we pass from a slight bit of knowledge to some more extensive one, from indifference to love, and from pain to pleasure, the mind does not remain the same. It does not go from nothing to nothing, the change in it is real. Nevertheless, because it is simple it cannot really change except by receiving some degree of new being or losing some degree of old being. For I can only conceive, he adds, of genuinely different modalities in the same entity in two ways; one, by the different arrangement of its parts, which pertains only to matter; the other, by the degrees of being added or taken away, which must pertain to the mind.

It is from these more or less extensive reasons that this author concludes that all our knowledge and all our loves, as well as degrees of knowledge and love, are so many entities or degrees of being. He uses this conclusion as an incontestable principle.

When I am well filled with this system, I get real pleasure from continually opening, closing, and reopening my eyes. With a glance I produce, annihilate, and reproduce entities without number. It seems further that with everything I hear, I feel my mind expand. If I learn, for example, that after a battle 10,000 men remained on the field, at that instant my mind increases 10,000 degrees of being, one for each man killed. If it increases by only 9,999 degrees, I do not know that the ten-thousandth one died. For the knowledge of the death of this ten thousandth man is not *a nothing, a nullity, or a chimera; it is an entity, a reality, a degree of being.* So true is it that in this system my mind derives some benefit from everything. Therein lies a great deal of philosophy.

It is a great pity that this system is unintelligible. It is a pity that the author can give no idea of these entities which he values so highly and proliferates so lavishly. Do we understand that at every instant new entities are added to our substance and together constitute only a single indivisible entity? Do we understand that something can be taken away from a substance that is not compound, or that something can be added to it without its losing any of its simplicity? I cannot conceive, you may say, how the thing can happen differently. I wish it were so, but can you conceive how it could occur as you say? Do you have some idea of these entities that are added to the mind but that do not deprive it of its simplicity, and yet increase it millions of times? Probably no. It thus would be better to leave the question unresolved than to pose it in a way that neither of us understands.

But let us pass on to the second principle. The author is attempting to prove that it is God who creates all the entities that our mind can increase at every instant.

"One cannot give," he says, "what one does not have, nor consequently more than one has"; or in other words, "with less one cannot do more." From which he infers that a created mind will never increase its being all by itself. Having, for example, only four degrees of being at moment A, the mind cannot give itself a fifth degree of being at moment B. For it would be giving itself what it does not have, giving itself more than it has, with less, it would be making more. Thus if at moment A it has only the power of knowing and loving, at moment B it will not perform by itself an act of knowledge or love, since by hypothesis this act is an entity that it does not have.

The author extends and turns over this argument in a thousand different ways, and supports it with the principle that "a cause must contain its effect." Now a mind that lacks some piece of knowledge does not contain it. Thus, for example, it cannot by itself give itself this knowledge. If, for example, it has only one piece of knowledge, it will never by itself make any judgment or argument. For two pieces of knowledge are necessary for a judgment, and three for an argument. Now one does not contain two, let alone three. Thus a mind with only one bit of knowledge cannot by itself give itself a second or a third one.

This writer argues in about the same way about the different loves arising in the human heart, and concludes that the mind acquires a piece of knowledge and performs an act of love only when God creates the being of both and adds it to His substance.

The first time I quoted from this system, I applied, without realizing it, to the capability what its author says only about the act, and I concluded that the mind cannot give itself an act of knowledge or love. I did not know by what fit of absent-mindedness this mistake escaped me, for I thought I had read this system attentively. I worked on a new quotation, but I observed that I had to guard against once again falling into the same error. I searched for its cause, and thought I had discovered it when in reviewing its principles, it seemed to me as natural to infer from them that the mind could give itself either knowledge or love only by concluding that it would give itself neither one. If, I said, one does not give oneself what one does not have, if one does not give oneself more than one has, if with less one cannot make more, if a cause must contain its effect, then the mind that lacks some particular piece of knowledge or a particular love, that has less than this knowledge or love, that contains neither this knowledge nor this love, cannot give itself either one. If the following principles are true, "one does not give oneself what one does not have, one does not give oneself more than one has, with less one does not do more," the following ones seem no less true: "one cannot give what one does not have, one cannot give more than one has, with less one cannot do more." From which we can certainly conclude that the mind cannot give itself knowledge or love that it does not yet have.

I continued and said: not only does the mind by itself not give itself either knowledge or love, it does not give them to itself even with the help of God, it does not enter into their production. To enter in this way, it is not enough for the mind to produce partially the act of knowledge or love, it must produce it in its entirety, and it must be the total cause, as God is. But if one does not give what one does not have, how does one take part in giving in its entirety what one does not have? If one cannot give more than one has, if with less one cannot do more, how can one take part in giving in its entirety what one has only in part? I resorted to the author because, withthe intention of reconciling his system with mental activity, he makes several attempts to resolve this difficulty. He thus undertakes to prove that God, by creating in us a new being of knowledge or love, uses the degrees of being that he finds in our mind and makes them take part in this production. This is his third principle.

We do not have much difficulty in conceiving that God bringing about all the mind's being, knowledge or love, puts to work the degrees of being that are already there and sees to it that one of these degrees really does have an effect on the production of another, that an old piece of knowledge has an effect on the production of a new one, that the degrees that were already in the mind cooperate and contribute along with what God adds to it to create a new action, that in short God, in giving the mind all its reality, nevertheless makes his actions be genuinely, physically, and immediately produced by the mind itself.

He tries to explain this as follows:

From the bottom of our minds God draws a new degree of kowledge, which unites, incorporates, elaborates it, and expands the old one. For (which is to be particularly observed) this new degree is merely the elaboration of the old one. But what provides this new degree is the current attention and the knowledge reflected which thereby cooperate and contribute to this new knowledge.

We must say the same thing about love. When we love some good as our end, and when this love is to be increased, the old degrees of love contribute to form the greater love. It is the reflected love, I mean the will to love or the love of love that provides and makes use of these old degrees.

As an example he uses the love of God and shows that before having this love we find in ourselves the idea of the infinitely perfect being, and that in the love of created things themselves, we love many of the perfections of the divinity. We would like, he says, to possess created things truly, eternally, immutably, infinitely. Thus we love truth, eternity, immutability, infinity. Nor do we fail to love God's other perfections such as His justice and holiness. Now to give us these latter loves, God does not cancel out the former loves which are good in their capacity as beings. On the contrary, He

---

[47]De l'Action de Dieu sur les Créatures, Traité dans lequel on prouve la Prémotion physique par le Raisonnement et où l'on examine plusieurs Questions qui ont Rapport à la Nature des Esprits et à la Grâce, 2 vols. Lille and Paris: 1713. P. Boursier.

uses them as much as the idea of the infinitely perfect being, and through these loves and through this idea He produces what is missing from these loves so that all of them become the love of God.

Finally, the author seeks a final solution to this difficulty in the idea of the infinitely perfect being. He believes that all we have to do is consider this idea and we will see what influence our first pieces of knowledge have on our final ones.

> Since we know the finite through the infinite, everything we know is united in our knowledge of the being of beings. Thus when God gives us some new knowledge, he does not place it in the mind as detached and independent of this primitive idea. He draws it from this fundamental knowledge. He makes this innate idea extend, evolve, and increase. And in this way he makes the mind true, real and efficient cause.

These answers gave me new material for reflection. Yes, I say, I can conceive without much difficulty that some knowledge and love can and do contribute to other knowledge and another love, but only when I consult experience which makes me daily sensitive to it. On the contrary, according to your principles, the thing seems to me utterly inconceivable.

At moment A my mind (I suppose it the same with you) has only four degrees of being. At moment B it has five. But it does not have this fifth degree. None of the first four degrees contains it. Thus neither my mind nor the first four degrees form the fifth if God himself does not produce it, you will agree. But I add that in creating the fifth degree, God does not have the mind give it to itself or make the mind take part in its production. For God would be using all His omnipotence to no purpose in making me give what I do not have. God cannot make a true principle become false, which is what would happen if it depended on Him for the mind to give itself what it does not have or more than it has.

The more I go over your words, the more difficulties I find. "God," you say, "puts into operation the first degrees of being that are already in the mind." Would your language not lead us to think that only God acts and that in the hands of God the first beings are like something purely passive, like clay in the hands of a potter? You add that, "God acts so that the degrees that were formerly in the mind cooperated, and contributed with what God adds to it, to form a new action." I find three things in this claim: (1) the cooperation of the old degrees of being; (2) what God adds; and (3) the resultant action. It thereby appears that we are not dealing with two causes, one subordinate to the other and each producing in its entirety one and the same action, but two parallel causes each creating a part of the action. For the cooperation of the old degrees and what God adds are two very different things. Now either the cooperation of the old degrees produces something or it does not. But what would it produce? Not what God adds—only God can be the cause of that. Will it be some other being? Here then is something that belongs to the created thing and that it produces all by itself. Will it produce nothing? Then it does not do anything and has no part in the action.

Or do the old degrees contain the action's being in its entirety? Their operation alone will then produce it, and there is no need for God to add His action to it. Do they not contain this being in its entirety? Their operation will thus not produce it in its entirety, even with God's help.

Or further, what does God add, and what is so distinctive in the cooperation of the old degrees? Is it the new action? Is it its being? In this case, the meaning of your words (if they have any) is at the very least quite obscure, and this is how it should be expressed. "God acts so that the old degrees of being cooperate with the new action that He himself adds to form this same action." I do not understand what it is to add an action before forming it. If the action is added, it is formed, and the cooperation of the old degrees in its production becomes superfluous.

Finally, will what God adds be something less than the action, than the being of the action? Then the action will never result from it, the old degrees will have produced something that they did not contain, and will have created something without God's help. Once again, we must ask what it is that God adds, according to your system?

Nor are the other explanations any more felicitous. According to you, God draws a new degree of being from the bottom of our mind, and this new degree is just an elaboration of the old one. But nothing will ever be drawn from the bottom of our mind except what it already contains; in vain will a being evolve from which we can ever extract anything except what is included in it. My mind's current attention, to which you appeal, or its reflected knowledge, will never on its own bring to light the slightest degree of knowledge as long as it is not there. I would say the same of your "reflected love," "the will to love," and "the love of love." Give it the powerful name love as many times as you like, and it would still have no greater power to draw from my mind what, following your principles, is not to be found there. Moreover, this current attention, reflected knowledge, and love of love are according to you so many beings. Now I ask how did the mind contribute to their creation? Will you appeal to a previous attention, reflection, or love?

As for the example that you are seeking in the love of God (an example more appropriate for obfuscating your subject than for illuminating it), I grant you that we loved God by loving creatures, and I suggest that we loved immutability, eternity, and so on, although this way of arguing seemed to me more strained than sound. At least it is certain that we do not love all the perfections of the divinity. What can you then reasonably conclude if not that the first loves will enter into the composition of the love of God as soon as the love of God fills our heart. But that is not enough for you. You still want the love of immutability and eternity to produce the love of holiness and goodness, although it does not include their reality, and according to your principles a cause should contain all the being of its effect.

You will say that we should not reason about mind the same way as we do about matter. Several bits of matter enter into the composition of an object but they do not influence each other. The mind is different. It is simple, and from a new degree of knowledge or love together with the old one, it forms a single being. But why and how can this simplicity bring a new degree of being to have an influence on the second one and produce it in its entirety? You will reply that it is because the second degree of being is merely *an elaboration of the first one, and because there is a genuine intercourse and a true and substantial communication between them.*

These are words that no doubt amount to proof. I could, however, ask whether this intercourse and communication take place between these entities before or after the production of new ones or at the very moment of their creation. If beforehand, how can there be some intercourse and communication between existing entities and nonexistent entities? If afterward, the new ones have been produced already. Consequently, this intercourse and communication occur too late to influence the former entities in the production of the latter ones. Finally, if it is at the very moment of creation that you claim to establish this intercourse between some and others, far from being imaginable as an influence of the old ones, it presupposes on the contrary that the new ones are produced by a source outside us. To have intercourse with an entity or to contribute to its creation are two very different things.

But I do not mean to insist too much. I will even not say anything about your principle that "we know the finite through the infinite"—that is an error produced by the prejudice of innate ideas. I would only have you notice the language that your imagination makes you use. Simple entities that extend themselves, expand, develop, increase, and blend together; spiritual creatures who, with only four degrees of being, cannot give themselves a fifth one, can still, by expanding, extending, and developing, provide, along with what God adds, this fifth degree; through their current attention, reflected love, their will to love, and their love of love, they can cooperate in the whole production of this new entity; finally they can draw it from their our foundation where it was not—simple entities which can be added to and taken away from without fear of harming their simplicity . . . Now all you need do is introduce a real intercourse and a genuine and substantial communication between the mind's old degrees of being and the new ones produced.

I reasoned this way, and seeing the confusions, obscurities, and contradictions of this system, I was increasingly persuaded that abstract principles are unsuitable for illuminating the mind, and that it would be a thousand times better to agree that we do not know things than to seek to know them in this way.

I stopped and took care to follow the author of this system in his application of his principles to freedom and grace. It is hardly believable how many different systems have been imagined on this subject, all of them based on abstract principles. To judge their abuses, we need only regard the divisiveness they have causes in the church. Theologians should confine themselves to what faith points out and philosophers to what experience teaches!

10 Eighth and Last Example: Spinozism Refuted

One unique, indivisible, and necessary substance from those whose nature all things necessarily follow as modifications expressing its essence, each in its own way—this is the universe according to Spinoza.

Spinoza's aim is thus to prove there exists just one single substance all of whose attributes, which we take for so many substances, are merely modifications, that everything that happens is a necessary consequence of the nature of the unique substance, and that consequently there is no difference between moral good and evil.

I am not proposing to make an extract of Spinoza's *Ethics*. It would be difficult or even impossible to succeed in doing so to every reader's satisfaction. I shall translate the first part literally because it includes the principles of the whole system. I shall consider all its expressions and analyze all its propositions. In making criticisms that cannot be glossed over, my plan is to give a clear example of how abstract systems are constructed and the abuses they entail. It will be recognized that no work is more appropriate for this than Spinoza's.

The title promises geometric proofs. Now two conditions are essential for these sorts of proofs: clarity of ideas and precision of signs. The question is one of knowing whether Spinoza met these conditions.

Article I: Definitions in the first part of Spinoza's Ethics

Definition I

By cause of itself I understand that whose essence includes existence or whose nature can only be conceived of as existing.

"Cause of itself" is an imprecise expression. The word "cause" implies a relationship to something independently identifiable, for an effect cannot produce itself. But the choice of a word is free. I am taking up Spinoza only to show that if in the following I say nothing about the many other such imprecise ways of speaking, it is not because they escape me but because I want to avoid going into details that could appear to be trifling. He thus means by "cause of itself" *that whose nature can only be conceived of as existing*. But Spinoza remembers using this expression and its definition only when he conceives the nature of a thing and sees that this nature includes existence. It would be irrational to apply the name "cause of itself" to a thing whose nature is unknown.

Definition II

We say a thing is finite of its kind when it can be bounded by another thing of the same nature. We say, for example, that a body is finite because we always can conceive of a larger body. Thus a thought is bounded by another thought. But a body is not bounded by a thought, nor a thought by a body.

What does Spinoza mean by this statement? *A body cannot be bounded by a thought nor a thought by a body.* Does he mean that a body, although finite in relation to bodies because it can be bounded by another body, is not finite in relation to thought because it cannot be bounded by a thought, and that a thought, although finite in relation to thought, is not finite in relation to body because it cannot be bounded by a body? What language! Is this much effort required to show what a finite thing is?

Moreover, of what relevance is it to the limitation of a thing that it be or not be bounded by another thing of the same nature? To judge whether a thing is finite, why is it necessary to have regard to the nature of what is outside it?

Is it not enough to consider what belongs to it? This obscurity will be doubtless useful for Spinoza's purpose.

Finally, a body is not finite because we can conceive of a larger one. But we can conceive of a larger one because it is finite.

Definition III

I understand by substance what exists in itself, and what is conceived by itself, that is, that the idea of which does not require the idea of another thing.

Since Spinoza wants to prove that there is only one single substance, it is essential that he give an exact idea of the thing that he makes the word "substance" mean. Otherwise everything he says about it will merely bear its name and shed no light on the nature of the thing. But neither he nor anyone else can meet this condition.

To prove our ignorance in this respect, I am refering only to the language of philosophers. When they say, "Substance is that which is in itself," and the like, "that which exists through itself,"[48] "that which can be conceived independently of anything else,"[49] "that which preserves the essential determination and constant attributes, while its modes vary and succeed each other,"[50] do not the words "that which" appear to refer to some unknown subject, "which is in itself, which exists by itself, which," and so forth? If we had some idea of its nature, would we indicate it in such a vague way? The names given to known modifications are clear. Why would it not be the same with the name given to this subject if, like them, it were understood?

But, Wolf will reply, nothing is more imaginary than the subject that you are trying to give to the essential determinations. These determinations are what is paramount in a substance. Three sides determine all the attributes of a triangle, and if we wanted something anterior to them, we would seek for it in vain. So the three sides are the subject of everything that pertains to this figure. It is the same with substance; it has a primary essential determination—its substratum. To ask for something anterior to it is a manifest contradiction.

I reply, first, that we should change the definition and say: "substance is a first essential determination that . . . " and I still doubt that the definition is any better. I agree, in the second place, that a substance has a first essential determination but that is a Proteus who gets pleasure from presenting himself to me under a thousand different forms and defies me to grasp him under any one of them. I must explain.

We can say of shapes as of substances that they are "that which preserves essential determinations and constant attributes," and so on—a notion so vague that someone who had no other idea of shape would in truth have no idea of any shape. This notion varies: here it is one determination, there another, and the Proteus takes different forms everywhere. Nevertheless he never escapes me, and I can always grasp the essential determination of each figure. But he is so subtle when he plays among substances that he always disappears at the moment I think I have hold of him. No philosopher knows how to fix him and show the essential determination of any substance whatever. This is the way that someone acquainted with shapes only through the vague notion that I have just given of them would be unable to indicate the essential determination of a single one.

---

[48]This is the definition given by the scholastics.

[49]This is how Descartes defines it. Malebranche expresses himself differently. He says that "substance is that which we can think of without thinking of anything else." All these definitions closely resemble Spinoza's.

[50]This is Wolf's definition. Elsewhere we have seen that Leibniz defines substance as what has in itself the principle of its changes.

But why leave metaphysics and resort to geometry to find examples of an entirely different kind? What leads us to this first determination by precise analyses of substance? The efforts would be superfluous. We will only be led to something we do not know and to which we will give the names *"essence,"* *"essential determination,"* *"support,"* *"substance."* But that is merely to make up words.

We observe different qualities in everything that comes within our ken. These qualities are divided, differently distributed, combined at different points, and form a multitude of distinct objects. We give them the names *"mode,"* *"modification,"* *"accident,"* *"properties,"* *"attributes,"* *"determination,"* *"essence,"* *"nature,"* depending on the relations from which we see them or think we do. But we cannot discover what serves as their foundation. Now if by the idea of substance we mean the idea of some qualities that are combined somewhere, we know what we call "substance." But if we mean the knowledge of what serves as a basis for the combination of these qualities, we do not know it at all.

This distinction suffices to show that the question here is not one of words. And if we tried to make ourselves understood, there would be no more dispute. Descartes did not doubt that he understood substance. Nevertheless he admits his ignorance when he takes the word in the sense in which I say that we do not have an idea of it.[51]

To come back to Spinoza's definition, substance is not conceived of by itself. It is not even conceived of but imagined so as to serve as a connection or support for the qualities that we do conceive of. And the vague idea of it given by the imagination can only be formed following some previous acquaintance with several other things.

We must conclude that Spinoza has given us no idea of what he wants to make the word "substance" mean. Consequently, nothing could be sillier than his proofs. Add that the ambiguity of the scholastic expression "in itself" is altogether appropriate for Spinoza's plan to prove that substance is independent by nature.

Definition IV

I understand by attribute what the understanding represents as constituting the essence of "substance."

---

[51]"Because we perceive some forms or attributes that must be attached to something in order to exist, we call the thing to which they are attached *substance.* We could still speak of substance after stripping it of all its attributes; but then we would be destroying all our knowledge of it, and we would not conceive clearly and distinctly the meaning of our words." He expresses himself in the same way in the fifth definition of his *Meditations* arranged geometrically. *(Reply to the Fourth Objection.)*

Elsewhere Spinoza says that he understands by attribute "everything that is conceived through itself and in itself, so that the idea of it does not include the idea of another thing. Extension is conceived through itself and in itself but not movement for it is conceived in another thing, and the idea of it includes that of extension."[52]

Here then are substance and attribute which are one and the same thing. Spinoza agrees with this and says[53] that he distinguishes attribute only in relation to the understanding which attributes a certain nature to substance.

The word "essence" doubtless means the same as "substance," if it is not in relation to the understanding that considers essence as something without which substance cannot neither exist or be conceived.[54]

Geometrical signs not only have different meanings in relation to the understanding, but also in relation to things. That is why everything that geometry proves about its signs is proven by objects themselves, assuming they exist. Nothing would be sillier than geometrical proofs if the terms had different senses in relation to the understanding. If for one thing Spinoza invents as many names as he pleases, he will prove nothing or will merely show what the nature of beings would be if it were as he supposed—which would be of very little interest to the reader.

Nothing reveals the weakness of the human mind better than its efforts to go beyond the limits prescribed for it. Although one had no idea of what is called substance, one took the word "essence" to mean that which constitutes substance. And in order that this term not be suspected of being meaningless, the word attribute was invented to refer to that which constitutes essence. Finally, when we can dispense with these distinctions, we can agree that substance, essence, and attribute are all one and the same thing. This is the way that a labyrinth of words serves to hide the profound ignorance of metaphysicians.

If, as I believe I have proven, we do not know substance at all, and if, as Spinoza agrees, substance, attributes, and attribute are actually one and the same thing, Spinoza has no more idea of attribute and essence than of substance itself.

Other philosophers also make a distinction between attribute and essence. They define attribute as that which necessarily flows from essence.

Definition V

I understand by mode, the affections of a substance or what is in another by which it is conceived.

---

[52]*Posthumous Works*, Letter 2.

[53]Letter 27.

[54]Part II, Definition 2.

We are so far from conceiving of modes through something else that we have no idea of the subject which serves them as support and by which, according to this definition, we should conceive of them. On the contrary, we can imagine the subject only after conceiving of modes. To use one of Spinoza's examples,[55] movement is conceived in extension, but it is not conceived through extension, for the notion of movement includes something more than the notion of extension.

We get the idea of a mode either from the sense impression received from objects or from abstractions formed in thinking about these impressions. In both cases it is obvious that the mode is known independently of the idea of its subject. Strictly, substances affect us only through their modes and come within our ken only through modes. It is thus absurd to suppose that we conceive of modes only through substances.

If Spinoza defined "mode" as what *is conceived through something else*, it is not because he reflected on the nature of the thing but because he tried to contrast "mode" with "substance" which he defined as *what is conceived of through itself*. Now by opposing these terms, he tacitly assumes that substance exists through its own nature. Why indeed does a mode exist in another thing by which it is conceived? Because it depends on that thing. Thus since substance is in itself, it depends only on itself; that is, according to Spinoza, substance is independent, necessary, and so on. When our definitions presuppose what we set out to prove, it is not very difficult to construct proofs.

Definition VI

I understand by God a being absolutely infinite, that is, a substance that includes an infinity of attributes, each of which expresses an eternal and infinite essence.

Explanation

I say absolutely infinite and not just of its kind. For we can deny an infinity of attributes to everything that is infinite merely of its kind. But, when a thing is absolutely infinite, everything that expresses its essence belongs to it and nothing can be denied of it.

Spinoza is very happy to be able to handle the ideas of the infinite with such ease. I admit that I have diffiulty following him, and that when he speaks of an attribute expressing an eternal and infinite essence, I find in the word "expresses" merely a figurative term with nothing precise about it.

---

[55]See what has just been noted about the preceding definition.

As for the idea Spinoza claims to have of the infinite, that is an error common to many other philosophers. It would take too long to attack it. I shall merely observe that Spinoza takes many precautions to be able to use his definition to conclude everything that will be advantageous to him. For, according to his definition, God is absolutely infinite only because nothing can be denied of Him and everything can be affirmed of Him.

Definition VII

A thing is called free when it exists only by the necessity of its nature and is determined to act only by itself. But it is necessary or rather constrained when it is determined by something else to exist and to act in a certain and determinate manner.

Definitions of words are said to be arbitrary; but the condition should be added that they will not be misused. We will soon see that Spinoza intends to prove that everything is necessary.

Definition VIII

By eternity, I understand existence itself as it is conceived that it necessarily follows from the definition alone of an eternal thing.

This is a curious definition. Would we not say that an eternal thing is better understood than eternity? The following is the explanation added by Spinoza: it does not shed much light on the definition.

Explanation

For such an existence is conceived, like the essence of a thing, as an eternal truth. That is why it cannot be explained either by either duration or time, although we conceive that duration has no beginning or end.

These are the definitions of the first part of Spinoza's *Ethics*. Far from being as precise as geometry requires, this language is merely the established jargon of the scholastics.

Article II: Axioms of the first part of Spinoza's Ethics

Axiom I

Everything that is, is in itself or in another thing.

The ambiguity of this axiom puts us in danger of confusing modes, which are said to exist in another thing, with everything that is dependent, and of confusing substance, which is said to exist in itself, with what is independent. Then it would not be difficult to prove that finite entities are merely modes of a single necessary substance.

In the Spinozistic language this axiom naturally applies to things as we suppose them in nature; to make it more precise, we would have to express ourselves in such a way that it could be understood only in the way in which we conceive of things. If we do not take this precaution, we run the risk of substituting our own imaginations for nature. This is what Spinoza does not try to guard against. So I would say: "everything that we conceive of, we represent as in itself or as in something else," that is, "as a subject or as a quality of a subject." But then this axiom would be of very limited use, for we could reasonably apply it only to things that we know. So it would become useless for Spinoza's purpose.

Axiom II

What cannot be conceived of through something else should be conceived of through itself.

This would be true if nothing existed that did not have to be conceived of either by itself or by something else.

As far as I can understand Spinoza, a thing is conceived through itself when we have the idea of it directly; and it is conceived through something else when the idea of it is included in the idea of something else that we know. Now from the fact that the idea of a thing is not found in any of the ideas that we already have, it does not follow that we must have it directly. We may have no idea of it at all.

Either Spinoza understands the word "conceive" in relation to us, in which case he is wrong not to observe that there are things that we do not conceive of, that is, of which we cannot form an idea, or he takes the word in relation to an intelligence that embraces everything and sees all things as they are, in which case the second axiom is true but Spinoza makes no application of it.

We should make a careful distinction between two kinds of language. One applies to things, and this would be the language of the supreme intelligence; the other applies to our way of conceiving of things, and it is the only one we should use. But Spinoza always confounds them. This observation could be made many times, but it should be enough to make it in regard to the following axiom.

Axiom III

Given a determinate cause the effect follows necessarily on the other hand, if the cause is not given, it is impossible for the effect to follow.

"Cause" and "effect" are relative terms, and the truth of this axiom depends on the way in which they are related. If by the word "cause" we understand a principle that is currently acting and producing, it is consequently related to a currently existing effect. Then it will be true that given a determinate cause, the effect will follow necessarily. But if by "cause" we understand only a principle that has the potentiality for acting and producing, it refers only to a possible effect, and although the cause is given, the effect does not follow necessarily.

Axiom IV

The knowledge of an effect depends on the knowledge of its cause, and includes it.

If Spinoza means that we can only know a thing as an effect because we know that it has a cause, the axiom is true, for the word "effect" is necessarily related to the word "cause." In this case the knowledge of the effect presupposes merely a vague knowledge of some cause. But if Spinoza means that we can have the idea of an effect only because we have the idea of its particular cause, so that the idea of the effect includes the idea of its true cause, nothing could be more false. There are many effects we know whose true causes we are ignorant of!

If the knowledge of an effect depends on the knowledge of its cause, the effect cannot be known by itself. Consequently, it is known through something else. Thus it is not a substance, but merely a mode. This axiom thus presupposes what is in question, and we see how useful its ambiguity is for Spinoza's plan.

Axiom V

Things that have nothing in common cannot be included in each other, or the idea of one of them does not include the idea of the other.

This axiom is false in that it assumes that entities with something in common can be included in each other, or that the notion of one of them includes that of the other. The ideas that we form of the thing by what it has in common with others are only partial ideas representing it in a vague, general, and consequently highly imperfect way. An example is the idea of an animal. It is formed only from the portion common to the notion of man and to the notion of everything that has life and sensation.

If entities have something in common, we can partially conceive of one through the other, or the idea of one partially includes the idea of the other. It includes what they have in common, but it does not contain the qualities that make them different. Spinoza assumes the notion of the one must unrestrictively include the notion of the other merely in order to prove that there cannot be several substances. For if there were, they would all be substances because of something they had in common. Thus by the fifth axiom, we can conceive the one through the other. Now by the third definition, that is absurd. There thus can only be one substance. This is how Spinoza always adjusts his definitions and axioms to suit the thesis he has set out to prove.

Axiom VI

A true idea must agree with its object.

When the Cartesians said: "We can affirm of a thing everything included in our clear and distinct idea of it," it was because they supposed that these sorts of ideas are true or conformable to the objects they refer to. Thus my previous observations concerning their principle can be applied to this sixth axiom. I refer the reader to it.

Brought up reading Descartes' works, Spinoza understood neither the origin nor the generation of ideas. We can judge this by his definitions of them.

By idea I understand the *concept* formed by the mind, as a thinking thing. I call it *concept* and not perception because the word *perception* seems to indicate that the mind endures whereas the word *concept* expresses the mind's action.[56]

But how can this idea produced by the mind's action be true or conformable to an object, and by which sign can we be certain of it? Spinoza has no answer to this question. He is content to assume that there are true ideas and he doubtless believes that they are his own.

It is easy for the imagination to form ideas, and it is just as easy for it to be persuaded that they are true. With this axiom of Spinoza we will conclude that they are conformable to the object they refer to. And by reasoning only about imaginary notions, people believe they are getting to the very nature of things. This is what happened to Spinoza.

Axiom VII

The essence of a thing does not include existence when this thing can be conceived as nonexistent.

---

[56]Part II, Definition 3.

It is no doubt surprising to see me reject generally received axioms. But it takes creatures as limited as we to imagine their manner of conceiving as the measure of the essence of things. It is the same prejudice that made this axiom and the preceding one fashionable. When we think we can affirm of an object everything contained in our ideas about it, it is natural for us to deny of it everything not contained in them.

If we accept this axiom, we could with as much reason agree with the following ones.

The essence of a thing does not include intelligence when this thing can be conceived of as nonintelligent. The essence of a thing does not include freedom, when this thing can be conceived of as being unfree.

In this case Spinoza would say: "I conceive that God could be without consciousness or freedom. Thus His essence does not include either of these." "But what kind of consciousness are you yourself," I would say to such a philosopher, "to want things only to be the way you conceive of them?" In truth, if this way of reasoning were not so widely adopted, I would be ashamed to attack it.

These are the materials with which Spinoza arranges all the would-be proofs of Part I of his work: eight definitions of words and seven somewhat imprecise and highly ambiguous axioms. It is rather curious to see how he goes from these to some real knowledge of the nature of things. I find it hard to believe that his proofs contain anything more than words. Let us follow him, and examine closely all his steps. This will be all the easier as we have already found in his definitions and axioms the assumption of everything that he sets out to prove.

Article III: Propositions that Spinoza undertakes to prove in the first part of his ethics

If my plan were merely to refute Spinoza, there would be no need to continue translating his work. We see that principles as silly as these cannot lead to true knowledge. But as I want to give an example of abstract systems, and I do not know where the methods that I am criticizing should be followed more carefully than Spinoza's, it is necessary to translate up to the point that everyone can get some idea of it.

Proposition I

Substance is anterior to its affections.

Proof

"This follows from definitions 3 and 5."

That is, what Spinoza calls substance, whether something in nature is similar to it or not, is, according to his way of conceiving it, anterior in nature to what he calls affections. For we must observe that this proposition and its proof can be applied only to the words "substance" and "affections" since he has not yet proven that there are entities fitting the definitions of substance and modes.

When we form the idea of the subject of substance in the way I have indicated, we reify this idea, however vague it is, and we then conceive of this subject as existing before the modes that successively come to be united with it. We then notice this relation and say: "The subject is anterior to its modes; a thing must exist before being a particular . . . " and so on. This means that after the violent abstractions that we have reified, we conceive that the subject exists before the modes and that a thing exists before being particular— extremely absurd propostions, which bear repetition by philosophers merely because all they often need are words. Indeed what does it matter to know the relation between reified abstractions? If we drop this ridiculous method, we will soon see that a thing cannot exist without being particular and that a thing cannot exist without having affections, and so forth.

But this way of reasoning is so widely adopted that Spinoza is right to use it with all the confidence of someone who does not suspect that there is anything wrong in his reasoning. We see here and by everything that has already been said that Spinoza's system often gets what little force it seems to have merely from the weakness of his opponents.

Proposition II

Two substances with different attributes have nothing in common.

Proof

This is again proven by the third definition. For every substance must exist in itself and be conceived by itself, or the notion of the one does not include that of the other.

Here Spinoza assumes, as in the fifth axiom, that of two entities with something in common, the notion of one of them includes the notion of the other. However it includes only a partial idea of it. Thus, the fact that the notion of substance (by the third definition) does not include the notion of something else does not imply that two substances have nothing in common. It merely implies that they do not have everything in common.

For Spinoza's conclusion to be precise, "substance" would have to be defined as follows: *for something to be a substance, the idea of it must not include anything belonging to the notion of anything else.* It even appears that this is the meaning that Spinoza himself attaches to his definition. In this way it is easy for him to prove that there is only one substance. For if there were several substances, it would only be insofar as they were referred to the same class. They would thus have something in common.

We should repeat here the remark we made about the preceding proposition. Nothing so far proves that something exists outside of us that is conformable to the definition of substance. Consequently, this definition cannot be used to prove what is common or not common to two substances, and the proof concerns merely words.

Our notion of substance is the idea of some properties and modes that we know to belong to a subject whose nature is unknown to us. In this sense, the notion of a substance can include the notion of another substance because we can represent the properties and the modes of one substance by the properties and modes of another substance. Although, the essence of gold, for example, is unknown to us, we can represent the properties of one particle of gold by the properties of another particle that we have analyzed. Spinoza assumes that we cannot represent one substance by another one merely because he has an abstract idea of substance that is real only in his imagination. There is the main defect in his reasoning.

Proposition III

"One thing cannot be the cause of another if the two things have nothing in common."

Proof

"If they have nothing in common between them (by Axiom 5), they cannot be conceived through each other; thus (by Axiom 4), the one cannot be the cause of the other."

This proof presupposes (by Axiom 4) that the knowledge of an effect includes the knowledge of its cause, as the knowledge of movement includes the knowledge of extension. This is false. Thus this proof is false as well.

Proposition IV

If two or more things are distinct, either they are so by the diversity of the attributes of substances, or by the diversity of the affections of substances.

Proof

Everything that is, exists in itself or in something else (by Axiom 1), that is (by Definitions III and V), that outside of the understanding there are only substances and their affections. Thus, outside of the understanding there are only substances, or, which comes to the same thing (Axiom 4), only their attributes and affections whereby several things can be distinguished.

At this point Spinoza begins to assume that his definitions of words have become definitions of things. "There are," he says, "outside of the understanding (by Definitions III and V) only substances and their affections." This is true if his definitions explain things as they are in themselves. But if the definitions include only certain ideas that it pleases him to attach to certain sounds, by what rule does he imagine he can use the definitions to judge the very nature of entities? He is free to make all the abstractions he wants. The problem is to go on from there to the nature of things. For however little we notice it in this passage, we easily notice the weak spot in his system.

Proposition V

In nature, there cannot be two or more substances of the same nature or attribute.

Proof

If there were several substances, they would be distinguished by the diversity of attributes or affections (preceding proposition). If they were distinguished merely by the diversity of attributes, there would only be one of the same attribute. But do we want them to be distinguished by the diversity of affections? In this case, as substance is anterior to its affections (Proposition 1), the affections apart, and substance considered in itself, that is, (Definition III and VI) considered as it must be, we cannot conceive of one substance as distinct from another, that is (preceding proposition), that there cannot be several substances, there can only be a single one.

First, I observe that not only could substances be distinguished by the diversity of attributes or affections, but perhaps numerically. That is, that there might be substances with the same attributes and affections, but that were distinct, because they could be several. At least this is the opinion of the Cartesians. A student of Decartes should not forget to refute it.

Second, I agree that if substances were distinguished only by the diversity of attributes, there would be only one substance with the same attribute. But I say that by the first proposition Spinoza has not proven that substance is in fact anterior to its affection, but merely that he conceives of it anterior to its affections. Now that does not give him the right to strip the substance of its affections or to conclude that several substances with the same attribute could not be distinguished by the diversity of affections.

Finally, I observe that it is fuitless to inquire whether there could be several substances of the same nature, inasmuch as Spinoza has not shown that there exists anything to which the name "substance" in his sense is applicable.

To get an abstract idea of substance, one can ignore what substances have in particular and consider only what they appear to have in common. Then, to conclude that there is only one substance, all one has to do is reify this abstraction. We thus have merely to construct all Spinoza's would-be proofs; we can with less expense construct a system like his, for the more we read him, the more convinced we will be that his reasoning ends up merely reifying an abstraction.

Proposition VI

One substance cannot be produced by another one.

Proof

In nature there cannot be two substances with the same attribute (preceding proposition), that is (Proposition II), which have something in common between them. Consequently (Proposition III), one cannot be the cause of another, or one cannot produce another.

That is, one substance in Spinoza's sense cannot be produced by another. Indeed, when we form the most abstract idea possible of a substance, we can see only one, and we cannot distinguish something productive from something produced. But that is merely an effect of our way of conceiving and we can conclude nothing from it when we are dealing with substances as they are in themselves and independent of our understanding. What I said about propositions II, III, and V shows how unsound this proof is.

Corollary

It thereby follows that there is nothing that can produce a substance; for in nature there are only substances and affections of substances (Axiom I, Definitions III and V). Now a substance cannot be produced by a substance (preceding proposition); therefore and so forth.

This proposition is also proven by the absurdity of its negation. For if a substance could be produced by some cause, the knowledge of it would have to depend on its cause (Axiom IV). Therefore (Definition III) it would not be a substance.

This corollary is no sounder than the proposition from which it was drawn. See what was said about the definitions and axioms on which it is based.

Proposition VII

It is in the nature of substance to exist.

Proof

Substance cannot be produced by any cause (Corollary of the preceding proposition). It is therefore the cause of itself; that is (Definition I), its essence includes existence, or it is in its nature to exist.

We have observed that Spinoza had to give the name "cause of itself" only to a thing whose nature he understood so well that he could see its existence included in it. Nevertheless he gives the name to an abstraction whose only reality is in his imagination. This proof is as frivolous as its dependent corollary.

Proposition VIII

Every substance is necessarily infinite.

Proof

There is only one substance with one and the same attribute (Proposition V). It is in its nature to exist (Proposition VII). It will therefore be in its nature to be finite or infinite; but not finite, for (Definition II) it must be bounded by another thing of the same nature which must exist necessarily as well (Proposition VII). In such a case there would be two substances with the same attribute, which is absurd (Proposition V). It is therefore infinite.

Here we can see why Spinoza's second definition is expressed so oddly. Because to deny the name substance to everything finite, "a finite thing" would have to mean *that which is bounded by another thing of the same nature*. Either I am very much mistaken or most of Spinoza's definitions and axioms were formulated only after their proofs.

I grow weary of pointing out that all these proofs deal only with the word "substance". One would say that nothing is better understood than an entity fitting Spinoza's definition of this term.

First Scholium

Since the finite carries some negation with it and since the infinite includes the absolute affirmation of the existence of some nature, the seventh proposition suffices to prove that every substance is infinite.

I do not know if anything in this definition of the infinite is comprehensible. But Spinoza's intent is to prove that as substance is infinite, it is everything that exists, so that nothing exists that does not belong to it as an attribute or modification.

Second Scholium

I do not doubt that all those who judge things confusedly and are unaccustomed to understanding them through their first causes will have trouble conceiving the proof of the seventh proposition because they do not distinguish between the modifications of substances and substances themselves, and because they do not know how things are produced. It thereby happens that they imagine that substances have a beginning, because they see that natural things have one. For those who do not know the true causes confound everything.

Spinoza has the good grace to criticize others for judging things confusedly and and for not knowing their first causes. Must he be so blind that he imagines that some word definitions and bad axioms will reveal the true springs of nature?

Notice that to understand things through their first causes, in Spinoza's manner, is to explain them by abstract notions. The absurdities he falls into are a new proof of the abuses of this method.

They find it no more repugnant to have trees speak than they do people. It costs their imagination nothing to represent men made with stones by way of generation, and to change any form whatever into any other form whatever. In the same way, those who confuse the divine nature with human nature glibly attribute human inclinations to God, especially when they do not know how these inclinations arise in our mind.

What relation does this verbiage have with the seventh proposition?

But if men reflected on the nature of substance, they would not have the slightest doubt about the truth of the seventh proposition. On the contrary, they would regard it as an axiom, and class it with the common notions. For by 'substance' they understand what is in itself and what is conceived through itself, that is, that the knowledge of which does not have need of the knowledge of anything else. And by 'modification,' they understand what exists in something else, and that the idea of which is formed by the idea of the thing in which it subsists.

Here Spinoza very clearly assumes that his definition of substance explains the truth about nature. He is also incorrect in suggesting that we form the notion of a modification by the idea of something else in which it subsists, since we have ideas of modifications without having any idea of their subject.

This means that we can have true ideas of modifications that do not exist; because although they do not actually exist outside of the understanding, their essence is so enclosed in another thing that they can be understood by that thing itself.

Once again nothing could be more false. We cannot derive the idea of any modification from an idea that we do not have, that is, from the idea of substance. All our knowledge comes from the senses; now our senses do not reach clear to the substance of things, they grasp only their qualities. If we believe there are modifications a knowledge of which is due to a knowledge of their subject, let us give a single example and we will soon recognize our mistake. Such is the blindness of philosophers when they are satisfied with vague notions: scarcely have they imagined substance in order to serve as the subject of modifications than they think they see it in itself and believe that it is only through substance that they have the idea of the modifications that revealed it to them.

But the truth about substances, outside of the understanding, lies nowhere else than in substances since they are conceived through themselves. Thus if someone said that he has a clear and distinct idea, that is, a true idea of substance, but that he doubts that such a substance exists, that would be the same thing as if he said that he had a true idea but that he did not know if it is false, as it is obvious to whoever tries to pay attention to it; or if he supposed that a substance is created, that would be to assume that a false idea has become true—which is the most ridiculous thing in the world. It must therefore be agreed that the existence of substance, thus of its essence, is an eternal truth.

All this would be true if Spinoza's definition of substance were the true idea of the thing.

... there are not two substances possessing the same nature. But in order to prove this methodically it is to be noted: (1) that the true definition of any one thing neither involves nor expresses anything except the nature of the thing defined. From which it follows:

(2) that a definition does not involve or express any number of individuals, since it expresses nothing but the nature of the things defined. For example, the definition of a triangle expresses nothing but the simple nature of a triangle and not any certain number of triangles.

(3) It is to be observed that in every existing thing there is some certain cause by reason of which it exists.

(4) Finally, it is to be observed that this cause by reason of which a thing exists, must either be contained in the nature itself and definition of the existing thing (simply because it pertains to the nature of the thing to exist), or it must exist outside the thing. This being granted, it follows that if a certain number of individuals exist in nature, there must necessarily be a cause why those individuals, and neither more nor fewer, exist. If, for example, there are twenty men in existence (whom, for the sake of greater clarity, I suppose existing at the same time, and that no others existed before them) it will not be sufficient, in order that we may give a reason why twenty men exist, to give a cause for human nature generally; but it will be necessary, in addition, to give a reason why neither more nor fewer than twenty exist, since, as we have already observed under the third head, there must necessarily be a cause why each exists. But this cause, as we have shown under the second and third heads, cannot be contained in human nature itself, since the true definition of a man does not involve the number twenty, and therefore, by the fourth head, the cause why these twenty men exist, and consequently the cause why each exists, must necessarily lie outside each one; and therefore we must conclude generally that whenever it is possible for several individuals of the same nature to exist, there must necessarily be an external cause for their existence.

Since it now pertains to the nature of the substance to exist (as we have shown in this scholium) its definition must involve necessary existence, and consequently from its definition alone its existence must be concluded. But from its definition (as we have already shown under the second and third heads), the existence of more substances than one cannot be deduced. It follows, therefore, from this definition necessarily that there cannot be two substances possessing the same nature.

Was so much verbiage really needed to get logically from an arbitrary definition to the existence of a chimera? All this reasoning is beside the mark for it assumes, in the first observation, that we know the nature of things well enough to include and express it in their definitions—a supposition that can be maintained only by philosophers who are wedded to their words.

Proposition IX

The more reality or being a thing possesses, the more attributes belong to it.

Proof

This is evident from Definition IV.

In advancing a proposition, we should give it a clear and determinate meaning before we go casting around for a proof for it. To prove a proposition that makes no sense or that proves nothing is the same thing. Now we have no idea of what is meant by the words "reality," "being," or "attribute"; I mention attributes that constitute essence because they are what we are dealing with (see Definition IV). Does "attribute" mean something different from "reality"? If so, what, and why does it have all the more attributes as it has all the more reality? If, on the other hand, the attribute, or what constitutes essence, is the same thing as reality, this proposition is completely silly. It says that the more reality a thing has, the more reality it has. Such a proposition would well deserve to be proven by a word definition. See what I said about Definition IV.

Proposition X

Each attribute of a substance must be conceived through itself.

Proof

For an attribute is that which the intellect perceives of substance, as if constituting its essence (Definition IV), and therefore (Definition III) it must be conceived through itself.

See what was said about the definitions used as proof in this so-called proof.

Scholium

From this it appears that although two attributes may be conceived as really distinct—that is, one without the assistance of the other—we cannot nevertheless then conclude that they constitute two different substances.

I myself would judge this matter quite differently. Substance is what is conceived through itself (Definition III). By the same definition, the attribute is also conceived through itself. Thus if there are two attributes, there are two substances.

For this is the nature of substance, that each of its attributes is conceived through itself, since all the attributes that substance possesses were always in it together, nor could one be produced by another; but each expresses the reality or being of substance. It is very far from being absurd, therefore, to ascribe to one substance a number of attributes, since nothing in nature is clearer than that each being must be conceived under some attribute, and the more reality or more being it has, the more attributes it possesses either expressing necessity or eternity and infinity.

Can the words "nature," "substance," "attribute," "being," "reality," "expresses," "eternity," and "infinity," after what little care that Spinoza took to determine their meaning, make some piece of discourse as clear as he says?

But if anyone now asks by what sign, therefore, we can distinguish between substances, let him read the following propositions, which show that in nature only one substance exists, and that it is absolutely infinite. For this reason, that sign would be sought for in vain.

Let us remember well the words "in nature" and we shall see whether they keep their promise.

Proposition XI

God, or substance consisting of infinite attributes, each one of which expresses eternal and infinite essence, necessarily exists.

First Proof

If this be denied, conceive, if it be possible, that God does not exist. Then it follows (Axiom VII) that His essence does not involve existence. But this (Proposition VII) is absurd. Therefore God necessarily exists.

Spinoza's reasoning is so infelicitous that one cannot agree with him even when he seems to come close to the truth. How can he propose to me to conceive that God exists or does not exist if his whole system has not yet taught me to conceive the ideas, not of the words but of the things *substance, infinity, attributes, essence,* or *God*? Moreover, if I conceive that God does not exist, it would follow that I had some extraordinary ideas, but it could not be concluded that God did not in fact exist or that His essence did not include existence. Finally, even if Proposition VII had been proven, it would not prove that it was absurd for the esssence of a substance containing an affinity of attributes, each of which expresses eternal and infinite essence, not to include existence; at most it would prove that it is of the nature of substance to exist (see Proposition VII). Now it seems to me that there is some difference between saying that it is in the nature of substance to exist and saying that it is in the nature of a substance containing an infinity of attributes, each of which expresses as eternal and infinite essence, to exist. It is obvious here that Spinoza is giving Proposition VII a greater extent than it had. It still remains for him to prove that this same substance which, by Proposition VII, exists of its nature, contains an infinity of attributes each of which expresses its eternal and infinite essence, which he never takes up.

Proof

For the existence or nonexistence of anything there must be a reason or cause. For example, if a triangle exists, there must be a reason or cause why it exists; and if it does not exist, there must be a reason or cause that hinders its existence or that negates it. But this reason or cause must either be contained in the nature of the thing or lie outside it. For example, the nature of the thing itself shows the reasons why a square circle does not exist, the reason being that a square circle involves a contradiction. And the reason, on the other hand, why substance exists, follows from its nature alone, which involves existence (see Proposition VII). But the reason why a circle or a triangle exists or does not exist is not drawn from their nature, but from the order of corporeal nature generally; for from that it must follow, either that a triangle necessarily exists, or that it is impossible for it to exist. This is self-evident. Therefore, it follows that if there be no cause nor reason that hinders a thing from existing, it exists necessarily. If, therefore, there be no reason or cause which hinders God from existing, or which negates His existence, we must conclude absolutely that He necessarily exists. But if there be such a reason or cause, it must be either in the nature itself of God or must lie outside it, that is to say, in another substance of another nature. For if the reason lay in a substance of the same nature, the existence of God would be by this very fact admitted. But substance possessing another nature could have nothing in common with God (Proposition II), and therefore it could not give him existence nor negate it.

Since, therefore, the reason or cause that could negate the divine existence cannot be outside the divine nature, it will necessarily, supposing that the divine nature does not exist, be in His nature itself, which would therefore involve a contradiction. But to affirm this of the being absolutely infinite and consummately perfect is absurd. Therefore neither in God nor outside God is there any cause or reason that can negate His existence, and therefore God necessarily exists.

"For the existence or nonexistence of anything there must be a reason or cause": does this mean that whatever idea that someone forms, we ought to say why there exists or does not exist something conformable to it? Would that be reasonable and should we take the trouble to prove that nothing in nature corresponds to the extravagant ideas that people sometimes have? Moreover, in addition to several defects in this proof that are a consequence of the preceding ones, it is assumed that we understand the causes or the reasons for the existence and nonexistence of things. I leave it to the reader to think whether that is true.

Proof III

Inability to exist is impotence, and, on the other hand, ability to exist is power, as is self-evident. If, therefore, there is nothing that necessarily exists excepting things finite, it follows that things finite are more powerful than the absolutely infinite being, and this (as is self-evident) is absurd; therefore, either nothing exists or being absolutely infinite also necessarily exists. But we ourselves exist, either in ourselves or in something else that necessarily exists (Axiom I and Proposition VII). Therefore, there is being absolutely infinite, that is to say (Definition VI), God, necessarily exists.

This proof is presented in a very singular and abstract manner. If someone denied the existence of God, can we prove it to him by saying that if God does not exist, that it would be through impotence?

Scholium

In this last demonstration I wish to prove the existence of God a posteriori, in order that the demonstration might be the more easily understood, and not because the existence of God does not follow a priori from the same grounds. For since the ability to exist is power, it follows that the more reality belongs to the nature of anything, the greater is the power for existence it derives from itself; and it also follows, therefore, that the absolutely infinite being, or God, has from Himself an absolutely infinite power of existence, and that He therefore necessarily exists.

It would be contradictory for a thing that we supposed to be absolutely infinite, and consequently to include existence, not to exist. Spinoza should have proven that there was in nature an object that fits his idea of God. Otherwise his proofs, at most true in relation to his way of conceiving, prove nothing about the thing itself.

When Spinoza says that God is infinite, he misuses this term to conclude that nothing exists that is not an attribute or a modification of God.

He continues and says that people who are accustomed to thinking of things produced by external causes and who judge that things can exist with difficulty when those people conceive that several realities belong to them will perhaps find it hard to follow his proof. To which he replies that in truth these things owe their existence and all their perfections to the virtue of their cause. But he adds that it is not a question of things and that he is only talking about substances that cannot be produced, and he concludes with these words:

For whatever perfection or reality those things may have that are produced by external causes, whether they consist of many parts or few, they owe it all to the virtue of an external cause, and therefore their existence springs from the perfection of an external cause alone and not from their own. On the other hand, whatever perfection substance has is due to no external cause. Therefore, its existence must follow from its nature alone, and is therefore nothing else than its essence. Perfection consequently does not prevent the existence of the thing, but establishes it; imperfection, on the other hand, prevents existence and so of no existence can we be more sure than of the existence of the absolutely infinite being or perfect being, that is to say, God. For since His essence shuts out all imperfections and involves absolute perfection, for this very reason all cause of doubt concerning His existence is taken away, and the highest certainty concerning it is given, a truth that I trust will be evident to anyone who bestows only moderate attention.

It is much more evident that the essence Spinoza is talking about is merely ideal, and consequently the existence that he infers from it is ideal as well.

Proposition XII

No attribute of substance can be truly conceived from which it follows that substance can be divided.

Proof

For the parts into which substance thus conceived would be divided will or will not retain the nature of substance. If they retain it, then (Proposition VIII) each part will be infinite, and (Proposition VI) the cause of itself, and will consist of an attribute different from that of any other part (Proposition V), so that from one substance, more substances could be formed, which (Proposition VI) is absurd. Moreover, the parts (Proposition II) would have nothing in common with their whole, and the whole (Definition IV and Proposition X) could be, and could be conceived without its parts, which no one will doubt to be an absurdity. But if the second case be supposed, namely, that the parts will not retain the nature of substance, then, since the whole substance might be divided into equal parts, it would lose the nature of substance and cease to be, which (Proposition VII) is absurd.

The further we go into Spinoza, the easier he is to refute, because the defects of his arguments increase as his final proofs assume a greater number of propositions. This proof has not only all the defects of propositions II, V, VI, VII, VIII, and X, but also all the others on which they depend. I refer the reader to what I have said.

Proposition XIII

An absolutely infinite substance is indivisible.

Proof

For if it were divisible, the parts into which it would be divided will or will not retain the nature of absolutely infinite substance. If they retain it, there will be a plurality of substances possessing the same nature, which (Proposition V) is absurd. If the second case be supposed, then (as above), absolutely infinite substance can cease to be, which (Proposition XI) is also absurd.

We can see that this proof goes wrong in the same way as the preceding one.

Corollary

Hence it follows that no substance, and consequently no bodily substance insofar as it is a substance, is divisible.

Scholium

That substance is indivisible is more easily to be understood from this consideration alone, that the nature of substance cannot be conceived unless as infinite, and that by a part of substance, nothing else can be understood than finite substance, which (Proposition VIII) involves a manifest contradiction.

Spinoza therefore agrees that bodily substance is divisible, but he denies that it is so *qua* substance. So it will be divisible *qua* mode. Thus he will soon say that bodily substance is only one affection of the attributes of God.

Proposition XIV

Besides God, no substance can be, nor can be conceived.

Proof

Since God is an absolutely infinite being, of whom no attribute can be denied which expresses the essence of substance (Definition VI), and since He necessarily exists (Proposition XI), it follows that if there were any substance besides God, it would have to be explained by some attribute of God, and thus two substances would exist possessing the same attribute, which (Proposition V) is absurd; and therefore there cannot be any subtance excepting God, and consequently none other can be conceived.

I would be repeating myself too often if I tried to show all the defects of this proof. I refer the reader to what I have said.

Corollary I

Hence it follows with the greatest clearness, firstly, that God is one, that is to say (Definition VI), *in nature* there is but one substance, and it is absolutely infinite, as (Scholium of Proposition X) we have already intimated.

Observe that the proof involves only a word definition and judge whether we would be justified in using the expression "in nature" in the corollary.

Corollary II

It follows, secondly, that the thing extended and the thing thinking are either attributes of God or (Axiom I) affections of the attributes of God.

Anyone can form an abstract idea of substance and reify this idea by supposing that it fits an object that does indeed exist in nature. That done, we can no longer represent finite beings as substances. For once we reify the abstract idea of substance, we will represent substance as everywhere the same, everywhere immutable and necessary; and whatever variety we assume in finite beings, we will no longer conceive of them as constituting a multitude.We will imagine them as one and the same substance differently modified. This is what happened to Spinoza.

The ancient philosophers also argued that there could be only one substance. But the way the Stoics explained matters, it appears that this substance is not properly one and that in fact it is a compound, a heap of substances. They said "one" merely because they thought of it under the abstract idea of everything and as being the collection of everything that exists, where they had never tried too hard to determine what constituted unity. Protecting himself from this criticism, Spinoza made it one by force of abstraction. But if the substance of the Stoics is too compound to be one, Spinoza's is too abstract to be something.

Proposition XV

Whatever is, is in God and nothing can either be or be conceived without God.

Proof

Besides God, there is no substance, nor can any be conceived (Proposition XIV), that is to say (Definition III), nothing is in itself and is conceived through itself. But modes (Definition V) can neither be or be conceived without substance; therefore, in the divine nature only they can be, and through it alone can they be conceived. But besides the substance and modes, nothing is assumed (Axiom I). Therefore, nothing can be or be conceived without God.

Created things thus are no more than modes of the divine substance, as Spinoza will say further on—too far-fetched and too ill-proven a supposition for us to stop here.

Always observe that Spinoza's demonstrations prove certain relations among words to which he had attached abstract ideas. But we can conclude nothing about things as they exist in nature.

Scholium

In this scholium, Spinoza replies to some objections raised by people who do not conceive that extended substance is an attribute of God and that matter belongs to the divine nature. But as his replies are based on the propositions that we have already refuted, I believe I can dispense with translating this extract.

Proposition XVI

From the necessity of the divine nature, infinite numbers of things in infinite ways (that is to say, all things that can be conceived by the infinite intellect) must follow.

Proof

This proposition must be plain to everyone who considers that from the given definition of anything, a number of properties necessarily following from it (that is to say, following from the essence of the thing itself) are inferred by the intellect, and just in proportion as the definition of the thing expresses a greater reality, that is to say, just in proportion as the essence of the thing defined involves a greater reality, will more properties be inferred. But the divine nature possesses absolutely infinite attributes (Definition VI), each one of which expresses infinite essence in its own kind (*in suo genere*) and therefore from the necessity of the divine nature, infinite numbers of things in infinite ways (that is to say, all things that can be conceived by the infinite intellect) must necessarily follow.

This definition (the sixth) is very fecund. I was right to observe the care with which Spinoza constructed it. In this demonstration, he obviously assumes that definition and essence are one and the same thing. Nevertheless Definition VI does not prove, whatever he says about it, that the divine nature *has an infinity of attributes*, of which each of its kind expresses an infinite essence. It merely teaches us what he understands by the word *God*.

Corollary I

Hence it follows that God is the efficient cause of all things perceived by the infinite intellect.

Corollary II

It follows secondly that God is cause through Himself, and not through that which is contingent (*per accidens*).

Corollary III

It follows ... that God is absolutely the first cause.

Spinoza did not define the words "cause," "efficient," "cause through itself," "cause by accident," or "first cause." Nevertheless, he had all the greater obligation to do so, as he appeared in the following to give them a very different sense than that which they commonly have.

Proposition XVII

God acts from the laws of his nature only, and is compelled by no one.

Proof

We have just shown (Proposition XVI) that from the necessity, or (which is the same thing) from the laws only of the divine nature, infinite numbers of things absolutely follow; and we have demonstrated (Proposition XV) that nothing can be, nor can be conceived, without God, but that all things are in God. Therefore, outside Himself, there can be nothing by which He may be determined or compelled to act; and therefore He acts from the laws of His own nature only, and is compelled by no one.

Corollary I

Hence it follows, first, that there is no cause, either external to God or within Him, that can excite Him to act except the perfection of His own nature.

Corollary II

It follows, second, that God alone is a free cause; for God alone exists from the necessity alone of His own nature (Proposition XI, and corollary of Proposition XIV), and acts from the necessity alone of His own nature (Proposition XVI). Therefore (Definition VII) He alone is a free cause.

This is what anyone else would call a necessary cause.

Scholium

Spinoza uses his principles to reply to some objections he formulates. To shorten this already overlengthy chapter, I shall not translate this scholium. I shall merely remark that in order to explain how all things follow from the divine nature he says that they follow from it by a necessity similar to the one by which it follows from all eternity, and will eternally follow from the nature of the triangle, that its three angles are equal to two right angles. That being so, I no longer know what it is to be a cause, for I do not know that it is ever advisable to say that the nature of a triangle was the *efficient and first cause by itself* of the equality of the three angles of the triangle to two right angles. Nor do I know what it is, in Spinoza's language, to act in relation to God, because I do not see how the nature of the triangle acts to produce the equality of its three angles to two right angles.

Thus, if everything follows from the divine nature by the same necessity as the equality of the three angles of the triangle to two right angles follows from the nature of a triangle, I infer an obvious contradiction from it. It is that in nature everything occurs without action. But it is not necessary to press Spinoza so strongly.

Proposition XVIII

God is the immanent and not the transient cause of all things.

Proof

All things that are, are in God and must be conceived through him (Proposition XV), and therefore (corollary I, Proposition XVI) He is the cause of the things that are in Himself. This is the first thing that was to be proved. Moreover, outside God there can be no substance (Proposition XIV), that is to say (Definition III), outside him nothing can exist that is in Himself. This was the second thing to be proved. God, therefore, is the immanent but not the transient cause of all things.

Whatever Spinoza means by the words "immanent cause" and "transient cause" which he has not defined, we understand the lack of solidity of the proposition on which he relies.

Proposition XIX

God is eternal, or in other words, all His attributes are eternal.

Proof

For God (definition VI) is substance, which (Proposition XI) necessarily exists, that is to say (Proposition VII), a substance to whose nature it pertains to exist, or *(which is the same thing) a substance from the definition of which it follows that it exists*, and therefore (Definition VIII) He is eternal. Again, by the attributes of God it is to be understood that which (Definition IV) expresses the essence of the divine substance, that is to say, that which pertains to substance.

It is this, I say, which the attributes themselves must involve. But eternity pertains to the nature of substance (Proposition VII). Therefore, each of the attributes must involve eternity, and therefore all are eternal.

This proposition, well explicated, is certainly true; but it appears from everything I have said, that it is inadequately proven.

Scholium

This proposition is as clear as possible, from the manner in which (Proposition XI) I have demonstrated the existence of God. From that demonstration I say it is plain that the existence of God, like His essence, is an eternal truth. Moreover, (Proposition XIX of the *Principles of Cartesian Philosophy*), I have demonstrated by another method the eternity of God, and there is no need to repeat the demonstration here.

Proposition XX

The existence of God and His essence are one and the same thing.

Proof

God (Proposition XIX) and all His attributes are eternal, that is to say, (Definition VIII) each one of His attributes expresses existence. The same attributes of God, therefore, which (Definition IV) manifest the eternal essence of God, at the same time manifest His eternal existence; that is to say, the very same thing that constitutes the essence of God constitutes at the same time His existence, and therefore His existence and His essence are one and the same thing.

Here are many words often repeated and about which I doubt we could forumlate clear and determinate ideas. When I give these proofs without comment, it is because I refer the reader to what I have observed about the propositions used as their basis. We can perceive that I do not discuss all the defects of the final proofs; but the criticisms that preceded them can reveal these defects.

Corollary I

Hence it follows that the existence of God, like His essence, is an eternal truth.

Corollary II

God is immutable, or (which is the same thing) all His attributes are immutable; for if they were changed as regards their existence, they must be changed also as regards their essence (Proposition XX); that is to say (as is self-evident), from being true, they would become false, which is absurd.

Proposition XXI

All things that follow from the absolute nature of any attribute of God must exist forever, and must be infinite; that is, through that same attribute they are eternal and infinite. [In this proposition and the next two succeeding Spinoza is referring to "infinite modes"].

Proof

Conceive, if possible (supposing that the truth of the proposition is denied), that in some attribute of God something which is finite and has a determinate existence or duration follows from the absolute nature of that attribute; for example, an idea of God in thought. [Not the idea that man forms of God, but rather of God's ideas] But thought, since it is admitted to be an attribute of God, is necessarily (Proposition XI) in its nature infinite. But so far as it has the idea of God it is by supposition finite. But (Definition II) it cannot be conceived as finite unless it be determined by thought itself so far as it constitutes the idea of God, for so far by supposition it is finite. Therefore it must be determined by thought so far as it does not constitute an idea of God, but which, nevertheless (Proposition XI) necessarily exists. Thought, therefore, exists but does not form the idea of God, and therefore its nature, insofar as it is absolute thought, the idea of God does not necessarily follow (for it is conceived as forming and as not forming the idea of God), which is contrary to the hypothesis. Therefore, if an idea of God in thought, or anything else in any attribute of God, follow from the necessity of the absolute nature of that attribute (for the demonstration being universal will apply in every case), that thing must necessarily be infinite, which was the first thing to be proved.

Again, that which thus follows from the necessity of the nature of any attribute cannot have a determinate duration. For, if the truth of this being denied, let it be supposed that in some attribute of God a thing exists that follows from the necessity of the nature of the attribute—for example, an idea of God in thought—and let it be supposed that at some time it has either not existed or will not exist. But since thought is supposed to be an attribute of God, it must exist both necessarily and unchangeably (Proposition XI and Corollary II, Proposition XX). Therefore, beyond the limits of the duration of the idea of God (for we are assuming that at some time this idea has either not existed or will not exist), thought must exist without the idea of God; but this is contrary to hypothesis, for the supposition is that thought being given, the idea of God necesarily follows. Therefore neither an idea of God in thought, nor anything else that necessarily follows from the absolute nature of any attribute of God, can have a determinate duration, but through the same attribute is eternal; which was the second thing to be proved. Observe that what we have affirmed here is true of everything that in any attribute of God necessarily follows from the absolute nature of God.

This manner of reasoning is so extraordinary that I do not imagine how it could occur to anyone if I did not know how blind one becomes once one has adopted a system. If this is an example of reasoning about clear ideas, I am very much mistaken. As for me, I cannot follow Spinoza's suppositions. "The idea of God in thought," "the thought now finite, now infinite, that constitutes or does not constitute the idea of God," are things that are too abstract, or rather they are words that I confess I understand not at all, or that I believe barely comprehensible. Spinoza should have used an example that gives his proof greater purchase.

Proposition XXII

Whatever follows from any attribute of God, insofar as it is modified by a modification that through the same attributes exists necessarily and infinitely, must also exist necessarily and infinitely.

Proof

This proposition is demonstrated in the same manner as the preceding proposition.

Thus it too is unintelligible.

Proposition XXIII

Every mode that exists necessarily and infinitely must necessarily follow either from the absolute nature of some attribute of God, or from some attribute modified by a modification that exists and infinitely.

Proof

A mode is that which is in something else through which it must be conceived (Definition V), that is to say (Proposition XV), it is in God alone, and through God alone can be conceived. If a mode, therefore, be conceived to exist necessarily and to be infinite, its necessary existence and infinitude must be concluded from some attribute of God or perceived through it, insofar as it is conceived to express infinitude and necessity of existence, that is to say (Definition VIII), eternity, or, in other words (Definition III and Proposition XIX), insofar as it is considered absolutely. A mode, therefore, that exists necessarily and infinitely must follow from the absolute nature of some attribute of God, either immediately (Proposition XXI), or immediately through some modification following from His absolute nature, that is to say (Proposition XXII), a modification that necessarily and infinitely exists.

I ask what a mode is that follows necessarily from the absolute nature of an attribute of God, either immediately or by means of some modification that modifies the attribute? Nowhere does Spinoza explain it or give any example. It is thus impossible to guess what truth this so-called proof contains.

Proposition XXIV

The essence of things produced by God does not involve existence.

Proof

This is evident from the first definition; for that thing whose nature (considered, that is to say, in itself) involves existence, is the cause of itself and exists from the necessity of its own nature alone.

Corollary

Hence it follows that God is not only the cause of the commencement of the existence of things, but also of their continuance in existence, or, in other words, (to use scholastic phraseology) God is the *causa essendi rerum*. For if we consider the essence of things, whether existing or nonexisting, we discover that it neither involves existence nor duration, and therefore the essence of existing things cannot be the cause of their existence nor of their duration, but God only is the cause, to whose nature alone existence pertains (Corollary I, Proposition XIV).

Proposition XXV

Suppose that God is not the cause of the essence of things; then (Axiom IV) the existence of things can be conceived without God, which (proposition XV) is absurd. Therefore, God is the cause of the essence of things.

Scholium

This proposition more clearly follows from Proposition XVI. For from this proposition it follows that, from the existence of the divine nature, both the essence of things and their existence must necessarily be concluded, or, in a word, in the same sense in which God is said to be the cause of Himself He must be called the cause of all things. This will appear still more clearly from the following corollary.

Corollary

Individual things are nothing but affections or modes of God's attributes, expressing those attributes in a certain and determinate manner. This is evident from Proposition XV and Definition V.

The more Spinoza uses the words "cause," "action," and "production," the more confusion we find. "God is the cause of everything in the same sense that He is the cause of Himself." But if He is the cause of Himself, then it is not because He acts to give Himself existence or that He produces Himself. He thus does not act to give existence to other things, he does not produce them, and there is properly in all nature no action or production or cause or effect.

Proposition XXVI

A thing that has been determined to any action was necessarily so determined by God, and that which has not been thus determined by God cannot determine itself to action.

Proof

That by which things are said to be determined to any action is necessarily something positive (as is self-evident); and therefore, God, from the necessity of His nature, is the efficient cause both of its essence and of its existence (Propositions XXV and XVI), which was the first thing to be proved. From this also the second part of the proposition follows most clearly. For if a thing that has not been determined by God could determine itself, the first part of the proposition would be false, and to suppose this possible is an absurdity, as we have shown.

Once again the same confusion. If in Spinoza the words "cause" and "action" mean nothing, the words "determine to act" have no more sense. It appears that Spinoza called God "cause of Himself" in order to be able to say that He is the cause of other things. It seemed absurd to Spinoza that an infinity of things existed and that there was no cause or effect. To speak in a way that seemed to make more sense, Spinoza had to say that God is the cause of Himself. But, since God is, strictly speaking, not the cause of Himself, it would follow from Spinoza's principles that He was not the cause of particular things.

Spinoza could have said that God is the effect of Himself. For if He is the cause of other things in the same sense that He is cause of Himself, He is the effect of Himself in the same sense that other things are the effect of Him. This relation is reciprocal. Now what are we to thing of a language that leads us to say that a substance produced itself? Could there be a greater misuse of these terms?

If the proposition "God is the cause of Himself" means that the essence of God includes His existence, as the first definition supposes, the proposition "God is the cause of particular things" means that God's essence includes the existence of particular things. For it is in the same sense that God is the cause in both cases. Thus God does not give more existence to particular things than to Himself. Particular things exist only because they belong like Him to the same essence; and strictly speaking, as I have already observed, there is neither action nor production. These conclusions necessarily follow in the Spinozistic system; but they refute themselves.

Proposition XXVII

A thing that has been determined by God to any action cannot render itself indeterminate.

Proof

This proposition is evident from Axiom III.

Proposition XXVIII

An individual thing, or a thing that is finite, and that has a determinate existence, cannot exist or be determined to action unless it be determined to existence and action by another cause that is also finite and has a determinate existence; and again, this cause cannot exist or be determined to action unless by another cause that is also finite and determined to existence and action, and so on ad infinitum.

Proof

Whatever is determined to existence and action is thus determined by God (Proposition XXVI and corollary of Proposition XXIV). But that which is finite and which has a determinate existence could not be produced by the absolute nature of any attribute of God, for whatever follows from the absolute nature of any attribute of God is infinite and eternal (Proposition XXI). The finite and determinate must therefore follow from God, or from some attribute of God, insofar as the latter is considered to be affected by some mode, for besides substance and modes nothing exists (Axiom I, and Definitions III and V), and modes (corollary of Proposition XXV) are nothing but affections of God's attributes. But the finite and determinate could not follow from God, or from any of His attributes, so far as that attribute is affected with the modification that is eternal and infinite (Proposition XXII). It must, therefore, follow or be determined to existence and action by God, or by some attribute of God, insofar as the attribute is modified by a modification that is finite, and that has as a determinate existence. This was the first thing to be proved. Again, this cause or this mode (by the same reasoning by which we have already demonstrated the first part of this proposition) must be determined by another cause, which is also finite, and which has a determinate existence, and this last cause (by the same reasoning) must, in its turn, be determined by another cause, and so on continually (by the same reasoning) ad infinitum.

God, or an infinitely perfect being, thus becomes superfluous in the Spinozistic system. Here is the proof. A finite thing can only be determined to exist and act by a finite cause (preceding Proposition). God as an infinite being does not determine finite things, He does not even determine Himself as modified by a finite modification. For if these things were determined by God as an infinite being, they would be infinite (Propositions XXI and XXII), which would be contrary to the supposition. So all finite causes are determined by other finite causes; so that an infinite progression is formed without our being able to reach an infinite cause that determined any one of them. Thus God as an infinite being does not determine finite things to exist or act. They can thus exist without God as an infinite being, that is (Definition VI), without God. Another absurdity is that as particular things are (corollary of Proposition XXV) modes of God, it follows that modes can exist without their substance.

If Spinoza wants God or the infinite being to determine the existence of all beings, his principles should lead him to conclude that everything is infinite and that we ourselves are infinite modes of divinity. Here is the proof.

God alone determines the existence of everything that exists (Propositions XVI and XVIII). Thus, we are determined to exist by Him. Now the things that follow from an infinite substance, or that are determined to exist by an infinite substance, are also infinite (Propositions XXI and XXII). God is an infinite substance (Definition VI). Thus each of us is infinite as well.

This ridiculous proposition could be maintained as well as a series of causes that by an infinite progression determine themselves without its being possible to reach the first one. The absurdity is the same on both sides.

If we examine this system carefully, we will recognize both that the finite beings seem to exist apart and independently of the infinite being (since they are sufficient unto themselves to determine their existence) and that they cannot be determined by God as an infinite being, that is, by God without becoming themselves infinite.

Scholium

Spinoza here observes that God is the proximate cause of things that He produces immediately; that He is not the cause of His own kind; and that finally we cannot say he is the remote cause of individual things. But Spinoza does not explain his thought either by examples or by precise definitions and he continues to be as obscure as ever.

Proposition XXIX

In nature there is nothing contingent, but all things are determined from the necessity of the divine nature to exist and act in a certain manner.

Proof

Whatever is, is in God (Proposition XV); but God cannot be called a contingent thing, for (Proposition XI) He exists necessarily and not contingently. Moreover, the modes of the divine nature have followed from it necessarily and not contingently (Proposition XVI), and that, too, whether it be considered absolutely (Proposition XXI), or as determined to action in a certain manner (Proposition XXVII). But God is the cause of these modes, not only insofar as they simply exist (Corollary of Proposition XXIV), but also (Proposition XXVI) insofar as they are considered as determined to any action. And if they are not determined by God (by the same proposition), it is an impossibility and not a contingency that they should determine themselves; and, on the other hand (Proposition XXVII), if they are determined by God, it is an impossibility and not a contingency that they should render themselves indeterminate. Wherefore all things are determined from a necessity of a divine nature, not only to exist, but to exist and act in a certain manner and there is nothing contingent.

Since every finite being must be determined by a finite cause (Proposition XXVII), whatever attempt Spinoza makes to prove that everything is determined by God, he cannot prevent the existence of two orders of completely independent things in his system. First, the order of infinite things that all follow from the absolute nature of God, or from one of his attributes modified by an infinite modification. Second, the order of finite things that all follow from each other without the possibility of going back to the first infinite cause that determined them to exist. How can these two orders of things constitute one and the same substance?

Scholium

Spinoza says here that he understands by *natura naturans* what is in itself and is conceived by itself, or every attribute that expresses an eternal and infinite essence, that is, (Corollary I of Proposition XIV, and Corollary II of Proposition XVII) God regarded as a free cause. But he understands by *natura naturata* everything that follows from the necessity of the nature of God, or from each of His attributes, that is, all the modes of the attributes of God insofar as they are regarded as things that are in God and that cannot exist or be conceived without Him.

The expressions *natura naturans* and *natura naturata* are so felicitous and energetic that it was a pity that Spinoza did not use them.

Proposition XXX

The actual intellect [distinguished from potential intellect], whether finite or infinite, must comprehend the attributes of God and His affections, and nothing else.

Proof

A true idea must agree with that of which it is the idea (Axiom VI), that is (as is self-evident), that which is objectively contained in the intellect must necessarily exist in nature. But in nature (Corollary I, Proposition XIV) only one substance exists, namely, God, and no affections (Proposition XV) excepting those that are in God, and that (by the same proposition) can neither be nor be conceived without God. Therefore, the actual intellect, whether finite or infinite, must comprehend the attributes of God and His affections, and nothing else.

Since the sense of the axiom "a true idea must agree with its object" is that things must be in nature as they are in the understanding, nothing is less certain than its truth. We see how right I was to point out this prejudice which still continues to hold sway and which Spinoza had found so well-established that no one could call it into question.

Proposition XXXI

The actual intellect, whether finite or infinite, together with the will, desire, love, and so forth, must be referred to the *natura naturata* and not to the *natura naturans*.

Proof

This proof was constructed only to give a new name to what Spinoza called the understanding as a finite or infinite act. This does not warrant our pausing here.

Scholium

The purpose of this scholium is to make us aware that when Spinoza is talking about an actual intellect, he does not agree that there is a potential intellect.

Proposition XXXII

The will cannot be called a free cause, but can be only called necessary.

Proof

The will is only a certain mode of thought, like the intellect, and therefore (Proposition XXVIII) no volition can exist or be determined to action unless it be determined by another cause, and this again by another, and so on ad infinitum. And if the will be supposed infinite, it must be determined to existence and action by God, not insofar as He is substance absolutely infinite, but insofar as He possesses an attribute that expresses the infinite and eternal essence of thought (Proposition XXIII). In whatever way, therefore, the will be conceived, whether as finite or infinite, it requires the cause by which it may be determined to existence and action, and therefore (Definition VII) it cannot be called a free cause but only necessary or compelled.

A volition determined by a series of causes ad infinitum, and an infinite will determined by God insofar as He has an attribute expressing the eternal and infinite essence of thought—these are big words but when has Spinoza given us adequate ideas of them? And how could he succeed if he tried to?

In the Spinozistic system everything occurs through blind necessity. If there is a first cause, it does not act out of knowledge, but because everything follows necessarily from its nature. Thus I do not see what utility the words "understanding" and "will" can have in this system. Indeed, what do "understanding" and "will" mean for a cause in the nature of which all things follow necessarily, as the equality of the three angles of a triangle to two right angles follows from the essence of a triangle? This is Spinoza's comparison. Thus he expressly denies God understanding and will,[57] although, by Propositions XXX and XXXI, he seems to admit an infinite understanding.

Corollary I

Hence it follows, first, that God does not act from freedom of the will.

Corollary II

It follows, second, that will and intellect are related to the nature of God as motion and rest, and absolutely as all natural things, which (Proposition XXIX) must be determined by God to existence and action in a certain manner. For the

---

[57]*Posthumous Works*, Letter 58.

will, like all other things, needs a cause by which it may be determined to existence and action in a certain manner, and although from a given will or intellect infinite things may follow, God cannot on this account be said to act from freedom of the will, any more than He can be said to act from freedom of motion and rest by reason of the things that follow from motion and rest (for from motion and rest infinite numbers of things follow). Therefore, will does not appertain to the nature of God more than other natural things, but is related to it as motion and rest and all other things are related to it; these all following, as we have shown, from the necessity of the divine nature, and being determined to existence and action in a certain manner.

What language! To use movement and rest to explain the will and understanding, and to relate them in the same way to the divine nature! We can see that Spinoza felt that in his principles the understanding and will are useless to God, but whether he accepts or rejects them, his system is always equally absurd.

Proposition XXXIII

Things could have been produced by God in no other manner and in no other order than that in which they have been produced.

Proof

All things have necessarily followed from the given nature of God (Proposition XVI), and from the necessity of His nature have been determined to existence and action in a certain manner (Proposition XXIX). If, therefore, things could have been of another nature, or could have been determined in another manner to action, so that the order of nature would have been different, the nature of God might then be different from that which it now is, and hence (Proposition XI) that different nature would necessarily exist, and there might consequently be two or more Gods, which (Corollary I, Proposition XIV) is absurd. Therefore, things could be produced by God in no other manner and in no other order than that in which they have been produced.

It is obvious that this proposition is merely a consequence of several inadequately proven propositions. It is the same with the three following ones.

Scholium I

In this scholium Spinoza tries to prove that if we judge that there are contingent things, it is only through ignorance, that is, that not knowing whether the essence of things includes some contradiction, we do not know whether they are impossible; or if we know that their essence does not include any contradiction, we do not know the causes from which they necessarily follow, and we do not know that they are necessary. Now, our ignorance about their necessity or impossibility makes us judge that they are contingent or possible.

Scholium II

In this second scholium Spinoza tries to prove Proposition XXXIII by arguing from the absurdity of contrary principles. I will not relate his reasoning on this subject, because it adds nothing to the truth of his system.

Proposition XXXIV

The power of God is His essence itself.

Proof

From the necessity alone of the existence of God it follows that God is the cause of Himself (Proposition XI), and (Proposition XVI and its corollary) the cause of all things. Therefore, the power of God, by which He Himself and all the things are and act, is His essence itself.

Proposition XXXV

Whatever we conceive to be in God's power necessarily exists.

Proof

For whatever is in God's power must (Proposition XXXIV) be so comprehended in His essence that it necessarily follows from it, and consequently exists necessarily.

Proposition XXXVI

Nothing exists from whose nature an effect does not follow.

Proof

Whatever exists expresses the nature or the essence of God in a certain and determinate manner (Corollary, Proposition XXV); that is to say (Proposition XXXIV), whatever exists expresses the power of God, which is the cause of all things, in a certain and determinate manner, and therefore (Proposition XVI) some effect must follow from it.

After all these propositions Spinoza ends the first part of his work by a kind of conclusion to which he gives the title *Appendix*.

Appendix

I have now explained the nature of God and His properties. I have shown that He necessarily exists; that He is one God; that from the necessity alone of His own nature He is and acts; that He is, and in what way He is, the free cause of all things; that all things are in Him, and so depend upon Him that without Him they can neither be nor be conceived; and, finally, that all things have been predetermined by Him, not indeed from freedom of will or from absolute good pleasure, but from His absolute nature or infinite power.

Spinoza adds that although he has kept away from preconceptions, there still remain many that can prevent one from grasping the chain of his proofs, and that the source of all the others is the widespread assumption that God and all natural things act, as we do, toward an end. Thus he is going to: (1) enquire why we assent to this prejudice; (2) prove, he claims, its falsity; (3) show how thereby originated the prejudices of good and evil, merit and demerit, praise and blame, order and disorder, and beauty and deformity. But as he then reasons only according to the principles he believes he has established, it would be boring and needless to follow his reasoning in detail.

This is the first part of Spinoza's *Ethics*. The four other parts are argued in the same style. The second discusses the origin and nature of the mind; the third, the origin and nature of affections; the fourth, the force of affections; the last one, human freedom. All four take as proven the propositions that I have just analyzed and that were ventured only according to very vague ideas. They are thus vulnerable to the same criticisms that I made about the first part.

Bayle has been criticized for misunderstanding Spinoza, and rightfully so if we judge the matter from the way he attacks him. Bayle treated charmingly all the matters he discussed and perhaps that was his only purpose. It appears that in general the choice of particular principles is indifferent to Bayle; that he is trying to get only one benefit from this, that of attacking all opinions, and that he undertakes to prove something only when he believes he has two proofs, one for and one against.

Did he think he had refuted Spinoza by arguing against all the conclusions he draws from the Spinozistic system? But if these conclusions do not follow from this system, he is no longer attacking Spinoza; and if they are valid conclusions, Spinoza will reply that they are not absurd at all and that they appear so only to people who do not know how to get back to the principles of things. Overthrow my principles, he will say, if you want to overturn my system; or if you let my principles to continue to exist, agree to the truth of the propositions necessarily implied by them.

As for me, I believe that my sole aim was to prove that Spinoza has no idea of the things he argues for, that his definitions are vague and his axioms inexact, and that these propositions are merely the work of his imagination and include nothing that can lead to a knowledge of things. That done, I stopped. It would have been as unreasonable for me to attack the phantasms arising from Spinozism as it was for the knights errant to combat the ghosts of the bewitchers. The wise thing to do was to break the spell.

It has often been said that Spinozism is a consequence of Cartesianism. This claim is not completely unjustified, but it must be agreed that in Spinozism the principles of Descartes are greatly altered. Spinoza has prejudices common to almost all philosophers, as one can see from my criticisms. But he borrowed very much from the Cartesians. Above all, he recognizes the principle that "we can affirm of a thing everything included in our clear and distinct idea of it," and he made application of it that Descartes would have disavowed. Rejecting creation, because he did not conceive of it or because he had no clear and distinct idea of it, Spinoza observes that finite beings exist and that existence is not included in our notion of them. From which he concludes that they do not exist by themselves. Now how can it be that finite beings, not existing by themselves, exist without creation occurring? This is what Spinoza proposes to clear up.

For this, he is careful to note that the notion of modes does not include existence, that they are not something created, and that they nevertheless exist. But how? In the substance on which they depend. So he believes he need only say that finite entities are modes of one and the same substance, as roundness and four-leggedness are modes of the body. A wonderful solution! Would we not say that this new way of explaining things is more conceivable? Nevertheless he undertakes to prove his hypothesis; and because he affects to follow the order of geometry, he believes he can construct proofs. As gross as it is, this mistake has been committed by many philosophers.

So let Spinoza's partisans choose between two alternatives: either they confess that they have hitherto declared themselves in favor of a system that means nothing, or that they work out in a clear and precise way the greater meaning presumably included in it. But one cannot waver about the judgment concerning Spinoza. Biased in favor of all scholastic prejudices, he did not doubt that our mind was capable of discovering the essence of things and of going back to their first principles. He formulated only vague notions with which he was always satisfied. And if he understood the art of arranging words and propositions in a geometric way, he did not understand the art of making up ideas similar to geometric ones. One thing persuades me that Spinoza could himself have been the dupe of his own arguments, and that is the art with which he fabricated them.

11 Conclusion of the Preceding Chapters

However little one has reflected about the examples I have cited, he will be convinced that we fall into error merely because we reason about principles whose ideas we have not clearly distinguished. Consequently, we do not take in these ideas with sufficiently clear and precise vision so as to understand their truth to its full extent, nor do we guard against what is vague and ambiguous in them. This is the true cause of philosophers' errors and the common peoples' prejudices. From which we can conclude that falsity of mind consists uniquely in the habit of reasoning with ill-determined principles, that is, about ideas that in fact we do not have and that we nevertheless regard as original knowledge necessarily leading us to other knowledge.

But education has so strongly accustomed people to be content with vague notions that few can resolve to give up the use of these principles.[58] Their drawbacks will be well understood only by those who remember the difficulties they had to overcome in order to familiarize themselves with them and who even recall sensing early on some of the contradictions involved. As for those who without aversion or reflection followed all these impressions produced by education, we cannot believe how wrong-thinking their minds have become and we should not wait for them to reform their manner of reasoning. This is how the sad effects of this method often become irremediable.

Having proved abstract principles useless and dangerous, it only remains for us to find principles that we can make use of. But we are very close to understanding the method that leads to truth when we understand the method that leads us away from it.

---

[58]I have explained elsewhere how education leads us to acquire this habit. *The Art of Thinking*, Part 2, Chapter 1.

12 Hypotheses

Philosophers are very much divided about the use of hypotheses. Some philosophers, predisposed in their favor by the success of hypotheses in astronomy or perhaps dazzled by the boldness of some hypotheses in physics, regard them as true principles. Other philosophers, considering the misuses made of hypotheses, would like to ban them from the sciences.

Abstract principles, even when they are true and highly determinate, are not strictly principles, since they are not original knowledge. Only the name "abstract" leads us to judge that they constitute knowledge that presupposes other knowledge.

Abstract principles are not even a proper means for leading us to discoveries, for as they are merely an abbreviated expression of our acquired knowledge, they can only take us back to this original knowledge. In short, they are maxims merely containing what we already know. And as the common people have proverbs, these so-called principles are philosophers' proverbs, and that is all they are.

So in the search for truth, abstract principles are faulty or at the very least useless, and they are good maxims or proverbs only because they are the abbreviated expression of what we already know through experience.

On the other hand, hypotheses or suppositions (for we use these words interchangeably) are not only means or hints in the search for truth, they can also be principles, that is, first truths that explain others.

They are means or hints because observations, as we have remarked, always begin by groping. But hypotheses are principles or first truths when they have been confirmed by new observations which we cannot doubt.

To assure ourselves of the truth of a supposition, we need two things: first, to be able to work out all the possible suppositions concerning some question; second, to have some means for confirming our choice or that makes us recognize our error.

When these two conditions are combined, there can be no doubt about the utility of suppositions; they are even absolutely necessary. Arithmetic proves this with examples that everyone can understand and that for this reason deserve preference over examples drawn from other branches of mathematics.

First, in solving arithmetical problems, we can always work out all the suppositions, for there are never more than a few of them. Second, we have the means for discovering whether a supposition is true or false, or even to use a false supposition to find out the number we are looking for. This is what is called *the rule of false position*.

We carry out our arithmetical operations with confidence because we have such precise ideas of numbers that we can go back to their simple elementary units and follow the generation of each particular number. It is no surprise that this knowledge provides us with the means for doing all sorts of compositions and decompositions, and of thereby making certain of the precision of the suppositions that we are obliged to use.

A science using suppositions without fear of error, or at least with the certitude of recognizing error, should serve as a model for all the sciences in which we want to use this method. So it would be desirable in all the sciences, as in arithmetic, to work out all suppositions exhaustively and for there being rules for ascertaining the best ones.

Now to have these rules, the other sciences would have to give us such clear and complete ideas that we could through analysis go back to the first elements of the things they treat, and follow the development of each one. These sciences are far from having all these desirable features, but insofar as they make up for them with others, we will be able to make greater use of hypotheses.

After pure mathematics, no science has been more successful with hypotheses than astronomy. For as a long series of observations has shown the periods in which the revolutions are repeated, it was hypothesized for each planet a movement and direction that explain perfectly their appearances with regard to each other.

The ideas formulated about this movement and direction are as precise as need be for the goodness of a hypothesis, since we see them so clearly give rise to phenomena that we can predict them with the highest precision.

Here observations indicate all the suppositions possible, and the explanation of phenomena confirms the suppositions chosen. So the hypothesis leaves nothing to be desired.

But if we are dissatisfied with explaining appearances and try to determine the absolute direction and movement of each planet—this is where our hypotheses will always prove inadequate.

We can judge the absolute movement of some object only insofar as we see it take some direction toward or away from some unmoving point. Now astronomical observations can never lead to the discovery of some celestial point whose immobility is certain. Thus no hypothesis can assure us of giving each planet the precise amount of movement proper to it.

As for direction, the planets could only have a simple one produced uniquely by the movement proper to each one, or they could have a compound movement produced by this original movement and from another one shared with the sun. By supposing the latter case, we would be thinking of them as similar to objects moving in a ship sailing through the waves. These are points about which experience cannot enlighten us; we cannot know the absolute direction of a planet. Consequently we must confine ourselves to judging direction and movement relative to the stars, and to be guided only according to observations. Our suppositions will be more felicitous, the more precise observers we are.

One first, and still rough observation led people to believe that the sun, planets, and fixed stars revolved around the earth. That is the origin of the Ptolemaic hypothesis. But more recent observations have taught us that Jupiter and the sun turn on their axes and that Mercury and Venus revolve around the sun. This observation indicates that the earth can also have two movements, one around itself and one around the sun. Consequently the Copernican hypothesis was confirmed as much by observations as by the phenomena that it explained more simply than any other. People wanted to go further and to know what circle the planets describe; they judged this by first appearances and supposed that the sun was at the center of this circle. But by bringing this supposition together with observations, people recognized its falsity, and saw that the sun could not be at the center of the circle. It is by continuing to observe precisely, by making hypotheses only as suggested by observations, and by correcting them only insofar as they are corrected by observations, that astronomers will imagine ever simpler systems, ones simultaneously more capable of explaining a greater number of phenomena. So we see that if their hypotheses do not indicate the absolute direction and movement of the stars, they do something equivalent for us when they explain appearances. They thereby become as useful as mathematical hypotheses.

Hypotheses in physics suffer from greater difficulties. They are dangerous if we do not formulate them with great caution, and it is often impossible to imagine any reasonable ones.

Located as we are on an atom that rolls around in a corner of the universe, who would believe that philosophers proposed as a physical proof of the original elements of things, to explain the generation of all phenomena, and to work out the mechanism of the entire world? It would be too much of a forecast of the progress of physics to imagine that we could ever have enough observations to formulate a universal system. The more materials experience furnishes, the more we appreciate what is lacking in such a vast edifice. There will always remain phenomena to be discovered. Some phenomena are too far from us to be observed, others depend on a mechanism that escapes us. We have no way to penetrate their springs. Now this ignorance leaves us unable to go back to the true causes that produce and tie together in a single system the few phenomena we are acquainted with. For, as everything is connected, the explanation for the things we do observe depends on an infinity of other things that we will never have a chance to observe. If we make hypotheses, we will do so without being able to exhaust all suppositions and without rules confirming our choice.

Let it not be said that the things we observe will enable us to imagine the things impossible for us to observe; that, combining some with others, we can imagine still new ones; and that, going back in this way from cause to cause, we can divine and explain all phenomena, even though experience acquaints us only a with few. There would be nothing solid in such a system, its principles would vary at the whim of each philosopher's imagination, and no one could be sure of coming across the truth.

Moreover, when things are such that we cannot observe them, the imagination can do no better than to represent them on the model of things that we do observe. Now how can we be sure that the principles that we imagine are the very principles of nature? And on what basis would we want nature to know how to do the things that it hides from us except in the same way that it does those that it does reveal to us? There is no analogy that allows us to divine its secrets. And probably, if it revealed them, we would see an entirely different world from the one we do see. In vain, for example, does the chemist flatter himself that he can use analysis to arrive at the primary elements. Nothing proves to him that what he takes for a simple and homogeneous element is not a compound of heterogeneous principles.

We have seen that arithmetic merely gives us rules for ascertaining the truth of a supposition because it enables us to analyze all sorts of numbers so well that we can go back to their first elements and follow their whole generation. If a physicist could in this way analyze some of the objects that concern him, for example, the human body; if observations led him as far as the first spring that gives movement to all the others and that gives him an insight into the mechanism of each part, then he could construct a system explaining everything that we observed in ourselves. But in the human body we distinguish only the grossest and most salient parts. And so, we can observe them only when death hides the whole trick. The others are a tissue of such fine, subtle fibers that we can distinguish nothing in them. We can understand neither the principle of their action nor the reason for the effects they produce. If a single body is an enigma for us, what an enigma the universe is!

What then must we think of Descartes' project, when with moving cubes he claims to explain the formation of the world, the generation of objects, and all phenomena? When from the security of his study, a philosopher tries to remake matter and arranges it to suit him, nothing resists him. It is because his imagination sees what pleases it and nothing more. But such arbitrary hypotheses shed the light on no truths; on the contrary, they retard scientific progress and become very dangerous because of the errors they cause to be adopted. We must attribute the chimeras of the alchemists, and the ignorance of the physicists for several centuries, to vague suppositions.

The misuses of this method made themselves felt most keenly in the practical sciences. Medicine is an example of this.

Because of our ignorance about the principles of life and health, medicine is all conjectures, that is, unprovable suppositions. And cases vary so widely that we cannot be sure of finding two perfectly similar ones. Physicians who follow the methods I am criticizing make a science of them that consistently conforms to certain principles. They all refer to general suppositions that they have adopted, they take no account either of the temperament of sick persons or of any of the circumstances that could upset their hypotheses. They thus commit all the evil that an ignorance of these things must naturally occasion.

Unfortunately, this method greatly abbreviates the practice of their art. With a general system, there are no illnesses whose causes and remedies they do not appear to discern at a glance. Being applicable to everything, their suppositions also give them a confident air and an ease of expression that for us takes the place of knowledge.

In spite of the uselessness and dangerous consequences of general hypotheses, physicists find it very difficult to give them up. They do not forget to cite hypotheses about astronomy. They thereby imagine their own hypotheses justified. But what a difference!

Astronomers propose to measure the respective movements of the stars—a promising inquiry. Physicists undertake to discover how the universe was formed and is preserved, and what the first principles of things are—idle curiosity doomed to failure.

Astronomers start off with a certain principle, which is that the sun or earth must revolve. Physicists begin with principles that they can never have a precise idea of. Do they say that the parts making up objects have a particular essence? They have no idea of the word "essence." Do they say that all the parts of matter are similar and thus form different objects according to the different forms they take and the amount of movement they receive? It is impossible for them to determine their shape and movement. Now what progress have we made when we know that the first principles of objects have a certain essence, a certain shape, and a certain movement, but we cannot indicate precisely what this essence, shape, and movement is? Would such knowledge add much to the occult qualities of the ancients?

It is enough for astronomers to suppose the existence of extension and movement. We have seen how they confine themselves to explaining appearances, and with what caution they construct their systems.

The physicists' hypotheses that I am criticizing are designed to give us insight into the nature of extension, movement, and all objects; and they are the work of people who usually make few observations or who even disdain to learn about the observations of others. I have heard of one physicist, congratulating himself on having a principle that explained all chemical phenomena, dared to communicate these ideas to a skilled chemist. Listening to him sympathetically, the chemist says to him that he sees only one difficulty, which is that the facts were completely different than he had supposed. "Well," said the physicist, "teach them to me so that I can explain them." This rejoinder betrays perfectly the character of someone who neglects to learn about the facts because he thinks he already has an understanding of all possible phenomena. Only vague hypotheses can yield such ill-founded confidence.

When our suppositions are false or uncertain, say these physicists, nothing prevents us from making use of them to arrive at important knowledge. It is in this way that in erecting a building, we use machines that become useless when it is finished. Are we not indebted to the Cartesian system for the most beautiful and important discoveries that have been made, either with intention of confirming it or with the intention of combatting it? The experiments of Huyghens, Boyle, Mariotte, Newton, on air, impact, light, and colors are well-known examples of this.

I reply first that suppositions are to a system what a foundation is to a building. Thus there is not enough grounds for comparing suppositions to the machines we use to construct a building.

I then say that the discoveries made about air, impact, light and colors are due to experience and not to some philosophers' arbitrary hypotheses. By itself Descartes's system gave birth only to errors. It led us to some truths only on the rebound, that is, by making us sufficiently curious to do certain experiments. It is to be hoped that in this sense the systems of modern physicist will someday be useless. Posterity will be greatly indebted to men who allowed themselves to be mistaken so that it might acquire knowledge by discovering their mistakes, knowledge that it would otherwise have obtained from them had they followed a wiser course.

Should all hypotheses be banished from physics? Certainly not. But there would be very little wisdom in adopting them without any choice; and above all we should distrust the most ingenious ones. For what is merely ingenious is not simple, and certainly the truth is simple.

To create the universe, Descartes requires of God only matter and movement. But when Descartes tries to carry out what he promises, he is merely ingenious.

First, Descartes observes, correctly, that the parts of matter should all tend to move in a straight line, and that if they encounter no obstacles, they will all continue to move in this direction.

He then supposes that everything is a plenum, or rather he concludes this from his idea of the body, and he sees that the parts of matter, straining in all possible directions, must be mutual obstacles to each other's movement. Will they thus be immobile? No. Descartes ingeniously explains how he imagines that they will move in a circular fashion and how they will form different whirls.

Newton found too many problems with this system. He rejects the plenum as a supposition that cannot be reconciled with movement. Without undertaking to recreate the world, he is satisfied to observe it—a less impressive project than Descartes's, or rather, less bold but wiser.

So Newton did not propose to divine or to imagine the first principles of nature. If he realized the advantage of a system that explains everything, he realized in this respect all our incapacity. He observed and looked among phenomena for one that could be considered as a principle, that is, as an original phenomenon capable of explaining others.

If he found it, he would construct a more limited system than nature's, and also more extensive than our knowledge can be. His purpose was to explain the revolutions of celestial bodies.

Newton observed and demonstrated that every body moving along a curved line necessarily obeys two forces: one tending to move it in a straight line, the other always turning it away from this line.

He thus supposed these two forces in all objects revolving around the sun. The first is what he calls force of projection; the second, attraction.

This supposition is not gratuitous or baseless. Since every moving object tends to move in a straight line, it obviously can turn away from this direction to describe a curve around a center only by obeying a second force continually directing it toward the center of the curve.

Newton does not designate this force with the name "impulsion" because, if there is impulsion in the movement of celestial bodies, it is at least certain that it is unobservable and nothing indicates it. He calls it "attraction" because attraction is indicated by weight. Indeed, on the earth's surface all the parts press toward a common center. At a certain distance from this surface, a body still presses toward this same center. It will be the same at a greater distance. The moon thus weighs on the earth. The earth and the moon thus weigh on the sun, and so forth. We see that analogy, observation, and the calculus will complete this system, which I have discussed elsewhere.[59]

The Cartesians criticize the Newtonians for having no idea of attraction. They are correct but they have no basis for judging that the idea of impulsion

[59]*The Art of Reasoning*, Book III.

is any more intelligible. If the Newtonian cannot explain how objects attract, he will challenge the Cartesian to explain the movement transmitted by impact. If it is merely a question of effects, they are understood. We have examples of attraction as we do of impulsion. If it is a question of principle, it is equally unknown in both systems.

The Cartesians understand it so poorly that they are obliged to assume that God has made it a law to move personally every object that is struck by another. But why do the Newtonians not assume that God makes it a law to attract objects toward a center inversely by the square of their distance? So the question would reduce to knowing which of these two laws God has prescribed, and I do not see why the Cartesians would be better informed on this subject.

Some hypotheses have no foundation. They bear on the comparison of two things that in fact are dissimilar and for this reason can only be conceived in a highly confused way. But because they do give an idea of some sort of mechanism, they explain the thing rather like the true mechanician would himself explain it if it were understood. These suppositions can be used when they make some practical truth clearer and teach us to do so to our advantage. But they should be taken for what they are, and that is what has not been done.

Do we want, for example, to argue that ease of thinking is acquired through practice, like all other habits, and that we cannot get to work too early to acquire it? First we take as a principle facts that no one can dispute: (1) that movement is the cause of all changes occurring to the human body; (2) that bodily organs have greater flexibility in proportion as they are given greater exercise.

We then suppose that all the fibers of the human body are so many small channels in which some very subtle liqueur (the animal spirits) circulates, which spreads in the part of the brain that is the seat of feeling or sentiment, and that creates different traces; that these traces are connected with our ideas and evoke them; and we conclude that, the more easily our ideas are evoked, the less obstacle we will find to thinking.

In the third place, we notice that the brain fibers are probably very soft and delicate in children, that with age the fibers harden, strengthen, and take on a certain consistency, that finally, on the one hand, age makes them so inflexible or rigid that they no longer obey the action of the spirits, and on the other hand, age dries out the body to the point that there is no longer enough spirits to overcome the resistance of the fibers.

Once these suppositions are admitted, it is not difficult to imagine how we can acquire the habit of thinking. I give Malebranche leave to speak, for this system belongs to him more than anyone else.

We hardly know how to be attentive to something if we do not imagine it and represent it in the brain. Now for us to imagine some objects, we have to make some parts of the brain fold or we have to impress some other movement on it so as to be able to form the traces to which the ideas representing these object to us are attached. So that if the brain fibers are hardened somewhat, they will only be capable of the bending and movement that they previously had. Thus the mind cannot imagine or consequently be attentive to what it wants, but only to familiar things.

Hence we should conclude that it is very beneficial to get early exercise in meditating on all sorts of subjects so as to acquire a certain facility in thinking about what we want to. For in the same way that we acquire a great facility in flexing our fingers in all ways and with great speed, by our frequent use of them by playing musical instruments, so the parts of our brain whose movement is necessary to imagine what we want, acquire through use a certain facility in folding, which means that we imagine the things we want to with great ease, promptness, and even cleanness.[60]

This hypothesis also provides Malebranche with explanations for many other phenomena. Among other things, he finds the reason for different personalities we encounter in people's minds. For this purpose, it is enough for him to combine abundance and dearth, agitation and slowness, largeness and smallness of animal spirits with the delicacy and grossness, wetness and dryness, and the rigidity and flexibility of the brain fibers. Indeed,

since imagination consists merely in the mind's power to form images of objects, in impressing them, so to speak, on the brain fibers, the greater and more distinct the vestiges of the animal spirits characteristic of these images, the more strongly and distinctly the mind will imagine these objects. Now in the same way that the size, profundity, and cleanness of the lines of some engravings depend on the power of the etcher's needle and the pliancy of the copper, thus the depth and the cleanness of the vestiges of the imagination depend on the power of the animal spirits and on the constitution of the brain fibers; and it is the variety found in these two things that is the source of almost all the great difference that we observe between minds.[61]

These explanations are ingenious, but, if we supposed that they gave us an exact idea of what happens in the brain, we would be very much mistaken. Such hypotheses do not give the real reason for things; they are not offered to lead to discoveries, and their use should be limited to making clear truths that experience does not allow us to doubt.

In astronomy, hypotheses have a quite different character. An astronomer

[60]*The Search for Truth*, Book 2, Part 2, Chapter 1.

[61]*The Search for Truth*, Book 2, Part 1, Chapter I, § 3.

has ideas of the stars, of the direction to which he fixes their courses, and of the resulting phenomena. But Malebranche inadequately depicts animal spirits, their circulation throughout the body, and the traces they leave on the brain. Nature conforms to the suppositions of the astronomer, and appears more disposed to open itself to him. For Malebranche, nature merely allows him to observe that the laws of mechanics are the principles of all the changes in the human body; and if the system of animal spirits has some relation to the truth, that is merely because it is some sort of mechanism. Could the relations be any more vague?

When a system gives the real reason for things, all its details are interesting. But the hypotheses we are discussing become absurd when their authors make it a law to elaborate them with great care. That is because the more they multiply vague explanations, the more they seem to congratulate themselves for having penetrated nature. And this mistake is unpardonable. These sorts of hypotheses are worth some brief discussion and require only the details needed to make some truth clear. We can judge whether Malebranche is absolutely exempt from criticism in this respect.

In my *Logic*[62] I have explained consciousness, memory, and consequently all mental habits. It is a system in which my reasoning is based on suppositions, but they are all indicated by analogy. Phenomena are worked out naturally and explained very simply. Nevertheless, I confess that suppositions like mine—when they are indicated merely by analogy—do not have the same certainty as the suppositions indicated and confirmed by experience. For if analogy cannot permit us to doubt a supposition, only experience can make it certain. And if we should not reject as false everything that is not obvious, neither should we regard all undoubted truths as evident truths.

Electrified objects present us with a great many phenomena: they attract, repel, give off light rays and sparks; they ignite vinous spirits, they produce violent commotions, and so forth. If we invented a hypothesis to explain these effects, such a clear analogy would have to be shown among them that they all explained each other. Experience shows us such an analogy among some of these phenomena. For example, we see that an electrified object attracts nonelectrified objects and repels those to which it has transmitted electricity. We also see that an electrified object loses all its power when touched by a nonelectrified object. Now these facts perfectly explain the movement of a small leaf that alternates between the finger touching it to the tube that repels it. It gets away from the tube when electricity is transmitted to it; it comes closer to it when it loses electricity by the finger touch.

By making us see some facts explained by others, experience provides a model of the way a hypothesis must explain everything. So to ensure the

---

[62]Part I, Chapter 9.

goodness of a supposition, we merely have to consider whether its explanations for certain phenomena accord with explanations that experience gives for other phenomena—if it explains them all without exception and all observations tend to confirm it. When all these advantages are combined, it must contribute to the progress of physics.

Thus we must not prohibit the use of hypotheses for intellects keen enough to get ahead occasionally of experience. Their suspicions, provided they are understood for what they are, may indicate the appropriate investigations and lead to discoveries. But we ought to urge these intellects to take all necessary precautions and never to be prejudiced in favor of their own suppositions. If Descartes had offered his ideas merely as conjectures, he would have no less provided the opportunity for making observations. But by presenting them as the true system of the world, he committed everyone who adopted his principles to error, and he put up obstacles to the progress of truth.

The result of all these reflections is that we can derive different benefits from hypotheses depending on the difference between the cases we use.

First, hypotheses are not only useful but even necessary when we can exhaust all the suppositions and when we have a rule for identifying the good one. Mathematics provides examples of this.

Second, in astronomy we cannot do without their help. But their use should be limited to explaining the apparent revolutions of the stars. So hypotheses begin to be less advantageous in astronomy than in mathematics.

Third, we ought not to reject them when they can facilitate observations or make clearer truths attested by experience. Examples, if we reduce them to their proper value, are several hypotheses in physics. But the best ones, which physicists seem to use, are those indicated by observations and which explain all phenomena in ways analogous to those provided by experience in some cases.

13 Of the Genius of Those Who With the Intent of Going Back to the Nature of Things Create Abstract Systems or Gratuitous Hypotheses

We will not be much surprised by the many abstract systems and gratuitous hypotheses that have been received with acclamation if we are aware of people's excessive curiosity, of the pride that prevents them from perceiving the limits of their intellects, and of the habit acquired in childhood of reasoning about vague notions.

Experience should have opened people's eyes to this abuse. But their minds were too prejudiced and the creation of these sorts of systems was regarded as an effort of genius, as was the revival of some long-forgotten ones.

Indeed models of this kind have everything required to create an illusion. More poets than philosophers, they give body to everything. They touch only the surfaces of things, but they depict it in the most vivid colors. They dazzle and are believed to enlighten. They have only imagination, and people do not hesitate to regard them as geniuses.

The principle of the imagination lies in the connection among ideas, which means that some ideas evoke others. If the connection is stronger, ideas are evoked more swiftly, and the imagination is keener. If the connection includes a greater number of ideas, the ideas are recalled in greater number, and the imagination is more extensive. Thus the imagination owes its liveliness to the force of the connection of ideas, and its extent to the multiplicity of ideas that are recalled on the occasion of a single one.

Because of the close connection between abstract notions and their original sensory ideas, the imagination is naturally led to represent these notions by concrete images. That is why we call it "imagination," for to imagine is to make clear by images. So this operation took its name not from its original function, which is to evoke ideas, but from its more salient function, which is to reclothe the images with which they are connected. Languages provide many examples of this kind, and they would provide as many examples as they do words if it were possible to go back first to the original meanings.

The greatest advantage of the imagination is to recall all the ideas with some connection to our subject and which are suitable for elaborating or embellishing it. This is the principle to which the mind owes all its discrimination, fecundity, and extent. But if, despite us, too many ideas are evoked, if those that ought to be the least connected were associated so strongly that the ones most distant from our subject were recalled as easily or more easily than others or even if, instead of being connected by their nature, they were connected by those sorts of circumstances that sometimes associate the most disparate ideas, we would unconsciously digress; we would suppose relations where none existed; we would take a vague image for a precise idea, and completely opposite ideas for the same ideas. So another operation is needed to direct, suspend, and arrest the imagination, and to prevent the deviations and errors that it cannot fail to occasion. This second operation is analysis. Analysis decomposes things and distinguishes everything that the imagination groundlessly supposes to exist in them.

Minds dominated by imagination are unsuited to philosophical inquiry. Accustomed to seeing poorly, they judge all the more confidently. They never doubt. A matter about which they are shown some difficulties has no attraction for them. Ever superficial, they esteem mere agreeableness and spread it without discernment. And their language is merely a tissue of ill-chosen metaphors and forced expressions that they themselves often do not understand.

On the other hand, people with so little imagination, or such a slow one, that they have a weak sense of the relation between abstract notions and sensory ideas have little taste for the poet's mixture of these ideas. Nothing appears more childish to these cold minds than fictions in which fame or glory is given a body or in which such abstract entities are made to move and act. They have respect only for the bottom of things. They love to examine. They make decisions only with extreme slowness. They see and they still doubt. And if they are capable of sometimes uncovering the errors of others, they are ill-suited for discovering the truth and even less suited for presenting it gracefully.

Because of an impoverished or excessive imagination, the intelligence is thus highly imperfect. For it not to be lacking something, imagination must be tempered by analysis, and the one must yield to the other depending on circumstances. The imagination should provide the philosopher with amusement without taking anything away from correctness, and analysis should give correctness to the poet without taking away any pleasure. A person in whom these two operations are in accord could combine the most opposite talents. But a person has opposite talents, and with greater or less defects, in proportion as he gets further away from this golden mean and approaches one or the other of these two extremes.

One would have to be at this mean to show its place to every person. Do we ever expect to have such an enlightened judge? If we had one, would we be capable of recognizing him? But it is easy to note minds at the extremes.

It is obvious, for example, that the philosophers I am criticizing are not at this golden mean where the understanding is the most perfect. We also see that when they stray from this mean, it is not because they have a share in this precise analysis which is so useful in the sciences and in which only adornment is lacking. They thus approach the extreme dominated by imagination. Consequently, they do not have the understanding required by the matters that concern them.

Although we commonly take the word "genius" to mean the highest point of perfection to which the human mind can aspire, nothing varies more than our applications of this word, for each of us uses it according to his own way of thinking and the compass of his mind. To be regarded as a genius by the common run of men, all one has to be is inventive. This quality is no doubt essential, but it must be combined with a right-thinking mind that consistently avoids error and that puts the truth in the most appropriate light for making it understandable.

To follow this notion precisely, we must not expect to find true geniuses. We are not naturally created infallible. Philosophers bestowed with this title know how to invent. We cannot even withold the advantages of genius from them when they are discussing matters that they make new through their discoveries about them or by their manner of presenting them. We appropriate everything we discuss better than others do. Thus, if they scarcely lead us beyond ideas that are already understood, they are merely better-than-average minds, at most men of talent. If they go astray, they are false minds. If they go from error to error, interlinking them and creating systems, they are visionaries. The history of philosophy provides examples of both kinds.

Nevertheless when we undertake to read these philosophers, the reputation gained by their imaginations predisposes us in their favor. We suppose that they are going to impart thousands and thousands of pieces of knowledge to us, and more inclined to believe that we lack understanding than to suspect them of not having any, we make every effort to understand them. Perhaps it would be more advantageous for us and for the truth to read them with a completely different frame of mind. At least it is certain that if we try to understand them, we have to differentiate sharply between conceiving and imagining, and to be satisfied with imagining most of the things that they think they have conceived. It would also be unreasonable to claim to go beyond this as it would be in reading these lines of Malherbe,

The poor man in his hut where the thatch covers him
Is subject to its laws;

And the guard who watches over the gates of the Louvre
Does not defend our kings from it.[63]

To try to conceive how guards could keep death away from the throne and to protect our kings from it. We can conceive with Malherbe that all men are mortal. But death personified, and the guards put in opposition to it because they are appointed to keep away from the throne every person who could make an attempt on the majesty of kings—these are things that he could only imagine, as we do ourselves.

This example is all the more suitable for clarifying my thought as errors of most philosophers stem from the fact that they have not carefully distinguished what we imagine from what we conceive, and from the fact that they thought they were conceiving things that existed only in their imagination. This is the prevailing error in their arguments.

Not that I want to deny the creators of abstract systems all the praise they receive. Some of their works force us to admire them. They resemble those palaces in which taste, comforts, grandeur, and magnificence converge to create an artistic masterpiece but which sit on such unsolid foundations that they appear to be supported merely by enchantment. We would no doubt praise the architect, but our praise would be very much offset by our criticisms of his imprudence. We would regard it as the most glaring folly to build such a superb edifice on such weak foundations, and although this was the product of a superior mind and the parts were arranged in an admirable order, no one would be so unwise as to want to live in it.

We can conclude from these considerations that we should be very cautious in reading philosophers. The surest way to guard against their systems is to study how they could have formed them. This is the touchstone of error and truth—go back to the origin of both and you can see how they entered into the mind, and you will distinguish them perfectly. That is a method that the philosophers I am criticizing barely understand the use of.

---

[63]Malherbe, *Stances, Consolation à M. du Perrier.*

14

Cases in Which We Can Construct Systems on Principles Established by Experience

Merely through the idea that we must form of a system, it is obvious that we would be incorrect to give the name systems to the books in which we claim to explain nature by means of some abstract principles.

When constructed according to the rules we have given, hypotheses can be the foundation of a system. We have shown their advantages.

But so as not to leave out anything desirable in a system, we should arrange the different parts of an art or science in an order in which they explain each other and in which they are all referred to a first, well-established fact on which they depend. This fact will be the principle of the system, for it will be the beginning of one.

It is obvious that we would be unsuccessful in arranging them this way if we did not know them all or did not see all their interrelations. The order invented for the parts that were known would not fit the parts that were not known. And as we acquired new knowledge, we would observe the inadequacy of principles adopted too hastily.

The rash people who have tried to construct systems can use their own experience to persuade themselves of what I am saying. They will recognize that insofar as they have not sufficiently worked out the matter they are trying to explain, they were not settled in their principles. They were obliged to extend, to restrict, and to change them; and they made them precise only in proportion as, by delving further into their subject, they distinguished more clearly all its parts.

So it would serve no purpose for us to undertake to construct systems about matters that we had not yet gone into deeply. What would it be like if we undertook others that were impossible to see through? I am imagining a person with no idea of watchmaking, or even of mechanics, who proposes to explain the effects of a pendulum. In vain does he observe the sounds that it makes at certain times, or note the movement of the clockhands; with no knowledge of statics, it is impossible for him to give a reasonable explanation of these phenomena.

Get him to make observations about the things that led to the invention of clockmaking, and he will succeed in inventing a mechanism producing much the same effects. For it seems perfectly possible for an art whose development is due to the works of several people to be the work of a single individual.

Finally, open up the clock and explain its mechanism to him. He will immediately grasp the arrangement of all its parts and how they interact, and he goes back to the first spring on which they depend. It is only by this movement that he can verify the true system that explains his observations.

This person is the philosopher studying nature. So let us conclude that we can construct true systems only in cases where we have enough obsevations to grasp the interconnection of phenomena. Now we have seen that we cannot observe either the elements of things or the original springs of living bodies. We can observe only their remote effects. Consequently the best principles that we can have in physics are phenomena that explain others but which themselves depend on unknown causes.

Systems can be constructed in any science or art but in some of them we aim to explain effects; in others, we aim to prepare effects and bring them about. The first aim is that of physics; the second, that of politics. There are sciences with both aims, such as chemistry and medicine.

The arts can also be classified according to which of these aims that we have particularly in mind. Levers, pulleys, wheels, and other machines were invented to produce certain effects. Thus in the mechanical arts, people began with facts that had to serve as principles for a system.

In the fine arts, on the other hand, taste alone produced the effects. People then sought principles, and ended where they had begun in the other arts. The rules we give in these matters are designed more to explain effects than to teach us how to produce them.

Examples are cases in which the systems can have facts for principles. All that remains is to discuss the precautions with which we should formulate them. I shall begin with political systems because they are the least perfect.

15 On the Necessity in Political Systems of Views and Precautions with which They Ought to be Constructed

If there is one topic about which we ought to be prejudiced against systems, it is politics. The public never judges except by the event; and because it has often been the victim of political schemes, it fears nothing so much as seeing them formed. Nevertheless, is it possible to govern a state without an overview of its parts or without connecting them so as to make them move in concert by one and the same spring? It is not the systems that ought to be blamed in this case, but the behavior of those who construct them.

The plans of a statesman cannot be useful, they will even be frequently dangerous, if they have not been preceded by a mature examination of everything that comes together in domestic and foreign government. Some unforeseeen circumstance will be sufficient to make the plans collapse.

A people is an artificial body. It is up to the magistrate watching out for its survival to maintain harmony and strength in all its members. He is the mechanic who must restore the springs and wind up the whole machine as often as circumstances require. But who is the wise man who would chance to repair the work of an artist if he had not previously studied its mechanism? Would he who made the attempt not run the risk of putting it even further out of order?

A statesman who does not take in all the parts, who does not grasp their interaction, will thus provoke greater abuses than the ones he was trying to remedy. To favor one class of citizens, he will harm another. If he looks after the interests of manufacture, he will forget agriculture; if he augments the nobility, he will destroy commerce. Soon there is no more equilibrium, conditions become confused, and the citizen has no rule other than his personal ambition, and the government undergoes increasing change and the state is ultimately overturned.

The sword, the robe, the church, commerce, finance, men of letters, and artisans of all kinds—these are the classes of citizens. In the system of governance, each citizen should be as happy as he can be without altering the general good of the whole body. That is what will give the state the sturdiest constitution. This includes two things: the behavior to be maintained with the people one governs and the behavior to be upheld with the neighboring powers.

To lead the people, one ought to establish a discipline that keeps a perfect equilibrium among all the classes and that thereby finds the interest of each citizen in the interest of the society as a whole. The citizens, by acting according to different views and each creating particular systems, must necessarily conform to the views of a general system. So the statesman ought to combine the riches and labor of different classes in order to favor them all without doing any harm to any one. He will succeed in this undertaking if his protection is never exclusive. On this depends the union that can maintain the equilibrium among all the parts.

Order thus established, the statesman will clearly see the powers and resources of the state. But he will still not know with what precaution he ought to use them against enemies. What makes a people powerful is as much the weakness of their neighbors as their own forces. From the combination of these things the statesman will learn how he should behave with foreigners.

It is not merely according to the natural resources of neighboring countries nor the industriousness of their inhabitants that the statesman should make these combinations, but mainly according to the nature of their government. For that is what creates the power or weakness of their people. So he should be acquainted the views of the people who govern—their systems, if any, and sometimes even court intrigues. Often the slightest means are the cause of great revolutions and if we go back to the source of the abuses that brought about the downfall of states, we would ordinarily see only some trifling matter that no one had dreamt of guarding against, for its consequences had not been foreseen.

Once he has acquired this knowledge, a king ought not to become two independent and separate systems, one for foreigners and one for his own people. In all his actions, he should have only a single purpose, and his foreign policy should be so subordinate to his prescriptions for domestic affairs that the two form a single unit. He will thereby acquire as much power as circumstances permit.

It is obvious that a system created by following these rules is absolutely relative to the situation. When this situation changes, the system will have to undergo a similar change, that is, the changes introduced must be so well combined with whatever is kept as is that the equilibrium continues to be maintained among all parts of society. That can only be done by the person who invented, or at least had done a complete study of, the system.

But as the heads of government do not have all the necessary knowledge, the public often suffers from changes they introduce. It immediately sets itself against any innovation, and because the new views of some statesman have not succeeded, the public judges that the views of others will succeed no better. We must, they say, stand by the established practices of our forefathers; they were good enough for their time, why will they not be good enough now?

People embracing such prejudices do not want to perceive that the springs sufficient for making a simple machine move are not enough if the machine becomes highly complex. Originally, societies were formed of only a few equal citizens. Judges and generals had superiority only during the exercise of their functions. Once this time passed, they returned to the class of the others. The citizen thus had no superior but the law. Later, societies grew larger, the number of citizens greatly increased, and the equality was altered. Then different orders were seen gradually to arise—warriors, judges, traders, and so forth. And each of these classes took its rank according to the authority that it had obtained. During the time of equality, the citizens all had the same interest, and a few very simple laws were enough to govern them. Once the equality was destroyed, the interests changed as the classes proliferated, and the original laws no longer sufficed. Only this consideration is needed to realize that the same system cannot be used to govern a society both at its beginning and during its growth period or decline.

So we cannot blame those who want to introduce changes in government, but we should invite them to acquire all the knowledge needed to do so strictly in accordance with the situation.

The most delicate occasion for a statesman or king is when a state that has been badly governed for several reigns seems to have no plan or even principles. So abuses arise in abundance, and the longer one waits to remedy them, the more obstacles there are to overcome.

To create a system in this case, one should not look to one's imagination for the most perfect government. One would merely create a piece of fiction. One must study the character of the people, search out the usages and customs, and identify the abuses. Then one will preserve what one was found to be good and replace what was found bad, but this will be in the ways more consistent with the citizens' mores. If the statesman offends them, this should merely be on the occasion in which he has enough authority to forestall the unfortunate natural consequences of sudden revolutions. Often he will not attempt to remove an abuse brusquely. He will appear to tolerate it and attack it only in a devious way. In short he will create such a sound combination of the changes with everything to be preserved, and with the power that he enjoys, that they will take place imperceptibly or at least with the approbation of some of the citizenry and without any fear on the part of its opponents.

Those who do not bring all this circumspection to governmental reform run the risk of precipitating the destruction of the state. Combining only a part of the things they should take account of, their projects are necessarily incomplete. But above all else, one should be far-seeing, I mean, seeing without prejudice, and that is what is difficult, especially for sovereigns. For in a democracy, the sovereign has only whims. In an aristocracy, he is a tyrant. In a monarchy, he is usually weak, and his weakness protects him against neither whims nor tyranny. If you review the course of history, you will prove the maxim that "opinion governs the world." Now what is opinion if not prejudices? This is what leads sovereigns.

Every government has maxims or rather every government behaves in ways that presuppose maxims that it often does not have or rather that it does not know it has. It unconsciously works out of habit; and without explaining to itself what it must do, it does as it has done in the past. In this way nations are generally blind to their own true interests, and swoop down upon each other. The experience that educates all persons does not educate nations. So nothing can educate them. Nevertheless I do not claim that one must not try to enlighten people, for the light will always produce some good effects. At least it will produce light among nations that have preserved civilized manners.

16 On the Use of Systems in Physics

Since physicists should confine themselves to systematizing the part of physics that they understand, their one purpose should be to observe phenomena, to grasp their interconnections, and to go back to the phenomena on which several others depend. But this dependence cannot consist in some vague relation. The effects must be so well-explained that their origin is made clear.

The first phenomenon we notice is extension; second is movement; and, by modifying extension, movement produces many others. So from the fact that we cannot go back any further we must not conclude that only extension and movement exist. Nor should we undertake to explain these phenomena. Experience would fail us, and we could merely imagine abstract principles whose lack of soundness we have seen.

It is important to observe, as much as possible, all the effects that movement can produce in extension, and especially the variations movement goes through when it passes from one object to another. But so that neither errors nor superfluous details slip into our experiments, we should not dwell just on what presents us with clear ideas. So we should not undertake to determine what is called an object's force—that is the name of a thing about which we have no idea. The senses give us an idea of its movement. We judge its speed and we measure its relative degrees by considering the space traversed in a certain amount of time. What more is needed? What light can be shed on our observations by our vain efforts to understand this force which we regard as the principle of movement? In only one case can we use the word "force." That is when we consider an object as a force in relation to some object on which it is acting. Horses, for example, are a force in relation to the wagon they are pulling. But here this term does not express the principle of movement, but simply designates some phenomenon.

So let us carefully distinguish between the different cases where we can observe moving objects. Are they solid or fluid, elastic or nonelastic substances? Which ones transmit movement to them? What are the media in which they move? Let us compare speeds and masses, and notice in what proportions movement is transmitted, increased, and diminishes when it runs down and how it takes different directions. If as we collect phenomena we arrange them in an order in which the first ones explain the last ones, we shall see them shed light on each other. This light will illuminate us about the experiments remaining to be done. It will suggest these experiments to us and help us formulate hypotheses that will frequently be confirmed by observations. In this way we will gradually discover the different laws of movement, and we will reduce the phenomena to be used as principles to a small number. Perhaps we will even find one law that will take the place of all laws because it will be applicable to every case. Then our system will be as perfect as possible and nothing will be lacking on the part of the physics that treats of the movement of objects.

In physics everything consists of explaining facts by facts. When a single fact does not suffice to explain similar facts, we must use two, three, or even more facts. Indeed, a system is still far from being perfect when its principles proliferate. Nevertheless we should not neglect to make use of them. By showing a connection among a certain number of phenomena, we can be led to the discovery of one phenomenon that suffices to explain them all. But one essential rule is to admit nothing that has not been confirmed by well-performed experiments.

More than one example proves how suitable certain facts are for explaining others and for suggesting experiments that will contribute to the progress of physics.

Among the many phenomena that the ancient philosophers could not explain was that of water rising above its level in a suction pump. Believing that air has a certain absolute buoyancy, they attributed all these effects to nature's so-called abhorrence of a vacuum. This principle was neither illuminating nor conducive to occasioning discoveries. So it was only when this principle appeared suspect that physicists thought of doing the experiments that showed them the true principle of these phenomena. Galileo observed the effects of suction pumps, and having ascertained that the water rose only to a height of 32 feet and that beyond that the pipe remained empty, he concluded that the true cause of this phenomenon was still unknown. Torricelli investigated this cause, and it is to him that we owe the first experiment of the inverted tube in which mercury reaches a height of 27½ inches. He compared the column of mercury with a column of water with the same base and a height of 32 feet and found they had exactly the same weight. He hypothesized that these columns could be reached only because they were each in equilibrium with a column of air. And this was the first proof of the weight of air.

Pascal, a distinguished man who lived long enough to become famous, but not long enough for the progress of the sciences, realized how important it was to evaluate Torricelli's hypothesis. He judged that if air has weight, its pressure should act like that of liquids, that it must decrease or increase according to the height of the atmosphere and that consequently the columns suspended in Torricelli's tube would be longer or shorter depending on the altitude of the place where the experiment was done. For this reason Puy-de-Dôme in Auvergne was chosen, and the experiment confirmed Pascal's reasoning.

Once the weight of air had been noted, there was a natural explanation for the effects that led people to imagine that nature abhors a vacuum. But this was not the only advantage of this principle.

The care taken in the many replications of Torricelli's experiment soon showed variations in the height of mercury in a tube. It was known that the weight of air is not constant. Observations were made of the degrees by which it varies, and the barometer was invented, a piece of apparatus whose effects are now known by everyone.

To judge still better the phenomena produced by the weight of air, people sought for a means for obtaining a space from which air could be pumped out. The pneumatic machine was invented.[64] Then several new phenomena were found that confirmed the weight of air and were explained by it.

This is the way that a principle should explain things and lead to discoveries. It would be desirable for physicists always to use this approach. As for suppositions that cannot be subject to observation, we have seen how limited their use can be.[65]

Hypotheses and facts that serve as principles differ in that a hypothesis becomes more uncertain as we discover more effects that it cannot explain whereas a fact always has the same certainty and cannot cease to be the principle of phenomena that it has once explained. If there are effects that it does not explain, it should not be rejected. We should work to discover phenomena connected with the principle and that make all of them into a single system.

There is another important difference between the principles of physics and those of politics. Physical principles are facts that experience does not allow us to doubt; political principles do not always have this advantage. Often the complexity of circumstances and the need to make quick decisions constrain the statesman to base his plans on the merely probable. Obliged to

---

[64]*Otto de Guerike was the inventor.*

[65]Chapter 12.

foresee or get ready for the future, he cannot have the same information as the physicist who reasons only about what he can see. Physics can erect systems only in particular cases; politics must have universal views and take in all aspects of government. In physics we cannot overthrow bad principles too completely, there are no precautionary measures to be taken, and we ought always to grasp unhesitatingly the measures provided by observation. In politics, we conform to circumstances and cannot always suddenly reject a faulty established system; we take measures, and we make only slow progress toward a more perfect system.

I am not talking about the use of systems in chemistry, medicine, and so forth. These sciences are properly parts of physics, and so their method should be the same. Moreover, every educated person is acquainted with the daily progress of chemistry and the procedures of the intelligent people now pursuing it are the methods appropriate to it.

17 On the Use of Systems in the Arts

The arts are divided into two classes: one class comprises all the fine arts, and the other, all the mechanical arts.

Mechanics teaches us to make use of the forces we observe in objects. It is based on the laws of movement, and by imitating nature, it produces phenomena.

Systems thus follow the same laws as physics. In a complex machine, a watch, for example, there is a progression of causes and effects whose principle lies in a first cause, or a progression of phenomena that is explained by a first cause. Thus the universe is just a huge machine.

If we conceive how a system is constructed in physics, we are conceiving how it is constructed in mechanics, and vice-versa. One revealing observation about the elements of mechanics is that all machines are merely levers going through different transformations. I have given the explanation for this in the *Art of Reasoning*. I have even shown in that book that according to Newton the system of the world reduces to a scales.

In the mechanical arts, we can do something only insofar as we have observed nature, since we can act as it does only after we have observed how it acts. So observation precedes the birth of these arts.

The fine arts, on the other hand, seem to precede observation, and to be reducible to a system, they must make progress. That is because they are less our work than nature's. It is nature that begins them when it creates us, and when we think to explain them, it has already perfected them.

All these arts are properly just the development of our own faculties. Our faculties are determined by our needs, and our needs are the effects of our biological constitution. In forming us, nature began everything. Thus I have shown in my *Logic* that nature is our first master in the art of thinking.

Indeed, as our biological constitution is given, so too is the language of action, and you can see in my *Grammar* how languages are modelled on this language.

As soon as languages begin, analogy, which begins with them, continually develops and enriches them. It shows, as it were, in the first signs that were found, all the signs that remain to be found.

The closest connection of ideas is based on this analogy. And this connection becomes the principle that gives the greatest clarity and precision to discourse, and character to every thought. When we know the arts of giving every thought its character, we have a system that includes all the genres of style. You can convince yourself of this by reading *Art of Writing*.

When we know how to give discourse the greatest clarity and precision, we understand the art of reasoning, since I have shown that this art reduces to a well-formed language.

All these arts thus come together in the art of speaking. They are merely the development of the same system, whose principle or beginning lies in our biological constitution.

We do not know how to go back to the first principle of our activities. We do not know how to show their beginning in the way we were constituted. That is why the arts of speaking, writing, reasoning, and thinking are formed and improve without our realizing it. While still primitive, they appear to be due to instinct, and when they are more developed, we attribute them to talent. But, in principle, instinct and talent are both the result of the same constitution. Instinct is the constitution that gives everyone the same faculties. Talent is the constitution that gives some people what it denies others.

Men of genius who have perfected the art of speaking doubtless observed their listeners and observed the impressions they made on them. They could thereby learn that a particular turn of phrase must produce a particular effect, but they did not learn why it produced it; and this art was for them merely an inexplicable groping. This is the way that poets and orators developed their talents.

To give the impression that they possessed an art, they already had to have made some progress. They were then credited with more art than they had. And because it was natural to look for rules in their works, the rules were proliferated as much as the observations that people believed these men must have made. So there were many rules, many exceptions, and many bad elementary texts. Good elements are formulated only insofar as rules for them are understood according to our way of conceiving; for, certainly, if we do not understand the human mind, we will not control it or we will have poor control over it. What has especially harmed these sorts of books is they have never been begun at the beginning. That is because definitions and axioms were thought to be principles and because synthesis was regarded as a doctrinal method. I have not talked about music, painting, sculpture, and so on, but we will judge that these arts should be treated like the others if we conceive that there is not and cannot be only one good method.

18 Considerations about Systems or about the Way to Study the Sciences

We are commonly led to believe that "abstract" and "difficult" mean the same. I do not understand this. But I do understand that there are writers who cannot be understood, not because they are abstract, but because they do not know how to analyze their own abstract ideas—two things that should not be confounded. If, as I believe I have shown, a well-conducted science is merely a well-formed language, any science should be within the reach of an intelligent mind, since every well-formed language is comprehensible. If you never understand me, it is because I do not know how to write; and if you happen sometimes not to understand me, that is because I sometimes write badly. So do not blame yourself when you do not understand me; and I will blame you only when you have been reading inattentively.

Indeed, why should abstract ideas be so difficult? We cannot speak without using them. Now if we continually use them in discourse, why can we not use them in our studies?

But a science, it will be said ... well! A science doubtless requires sustained attention. But if you are capable of attention, why would a science be incomprehensible? Why would it even be difficult? You easily overcome other difficulties when you learned your language in childhood.

A well-conducted science is a well-constructed system. Now in a system, there are generally two things, principles and conclusions.

Whatever the principles, once they are admitted, it is not the conclusions that are difficult to grasp. One would have to be very absent-minded or preoccupied to miss them and we are naturally rational.

Thus when we do not trouble ourselves overmuch with principles, which is rather common, systems construct themselves. Observe the human mind and you will see that in every century everything is systematic for the common

151

people as for the philosopher. You will observe that we naturally go from one preconception to another, and from opinion to opinion, from error to error, as we would go from truth to truth; but bad systems are constructed no differently from good ones.

You can understand how easily we ought to create systems if you consider that nature does so with our faculties, our needs, and things related to us. We think according to this system, as well as produce and combine our opinions, whatever they are. How else would our opinions be formed? Certainly we find such systems among even primitive and ignorant societies.

Now if the bad systems are rational, but nevertheless created so naturally and easily, a good system will not be hard to understand because of its conclusions. Then is it because of its principles?

I agree that the best system can only be understood with difficulty, if one has chosen to explain it by synthesis. And that is not surprising, since the synthetic method always begins with things that are not understood.

But when a system is worked out by analysis, it begins with the principle, with the beginning, and this beginning is so simple that a good system is constructed as easily as a bad one. We go naturally from discovery to discovery: All that is required is to be consistent. Where then does the difficulty come from? For it must be agreed that there is a difficulty.

When you study a new science, if it is well laid out, its beginnings should be as easy as possible. For you are led from the known to the unknown. Thus you are led to find in your present knowledge the first things that you are made to notice and it seems that you knew them before you learned them.

Nevertheless, the easier this beginning is, the more impatient you become to forge ahead. You have understood it and you think that is enough. But notice that you have a language to learn, and that a language is not known merely by once having seen its words. You have to speak it and make it familiar. Thus do not be so surprised if, after having understood a first chapter you have some difficulty understanding the second, which you pass on to too rapidly. In continuing this way, it will be even more difficult for you to understand the third one. So begin slowly, and expect everything to be easy when the beginning is familiar.

Nevertheless one difficulty remains and it is a big one. It comes from the fact that before studying the sciences, you already speak their language, and you speak it badly. For with the exception of a few new words, their language is your own. Now you agree that you often speak your language without really understanding what you are saying or that at most you understand yourself only approximately. This is nevertheless sufficient for you and for others, because they pay you in coin. It seems that to maintain our conversations we tacitly agreed that words can take the place of ideas, as in games chips take the place of money. And although there is only one cry of protest against those imprudent enough to play without having learned the value of chips, everyone can with impunity speak without having learned the value of words.

Do you wish to learn the sciences easily? Begin by learning your language.

BOOK II:
A TREATISE
ON THE SENSATIONS

Ut potero, explicabo: nec tamen, ut Pythius Apollo, certa ut sint et fixa, quae dixero: sed ut homunculus, probabilia conjectura sequens. (Cicero)

IMPORTANT NOTICE TO THE READER

I forgot to alert the reader to something I ought to have mentioned and perhaps repeated several times in this work. But I trust that acknowledging this oversight is just as effective and avoids the inconvenience of repetition. Thus I forewarn the reader that it is very important to put himself exactly in the place of the statue we are going to observe. He should begin to live when it does, have only a single sense when it has only one, acquire only those ideas that it acquires, contract only the habits that it contracts: in short, he must be only what it is. The statue will judge things as we do only when it has all the senses and all the experiences we do: and we will judge in the same way it judges only when we suppose ourselves deprived of everything that it lacks. I believe that readers who put themselves exactly in its place will have little difficulty in understanding this work; others who do not will meet with innumerable difficulties.

As yet the reader does not understand what the statue is that I propose to observe, and this warning will doubtless seem misplaced; but that will be one further reason for taking heed and remembering it.

PRÉCIS OF THE TREATISE ON SENSATIONS

The main purpose of this work is to show how all our knowledge and all our faculties come from the senses or, to be more precise, from sensation: For in truth, the senses are only occasional causes. They do not have sensations, it is the mind alone that has sensations as occasioned by the sense organs; and the mind draws, from the sensations that modify it, all its knowledge and all its faculties.

This inquiry can contribute enormously to advancing the art of reasoning; it alone can explicate that art right down to its underpinnings. Indeed, we will not discover a reliable way of steadily guiding our thoughts if we do not know how they were formed. What to we expect of thos philosophers who have continual recourse to the notion of an instinct that they cannot define? Do they fancy that they can exhaust the source of our errors, as long as they impute such mysterious ways to the mind? We must then observe ourselves from the first sensations that we experience; we must sort out the principle of our first mental opertions, go back to the origin of our ideas, spell out their elaboration, follow them up to the limits that nature has prescribed for us: in short, we must, as Bacon said, renew all human understanding.

But, it may be objected, everything has been said, once we repeat, following Aristotle, that our knowledge comes from the senses. There is no one with a keen mind who cannot conduct this explication that you think so

---

[1] Book 2, Ch. 20, Sec. 6

necessary, and nothing is so useless as to dwell with Locke on the details. Aristotle shows much more genius when he is satisfied with embracing the whole structure of our knowledge in a general maxim.

Aristotle, I agree, was one of the greatest geniuses of antiquity, and those who make this objection are doubtlessly clever. But in order to convince oneself how unfounded their criticism of Locke is and how useful it would be for them to study this philosopher instead of criticizing him, it is sufficient to hear them reason, or to read their works if they have written on philosophical matters.

If these men combined a precise method with much clarity and precision, they would have some right to consider useless the efforts that metaphysics has made to know the human mind; but we could well suspect them of estimating Aristotle so highly only in order to deprecate Locke; and of deprecating Locke only in the hope of casting aspersions on all metaphysicians.

A long time ago it was said that all our knowledge originated with the senses. Nonetheless, the Peripatetics were so far from knowing this truth that despite their considerable intelligence, they never knew how to explicate it, and after several centuries, it still remained to be discovered.

A philosopher often declares himself in favor of the truth without knowing what it is: sometimes he follows the crowd, he concurs with the opinion of the majority; sometimes more ambitious than docile, he resists, he struggles, and sometimes he succeeds in leading the masses astray.

Thus almost all sects were formed: they often reasoned haphazardly; but sooner or later some were bound to be sometimes right since they always contradicted each other. I do not know what was Aristotle's motive when he proposed his principle on the origin of our knowledge. But what I do know is that he left us no work where this principle was developed and that, moreover, he sought to be in contradiction with the opinions of Plato in every respect.

Immediately after Aristotle came Locke, for we must not count the other philosophers who wrote on the same subject. This Englishman doubtless shed a lot of light on the matter, but there still remained some obscurity. We shall see that most of the judgments that are intermingled with our sensations escaped his notice; that he did not appreciate how much we need to learn to touch, to see, to hear, and so forth; that all the faculties of the mind appeared to him to be innate qualities; and that he did not suspect that they could take their origin from sensation itself.

He was so far from compassing the full extent of the nature of man that, were it not for Molyneux, perhaps he would never had occasion to observe that he mixes up judgments with visual sensations. He explicitly denied that this was the case with the other senses. Thus he believed that we naturally use them by a kind of instinct, without reflection having contributed to our using them.

M. de Buffon, who tried to trace the history of our thoughts, creates an imaginary man and invests him in a single stroke with habits that he should have made him acquire. He did not know by what series of judgments each sense developed. He says that in animals, the smell is the first sense; that it alone will take the place of all the others, and that right from the start before receiving the lessons of touch, it determines and directs all animal movements.

This *Treatise on Sensations* is the only work which strips man of all his habits. By observing the birth of sensation, we show how we acquire the use of our faculties; and those who have grasped the system of our sensations will agree that it is no longer necessary to have recourse to vague words such as instinct, involuntary response, and the like, or that if we do use them, at least we can form precise ideas of them.

But to fulfill the goal of this work, it was absolutely necesary to put before our eyes the basic source of all our mental operations: thus we would never lose sight of them. It will be sufficient to indicate it in this précis.

If man had no interest in attending to his sensations, the impressions that objects make on him would pass as shadows and leave no trace. After several years, he would be as at the first instant, without having acquired any knowledge and without any mental processes other than that of having sensations. But the nature of his sensations does not allow him to remain suspended in this trance. As they are necessarily agreeable or disagreeable, he is interested in finding the one and in ridding himself of the other; and the more keen the contrast between pleasures and pains, the more it occasions action in the mind.

Then the privation of an object that we judge necessary for our happiness gives us this malaise, this disquiet that we call "need," and from which arise desires. These needs recur depending on conditions, often new ones even arise, and it is this that develops our knowledge and our faculties.

Locke is the first to observe that the disquiet caused by the privation of an object is the basic source of our motives. But he has it born of desire, whereas precisely the opposite is true; moreover, he makes more of a difference between desire and will than there in fact is; finally, he examines the influence of this disquiet only in a man with the use of all his senses and all his faculties.

It thus remains to show how this disquiet is the mainspring of our actions given us by our habits of touch, sight, hearing, feeling, taste, comparison, judging, reflection, desiring, loving, hating, fearing, hoping, wanting; in short, that all the habits of the mind and body arise through this disquiet.

For this, it was necessary to go further back than this philosopher did. But since we are unable to observe our first thoughts and our first movements, it was necessary to make inferences, and consequently to make different assumptions.

Nevertheless, it was not yet enough to go back to sensation. In order to discover the progress of all our knowledge and of all our faculties, it was important to distinguish what we owed to each sense, an inquiry that had not yet been attempted. Thereby the four parts of this *Treatise on Sensations* are formed: The first, which treats the senses that by themselves do not judge external objects; The second, on touch, or the only sense that judges external objects by itself; Third, how touch teaches the other sense to judge external objects; Fourth, on needs, ideas, and the activities of an isolated man who enjoys the use of all his senses.

This discussion shows clearly that the object of this work is to reveal which are the ideas that we owe to each sense and how, when they are reunited, they give us all the knowledge necessary for our survival.

It is thus sensations that give rise to the whole system of man: A complete system of which all the parts are connected and mutually sustaining. It is a sequence of truths: the first observations prepare the way for those that must follow them; the last ones confirm those that preceded them. If, for example, in reading the first part, we begin to think that it may well be the case that the eye does not judge sizes, shapes, locations, and distances by itself, we are completely convinced when we learn in the third how the sense of touch gave him all these ideas.

Although this system rests on assumptions, all the conclusions that we draw from it are attested to by our experience. There is no man, for example, limited to the sense of smell; such an animal could not safeguard its own survival; but for the truth of the arguments that we have advanced in observing him, only a little reflection on ourselves is needed make us recognize that we could owe to the senses of smell all the ideas and faculties that we discover in this man and that it would not be possible for us to acquire others with this single sense. We could have been content merely to consider the sense of smell by abstracting from the senses of sight, hearing, taste, and touch: if we made some assumptions, it is because they make this abstraction easier.

PRÉCIS OF THE FIRST PART

Locke distinguishes two sources of our ideas, the senses and reflection. It would be more precise to recognize only a single one, either because reflection is underlying only sensation itself, or because it is less the source of ideas than the channel by which they are derived from the senses.

This imprecision, as slight as it may seem, is responsible for a lot of obscurity in his system; for it makes him powerless to explicate its rudiments. Thus this philosopher is content to recognize that the mind perceives, thinks, doubts, believes, reasons, knows, wills, reflects; that we are convinced of the existence of these operations because we find them in ourselves, and that they contribute to the progress of our knowledge; but he did not feel the necessity of discovering their bases and elaboration, he did not suspect that they could be only acquired habits; he seems to have regarded them as something innate, and he says only that they are perfected through use.

In 1746 I tried to explain the development of the faculties of the mind. This attempt appeared novel, and had some success; but it owed this success to the abstruse way in which I carried it out. For such is the fate of discoveries about the human mind: when they are exposed in broad daylight they seem so simple that we read things we never suspected and yet believe that we have learned nothing.

There you have the flaw in the *Treatise on Sensations*. When the reader finds in the introduction: "Judgment, reflection, passion, all the operations of the mind, in short, are only sensation itself variously transformed," he believes he sees a paradox denuded of any kind of proof; but hardly has he finished reading this work than he is tempted to say: "This is a very simple truth and no one would be ignorant of it." Many readers have not resisted this temptation.

This truth is the chief object of the first part of the *Treatise on Sensations*. But as it can be demonstrated considering all our senses at once, I shall not separate them at this point and that will be an occasion to present it in a new light.

If a multitude of sensations occur all at once with the same degree of liveliness, or nearly, man is up to this point only an animal that has sensations: experience alone suffices to convince us that, in this case, the multitude of impressions suppresses all mental activity.

But let us allow only a single sensation to remain, or even, without entirely taking away the others, let us only diminish their force: immediately the mind is more particularly occupied with the sensation that preserves all its liveliness, and this sensation becomes attention, without it being necessary to assume anything additional in the mind.

I am, for example, not very attentive to what I am seeing, I am even completely inattentive, if all my senses assail my mind on all sides; but the visual sensations become attention as soon as my eyes devote themselves exclusively to the action of objects. However, the impressions that I experience can then be, and sometimes are, so extensive, varied and numerous, that I perceive an infinity of things without being attentive to any one of them; but hardly do I rest my gaze on an object than the particular sensations that I receive from it are the very attention that I give to it. Thus a sensation is attention, either because it is alone, or because it is livelier than all the others. Let a newly acquired sensation have more liveliness than the first one, it in turn becomes attention. But the more forceful the former, the more enduring the impression that it made. Experience proves this.

Our capacity for having sensations is thus shared between the sensation that we had and the one we are having. We perceive them both at the same time; but we percieve them differently: one seems past, the other present.

To perceive or to experience these two sensations is the same thing: now this experience takes the name "sensation" when the impression is being made on the senses, and it takes the name "memory" when this sensation, which is not currently occurring, presents itself to us as a sensation that occurred. Memory is thus only sensation transformed. We are thereby capable of two kinds of attention: the one exercised by memory and the other by the senses.

As soon as there is twofold attention, there is comparison; for to be attentive to two ideas or to compare them is the same thing. Now we cannot compare them without perceiving some difference between them or some resemblance: to perceive such relations is to judge. The actions of comparing and judging are thus only attention itself: thus sensation becomes successively attention, comparison, and judgment.

The objects that we compare have a multitude of relations, either because the impressions which they make on us are completely different, or because they only differ by degree, or because while similar, they combine differently in each object. In this case the attention that we give to the objects first includes all the sensations that they occasion. But as this attention is so divided, our comparisons are vague, we grasp only confused relations, our judgments are imperfect or uncertain: we are thus obliged to shift our attention from one object to another, considering their properties separately. Having, for example, judged their color, we judge their shape, to judge next their size; and in this way running over all the sensations that they evoke, we will discover through a series of comparisons and judgments the relations among them, and the result of these judgments is the idea that we form of each object. Attention thus guided is like a light that reflects from one body to another to illuminate both, and I call it "reflection." Sensation, after having been attention, comparison, judgment, thus becomes reflection itself.

And there you have enough to give an idea of the way in which the faculties of the understanding are unfolded in the *Treatise on Sensations*, and to show that it is not a desire to generalize that led us to say that these faculties all arise from the same origin. This is a system that, as it were, developed by itself, and it is all the more solidly established for that. I will add a work to make equally clear the development of the faculties of the will.

The feelings that are most familiar to us are sometimes those that we have the most difficulty explaining. What we call "desire" is one example of this. Malebranche defined it as "the movement of the mind" and in that he speaks like everyone else. It happens all too often to philosophers to take a metaphor for a precise notion. Nonetheless, Locke is free from reproach here; but in wanting to define desire, he confused it with the cause that produces it. "The disquiet," he says, "that a man finds in himself through the absence of a thing which would give him pleasure were it present is what we call desire." You will soon be convinced that desire is something other than this disquiet.

There are no indifferent sensations except by comparison: each one in itself is pleasant or unpleasant: to feel and not to feel good or bad are expressions that are completely contradictory.

Consequently, it is pleasure or pain that, engaging our capacity for feeling, produces this attention from which memory and judgment are formed.

We thus cannot feel bad or less good than we did except by comparing the state we are in with those through which we have passed. The more we make this comparison the more we feel this disquiet that leads us to believe it is important for us to change our condition: we feel the need of something better. Soon, memory recalls the object that we believe can contribute to our happiness, and in an instant, the action of all our faculties is focused on this object. Now this action of the faculties is what we call "desire."

Indeed, what do we do when we desire? We judge that the enjoyment of some good is necessary for us. Immediately our reflection is entirely devoted to this end alone. If it is present, we fix our eyes on it, we extend our arms to grasp it. If it is absent, the imagination recalls it, and vividly paints the pleasure of enjoying it. Desire is thus only the action of the same faculties that we attribute to the understanding; when this action is fixed on an object by the disquiet caused by its privation, it also determines the actions of the faculties of the body. Now desire gives rise to the passions, love, hate, hope, fear and the will. All that is still only sensation transformed.

The reader will find the details of these matters in the *Treatise on Sensations*. It explains how, in passing from need to need, from desire to desire, imagination takes shape, the passions arise, the mind acquires more activity in a trice and develops from one bit of knowledge to the next.

It is especially the first part that is devoted to showing the influence of pleasures and pains. This principle is not lost sight of in the course of the work, and we never suppose any mental proces in the statute, any movement in its body, without showing the motive that determines it.

This first part has the further goal of considering smell, hearing, taste, and sight separately and together; and a truth that we encounter first is that our senses by themselves give us no knowledge of external objects. If philosophers believed the opposite, if they were so mistaken as to suppose that smell alone could regulate the movements of animals, it is because, for want of having analyzed sensation, they took for the effect of a single sense the actions to which several contributed.

A creature limited to the sense of smell would only sense itself in the sensations that he would experience. Present him with aromatic bodies, he would have the sense of his existence; but offer him nothing of the kind and he will not sense himself. He exists with respect to himself only because of odors, only in the odors; he believes himself to be and he can only believe himself to be the odors themselves.

We have little difficulty in recognizing this truth, when it is a matter only of smell and of hearing. But the habit of judging sizes, shapes, arrangements, and distances by sight is so great that we do not imagine how there could have been a time when we opened our eyes without seeing as we now see.

It was not difficult to foresee the poor reasoning that preconceptions would yield on this topic because I had committed some myself in the *Essay on the Origins of Human Knowledge*. It did not seem necessary to take this up in the *Treatise of Sensations*. We would have become lost in details that intelligent readers would find tiresome. It seemed that the observations made on smell and hearing could ward off all the bias concerning vision. Indeed, this could be accomplished simply by reasoning carefully; but that is no little task, when we have prejudices to combat.

If the senses of smell and hearing give no idea of external objects, it is because by themselves they are limited to modifying the mind and they can show it nothing external. It is the same with the sense of sight. The extremity of the ray hitting the retina produces a sensation. But this sensation does not by itself refer to the other extremity of the light ray. It remains in the eye, does not extend beyond it, and the eye is then in the same category as a hand that at the first moment it touches grasps the end of a stick. It is obvious that this hand will know only the end that it is holding: it cannot yet discover anything more in the sensation. Chapter 8 in the second half of the *Treatise on Sensations* was written to show how just this comparison is, and to lay the way for what remained to said about sight.

But, one might object, the eye does not need to learn from touch to distinguish colors. Thus at least it sees in itself sizes and shapes. If, for example, we present it with a red sphere on a white background, it will discern the boundaries of the sphere.

Discern! There's a word whose full force is not appreciated. Discernment is not something innate. Our experience teaches us that it improves. Now, if it improves, it began. Thus it should not be believed that we discern as soon as we see. If, for example, at the moment someone shows you a painting, it is covered with a veil, you cannot say what you have seen. Why? Because you have seen without discerning. A painter will discern in this painting more things than you or I because his eyes are better educated. But, although we discern fewer things than he, we discern more than a child who has never seen a painting and whose eyes are less educated than ours. Finally, if we continue to go from those who discern less to those who discern still less, we will conclude that we can only begin to discern something insofar as we look at it with eyes that begin to instruct themselves.

Therefore, I say that the eye naturally sees everything that makes some impression on it, but I add that it discerns only insofar as it learns to look, and we will show that, to discern the simplest shape, it is not sufficient to see it.

"Nothing is more difficult," one might further object, "than to explain how the sense of touch would go about teaching the eye to perceive if the use of the eye was absolutely impossible without the aid of touch"; and there you have one of the reasons that lead us to believe that the eye sees sizes and shapes by itself.[2] This difficult matter will be explained in the third part.

Finally, the last goal of the first part is to show the extent and limits of the discernment of the senses that it discusses. We see how the statue, limited to the sense of smell, has particular ideas, abstract ideas, and ideas of number; what sort of particular and general truths it knows, what notions it forms of the possible and the impossible; how it judges duration by the succession of sensations.

We discuss its sleep, its dreams, and its "I," and we show that it has with a single sense the germ of all our mental faculties.

From there we go on to hearing, taste, and sight. We leave to the reader the task of applying to them the observations made about the sense of smell; we dwell only on what is particular to them, or if we sometimes take the liberty of repeating ourselves, it is to recall principles that, brought up recurrently, will make it easier to understand the whole system.

It is sufficient for me to indicate these details, because they are spelled out by a series of analyses, for which an extract would give only a very inadequate idea.

PRÉCIS OF THE SECOND PART

On the one hand, all our knowledge comes from the senses; on the other, our sensations are only ways of being. How thus can we see objects outside of us? Indeed, it seems that we ought only to see our minds variously modified.

I agree that this problem was poorly resolved in the first edition of the *Treatise on Sensations*. Mlle. Ferrand would have no doubts spotted this. Although she had a greater hand in this work than I did, she was not pleased with it; when I lost her, she was of the opinion that there was a lot to do over again. I completed the revision alone, and I reasoned poorly because at that time I did not know how to state the question. What is more surprising is that all of those who took it on themselves to criticize me directly or indirectly did

---

[2]*Lettre sur les aveugles*, p. 171

not know how to put the question better than I did, and reasoned poorly also.

Questions well put are questions resolved: thus the difficulty is in stating them well, and often this is a considerable difficulty, especially in metaphysics. The language of this science does not naturally have the simplicity of algebra, and we find it hard to make it simple because our mind has so much difficulty in being simple itself. However, we can formulate good questions only insofar as we speak with the greatest simplicity. But because we are often metaphysicians more by virtue of what we read than how we reflect, we pose a problem as it was posed previously, we speak of it as other people have spoken, and it remains to be resolved.

We have proven that with the sensations of smell, hearing, taste, and sight, man would believe himself to be smell, sound, taste, color; and that he would acquire no knowledge of external objects.

It is equally certain that with the sense of touch he would be in the same state of ignorance if he remained immobile. He would perceive only those sensations that the surrounding air might provoke; he would be hot or cold, he would have pleasure or pain; and those are states in which he would perceive neither the surrounding air nor any object; he would sense in these only himself.

Three things are necessary for this man to judge that there are objects: first that his limbs are induced to move; second, that his hands, the chief organ of touch, are placed on him and on the things around him; and lastly that, among the sensations that his hands feel, there is one that necessarily represents objects.

Now, one part of an extension is a continuum formed by the contiguity of other extended parts: an object is the continuum formed by the contiguity of other objects; and in general a continuum is formed by the contiguity of other continua. Thus it is that we judge them, and it is not possible for us to have any other idea of them because we can construct extension only with extension, and objects only with objects.

Consequently, either the sense of touch will give us no knowledge of objects, or among the sensations that we owe to it, there will be one that we shall not perceive as our state but rather as the state of a continuum formed by the contiguity of other continua. We must be forced to judge this sensation itself as extended.

If we suppose then that the statue reasons in order to proceed from itself to objects, we suppose wrongly; for certainly there is no reasoning that can make it leap this hurdle, and moreover, it cannot begin by reasoning.

But nature reasoned for it: she constituted it to be moved, to touch, and to have in touching a sensation that makes it judge that there are, outside of its sentient being, continuua formed by the contiguity of other continua, and consequently, extension and objects. This is what is spelled out in the second part of the *Treatise on Sensations*.

PRÉCIS OF THE THIRD PART

When we say that the eye does not naturally see the exterior of colored objects, even the philosopher protests a proposition that conflicts with his preconceptions. Nevertheless, everyone recognizes nowadays that colors are only modifications of our mind. Is this not a contradiction? Would one think that the mind perceives colors outside of itself for the sole reason that is experiences them in itself, if one reasoned consistently? Let us forget for a moment all our habits, let us transport ourselves to the creation of the world and suppose that God says to us: "I am going to produce a mind to which I will give certain sensations that will be only modifications of its substance." Would we conclude that it would see its sensations outside of itself? And if God added that it would perceive them in this way, would we not ask ourselves how this could be done? Now the eye, like smell, hearing, and taste, is an organ that is limited to modifying the mind.

It is touch that educates these senses. Scarcely do objects in hand take on certain forms, certain sizes, than smell, hearing, sight, and taste, outdo each other in lavishing their sensations on them, and the modifications of the mind become the properties of everything that exists outside it.

Having acquired these habits, we have difficulty in distinguishing what belongs to each sense. Nevertheless, their domains are quite separate: touch alone has within it the wherewithal to transmit the ideas of sizes, shapes, and so forth, and sight, deprived of the help of touch, only sends to the mind those simple modifications called "colors"; as smells only sends it those simple modifications we call "odors."

At the first moment that our eye opens to the light, our mind is modified: these modifications exist only in themselves, and they cannot yet be either extended or shaped.

Some circumstance makes us put our hand on our eyes, and promptly the sensation that we were experiencing grows weaker or completely disappears. We withdraw our hand and this sensation is reproduced. Surprised, we repeat these experiments, and we judge these sensations of our mind to be on the organ touched by our hand.

But to attribute them to this organ is to extend them over the entire external surface that the hand feels. Then, there you already have the simple modifications of the mind that produce at the surface of the eyes the phenomenon of something extended; this is the state in which the blind man of Cheselden first found himself when he had his cataracts removed.

Through curiosity or restlessness, we put our hand before our eyes, we hold it farther away, we bring it nearer, and the surface that we see appears to us to change. We attribute these changes to the movement of our hand and we begin to judge that the colors are at some distance from our eyes.

Then we touch a body on which our sight is fixed: I assume it to have a single color, blue, for example. Assuming this, the blue, which previously appeared at some indeterminate distance, must presently appear at the same distance as the surface that the hand touches, and this color extends over this surface as it first extended over the exterior surface of the eye. The hand says, as it were, to sight, "the blue is on each part that I skim over"; and sight, by dint of repeating this judgment, makes such a strong habit of this that it comes to feel the blue where it judged it to be.

With continual practice, sight feels itself animated by a force that becomes natural to it, it leaps in an instant to the greatest distances; it takes in and manipulates objects that touch cannot reach, and it scans all of space with astonishing speed.

It is easy to understand why the eye alone has the advantage over the other senses of learning from touch to give extension to its sensations.

If the light rays reflected did not always travel in a straight line in a constant medium, if, traversing different media, they did not always refract according to constant laws, if, for example, the slightest agitation of the air continually changed their direction, then the rays reflected by different objects would come together, those that came from the same object would be separated, and the eye could never judge either sizes or shapes because it could have only confused sensations.

Even if the directions of the rays were constantly subject to the laws of dioptrics, the eye would still be in the same predicament if the opening of the pupil was as large as the retina: for then the rays that come from every direction would strike it in a confused manner.

In this hypothetical condition, vision would be like smell; the colors would act on the eye as odors on the nose, and it would learn from touch only what smell itself learns from it. We would perceive all the colors pell-mell, at most we would distinguish the dominant colors; but it would not be possible for us to extend them over surfaces, and we would be far from suspecting that these sensations were, by themselves, capable of representing something extended.

But the rays, by the way they are reflected right up to the retina, are precisely to the eye what two crossed sticks are to the hand. Thereby, there is a close analogy between the way in which we see and that in which we touch with the help of two sticks; so that the hands can say to the eyes, "do like us," and immediately they do like them.

We could suppose a situation in which the sense of smell would learn to judge sizes, shapes, locations, and distances perfectly. It would be sufficient, on the one hand, to submit the odorous particles to the laws of dioptrics and, on the other hand, to construct the organ of smell a bit like that of sight; so that the odorous rays, having crossed at the opening, would strike an interior membrane at as many distinct points as there are on the surfaces from which they would be reflected.

In such a case, we would soon acquire the habit of extending odors over objects, and philosophers would not fail to say that the sense of smell had no need of the sense of touch in order to perceive sizes and shapes.

God could have established that light rays were the occasional cause of odors, as they are for colors. Now, it seems to me easy to understand that, in a world where that took place, the eyes could—as here—learn to judge sizes, shapes, location, and distances.

Readers who reason will yield, I believe, to these last reflections. As to those who know how to decide only according to their habits, I have nothing to say to them. They will doubtless find very strange the suppositions that I have just made.

Such are the principles on which the third part of the *Treatise on Sensations* bears. It is sufficient here to have established them. The reader is referred to the work itself for further elaboration, and for the conclusions that follow. He will see above all the ideas that result from the joint action of the five senses.

PRÉCIS OF THE FOURTH PART

With all the senses instructed, there remains only the question of examining the needs that must be satisfied for our survival. The fourth part shows the influence of these needs, in what order they engage us in studying the objects that concern us, how we become capable of foresight and industry and the circumstances that contribute to them, and what are our first judgments on the goodness and beauty of things. In short, we see how man, having been at first only a sentient animal, becomes a reflecting animal capable of safeguarding his survival himself.

This completes the system of ideas that began with this work. I will now summarize it.

The word "idea" expresses something that no one, I dare say, has yet explained well. That is why people argue over the origin of ideas.

A sensation is not yet an idea, insofar as it is considered only as a feeling limited to modifying the mind. If I am currently experiencing pain, I would not say that I have the idea of pain, I would say that I feel it.

But if I remember some past pain, the memory and the idea are then the same thing; and if I say that I have formed the idea of a pain that someone is telling me about and that I have never felt, it is because I judge according to a pain that I have experienced, or according to one that I am currently suffering. In the first case, the idea and the memory do not yet differ at all. In the second, the idea is the feeling of a current pain modified by judgments that I make in order to portray for myself someone else's pain.

Current sensations of hearing, taste, sight, and smell are only feelings as long as these senses have not yet been instructed by the sense of touch, because the mind can then take them only for modifications of itself. But if these feelings exist only in the memory that recalls them, they become ideas.

We do not say: "I have the feeling of what I was"; we say: "I have the memory of it or the idea of it".

The current sensation, like the past sensation, of solidity is the only one that is by itself at once feeling and idea. It is feeling by virtue of the relation it has to the mind that it modifies; it is an idea by virtue of the relation it has to something external.

This sensation soon forces us to judge as outside of ourselves all the modifications the mind receives from touch; that is why each sensation of touch proves to be representative of the objects that the hand grasps.

The sense of touch, accustomed to attributing its sensations to external objects, leads the other senses to acquire the same habit. All our sensations seem to be the properties of objects that surround us: they thus represent them, they are ideas.

But it is obvious that these ideas do not lead us to know what beings are of themselves; they only picture them in relation to us, and that alone shows how superfluous are the efforts of philosophers who claim to penetrate into the nature of things.

Our sensations gather outside of us, and form as many collections as we distinguish perceptible objects. Whence, two kinds of ideas: simple ideas and complex ones.

Each sensation, taken separately, can be regarded as a simple idea: but a complex idea is formed from several sensations that we unite outside of us. the whiteness of this paper, for example, is a simple idea; and the collection of several sensations, such as solidity, form, whiteness, and so forth, is a complex idea.

Complex ideas are complete or incomplete: the former include all the properties of the things they represent, the latter include only a part of them. Since we do not know the nature of beings, we can form a complete idea of none of them, and we ought to confine ourselves to discovering the properties that they have in relation to us. We have complete ideas only in mathematics, because this science has only abstract notions as its object of study.

If it is asked then what an object is, it must be replied: "it is this collection of properties that you touch, see, and so forth, when the object is present; and when the object is absent it is the memory of those properties that you have touched, seen, and so forth." Here the ideas are further divided into two kinds: I call the one kind sensory, the others intellectual. Sensory ideas represent objects that are currently acting on our senses; intellectual ideas represent those that have disappeared after having made their impression: these ideas differ from each other only as memory differs from sensation.

The more memory one has, the more one is consequently, capable of acquiring intellectual ideas. These ideas are the stock of our knowledge, just as sensory ideas are its origins.

This stock becomes the object of our reflection, at times we can devote ourselves to it exclusively and make no use of our senses. That is why it appears in us if it had always been there. One would say that it had preceded every kind of sensation, and we no longer know how to think of it in terms of its basic character: whence the error of innate ideas.

Intellectual ideas, if they are familiar, are recalled almost every time that we want them to be. They enable us to better judge the objects that we come across. They continually compare themselves with sensory ideas, and they enable us to discover relations that are new intellectual ideas, which enriches the stock of our knowledge.

In considering relations of resemblance, we put in the same class all the individual things that we notice have the same properties; in considering relations of difference, we generate classes, we subordinate them to each other, or we distinguish them in every respect. Whence, species, genera, abstract and general ideas.

But we have no general idea that was not particul; r. A first object that we chanced to notice is a model to which we relate everything that resembles it: and this idea, which was at first only singular, becomes all the more general as our discrimination is less developed.

Thus we suddenly pass from particular ideas to very general ones, and we descend to subordinate ideas only to the degree that we overlook the differences among things less.

All these ideas make up a single chain: the sensory ones are linked to the notion of extension; so that all objects appear to us to be only extension variously modified; the intellectual ideas are connected to the sensory ones from which they derive their origins; thus they are often reawakened on the occasion of the slightest sensory impression. The need that gave them to us originally is the motive that gives them to us again; and if they come to mind over and over again it is because our needs are repeated and follow one another continually.

This is in general the system of our ideas. To make it so simple and clear, it was necessary to have analyzed the operation of the senses. Philosophers have been unacquainted with this analysis and that is why they have reasoned badly on this subject.[3]

---

[3] "When we speak of ideas," says the author of the *Logique de Port-Royal*, part I, ch. I, "we do not attribute this term at all to the images that are painted in imagination but to all that is in our mind when we can say truthfully that we conceive of something in whatever way we conceive of it." We see how vague that is. Descartes was as thoroughly confused on this topic. Malebranche and Leibnitz only made up clever systems. Locke had more success but he still leaves much unclarity because he did not sufficiently sort out all the sensory operations. Finally, M. de Buffon says that "ideas are only sensations compared" and he gives no further explanation. Perhaps it is my fault but I do not understand this language. It seems to me that to compare two sensations one must already have some idea of the one and the other. And there you have ideas before having compared anything.

THE PLAN OF THIS WORK
Dedication to the Countess of Vassé

We cannot recall the ignorance in which we were born. That state leaves no trace. We only remember being ignorant of something that we remember having learned. To notice what we are learning, we must already know something. We must experience some ideas in order to observe that we experience ideas that we once lacked. This reflective memory, which now makes it so evident when we go from one bit of knowledge to another, cannot work its way back to original knowledge; on the contrary, it presupposes that knowledge, and this is the origin of our propensity to believe that we were born with it. To say that we have learned to see, hear, taste, smell and touch seems the oddest paradox. It gives the impression that nature gave us the full use of our senses at the same instant that it created them, and that we have always used them without study, because now we are no longer obliged to study them.

When I published my *Essay on the Origin of Human Knowledge*, I myself had these same prejudices. I could not be convinced by Locke's reasoning about a man born blind who was given the sense of sight; and I maintained that, contrary to this philosopher, the eye naturally judges shapes, sizes, locations, and distances.

You know, Madame, to whom I am beholden for enlightenment that finally made my prejudices evaporate, you know the part played in this work by someone who was so dear to you and so worthy of your esteem and friendship.[4] It is to her memory that I dedicate this work, and I address it to you so that I may enjoy at the same time both the delight of speaking of her and the pain of regretting her loss. Let this monument perpetuate the memory of your friendship and of the honor I had in receiving your mutual esteem.

But may I not hope for success when I consider how much this treatise owes to her. Its sharpest insights are due to the soundness of her mind and to the liveliness of her imagination—qualities that she united to such a point that they seemed almost incompatible. She felt the necessity of considering our senses separately, of distinguishing precisely the ideas that we owe to each, and of observing how they instruct and help each other.

For this purpose, we imagined a statue internally organized like ourselves, and animated by a mind deprived of every kind of idea. We further supposed that its marble exterior did not allow it the use of any of its senses, and we reserved for ourselves the freedom to open them at will to the different impressions they are susceptible of.

We believed we ought to begin with the sense of smell, because of all the

---

[4]It is she who advised me to choose the epigraph *Ut potero, explicabo*, etc.

senses it is the one that seems to contribute the least to the knowledge of the human mind. The others were then the object of our inquiry, and after having considered them separately and together, we saw the statue become a living being capable of safeguarding its own survival.

The principle determining the development of its faculties is simple; sensations themselves contain it; for since each is necessarily pleasant or unpleasant, the statue is interested in enjoying some and ridding itself of others. Now we shall become convinced that this interest is sufficient to give rise to the activities of understanding and volition. Judgment, reflection, desires, passions, and so forth are only sensation itself differently transformed.[5]

That is why it seemed to us useless to suppose that the mind receives immediately from nature all the faculties with which it is endowed. Nature gives us sense organs so that pleasure can alert us to what we must seek, and pain to what we must avoid. But it stops there, it leaves to experience the task of making us acquire habits and of finishing the work that it began. This plan is original, and it shows all the simplicity of the methods employed by the author of nature. Must we not admire the fact that man had only to be made sensitive to pleasure and pain in order for there to arise in him ideas, desires, habits, and talents of every kind?

There are no doubt many difficulties to overcome in order to expound the whole system; I have often felt how far such an undertaking is beyond my powers. Mademoiselle Ferrand enlightened me on the principles, plan, and finest details. I must be all the more grateful as her purpose was neither to instruct me nor to produce a book. She did not realize she was becoming an author, nor had she any design other than to discuss with me matters in which I took some interest. Thus, she was never prejudiced in favor of her opinions. If I almost always preferred hers over those I had at first, I had the pleasure only of attaining enlightenment. I esteemed her too highly to adopt her views for any other reason. And she herself would have been offended had I done so. Nevertheless, I recognized the superior wisdom of her views so often that I could not avoid the suspicion of being too acquiescent. Sometimes she reproached me for this; she feared, she said, spoiling my work. Scrupulously

---

[5] But, it will be said, animals have sensations and yet their minds are not capable of the same faculties as man's. That is true, and reading this work will make the reason evident. The organ of touch is less perfect in animals; as a result it cannot be the occasional cause of all the activities that can be obseved in us. I say "occasional cause" because sensations are the natural modifications of the mind and the organs can only occasion them. From which the philosopher should conclude, in accord with the teachings of the faith, that the mind of animals is of an essentially different order than that of man. For would it be a part of God's wisdom that a mind capable of attaining all kinds of knowledge, of discovering its duties, of being worthy and unworthy, should be subjected to a body that would only occasion in it the faculties necessary for animal survival?

examining the opinions that I forsook, she tried to convince herself that her criticisms were unfounded.

If she had taken up her pen herself, this work would be a better proof of her talents. But her delicacy did not allow her even to think of it. Although I was obliged to approve of this when I considered her motives, I also blamed her because I saw in her advice what she would have wanted to do herself. The treatise is thus unfortunately only the result of my conversations with her, and I very much fear that I have not always known how to present her thoughts in their true light. It is distressing that she could not enlighten me right up to the time of publication. I am especially sorry that there were two or three questions on which we were not entirely in agreement.

I would not presume to give Mademoiselle Ferrand her due if she were still alive. Solely protective of the glory of her friends, and considering as theirs all that she may have contributed to it, she would not have acknowledged at all the part that she played in this work, she would have prohibited me from acknowledging it, and I would have obeyed. But now, ought I to refuse myself the pleasure of doing her this justice? It is all that I have left after the loss of this wise advisor, enlightened critic, and loyal friend.

You will share this pleasure with me, Madame, you who will forever regret her loss, and thus it is with you that I want to speak of her. Both equally worthy of esteem, you both had the discernment which reveals all the value of what is loved and without which we do not know how to love at all. You knew the principles, truth, and courage that shaped you for one another. These qualities were the links of your friendship, and you found in your relations that happiness characteristic of virtuous and sensitive souls.

This happiness was then fated to end. In the final moments, she needed no other consolation than that she would not have to survive you. I saw that she was indeed happy about that. It was sufficient for her to live in your memory. She took pleasure in this idea but she would have effaced from it the image of your pain. "Talk about me sometimes with Madame de Vassé," she said, "and let it be with a kind of pleasure." She knew, in truth, that pain is not the only mark of regret, and that in such a case the more pleasure we find in thinking of a friend, the more keenly we feel the loss we have suffered.

How honored I am, Madame, that she thought me worthy of sharing with you this plan and this pleasure, and that you think the same. How could either of you give me any greater proof of your esteem and your friendship?

PART ONE:
ON SENSES THAT BY THEMSELVES DO NOT JUDGE EXTERNAL OBJECTS

1 Of the First Knowledge of a Man Limited to the Sense of Smell

1. *The statue limited to the sense of smell can only know odors.* Our statue's knowledge, limited to the sense of smell, can extend only to smells. It can no more have ideas of extension, shape, or of anything outside of itself, or outside of its sensations, than it can have of color, sound, or taste.

2. *It is, in relation to itself, only the odors that it smells.* If we present it with a rose, to us it will be a statue that smells a rose; but to itself, it will be the smell itself of this flower.

Thus it will be the smell of a rose, a carnation, a jasmine, or a violet according to the objects that act on its sense organ. In short, smells are for it only its own modifications or states. And it cannot think of itself as anything else since these are the only sensations of which it is capable.

3. *It has no idea whatever of matter.* Let philosophers to whom it seems obvious that everything is material put themselves in its place for a moment and let them imagine how they could suspect that there exists something that resembles what we call "matter."

4. *One cannot be more limited in knowledge.* Thus we can already convince ourselves that it would be sufficient to increase or diminish the number of our senses to cause us to make judgments quite different from those that are now so natural to us. And our statue limited to the sense of smell can give us an idea of the class of beings whose knowledge is the least extensive.

2

On Mental Processes in a Man Limited to the Sense of Smell, and How Different Degrees of Pleasure and Pain Are the Mainspring of These Processes

1. The statue is capable of attention. At the first smell our statue's capacity for having sensations is wholly devoted to the impression made on its sense organ. This is what I call attention.

2. *Of enjoyment and suffering*. From this instant on, it begins to enjoy or to suffer. For if the capacity of having sensation is entirely devoted to a pleasant smell, there is pleasure. And if it is entirely devoted to an unpleasant smell, there is distress.

3. *But incapable of forming desires*. But as yet our statue has no idea of the different changes it can undergo. Thus it is well off without wishing to be better, or badly off without wishing to be well off. Distress can no more make it desire some good that it does not know than enjoyment can make it fear some evil that it does not know any better. Consequently, however unpleasant the first sensation may be, even if it were on the verge of harming the sense organ and causing violent pain, it cannot give rise to desire.

If this distress is always accompanied in us by the desire not to suffer, it cannot be the same with our statue. The pain occasions this desire in us only because we are already acquainted with this state. The habit we have acquired of regarding pain as something that we have been without, and that we can again be without, makes it impossible for us to suffer pain without wishing immediately not to suffer, and this desire is inseparable from a painful state.

But the statue that initially experiences itself only through the pain that it is undergoing does not know whether it can cease being in that state and become something else, or become nothing at all. As yet it has no idea of change, succession, or duration. Thus it exists without being able to form desires.

4. *Pleasure and pain the impetus for its mental processes.* When the statue notices that it can stop being what it is in order to become what it was, we will see its state of pain give rise to desires, for it compares a state of pain with a state of pleasure that memory recalls. It is by this stratagem that pleasure and pain form the single driving force that, determining all mental processes, must raise the mind by degrees to all the knowledge of which it is capable. To discern the progress that the mind may make, we will only need to note the pleasures that it will come to desire, the pains that it will come to fear, and the influence of each according to circumstances.

5. *How limited it would be without memory.* If it retained no memory of its modifications, each time it would believe it was having sensations for the first time. Whole years would be lost at each present moment. Thus always limiting its attention to a single state, it would never take account of two together, and it would never judge their relations. It would enjoy or suffer without yet having either desire or fear.

6. *Birth of memory.* But the smell that it smells is not completely forgotten when the odorous body stops acting on its sense organ. The attention the statue gave it still retains it, and a more or less keen impression of it remains according as the attention itself was more or less concentrated. This is memory.

7. *Smell and memory share the capacity of sensation.* When our statue is a new smell, it still has present the smell that it was the preceding moment. Its capacity for having sensation is divided between memory and the sense of smell. The faculty of memory is attentive to the past sensation while that of smell is attentive to the current sensation.

8. *Memory is thus only a way of having sensation.* Thus the statue has two ways of having sensation, which differ only in that one relates to a current sensation and the other to a sensation that no longer exists but whose impression still remains. Not knowing that there are objects that act on it or even that it has a sense organ, it usually distinguishes the memory of a sensation from a current sensation only as a weak feeling of what it was and a keen feeling of what it is.

9. *Recalled sensations can be more vivid than current ones.* I say "usually" because the memory is not always a weak feeling, nor the sensation always keen. For whenever the memory recollects these ways of being very forcibly and the sense organ, on the other hand, receives only slight impressions, then the feeling of a current sensation will be less keen than the memory of a past sensation.

10. *The statue distinguishes succession in itself.* Thus when a smell is present to the olfactory sense through the impression made by an odorous body on the sense organ itself, another smell is present in memory because the impression of another odorous body continues to exist in the brain, where the sense organ had transmitted it. By passing as it were through two states,

the statue feels that it no longer is what it was. The knowledge of this change makes it refer the first smell to a different moment from the one in which it is experiencing the second. And this is what makes it differentiate between existing in one state and remembering having existed in another.

11. *How it is active and passive.* The statue is active in regard to one of its two states of feeling and passive in regard to the other. It is active when it remembers a sensation, because it has in itself the cause that recalls it, that is, memory. It is passive at the moment it is experiencing a sensation, because the cause that produces the sensation is outside of it, that is, in the odorous bodies acting on its sense organs.[6]

12. *It cannot distinguish these two states.* Unable to suspect the action of external objects on itself, the statue cannot differentiate between an internal cause and an external cause. All its modifications are for it as if it owed them only to itself; and whether it experiences a sensation or only recalls one, it never perceives anything else, except that it is or was in a certain state. Consequently, it cannot notice any difference between the state in which it is active and that in which it is entirely passive.

13. *Memory becomes a habit.* Nevertheless, the more memory is exercised, the more easily it acts. In this way, the statue acquires a habit of effortlessly recalling the changes it has passed through, and of dividing its attention between what it is and what it has been. For habit is only the facility of repeating what one has already done, and this facility is acquired by the repetition of acts.[7]

14. *The statue compares.* If, having repeatedly smelled a rose and a carnation, the statue once again smells a rose, passive attention, which occurs through the sense of smell, will be entirely devoted to the current smell of the rose, and active attention, which occurs through memory, will be divided between the memory that remains of the rose's smell and that of the carnation. Now the states of being can share the capacity for having sensations only insofar as they are compared, for to compare is nothing other than to attend to two ideas simultaneously.

15. *Judges.* When there is comparison, there is judgment. Our statue cannot attend simultaneously to the smell of a rose and to that of a carnation without perceiving that the one is not the other, and it cannot attend to the

---

[6]There is in us an impetus for our actions that we feel but cannot define; it is called *force*. We are likewise active in relation to everything this force produces in us or outside of us. We are active, for example, when we reflect, or when we move some object. By analogy, we suppose a force in all objects that produces some change, one with which we are even less familiar; and we are passive in relation to the impressions these objects make on us. Thus a being is active or passive depending on whether the cause of the effect produced is in it or outside of it.

[7]I am speaking here, and throughout this work, only of habits that are acquired naturally; in the supernatural order everything is subject to other laws.

scent of a rose that it is smelling and to that of a rose that it has smelled without perceiving that they are the same change in its state. A judgment is thus only the perception of a relation between two ideas that are compared.

16. *These processes become habits.* As comparisons and judgments are repeated, our statue makes them more easily. It thus acquires the habit of comparing and judging. Consequently, we need only to make it smell other smells in order to get it to make new comparisons, form new judgments, and acquire new habits.

17. *It becomes capable of surprise.* The statue is not at all surprised at its first sensation, for it is not yet accustomed to any sort of judgment.

Nor is it surprised when, smelling several odors in succession, it perceives each of them for only an instant. Then it does not hold to any of the judgments it makes, and the more it changes, the more it must feel itself naturally inclined to change.

Nor will it be any the more surprised if we lead it by imperceptible gradations from the habit of believing itself one smell, to that of judging that it is some other one. For it changes without being able to notice it.

But it will be surprised if it suddenly passes from one state to which it was accustomed to a quite different state of which it had as yet no idea.

18. *This surprise activates mental processes.* This surprise makes it feel more keenly the difference between its states of being. The more abrupt the transition from some of them to others, the greater its surprise and also the more striking the contrast between the pleasures and pains accompanying the changes. Its attention, dominated by the pains that are more strongly felt, is devoted more keenly to all the succeeding sensations. It then compares them with greater care, and thus judges their relations better. Consequently, surprise increases the activity of its mental processes. But since it increases this activity only by making the statue notice a more perceptible contrast between pleasant and unpleasant feelings, pleasure and pain are always the prime movers of its faculties.

19. *The ideas preserved in memory.* If odors each attract the statue's attention equally, they will be preserved in the statue's memory according to their order of succession, and will be held in memory by this means.

If this succession includes a great number of them, the impression of the final ones, since they are the most recent, will be strongest; that of the first ones will weaken by imperceptible degrees, will be completely extinguished, and it will be as if they had not occurred.

But those that receive only very slight attention will leave no impression and will be forgotten as soon as they are perceived.

Finally those that have been the most striking will be recalled more vividly and will preoccupy the statue so completely that they will be capable of making it forget the others.

20. *Connection of ideas.* Memory is thus a sequence of ideas forming a

kind of chain. This linkage provides the means of passing from one idea to another and of recalling the remotest ones. Consequently we recall an idea we have had some time ago only because we recall the intermediate ideas more or less quickly.

21. *Pleasure guides memory.* At its second sensation our statue's memory has no choice to make, for it can remember only the first one. It will act only with more force if it is led to do so by the keenness of the pleasure and pain.

But when there has been a series of modifications, the statue, keeping in mind that there were many of them, will be led to recall preferentially those that can contribute more to its happiness. It will pass rapidly over the others, or will stop only in spite of itself.

To put this truth in its full light, we must recognize the different degrees of pleasure and pain to which we are liable, and the comparisons we may make of them.

22. *Two kinds of pleasure and pain.* Pleasures and pains are of two kinds. Some belong more particularly to the body; they are sensory. Others lie in the memory and in all of the faculties of the mind; they are intellectual or mental. But this is a difference that the statue is incapable of noticing.

This ignorance keeps it from an error that we have great difficulty avoiding. For these feelings do not differ as much as we imagine. In truth, they are all intellectual or mental because in the strict sense only the mind feels. If you like, they are all also in one sense sensory or corporeal because the body is their only occasional cause. We can sort them into two kinds only by considering them with respect to the faculties of the body or to those of the mind.

23. *Different degrees of each.* Pleasure can diminish or increase by degrees. In decreasing, it tends to extinguish and vanishes with the sensation. In increasing, on the other hand, it can lead to pain because the impression becomes too strong for the sense organ. Thus there are two limits to pleasure. The weakest is where sensation begins with the least force; it is the first step from nothingness to feeling. The strongest is where the sensation cannot increase withot ceasing to be pleasant. It is the state closest to pain.

The impression of a mild pleasure seems to be concentrated in the sense organ that transmits it to the mind. But if it has a certain degree of vividness, it is accompanied by an emotion that spreads throughout the whole body. This emotion is a fact that our experience does not permit us to call into question.

Pain can likewise increase or diminish. In increasing, it tends toward the total destruction of the animal; but in diminishing, it does not lead, like pleasure, to the privation of all feeling. On the contrary, the moment that terminates pain is always pleasurable.

24. *Indifferent states exist only by comparison.* Among these different degrees, it is impossible to find a state of indifference. At the first sensation, however weak, the statue is necessarily contented or discontented. But when it has experienced the sharpest pains and the deepest pleasures successively, it will judge that the weakest sensations, which it will have compared with the strongest, are indifferent; it will cease to regard them as pleasant or unpleasant.

We can thus suppose that it has pleasant and unpleasant states in different degrees, and states that it regards as indifferent.

25. *The origin of need.* Whenever it is badly off, or less well off, it remembers its past sensations, compares them with its current ones, and feels the importance of returning to what it was. From this arises need, or its knowledge of some good that it judges necessary to enjoy.

The statue thus knows about needs only because it compares the pain that it suffers with the pleasures that it has enjoyed. Take away the memory of these pleasures, and the statue will be uncomfortable without suspecting that it had any needs. For to feel in need of something, one must have some knowledge of it. Now, following the supposition that we have just made, the statue knows of no other state than the one in which it finds itself. But when it remembers a happier state, its current situation makes it immediately feel the need for that state. Thus pleasure and pain will always determine its mental processes.

26. *How need determines mental processes.* Its need can be occasioned by a genuine pain, by an unpleasant sensation, by a sensation less agreeable than some of those that preceded it, or finally by apathy in which it is reduced to one of its states that it is accustomed to find indifferent.

If its need is caused by an odor that gives rise to acute pain, this need preempts almost all its capacity for feeling, and it leaves memory some power only to remind the statue that it was not always so badly off. Then it is unable to compare the different states it has gone through, and it cannot judge what the most pleasant one is. The only thing that interests it is to get out of this state in order to enjoy some other one, whatever it may be. And if it knows some means that can put an end to its suffering, it will apply all its faculties to put it to use. Thus in serious illnesses we stop desiring pleasures that we have sought so fervently and we long only to recover our health.

If the need is generated by a sensation less pleasant than some prior ones, we must distinguish between two cases. Either the pleasures the statue compares it with have been keen and accompanied by the greatest emotion, or they have been less keen and have hardly evoked any emotion.

In the first case, the past happiness is evoked with all the more force as it differs from the current sensation. The emotion accompanying it is partly reproduced, and appropriating almost all capacity for feeling, it does not allow the statue to notice the pleasant sensations that followed or preceded it.

The statue is thus not distracted at all, and better compares this happiness with its present state. It appreciates the difference better and, applying itself to picturing that happiness in the most vivid way, the privation of this happiness brings about a greater need and acquiring it becomes all the more necessary.

In the second case, on the other hand, the past happiness is recalled with less intensity; other pleasures divide the statue's attention. The benefit offered by the past happiness is felt less; and it reawakens little or no emotion. The statue is thus not interested as much in the return of the pleasure, and it does not apply its faculties to it as much.

Finally, if the need is caused by one of those sensations that the statue is accustomed to judge indifferent, it endures at first without experiencing pain or pleasure. But this state, compared with the happy situations in which it has found itself, soon becomes rather unpleasant, and the discomfort it suffers is what we call "boredom." However, the boredom persists, increases, becomes unbearable, and forcibly directs all the statue's faculties toward recovering the happiness whose loss it feels.

This boredom can be as overwhelming as pain, in which case the statue has no other interest than to escape from it, and it turns indiscriminately toward all states that can dispel it. But if we alleviate the boredom, its state will be less unhappy and getting rid of it will matter less. It can turn its attention to all the pleasant sensations that it has some memory of, and whichever pleasure it recalls most vividly will engage all its faculties.

27. *How it activates memory.* There are thus two principles that determine the level of activity of its faculties. One is the vividness of a good that it no longer has. The other is the meager pleasure of a current sensation, or the pain that accompanies it.

When these two prinicples are united, the statue makes a greater effort to recall what it has ceased to be, and it feels less what it is. Since its capacity for sensation necessarily has limits, memory appropriates a part only at the expense of smell. If indeed this faculty's action is strong enough to take over the whole capacity for having sensation, the statue will no longer notice the impression made on its sense organ, and it will recall so vividly what it has been that it will seem that it still is in that state.[8]

28. *The activity ends when the need does.* But if its current state is the happiest it knows, then pleasure leads the statue to enjoy it in preference to all others. Nothing remains that can set memory into action with sufficient force to encroach upon the sense of smell as far as extinguishing its sensations. Pleasure, on the contrary, fixes at least the greatest part of the

---

[8] Our experience proves this. For there is perhaps no one who has not recalled past pleasures with as much vividness as if he were presently experiencing them; or at least with enough vividness to cause him to give no attention to the state he is in, even though it may be distressing.

attention, or the capacity for having sensation, on the current sensation. If the statue still remembers what it has been, that is because the comparison it makes between the past and the present enables it better to relish its happiness.

29. *Difference between memory and imagination.* There are then two effects of memory. One is a sensation that is recalled as vividly as if it came from the organ itself; the other is a sensation of which only a faint memory remains.

Thus there are in this mental process two degrees that we can distinguish: the weakest is that where the statue barely experiences the past event; the strongest is that where it experiences the event as if it were present.

Now this mental process keeps the name "memory" when it only recalls things as past. And it takes the name "imagination" when it recalls them so forcefully that they seem to be present. Imagination as well as memory thus occur in our statue, and these two processes only differ in degree. Memory is the beginning of an imagination that has as yet but little force; imagination is meory itself invested with all possible vividness.

As we have distinguished two kinds of attention that take place in our statue—the one through the sense of smell, the other through memory—we can now observe a third achieved through imagination, and whose character is to stop sensory impressions in order to substitute a sensation independent of the action of external objects.[9]

30. *This difference eludes the statue.* When, however, the statue imagines a sensation that it no longer has, and recreates it as vividly as if it still were having it, it does not know that it contains a cause producing the same effect as an odorous object acting on its sense organ. Thus it cannot distinguish as we do between imagining a sensation and having one.

31. *Its imagination more active than ours.* But we have reason to presume that its imagination is more active than ours. As its capacity for sensation is confined entirely to a single kind of sensation, and all the force of its faculties is applied uniquely to smells, nothing can distract it. As for us, we are divided among a multitude of sensations and ideas that constantly assail us and we imagine feebly since we reserve for imagination only a part of our powers. Moreover, our senses are always on guard against our imagination, and incessantly call our attention to objects that we want to imagine. On the other hand, everything gives free rein to the imagination of our statue. It thus

---

[9] A thousand facts prove the power of imagination over the senses. A man lost in thought will not see at all the objects before his eyes, nor hear the noise that strikes his ears. Everyone knows the story about Archimedes. If imagination is engaged even more vigorously, we can be pricked or burned without feeling pain and the mind appears denuded of all sensory impressions. To understand how such things can be, we need only notice that, since our capacity to have sensations is limited, we will be absolutely insensitive to sensory impressions whenever imagination devotes this capacity fully to some object.

recalls without impedment a smell it has experienced, and it experiences it in fact as if its sense organ were presently affected by it, Finally, our ease in averting objects harmful to us and in seeking those whose enjoyment is dear to us further contributes to making our imagination lazy. But since our statue can only get rid on an unpleasant feeling by vividly imagining some pleasant state, its imagination receives greater exercise, and it must produce effects that ours is powerless to provide.[10]

32. *Special case in which the statue's imagination is inactive.* There is one circumstance, however, where imagination's activity, and even that of memory, is absolutely suspended. This happens when a sensation is vivid enough to take complete possession of the capacity for experiencing sensations. Then the statue is utterly passive. Pleasure becomes a kind of intoxication which it hardly enjoys; and pain becomes an overwhelming experience in which it hardly suffers at all.

33. *How it resumes its activity.* But let this sensation lose some degree of vividness, and immediately the faculties of the mind come back into play, and need again becomes the cause that controls them.

34. *And gives a new order to ideas.* The most pleasurable modifications for the statue are not always its most recent ones. They can be found in the beginning or middle of its chain of knowledge as at the end. Thus imagination is often obliged to pass rapidly over intermediate ideas. It brings together the most distant ones, changes the order they had in memory, and forms an entirely new chain.

The connection among ideas thus does not follow the same order in its faculties. The more familiar the order the statue has in imagination, the less it keeps the order that memory gave it. By this means ideas are connected in a thousand different ways, and often the statue remembers less the order in which it has experienced sensations than that in which it has imagined them.

35. *Ideas are variously connected because of new comparisons.* But it forms all its chains only by comparisons made of each link with the ones preceding and following, and by judgments made about their relations. This connection becomes stronger as the exercise of its faculties strengthens the habits of remembering and imagining. Thereby we get the surprising benefit of recognizing sensations we have had previously.

36. *The statue recognizes former states from these connections.* In fact, if we make our statue smell a familiar smell, we than have a state that it has compared, judged, and connected to some parts of the chain that its memory has the habit of scanning. That is how it judges that its current state is the

---

[10]However surprising the effects of imagination may be, we cannot doubt them at all if we reflect on what happens to us when dreaming. Then we see, we hear and we touch objects that do not act on our senses at all; and there is every reason to believe that imagination has such great power only because we are not distracted by the multitude of ideas and sensations that occupy us when we are awake.

same as one of its past states. But this does not apply to an odor that it has not yet smelled. It must than seem completely new to the statue.

37. *It cannot explain this phenomenon.* It is needless to observe that when the statue recognizes some state, it is incapable of giving an account of it. The cause of such a phenomenon is so difficult to identify that it escapes every person who does not know how to observe and analyze what goes on within himself.

38. *How ideas are preserved and reviewed in memory.* When the statue goes for a long time without thinking of a certain state, what happens during this whole interval to the acquired idea of this state? Where does this idea come from when it is later recalled to memory? Is it preserved in the mind or the body? In neither.

It is not in the mind, since a malfunction in the brain is sufficient to take away the power or recalling it.

It is not in the body. Only the physical cause could preserve itself in the body, and for that we should have to suppose that the brain remained absolutely in the state it was put in by the sensation that the statue recalls. But how should we reconcile this assumption with the ceaseless activity of the mind? How to reconcile it especially when we consider the multitude of ideas that enrich the memory? We can explain this phenomenon much more simply.

I have a sensation when some action occurring in one of my sense organs is transmitted to the brain. If this action begins in the brain and extends as far as the sense organ, I believe I have a sensation that I in fact do not have: it is an illusion. But if the action begins and ends in the brain, I remember the sensation that I have had. When the statue recalls an idea, it is not because the idea is preserved in either the body or the mind. Rather, the action that is its physical and occasional cause is reproduced in the brain.[11] But this is not the place to hazard guesses about the mechanism of memory. We preserve the memory of our sesations. We recall them after having gone a long time without thinking of them. For this, it is enough that they have made a vivid impression on us, or that we have experienced them several times over. These facts allow me to suppose that our statue, constituted as we are, is like us capable of memory.

39. *Enumeration of the habits acquired by the statue.* Let us conclude that the statue has acquired several habits—one habit of attending, another of remembering, a third of comparing, fourth of judging, fifth of imagining, and last one of recognizing.

40. *How these habits are sustained.* The same causes that have produced habits are the only ones capable of maintaining them. I mean that

---

[11] See the *Logic*, part 1, ch. 9.

habits will be lost if they are not renewed by acts that are repeated from time to time. Then our statue will not recall either the comparisons that it made with some state of being or the judgments that it made about it, and it will experience the state for the third or fourth time without being capable or recognizing it.

41. *Reinforce each other.* But we ourselves can contribute to maintaining the statue's use of its memory and all its other faculties. We need only interest it with different degrees of pleasure or pain in preserving its states or in escaping them. The skill with which we will control its sensations could thus give us the means to strengthen and to extend its habits further and further. There is even reason to suppose that it will distinguish in a succession of smells differences that escape us. Since it must apply all its faculties to a single kind of sensation, will it not be able to bring to this study more discernment than we do?

42. *The limits of its discernment.* Nevertheless, the statue's judgments enable it to discover very few relations. It knows only that some state is the same or different as one it already experienced, that one state is pleasant another unpleasant, or that they are so to a matter of degree.

But will it distinguish several smells that are smelled together? We ourselves acquire such discrimination only after a good deal of practice and then it is still confined within very narrow limits, for no one can recognize by the sense of smell all the odors in a sachet. Now every mixture of smells, it seems to me, must be a sachet for our statue.

It is a knowledge of odorous objects, as we shall see further on, that has taught us to recognize two smells in a third. Having smelled in turn a rose and a jonquil, we smell them together, and we thereby learn that the sensation that these combined flowers evoke is composed of two other ones. If we increase the number of odors, we will distinguish only the predominant ones, and we will not even make this discrimination if the mixture is done with enough skill that no particular smell prevails. In this case they appear to merge much like colors blended together; they are combined and mixed so well that not one of them remains unchanged; and several result in just a single one.

If our statue smells two smells at the first moment of its existence, it will not judge then that it is in two states at the same time. But suppose that having learned to recognize them separately, it smells them together, will it recognize them? That does not seem likely to me. Since it does not know that they come from two different objects, nothing can make it suspect that the sensation that it is experiencing is formed of two other ones. In fact, if neither smell predominates, even we ourselves will confound them. And if one is weaker, it will only change the strongest, and together they will seem like a simple state. To become convinced of this, we have only to smell odors that we have not made a habit of associating with different objects. I am persuaded that we would not venture to say if they are only one or if they are several. This is precisely the case of our statue.

The statue thus acquires discernment only through its simultaneous attention to a state it is experiencing, and to another it has experienced. Thus its judgment is not developed by two odors smelled at the same time; it only bears on sensations that follow one another.

3 The Desires, Passions, Love, Hate, Hope, Fear, and Will in a Man Limited to the Sense of Smell

1. *Desire is only the action of the faculties.* We have just shown how the different sorts of needs are constituted and how they are the cause of the level of activity of mental processes that seek some good whose enjoyment becomes necessary. Now desire is only the action itself of these processes directed toward something that we feel the need of.[12]

2. *What makes them strong or weak.* Every desire thus supposes that the statue has the idea of something better than its current state, and that it judges the difference between two states that follw each other. The less the difference, the less the statue suffers from the deprivation of the state it desires, and I call the emotion it experiences "discomfort" or "slight discontentment"; in this case, the actions of its mental processes, its desires, are weaker. On the other hand, if the difference is great, it suffers much more, and I call the impression that it feels "uneasiness" or even "torment"; in this case, its mental processes are livelier, its desires more intense. The measure of desire is thus the difference perceived between these two states. We need only remember how mental processes can gain or lose liveliness in order to realize all the degrees of which desires are susceptible.

3. *A passion is a dominant desire.* For example, desires are never more violent than when the statue's mental processes are focused on some good whose privation makes it all the more uneasy as it differs more from the present situation. In such a case, nothing can distract it from this object: it remembers it, it imagines it; all its mental processes are entirely occupied with it. Consequently, the more it desires it, the more accustomed it gets to

---

[12]*Logic. Preliminary lessons of the Course of Study.*

desiring it. In short, it has what we call a "passion," that is, a desire that drives out all others, or that at least is the most dominant.

4. *How one passion follows another*. This passion continues to exist as long as the good that is its object continues to seem the most pleasant, and as long as its privation is accompanied by the same disquiet. But it can be replaced by another if the statue has the opportunity to get used to a new good that it prefers.

5. *What love and hate are*. When the statue has enjoyment, suffering, need, desire, and passion, it also has love and hate. For it loves a pleasant smell that it enjoys or desires. It hates an unpleasant smell that makes it uncomfortable. Finally, it likes less a less agreeable odor that it would like to exchange for another. To be convinced of this, it is enough to consider that "to love" is synonymous with "to enjoy" or "to desire," and that "to hate" is synonymous with "to suffer from malaise, from discontent" in the presence of an object.

6. *Each can have different degrees*. As there can be several degrees in the disquiet caused by the privation of some loved object and in the discontent that the sight of an odious object brings, we must likewise distinguish degrees in both love and hate. We even have words for this usage, such as "a taste for, a liking, an inclination; an aversion, repugnance, disgust." Although we cannot substitute love and hate for these expressions, the feelings they express are nevertheless the beginnings of these passions. They differ from them only in that they are weaker in degree.

7. *The statue can only love itself*. Moreover, the only love our statue is capable of is what we call self-love. In truth, it loves only itself, since the things it loves are only its own states of being.

8. *Source of hope and fear*. Hope and fear arise from the same source as love and hate. Our statue's habit of experiencing pleasant and unpleasant sensations makes it judge that it can experience them again. If this judgment is joined to the love of a pleasing sensation, it produces hope. It it is joined to the hatred of an unpleasant sensation, it produces fear. Indeed, to hope is to anticipate the enjoyment of some good; and to fear is to see oneself threatened by some evil. We can observe that hope and fear contribute to increasing desire. It is the struggle of these two feelings that gives rise to the strongest passions.

9. *How the will develops*. The memory of having satisfied some of its desires makes the statue hope all the more to be able to satisfy others. Unacquainted with the obstacles that oppose it, it cannot see that what it desires is not within its power, as what it desired was on other occasions. In truth, it cannot be certain of it, but also it has no proof of the contrary. If it remembers that this same desire has on other occasions been followed by satisfaction, the greater its need, the more it will count on this outcome. Thus

two causes contribute to its confidence: the experience of having satisfied such a desire, and its interest in doing so again.[13] From then on it no longer confines itself to desiring, it wills. "Will" means an absolute desire such that we believe the thing desired is within our power.

---

[13] It is the same with our statue as with all men. We behave according to experience and we construct different rules of probability depending on our guiding interests. If that interest is great, the slightest degree of probability ordinarily suffices. When we are circumspect enough to act only on well-founded probabilities it is often only because we are little motivated to act.

4 The Ideas of a Man Limited to the Sense of Smell

1. *The statue has the ideas of satisfaction and dissatisfaction.* Our statue cannot be successively in several states, some pleasing to it and other displeasing, without observing that it is passing in turn through states of pleasure and pain. With the former, it is contentment or enjoyment; with the latter, it is discontent or suffering. Its memory thus preserves the ideas of satisfaction and dissatisfaction common to several states of being. And it has only to consider its sensations from these two points of view to sort them into two classes in which it will learn to distinguish various nuances as it gains further practice with them.

2. *These ideas are abstract and general.* To abstract is to separate one idea from another with which it appears naturally united. Now in considering that the ideas of satisfaction and dissatisfaction are common to several of its states, the statue acquires the habit of separating them from any particular state which at first it did not distinguish. It thus forms abstract notions, and these notions become general because they are common to several of its states.

3. *An odor is only a particular idea for the statue.* But when the statue smells several flowers of the same kind successively, it always experiences the same state, and it will have only one particular idea about this object. The smell of violets, for example, cannot be an abstract idea for it, common to several flowers, since it does not know that violets exist. It is thus only the particular idea of its own state. Consequently, all its abstractions are limited to more or less pleasant states and to others that are more or less unpleasant.

4. *How pleasure in general becomes the object of its will.* As long as the statue had only particular ideas, it could only desire one or another particular

state. But as soon as it has abstract notions, its desires, love, hate, hope, fear and will can have pleasure or pain in general as their object.

This love of the good in general occurs, however, only when the statue does not yet distinguish what ought to please it the most among the many ideas that its memory vaguely recalls. But as soon as it thinks it has perceived it, then all its desires turn toward that one particular state of being.

5. *It has ideas of number.* Since the statue distinguishes the states it passes through, it has some idea of number. It has the idea of unity each time it experiences a sensation or remembers one, and it has the ideas of two and three each time its memory recalls two or three distinct states. For it then takes note of itself as one odor or having been two or three in succession.

6. *Owing to memory.* It cannot distinguish two smells that it smells at the same time. The sense of smell by itself can thus give it only the idea of unity, and it owes the ideas of numbers to memory exclusively.

7. *How far it can extend them.* But it does not extend its knowledge of numbers very far. Just like a child who has not learned to count, it cannot determine the number of its ideas when the succession becomes somewhat long.

It seems to me that to discover the greatest number of ideas the statue is capable of knowing distinctly, we need only consider how far we ourselves could count with the sign "one." When the collections formed by the repetition of this word cannot be grasped distinctly all at the same time, we would be right to conclude that the precise ideas of the numbers included in them cannot be acquired by memory alone.

Now in saying "one and one," I have the idea of two. And in saying "one, one, and one," I have the idea of three. But if to express ten, fifteen, twenty, I had only the repetition of this sign, I could never fix the ideas of these higher numbers. For I could not be sure by memory that I had repeated "one" as many times as each of these numbers requires. It even seems to me that I could not reach the idea of four by this means. And I need some contrivance to be sure I did not repeat the sign of unity either too often or not often enough. I say, for example, "one, one," and then "one, one." But that alone proves that memory does not distinctly grasp four units at once. Beyond three, then, it presents only an indefinite multitude. Those who believe that memory alone can extend out ideas further will substitute another number for that of three. It is enough for my argument to agree that there is a number beyond which memory does not allow us to perceive more than an indefinitely vague multitude. It is the art of using signs that has taught us how to exceed that limit. But however great the numbers we can distinguish, there always remains a multitide that is it not possible to specify, and which for this reason we call "infinite," and that we should more accurately call "indefinite." This change of name alone would have prevented errors.[14]

We may thus conclude that our statue apprehends distinctly only up to three of these states. Beyond that, it will see a multitude of them that will be for it what the so-called notion of the infinite is for us. It will even be much more excusable for it to make a mistake, for it is incapable of reflections that could save it from error. It will thus perceive the infinite in this multitude as if it were really there.

Finally, we observe that the statue's idea of unity is abstract, for it perceives all of its states in this general way, each distinguished from every other.

8. *It knows two kinds of truths.* As it has both particular and general ideas, it knows two sorts of truths.

Particular truths. The smells of each kind of flower are for it only particular ideas. Therefore it will be the same way for all the truths that it apprehends when it distinguishes one smell from another.

General truths. But it has abstract notions of pleasant and unpleasant states. It will thus know general truths on this topic. It knows that in general its states differ from each other and that they are more or less pleasing or displeasing.

But this general knowledge presupposes particular knowledge in it, since the particular ideas preceded the abstract notions.

9. *It has some idea of the possible.* Since the statue is in the habit of being, ceasing to be, and becoming again the same smell, it will judge that when it is not this smell, it can become it, and when it is this smell, that it can cease to be it. It will thus have occasion to consider its states as capable of existing or not existing. But this notion of the possible will not bring with it the knowledge of the causes that can produce an effect. On the contrary, it supposes ignorance of causes, since it is founded on a judgment of what is habitual. When the statue thinks, for example, that it can cease to be the smell of a rose and become again the smell of a violet, it does not know that some external being is the sole cause of its sensations. For to make it err in its judgment, it is enough for us to make it continually smell the same smell. It is true that its imagination can sometimes come to its aid, but this will only happen when its desires are violent, and even then it will not always succeed.

10. *Even perhaps of the impossible.* Perhaps by following its judgments of what habitually happens, the statue could also form some idea of the impossible. Accustomed to losing one state as soon as it has acquired a new one, it is impossible according to its way of conceiving for it to have two states at a time. The only case where it would believe the opposite would be that in which its imagination acts forcefully enough to recall two sensations

---

[14]Principally, the error of believing that we have a positive idea of the infinite, whence much bad reasoning by metaphysicians and sometimes even by geometers.

with the same vividness as if it were actually experiencing them. But that is scarcely likely to happen. It is natural for its imagination to conform to the habits it has acquired. Thus having experienced its states one after the other, it will imagine them in that order. In addition, its memory will probably not be powerful enough to recreate two sensations that the statue has had and no longer has.

But what seems to me more probable is that its habit of judging that what has happened to it can happen again includes the idea of the possible. It is very difficult, however, for it to have occasion to form judgments in which we can discover our idea of the impossible. For that it would have to concern itself with what is has not yet experienced. But it is far more natural to suppose it is completely occupied with what it is experiencing.

11.   *It has the idea of a past duration.* The statue's ability to discriminate different smells gives rise to an idea of succession. For it cannot feel that it has ceased to be what it was without representing in this change a duration of two instants.

As the statue takes in only up to three smells distinctly, it will also differentiate only three instants in its duration. Beyond three it will perceive only an indefinite succession.

If we suppose that its memory can distinctly recall up to four, five, six states, it will consequently distinguish four, five, or six instants in its duration. Each of us can state hypotheses on this topic that he thinks appropriate and substitute them for those that I thought preferable.

12.   *Of future duration.* The transition from one smell to another gives our statue only the idea of the past. To have an idea of the future, it must have had several repetitions of the same series of sensations and it must have formed the habit of judging that after one state another must follow.

Take for example the series: jonquil, rose and violet. When these smells are constantly connected in this order, one of them cannot affect its sense organ without memory immediately calling the others to mind in their relations with the smell experienced. Thus on the occasion of the smell of violet, the other two are recalled as having come before it, and the statue conceives of past duration; likewise, on the occasion of the smell of the jonquil, those of the rose and violet will be recalled as yet to follow, and it will conceive of future duration.

13.   *Of indefinite duration.* The smells of jonquil, rose and violet can thus mark off the three instants that the statue apprehends distinctly. For the same reason, the odors that come before and those that typically follow will mark off the instants that it perceives vaguely in the past and future. Thus, when the statue smells a rose, its memory will distinctly recall the smells of jonquil and violet, and will portray an indefinite duration that came before the instant in which it smelled the jonquil, and one that must follow the instant in which it will smell the violet.

14. *This duration is an eternity for the statue.* Perceiving this duration as indefinite, the statue can distinguish neither its beginning nor its end; it cannot even suspect the existence of either. Thus for the statue this duration is an absolute eternity that seems as if it had always been and ought never to stop being.

In fact, it is not reflection about the seccession of our ideas that teaches us that we had a beginning and will have an end, but the attention we give to beings of our own species whom we see born and die. A man who was aware only of his own existence would have no idea of death.

15. *It has two successions in itself.* The idea of duration first produced by the succession of impressions made on the sense organ is preserved or reproduced by the succession of sensations that memory recalls. Thus, even when odorous bodies no longer affect our statue, it continues to have ideas of the present, past, and future: the present through its present state; the past through its memory of what it was; the future, because it judges that, having had the same sensations several times over, it can have them again.

Thus it has two successions: that of impressions made on its sense organ, and that of sensations recalled in memory.

16. *One of these successions measures the moments of the other.* Several impressions may succeed each other in the sense organ, while the memory of one and the same sensation is present in memory. And several sensations can be recalled successively in memory while one and the same impression is being felt in the sense organ. In the first case, the sequence of impressions made on the sense of smell measures the duration of the memory of a sensation. In the second case, the sequence of sensations produced by memory measures the duration of the impression received by the sense of smell.

If, for example, while the statue smells a rose, it remembers the smells of the tuberose, jonquil, and violet, it judges the duration of its sensation by the succession that occurs in its memory. And if, while it recalls the smell of a rose, I quickly present it with a series of odorous objects, it judges the duration of the recollection of this sensation by the succession occurring in its sense organ. It thus perceives that every one of its states can endure. Duration becomes a way in which the statue considers all its states in general and it forms a notion of duration in the abstract.

If while it is smelling a rose, it remembers the smells of violet, jasmine, and lavender, successively, it will perceive itself as the smell of a rose that lasts three instants; and if it recalls a series of twenty smells, it will perceive itself as having been the smell of a rose for some indefinite time. It will no longer judge that it began to be the smell of rose, but will believe that it is so for all eternity.

17. *The idea of duration is not absolute.* Thus only a succession of smells transmitted by the sense organ, or recalled by memory, can give the

statue some idea of duration. It could have known only an instant if the first odorous object had affected it uniformly for an hour, a day, or longer, or if the object's actions had varied by gradations so fine that it could never have noticed them.

The same thing will occur if, having acquired the idea of duration, the statue sustains a sensation without using its memory, without successively recalling some of the states it passed through. For how then would it distinguish instants? And if the statue does not distinguish instants, how could it perceive duration?

The idea of duration is thus not absolute, and when we say that time passes quickly or slowly, that means only that the revolutions serving to measure time occur more quickly or slowly than our ideas succeed each other. We can convince ourselves of this by a supposition.

18.   *Supposition that makes it clear.* If we imagine a world made up of as many parts as our own that was no bigger than a hazelnut, it is beyond doubt that the stars would rise and set there thousands of times in one of our hours and that, constituted as we are, we could not follow their movements. The organs of the intelligent beings destined to inhabit that world would have to be matched to such swift revolutions.[15]

Thus, while the earth of this little world is turning on its axis, and revolving around its sun, its inhabitants will be receiving as many ideas as we do during the time that our earth makes similar revolutions. Therefore, it is obvious that their days and years will seem as long to them as ours do to us.

In supposing another world to which ours would be as inferior as it is superior to that one that I have just imagined, we would have to give its inhabitants sense organs whose actions would be too slow to allow them to perceive the revolutions of our stars. They would stand in relation to our world as we stand in relation to the one no bigger than a hazelnut. They could not distinguish any succession of movement.

Let us then ask the inhabitants of these worlds what their durations are. Those of the smaller one would reckon millions of centuries, and those of the larger ones, with their eyes barely yet open, would reply that they had just been born.

The notion of duration is thus entirely relative. Each person judges it only by the succession of his ideas, and probably at a given time no two men count an equal number of instants. For there is reason to presume that there are no two men whose memories always recall ideas with the same speed.

Consequently, a sensation uniformly sustained for a year, or a thousand if you wish, will be only an instant for our statue; just as an idea that we preserve while the inhabitants of the small world were counting centuries, is

---

[15]Malebranche makes a like supposition to show that we judge the size of bodies only by the relations that exist between them and us. *Recherche de la Vérité*, book 1, Ch. 6.

an instant to us.[16] It is thus a mistakle to think that all beings count the same number of instants. Since the presence of one unchanging idea is only an instant for me, it follows that one instant in my duration can coexist with several instants in the duration of someone else.

---

[16]The hypothesis of these worlds makes it clear that to imagine some older than others we do not need a successive eternity in which some were created sooner or later; it is sufficient to vary the number of revolutions in each world and to match the sense organs of the inhabitants.

This supposition leads us further to realize that an instant in the duration of one being can coexist, and coexist in fact with several instants in the duration of another. We can then imagine intelligent beings who perceived all at once ideas that we have only successively, and make our way as it were up to a mind that in an instant embraces all the knowledge that creatures have only in a series of centuries and that consequently undergoes no succession. It would be as if it were in the center of all these worlds where duration is judged so differently, and, capturing in a glimpse all that is happening to them, it would see all at once the past, the present, and the future.

In this way we elaborate, as far as it is within our power, the idea of an indivisible and permanent instant with which the instants of creatures coexist and in which they succeed one another. I say "as far as it is within our power," for here we have only the idea of comparison. Neither we nor any other creature can have a perfect notion of eternity. God alone knows it, for he alone experiences it.

5 Of the Sleep and Dreams of a Man Limited to the Sense of Smell

1. *How the action of the faculties is slowed down.* Our statue can be reduced to being only the memory of a smell, and then the sense of its own existence seems to elude it. It feels less that it exists than that it has existed and to the degree that its memory recalls ideas less vividly, this remnant of feeling is still further weakened. Like a light that is gradually extinguished, it ceases completely when this faculty falls into complete inaction.

2. *State of sleep.* Now our own experience teaches us that exercise must finally tire out our statue's imagination and memory. Let us consider then these faculties in repose, with no sensation exciting them. This will be the state of sleep.

3. *State of dreaming.* If their repose is such that the faculties are completely inactive, we can notice nothing other than the deepest possible sleep. If, on the other hand, memory and imagination still continue to act, it will only be on a part of the acquired ideas. Several links of the chain will thus be broken and the order of ideas in sleep will not be the same as in waking. Pleasure will no longer be the only cause controlling imagination. This faculty will evoke only the ideas it still has power over, and it will contribute as often to the unhappiness of our statue as to its happiness.

4. *How it differs from waking.* This is the state of dreaming. It differs from that of waking only in that ideas are not preserved in the same order, and that pleasure is not always the law that controls the imagination. Every dream thus supposes some intercepted ideas that mental processes can no longer act on.

5. *The statue could not distinguish them.* Since our statue does not know the difference between imagining vividly and having sensations, it cannot distinguish between dreaming and waking. Everything it experiences while asleep is thus as real for it as what it experienced before it went to sleep.

6 Of the Self, or the Personality of a Man Limited to the Sense of Smell

1. *Of the personality of the statue*. As our statue is capable of memory, it is never one smell without recalling that it was once another smell. This is its personality. If it could say "I," it would say it every instant of its duration, and each time its "I" would include every moment it remembered.

2. *It cannot say "I" in the first moment of its existence*. In truth, it would not say "I" at the first smell. What we understand by this word seems to me suited only for a being who notices that at the present moment he no longer is what he was. As long as this being does not change, he exists without any reflection on himself. But as soon as he changes, he judges that he is one and the same being as he previously was in another state, and he says "I."

This observation makes it clear that at the first moment of its existence, the statue is not able to form desires, for before being able to say "I desire," it must have said "me" or "I."

3. *Its "I" is at the same time an awareness of what it is and the memory of what it was*. The smells the statue does not remember thus do not enter into its idea of its person. As foreign to its "I" as the colors and sounds that the statue has no knowledge of, they are for it as if it had never smelled them. Its "I" is only the collection of sensations it experiences, and of those that its

memory recalls.[17] In short, it is at once the consciousness of what it is and the memory of what it was.

---

[17]"Does the man who loves a lady for her beauty," said Pascal (c. 24, n. 14), "truly love her? No; for smallpox which will take away her beauty without killing her will lead him to love her no longer. And if I am loved for my judgment or my memory, am I truly loved? No; for I can lose these qualities without ceasing to exist. Where then is the 'I' if it is neither in my body nor in my mind? And how else shall we love the body and the mind if not for those qualities that do not constitute the 'I' at all, since they may perish? Should we then love the mind of a person abstractly with such qualities as it might possess? This is impossible and unreasonable. Thus, we never love a person but only qualities. When we say we love a person we must mean that we love the collection of qualities that make up the person."

But it is not the collection of qualities that make the person, for then the same man, young or old, beautiful or ugly, wise or foolish, would be as many different people. Whatever the qualities for which you love me, it is always me you love, for the qualities are only me modified differently. If someone treading on my toe were to say to me "I have not hurt *you* for you could lose your toe and still be you," should I be convinced that I was not hurt? Why then should I think that, because I can lose my memory and my judgment, I am not loved if I am loved for these qualities? So what if they are perishable? Is the *me* a necessity of one's nature? Does it not perish in animals? And is not man's immortality a special gift of God? In Pascal's meaning, God alone can say "I."

7 Conclusion of the Preceding Chapters

1. *With only one sense the mind has the basis of all its faculties.* Having proven that our statue is capable of attending, remembering, comparing, judging, and imagining; that it has abstract notions, ideas of number and duration; that it knows general and particular truths; that it forms desires, expresses passions and loves, hates, and wills; that it is capable of hope, fear, and surprise; and that finally, it acquires habits, we must conlcude that with one sense alone, the mind has as many faculties as with the five of them combined. We shall see that those faculties that seem to us special are only the same faculties we have considered already applied to a greater number of objects and accordingly further developed.

2. *Sensation contains all mental faculties.* If we bear in mind that remembering, comparing, judging, discerning, imagining, being surprised, having abstract ideas and ideas of number and duration, and knowing general and particular truths are only different modes of attending; that having passions, loving, hating, hoping, fearing, and willing are only different modes of desiring; and finally, that to attend and to desire are originally to have sensations, we shall conclude that sensation contains all mental processes.

3. *Pleasure and pain are the sole motives.* Finally, if we bear in mind that there are no absolutely indifferent sensations, we shall further conclude that the different degrees of pleasure and pain are the law by which the germ of everything we are develops in order to produce all our mental process.

This principle can take the names of need, surprise, and others, that we will give it further on. Yet the principle is always the same, for we are always moved by pleasure or pain in everything that need or surprise can made us do.

In fact, our first ideas are only pain or pleasure. Soon others follow and give rise to comparisons from which our first needs and desires arise. Our attempts to satisfy them give us other ideas that produce further new desires. The surprise that contributes to making us feel keenly whatever out of the ordinary happens to us occasionally increases the activity of our mental processes. A chain develops whose links are in turn ideas and desires. We have only to follow this chain to discover the progress of all human knowledge.

4. *What has just been said of smell applies to the other senses.* Almost everything I have said about mental processes in discussing smell I could have said beginning with any of the other senses. It is easy to make the extension. All that remains for me is to examine what is peculiar to each of the other senses.

8 Of a Man Limited to the Sense of Hearing

1. *The statue limited to hearing is what is hears*. Let us limit our statue to the sense of hearing, and reason the way we did when it had only the sense of smell.

When its ear is struck, the statue becomes the sensation that it experiences. It is like the echo of which Ovid says: *sonus est qui vivit in illa*; it is the sound that lives in it. Thus at will we transform the statue into a noise, a sound or a symphony, for it does not suspect that anything other than itself exists. Hearing does not give it the idea of an object located at a certain distance. The proximity of distance of sonorous bodies produces only a stronger or weaker sound for it, and the statue feels its own existence only more or less.

2. *Two kinds of auditory sensation*. The ear yields two sorts of sensation: one is sound, the other is noise.[1]

The ear is organized to grasp a definite relation between one sound and another. But it can grasp only a vague relation between one noise and another. Noise is to the sense of hearing rather like what a multitude of smells is to the sense of smell.

3. *The statue distinguishes several noises only if they follow one another*. If at the first instant our statue hears several noises all together, the loudest one will envelop the weakest, and they will mix so thoroughly that the

---

[1] It has been noticed in the resonance of sonorous bodies, that when a dominant is struck, two other notes are heard which have a definite relation to the dominant and are calculable. These are called the harmonics of the dominant. They are the twelfth and the seventeenth above the dominant and from them we get the third and the fifth. A healthy ear is able to discern these sounds and that is why we say that it measures sounds. Sound in the strict meaning may be defined as measurable sound.

consequence for the statue will be only a simple state in which they are confounded.

If the noises follow each other, however, the statue retains the memory of its past. If the series was heard repeatedly it distinguishes its different states, compares them, judges them, and forms a sequence that its memory retains in the order in which they were compared. It will thus recognize these noises when the succeed each other again, but it will not recognize them when it hears them at the same time. We must reason on this subject as we did about smells.

4.   *The same for sounds.* As for sounds in the strict sense, since the ear is contituted to register their relations exactly, it brings a fine and more extensive discernment to bear. Its fibers seem to divide up the vibrations of sonorous bodies, and it can hear distinctly several sounds at the same time. Nevertheless, it is enough to consider that the ear does not have all this discernment in people who are not versed in music to be convinced that at least initially our statue will not distinguish two sounds that it hears together.

But will it distinguish them if it has studied them separately? This seems to me improbable. Although the mechanism of the ear is capable of distinguishing the difference between them, the sounds are so analogous that there is reason to presume that the statue will continue to get them confused since it is not aided by judgments that accustom it to relating them to different objects.

5.   *It acquires the same faculties as with smell.* Be this as it may, the degrees of pleasure and pain will cause the statue to acquire the same faculties it acquired by the sense of smell. But there are a few special remarks to be made on this subject.

6.   *The pleasures of hearing consist mainly in melody.* First, the pleasures of hearing consist chiefly in melody, that is, in a succession of harmonious sounds to which measure gives different characters. Our statue's desires are thus not limited to having a sound as their object, and it will hope to become an entire tune.

7.   *Melody causes an emotion that does not presuppose acquired ideas.* Second, the pleasures of the ear have a very different character from those of smell. Since sounds are more suited than smells to stirring the emotions, they

---

Noise, on the other hand, is the result of several sounds with no common harmonics. It is a multitude of dominant and harmonic sounds in confusion. We can define noise as inappreciable sound.

Let us imagine twelve violins playing in unison. If they play the same chord, they produce a sound together that is properly called an appreciable sound because we can distinguish the third and the fifth in it. But if we suppose them all playing discordant notes, they will only be making a noise because the total sound they emit has no harmonics. The same *me* and the same *so* which are the harmonics of the *do* of one of these violins are not the harmonics of the *do* that the others emit. It is then the confusion of many sounds that yields noise.

will, for example, give our statue that sadness or joy, independent of acquired ideas, that arises solely from certain bodily changes.[19]

8. *These pleasures are, like those of smell, susceptible of different degrees.* Third, these pleasures like those of smell begin with the slightest sensation. The first noise, however weak it may be, is thus a pleasure for our statue. Let the noise increase, and the pleasure will also increase and will stop only when the vibrations hurt the eardrum.

9. *The keenest require a trained ear.* As for music, it will give the statue greater pleasure the more it is suited to its ear's lack of training. At first simple and crude songs will be capable of delighting it. If we then accustom it by degrees to more complex songs, the ear will acquire the habit of the exertions they demand, and the statue will learn new pleasures.

10. *And above all, a healthy ear.* Moreover, this progression is only for healthy ears. If the nerve fibers do not have certain relations, the ear will be out of tune, like a badly strung instrument. The greater this defect, the less sensitive the ear will be to music; it can even be as indiscriminate as with noise.

11. *The statue can come to distinguish a noise and song heard together.* Fourth, since the pleasure of a succession of sounds is so superior to that of a continuous noise, we have reason to conjecture that if the statue simultaneously hears a noise and a melody, neither of which is dominant and each of which it has learned to recognize separately, it will not confuse them.

If, at the first moment of its existence, it had heard them together, it would not have distinguished between them. For we know from our own experience that we distinguish among sensory impressions only what we could have noticed and that we notice only ideas that we have successively attended to. But if our statue has been in turn a song and the noise of a brook, and has made a habit of distinguishing these two states and of dividing its attention between them, they are, it seems to me, too unalike ever to be confused further every time it experiences them together, especially if, as I suppose, neither of them is dominant. The statue thus cannot help noticing that it is at the same time the noise and the song that it remembers as two states that had succeeded each other.

My basic principle here will become clearer in the rest of this work because I will have occasion to apply it to even more obvious examples. We shall see how, as a result of the way we judge our sensations, we can distinguish only what circumstances have taught us to notice: that all the rest is confused and

---

[19]We find in music the pleasures of imitation when it imitates the song of birds, thunder, storms, sighs, lamentations and cries of joy; and when, by its measure, it invites our bodies to take the positions and movements of the various passions. Our statue is not made for these sorts of pleasures because they suppose judgments and habits that it is not capable of. But independent of this imitation, music transmits to the brain impressions that spread throughout the body and produce emotions in which our statue will surely find pleasure and pain.

that we do not retain any ideas except insofar as we have had some experience of them. This is one of the causes that make people experiencing the same sensations have such different knowledge. This potential is the same everywhere, but it remains undeveloped in some of them, while in others it develops, is nourished and grows.

12. *A succession of sounds is more easily united in memory than a succession of noises.* Finally, since noises are to the ear what smells are to the nose, their connection in memory will be the same as that of smells. But as sounds are much more closely connected by their nature and that of the sense organ, memory will preserve their succession more easily.

9 Of the Senses of Smell and Hearing United

1. *These two senses together give no idea of anything external.* Since these senses taken separately do not give our statue the idea of anything external, they will not do so any the more when they are united. It will not suspect that it has two different sense organs.

2. *At first the statue does not distinguish sounds and odors that come together.* Even if at the first moment of its existence it heard sounds and smelled smells, it could not yet distinguish two states in itself. The sounds and smells will be confounded as if they were only one simple state. For we have already observed that it distinguishes in its sensations only those ideas that it has had occasion to take note of individually.

3. *It learns to distinguish sounds from odors.* But if it has considered sounds separately from smells, it will be capable of distinguishing them when it experiences them together, for provided that the enjoyment of the one does not completely distract it from enjoying the other, it will recognize that it is simultaneously what it formerly was successively. The nature of these sensations does not lead to their confusion, as with two odors: they differ too much not to be distinguished from the memory that remains of each one. Thus the statue owes to memory the benefit of distinguishing the impressions simultaneously transmitted to it by different sense organs.

4. *It will seem to acquire a double existence.* Then it has the impression that its being enlarges and that it acquires a double existence. This is a major change in its habitual judgment. For before the union of hearing and smell, it had not imagined that it could be in two such different states at the same time.

5. *Its memory is more extensive than with a single sense.* It is obvious that the statue will acquire the same faculties as when it had these two senses separately. Its memory will increase because its chain of ideas will be more

varied and extensive. Sometimes a sound will remind it of a series of smells, sometimes a smell will remind it of a series of sounds. But we must observe that these two kinds of sensations united, are subject to the same law as before their union; that is, the most vivid ones can sometimes cause the others to be forgotten and prevent them from being noticed even at the moment that they occur.

6. *It has more numerous abstract ideas.* It further seems to me that the statue can have more ideas that are abstract than with a single sense. In general it knew only two states, one pleasant, the other unpleasant; but now that it distinguishes sounds from smells, it cannot help thinking of them as two different states. Perhaps also noise will seem to it so different from harmonious sounds that if we could make it understand that its sensations were transmitted to it by different sense organs, it could very will imagine that it had three senses: one for smells, another for noise, and a third for harmonious sounds.

10 Of Taste Alone and of Taste Joined to the Senses of Smell and Hearing

1. *The statue acquires the same faculties as with smell.* Having given sentience only to the inside of our statue's mouth, I cannot lead it to take nourishment. But I suppose that the air brings it, at my pleasure, all sorts of tastes, and serves to nourish it whenever I judge it necessary.

The statue will acquire the same mental processes as with hearing and smell; and because its mouth is to tastes what the nose is to smells and the ears to noise, several tastes combined will seem to it like a single one, and it will distinguish among them only insofar as they are successive.

2. *Taste contributes more to its happiness and unhappiness than smell or hearing.* Taste can usually contribute more than smell to its happiness or unhappiness, for flavors commonly move us more than odors do. It even contributes more than harmonious sounds do because the need for nourishment makes tastes more necessary, and consequently makes the statue taste more eagerly. Hunger can make it unhappy, but as soon as it has noticed sensations suited to satisfying it, it will turn its attention more toward them, will desire them more avidly, and will enjoy them with more delight.

3. *Its discriminations among its sensations.* If we combine taste with hearing and smell, the statue will begin to distinguish sensations transmitted to it at the same time, because it has learned to recognize them separately, provided that its attention is fairly evenly divided among them. Thus, its existence is, as it were, tripled.

It is true that it will not always be as easy for it to differentiate between a flavor and a smell as between a flavor and a sound. The senses of smell and taste are so similar that their sensations must sometimes be confused.[20]

---

[20]Everyone has noticed that he sometimes attributes to a dish he is eating the odors that strike

4. *Taste can be detrimental to the other senses*. As we have just seen that tastes must interest the statue more than any other sensation, the greater its hunger, the more it will be interested in them. Taste can thus be a hindrance to the other senses to the point of making the statue insensitive to smells and harmony.

5. *Advantages resulting from the union of these senses*. The combination of these senses will extend and give greater variety to the statue's chain of ideas, increase the number of its desires, and make it acquire new habits.

6. *A doubt concerning their effects*. It is, however, very difficult to determine how far the statue can distinguish the states that it owes to the different senses. Perhaps its discernment is less extensive than I have imagined[21], perhaps more so. To judge this matter, it would be necessary to put oneself entirely in its place, and to rid oneself entirely of all habits. But I do not flatter myself that I have always succeeded in doing so.

The habit of referring each kind of sensation to a particular sense organ must contribute a lot to our differentiating among them: without it, perhaps our sensations would be chaotic. In this case the statue's discernment would be very limited.

But it must be observed that the uncertainty or even the falsity of some of our conjectures could not invalidate the basis of this work. When I observe the statue, it is less to determine what is taking place in it than to discover what is taking place in us. I may be wrong in attributing to it mental processes that it is not yet capable of, but such mistakes are of little consequence if they put the reader in a position to observe how these processes take place in himself.

---

his sense of smell. What gives further proof of this relation is that people have a more refined sense of taste the more they have a refined sense of smell.

[21]This was Mlle. Ferrand's opinion.

11 Of a Man Limited to the Sense of Sight

1. *A prejudice and countervailing considerations.* No doubt it will seem extraordinary to many readers when I say that the eye is incapable by itself of seeing external space. We have such a strongly ingrained habit of judging surrounding objects by sight, that we find it hard to imagine how it could have been otherwise when our eyes first opened to the light.

Reason has very little force, and its progress is very slow when it has to remove errors to which we are all prone, errors that began with the initial development of our senses, and whose roots are buried in a time long forgotten. At first, we think we have always seen as we now do, that all our ideas are born with us, and that our first years are like that fabulous age of the poets in which the gods supposedly gave man all the knowledge that he does not remember acquiring by himself.

If a philosopher suspects that all our knowledge can very well have originated with the senses, the great minds at once cry out against an opinion that seems so strange to them. What is the color of thought, he would be asked, that it comes the mind through sight? What is its taste or its smell, and so on, for it to be due to taste, smell, etc.? Finally, he is overwhelmed with a thousand difficulties of this kind advanced with all the assurance arising from a generally accepted preconception. The philosopher who spoke quickly before having worked out the origin of all our ideas is hard pressed. And it is thought that doubtlessly this is a proof of the falsity of his opinion.

Philosophy takes a new step: it discovers that our sensations are not the properties themselves of objects and that, on the contrary, they are only modifications of our mind. It examines each sensation in particular, and as it finds few difficulties in this investigation, it hardly seems to have made a discovery.

From this it was easy to conclude that we perceive nothing except what is in ourselves and that, consequently, a man limited to the sense of smell would have been only a smell; limited to taste, a flavor; to hearing, a noise or a sound; to sight, light and color. Then the most difficut thing would have been to imagine how we acquire the habit of referring our sensations to the external world. In fact, it seems very surprising that with the senses, which experience only what is in themselves and which have no means of suspecting an external space, we could refer these sensations to objects that occasion them. How can sensation be extended beyond the organ that experiences and limits it?

But by considering the properties of touch, we would have recognized that it is capable of discovering this space and of teaching the other senses to refer their sensations to surrounding objects. Then even those persons whose biases kept them furthest from this truth would have begun to entertain at least some doubt. We would have agreed that with the senses of smell or taste we would have thought ourselves only a smell or a flavor. Hearing would have provided a bit more difficulty, because of our habit of hearing sound as if it were outside us. But this sense has so much difficulty in judging distances and locations, and it is so often mistaken, that we would finally have agreed that it judges nothing by itself. We would have regarded it like a pupil that had forgotten the lessons of touch.

But how could sight have learned from touch, sight which judges distances that touch cannot reach; that encompass in an instant objects that touch skims only slowly or can never grasp all together?

Analogy might have led us to assume that sight must be like the other senses: the sensation, the impression of light, is entirely in the eyes, we could speculate that they must see only in themselves, as long as they have not learned to refer their sensations to objects. In fact, if they saw only according to their sensations, could they suspect that there is external space, and in it objects that act on them?

We might then have assumed that by themselves the eyes have knowledge only of light and color, and having explained all phenomena according to this hypothesis, having explained how with the help of touch they come to judge objects in space, we would only have lacked experiments to remove all our prejudices.

We must credit M. Molyneux with being the first to make conjectures on this subject. He communicated his thought to a philosopher; that was the only means of gaining a spokesman. Locke agreed with him that someone born blind whose eyes were later opened to the light would not distinguish a globe from a cube. This conjecture has since been confirmed by Cheselden's experiments, to which it gave rise. It seems to me that we can now sort out with some precision what is due to the eyes themselves and what they owe to the sense of touch.

2. *The statue perceives colors only as states.* Thus I believe I am justified in saying that our statue sees only light and colors, and that it cannot judge that there is anything outside itself.

That being the case, it perceives in the action of light rays only its own states. The statue is with this sense as it was with those whose effects we have already examined, and it acquires the same mental processes.

3. *At first, it sees them indistinctly.* If from the first instant it perceives several colors equally, it seems to me that it cannot yet notice any one of them in particular. Its attention is too much divided up and embraces them all confusedly. Let us see how it learns to distiguish them.

4. *How it then distinguishes them one after another.* Of all the senses the eye is the one whose mechanism we know best. Several experiments have taught us how to follow the light rays as far as the retina, and we know that there they make the distinct impressions. Admittedly, we do not know how these impressions are transmitted to the mind by the optic nerve. But it seems beyond doubt that they reach it without confusion, for would the author of nature have taken the precaution of separating them so carefully on the retina only to allow them to get confused slightly further along? And if that did happen, how would the mind ever learn to distinguish them?

Thus colors are by their nature sensations that tend to be distinguished. Here is how I imagine our statue comes to notice a certain number of them.

Among the colors that suffuse its eyes at the first instant and that project onto the retina, there may be one that the statue singles out, one that it sees as apart: the color will be one on which pleasure fixes its attention with a certain intensity. If the statue did not notice it more than the others, it still would not distinguish it. Thus, we would discern nothing in a landscape in which we try to see everything equally well at one and the same time.

If the statue could attend with the same intensity to two colors together, it would notice them with the same ease as one alone; if it could consider three in this way, it would notice them equally well. But it does not seem to me that it is yet able to do this. The pleasure of considering them one after another must prepare it for the pleasure of considering several at the same time.

The statue probably stands in the same relation to two or three colors presented along with many others as we ourselves stand in relation to a somewhat complex picture whose subject is unfamiliar. At first we perceive its details indistinctly. Then our eyes fix on one form, then on another, and only after we had observed them successively do we come to judge them as a whole.

The confusion in the first glimpse is not the effect of an absolute, determinate number of objects, so that what is indistinct for me must be so for everyone else. It is the result of too great a multitude of objects in relation to the limited training of my eyes. Both the painter and I see all the parts of a picture; but while he distinguishes them quickly, I discover them with so much difficulty that it seems to me that, at each instant, I see something I have not seen before.

Thus it is that in this picture there are more things that are distinct to his eyes and fewer to mine. Among all the colors our statue sees at the first instant, it will probably notice only one, since its eyes have not yet been trained.

Thus, while other colors project distinctly on its retina and consequently it sees them, they are as confused for it as if they were mixed together in fact.

As long as it is totally concerned with the color that it notices, it thus has no real knowledge of other colors.

Its eyes become tired, however, either because this color is intense, or because it takes some effort to keep gazing at the same color. Thus they shift automatically. They change position again if by chance they are struck by a color that is too intense to be pleasing; and they come to rest only when they hit on a color that is more pleasant, because it is restful.

After a time they become tired again and pass on to a less intense color. Thus they gradually come to get their greatest pleasure from seeing only black. Finally, the weariness can be carried to such a point that they will close and completely shut out the light.

If our statue, having distinguished colors in this successive order, could never notice several colors simultaneously, it would be precisely the same with the sight as it was with the sense of smell. For although hitherto it has always seen several colors together, all those it has not noticed are for it as if it had never seen them. It can take no account of any of them. But it seems to me that it must learn to distinguish several at a time.

5. *How it distinguishes several at once.* Red, I suppose, is the first color to strike it most, and the first it notices. When its eyes become tired, they change position and encounter another color, yellow, for example. It enjoys this new state, but it does not forget the red, or the pleasure red gave it. Its attention is then divided between these two colors. If it apprehends the yellow as a state it is currently experiencing, it apprehends red as a state that it has experienced in the past.

But red cannot attract its attention and continue to appear to it only as a state that no longer exists if the sensation of red is, as I suppose, as present as that of yellow. After remembering that it was red and yellow in succession, the statue then notices that it is both red and yellow at the same time.

Let its eyes tire and turn to a third color, green, for example. Its attention, fixed on this state, abandons the first two. It is not preempted, however, to the point that the statue completely forgets what it was. It still perceives red and yellow as two states that came before green.

This memory gains its attention to the degree that the sense organ fixed on green becomes tired. Little by little it comes to occupy as large a place in attention as the color currently observed. Thus the statue distinguishes that it was red and yellow with the same force as it distinguishes that it is green. Henceforth, it notices that it is all three colors at the same time. And how would it constrain itself to considering two of them as past when all three sensations are in its eyes concurrently and distinctly?

It is then with the help of memory that the eye comes to notice up to two or three colors presented together. If when it perceives the second one, the first were totally forgotten, it would never come to judge that it is in two states at the same time. But when the memory of the final state stays with it, attention is divided between the two; and as soon as it has noticed that it was in two states successively, it judges that it is in two at the same time.

6. *Limits of its color discrimination.* As we have taught it to know three colors in succession, we can teach it to know a greater number of them. But in all this succession it will never apprehend more than three of them distinctly; for our statue's ideas about number are no more extensive than they were with the sense of smell.

If we then present it with all these colors together, it will distinguish equally only three at a time, and it cannot determine how many others there are. Having shown that the eye requires memory to distinguish them, it is beyond all doubt that the eye will distinguish no more than memory itself does.

7. *It has with sight another means of obtaining what it desires.* Casting its gaze from one color to another, our statue does not always experience the state it remembers as having been the most pleasant. Since its imagination is at work to portray vividly the object of its desire, it cannot fail to act on the statue's eyes. Then it leads them unwittingly to scan several colors until they encounter the one they are looking for. Consequently, the statue has with sight one more means than with the preceding senses of obtaining the enjoyment of what it desires. It can even be that, having first found a color as if by chance, its eyes will acquire the habit of movement needed to enable them to find it again. And that will happen, provided that the objects in view do not change their locations.

8. *How it feels itself extended.* A sensation of sound cannot convey extension to the mind that experiences it because a sound is not extended. It is not the same with a sensation of color, which does convey extension to the mind experiencing it because color is itself extended. This is a fact that we cannot call into question. Observation proves it. Thus it is impossible to conceive a color without extension, as it is impossible to conceive of a sound that is extended.

Since every color is extended, several contiguous colors necessarily form a continuum of several parts that are extended and distinct from each other.

This phenomenon is a colored surface. This at least is how we ourselves perceive it.

When our statue judges that it is several colors at the same time, it would therefore sense itself to be a colored surface.

The idea of extension presupposes the perception of several things that, being outside each other, are contiguous and consequently each extended: for unextended things cannot be contiguous. Now we cannot deny the statue this perception, for it senses that it repeats itself, outside of itself, as often as there are colors that modify its states. Insofar as it is red, it senses that it is outside green; insofar as it is green, that it is outside red, and so forth.

It thus feels itself a colored extension, but this extension has neither a surface nor a definite size.

It is not a surface because the idea of a surface presupposes the idea of a solid, an idea that it does not and cannot have.

Nor does it have a definite size, for any such size is an extended thing enclosed within circumscribing limits. Now the statue's "I" cannot feel itself circumscribed within limits. It is at the same time all the colors that modify it concurrently. And since it sees nothing beyond that, it cannot perceive itself as circumscribed. Because it is modified at the same time by several colors, and because it discovers itself in each, it senses itself as extended, and because it perceives nothing that circumscribes it, it has only a vague impression of its extension. It is an extension without limits. It seems to the statue that it endlessly repeats itself, and knowing nothing beyond the colors that it believes itself to be, to itself it is immense, everywhere, and everything.

But in its extension that seems immense to it, the different colors mutually limit each other and thus they define shapes. Now will the statue also believe that it is these shapes? Does it have ideas of shapes, as soon as it has sensations of color?

"A sensation involves a particular idea: thus when we have that sensation, we have that idea." Bad metaphysicians never fail to draw this conclusion. Nevertheless, we do not have all the ideas involved in our sensations. We have only those that we know how to notice. Thus we can see the same objects, but because we do not have the same interest in observing them, we each have very different ideas about them. You may notice what escapes me, and often when you can give an exact account of it, I am as ignorant as if I had seen nothing.

Now since light and colors are the most obvious means for the statue to know itself, for it to experience itself, it will be more inclined to consider its states as illuminated and colored than as shaped. Completely absorbed in judging colors by their distinctive shades, the statue will not think about the different ways in which we suppose them bounded.

Moreover, it is not enough for the eye to see all of a shape in order to have an idea of it; the way it is enough for it to see a color to know it. It grasps the whole of the simplest shape only when it has analyzed it, that is, when it has observed all its parts in succession. It must make a judgment about each particular part, and another judgment that combines them. It must say to itself: here is one side, here is a second, and here is a third; here is a space bounded by these three sides, and from all that, this triangle results.

Thus, just as the eyes have learned to distinguish three colors at a time only because, having considered them in succession, they observed the impression they make together, so likewise, they learn to distinguish the three sides of a triangle only insofar as, having noticed them one after another, they observe them all together, and judge the way in which they are combined. But this is a judgment the statue will have no opportunity to make.

Shapes are, we suppose, involved in the sensations that the statue experiences. But our own experience makes it sufficiently clear that we do not have all the ideas that our sensations bring with them. Our knowledge is limited solely to the ideas that we have learned to notice. Our needs are the sole cause that directs our attention to some more than others. And those that require a greater number of judgments are also those that we acquire last. Now I cannot imagine what sort of needs could lead our statue to make all the judgments necessary for it to have the idea of even the simplest shape.

What happy chance, moreover, could control the movement of its eyes to make them follow the outline of the shape? And when they do follow it, how could the statue be assured that it is not continually passing from one shape to another? By what means could the statue judge that three sides that it has seen one after another form a triangle? It is much more likely that its sight, responding only to the light, would get lost in a chaos of shapes—a scene in flux whose parts each slip away in turn.

It is true that we do not notice the judgments we make in order to grasp the whole of a circle or square. But neither do we observe those that make us see colors external to us. I shall prove, however, that this appearance is the effect of certain judgments with which habit has familiarized us. When someone shows us a very complex picture, we are aware that we study it. We perceive that we count the persons in it, review their poses and features, and make a series of judgments on all these things and that is only after all these operations that we take them all in at a single glance. Now in order to see a whole shape, our statue's eyes would be obliged to do what ours do in order to see a whole picture. We doubtless did this ourselves the first time we learned to see a square. But now the quickness with which we habitually run over the sides of a square does not allow us to perceive the sequence of our judgments. It is reasonable to think that, when our eyes were untrained, they had to act in order to see the simplest objects as they now act in order to see the most complex ones.

9. *It has no idea of location or movement.* We judge locations only because we see objects in a place where they each occupy a definite space. And we only judge movement because we see them change locations. Now the statue can observe nothing similar in the sensations that modify it. If it is by means of touch, as we shall show, that we learn to notice definite sizes or shapes in colors, it is again by touch that we learn to notice locations and movements in colors. Since the statue has only a confused and indefinite idea

of extension, without any idea of shape, place, arrangement, and movement, it feels only that it exists in many ways. If several objects change place without disappearing from view, the statue will continue to be the same colors that it was before. The only change it can experience is to be more clearly the one or the other, according to the different locations through which movement displaces various objects. When the statue is, for example, yellow, purple, and white at the same time, it will be at one moment more yellow, at another, more purple, and at a third, more white. It is all the colors it sees, but it is more particularly the color it is looking at.

12 On Sight with Smell, Hearing and Taste

1. *Effects produced by the union of these senses.* The combination of vision, smell, hearing and taste increases the number of our statue's states. Its chain of ideas becomes more extensive and varied. The objects of its attention, desires, and enjoyment are multiplied. It notices a new class of states, and seems to perceive in itself a host of different beings. But it continues to see only itself, and nothing can separate it from itself and take it outside itself.

2. *Ignorance from which the statue cannot escape.* The statue thus does not suspect that it owes its states to outside causes. It does not know that they come to it through its four senses. It sees, smells, tastes and hears without knowing that it has eyes, nose, mouth, or ears. It does not even know that it has a body. It notices only that it experiences these different kinds of sensations all together only after having studied them separately.

3. *Judgments it can make.* Supposing the statue remains the same color and we give it a succession of smells, tastes, and sounds, it will regard itself as a color that is successively odorous, savorous, and sonorous. If it were constantly the same smell, it would regard itself as a savorous, sonorous, and colored smell. And the same observation must be applied to all the suppositions of this kind. For it must find its "I" in its habitual state and it is this "I" that seems to it to be the subject of all the states to which it is susceptible.

Now when we are led to regard extension as the subject of all perceptible qualities, is it because it is in fact, their subject, or merely because, through some habit we have acquired, this idea always is everywhere the others are and always remains the same although the others change, so it appears to be modified by them without actually being so?

220

In the same way, when philosophers affirm that there is only extension, does there exist no other substance? Is it even true that extension is a substance? Or do they judge this way only because this idea is so familiar to them, and they find it everywhere? The statue would have as much reason for believing that it is only a color or smell, and that this color or smell is its being, its substance. But this is not the place to stop and discuss such systems and it is enough refutation to show that they are no better founded than the judgments that we have just attributed to our statue.

PART TWO:

ON TOUCH, OR THE ONLY
SENSE THAT JUDGES
EXTERNAL OBJECTS
ON ITS OWN

1 Of the Least Degree of Sensation to which a Man Can be Reduced Who is Limited to the Sense of Touch Alone

1. *Basic sentience of the statue*. Our statue, deprived of smell, of hearing, of taste, of vision, and limited to the sense of touch, exists first by its sensitivity to the action of the various parts of its body on each other, and above all to respiratory movements: and there you have the lowest degree of sentience to which it can be reduced. I will call this "basic sentience," because animal life begins and depends uniquely on this activity of the machine.

2. *It is subject to changes*. Exposed to the impressions of the surrounding air and to all that can provoke them, its basic sentience is subject to numerous modifications in all the parts of its body.

3. *It is the same as the "I."* Finally, we note that it can say "I" as soon as some change occurs to its basic sentience. This sentience and its "I" are therefore at the outset only one and in the same thing, and to discover what the statue is capable of with the sole aid of touch, we need only observe the different ways in which basic sentience or the "I" can be modified.

2 This Man Limited to the Lowest Degree of Sentience Has No Idea of Extension Or of Movement

1. *Existence limited to basic sentience*. If our statue is not struck by any object and if we place it in calm air of moderate temperature, where it will sense neither an increase nor a decrease in its natural warmth, it will be limited to basic sentience and it will know its own existence only by the vague impression that results from the movements to which it owes its life.

2. *This sentience gives no idea of extension*. This sentience is uniform and consequently simple with respect to the statue; it cannot detect from it the different parts of its body. It will not sense at all that some parts are exterior to others and contiguous with them. It is as if it existed only at a point and it is not yet possible for it to discover that it has extension.[22]

---

[22]We can become persuaded of this by observing what happens in ourselves. I judge that a uniform pain affecting my entire arm is extended only because I refer the pain to something that I feel to be extended. The use that I make of my arm teaches me to notice the different parts of its length; but it does not likewise teach me to notice the different parts of its diameter. Thus I am a much better judge of the length that a painful feeling occupies than I am of its volume. I know if it extends as far as the elbow or as far as the wrist; and I do not know if it affects a fourth, a third or half the thickness of the arm, or even more.

Countless experiences can confirm that we feel pain as if at a point whenever we refer it to some part of ourselves that we do not have the habit of measuring. For example, to discover the space occupied by a pain that we feel in the middle of the thigh, we must run our fingers over it. This is not true if the pain extends from the knee to the hip, because we know the separation of the latter two points.

Thus it is not a uniform feeling that gives us an idea of the extension of our body but rather it is the knowledge of the volume of our body that leads us to attribute extension to a uniform feeling.

Since our statue is reduced to the least degree of feeling, it has only a uniform feeling of its entire body: it therefore does not know that it is extended.

3. *Heightened sensation still does not convey extension*. Let us heighten this basic sentience, but let us preserve its uniformity; let us warm up the air, for example, or cool it; the statue will have throughout its body a uniform sensation of warm or of cold and I do not foresee any change other than that it will have a keener sense of its existence. For a single sensation, however vivid it may be, cannot give an idea of extension to a being that, since it does not know that it is extended itself, has not learned to give extension to this sensation by associating it with the different parts of its body.

As a result if our statue lived only by a sequence of uniform feelings, it would be as limited in its mental activity and in its knowledge as it had been with the sense of smell.

4. *Nor will a change in state.* If I strike it successively on the head and on the feet, I modify its basic sentience several times but these modifications are themselves uniform. None of them, therefore, can lead the statue to notice that it has extension. I might be asked if the statue, struck at the same time on the head and on the feet, would not sense that these modifications are distant from one another.

When I touch the statue, either the sensation that it experiences occupies it capacity for feeling so completely that it attracts its entire attention or its attention continues to be focused on the basic sentience of the other parts of its body. In the first case, our statue could not conceptualize an interval between its head and its feet, for it does not perceive at all what separates them. Nor could it in the second case, since basic sentience gives no idea of extension.

5. *The statue has no idea of movement in this state.* I move its arm and its "I" receives a new modification: will it then acquire an idea of movement? Probably not, for it does not yet know that it has an arm, nor that it can change its position. What it experiences in this moment is to feel its existence more particularly in the sensation that I give it without ever being able to comprehend what it is experiencing.

The same thing will result if I move the statue through the air. So for the statue everything comes down to an impression that modifies basic sentience completely and the statue cannot yet learn that it has a body that moves.

3 Of the Sensations that are Attributed to Touch and Nevertheless Give no Idea of Extension

1. *The statue distinguishes concurrent sensations only after noting them successively.* Let the feeling of our statue cease to be uniform, let us modify it variously throughout all the parts of its body, but at the same time and with the same intensity and it seems to me that it would not yet have any idea whatever of extension. Since these sensations come all at once, the result is a vague feeling in which the statue cannot distinguish them because it has not yet recognized them one after the other so it has not learned to recognize several of them together.

But if the heat and the cold are felt successively, the statue will distinguish them and preserve an idea of each of these sensations. If the statue subsequently experiences them together, it would compare its current impression with the ideas that memory calls to mind and it would recognize that it is in two different states concurrently.

We can likewise give it ideas of various other kinds of pleasure and of pain: for as it learns to notice sensations that succeed one another, it will become accustomed to notice them when they come several at once; and it will become able to sort out so many sensations in a single instant that it would not be able to specify the exact number.

Let us suppose, for example, that the statue feels at the same time warmth on one arm, cold on another, a pain in the head, a tickling in the feet, a discomfiture in the bowels, etc.; I believe that it would notice these states, provided that it had known them separately and that no one dominates over all the others so its attention is distributed equally among them. We must apply here the principles that we have established earlier in speaking of vision.

These states that it notices all at once coexist, are more or less distinguishable, and are in this respect outside of each other: but because neither contiguity nor continuity result, these states cannot give the statue any idea of extension any more than sounds or odors could. If we represent them as extended, it is not that they give this idea on their own; rather it is that knowing from other evidence that we have a body, we relate them to something of which the parts are external to one another and contiguous, forming a continuum. And there you have the sensations that belong to touch which however cannot produce the phenomenon of extension.

4 Preliminary Considerations for the Solution of the Question: How do We Go From Our Sensations to a Knowledge of Objects?

1. *How we conceive objects.* It is only with extension that we can make extension as it is only with objects that we can make objects; for we do not see how there can be contiguity among several nonextended things nor how as a result they can form a continuum. We necessarily conceptualize each object, however, as a continuum formed by the contiguity of several other extended objects. We are obliged to represent things for ourselves in this way just so long as they do not come within the purview of our senses: we judge that each of them is composed of other extended objects, which are composed of yet others, and we no longer know where to stop.

2. *The property of sensations that lead us to know objects.* It is thus evident that we will not proceed from our sensations to a knowledge of objects except insofar as those sensations produce the phenomenon of extension; and because an object is a continuum formed by the contiguity of other extended objects, the sensation that represents it must be a continuum formed by the contiguity of other extended sensations. We have not found this property in any of the sensations that we have observed: it remains to inquire whether we will find it in yet others.

3. *The sole means by which nature leads us to this knowledge.* Since sensations belong only to the mind, they cannot be anything other than states of this substance: they are concentrated in it, they do not extend beyond it whatsoever. Now if the mind only perceives them as states concentrated in it, it will only see itself in these sensations: it will therefore be impossible for it to discover that it has a body and that beyond this body there are yet others.

However this discovery is one of the first that it makes and it had to make it without delay. How could a newborn infant tend to its own needs if it had no knowledge whatever of its body and if it did not conceive as readily of the objects that can assuage its needs?

I have called attention several times, particularly in my *Logic*, to the fact that we only do something intentionally to the extent that we have already done it unintentionally. This is a fertile truth but I do not say a "principle" for this latter word has been so abused that I no longer know what it means.

It follows from this truth that nature begins everything in us: accordingly, I have shown that, in principle or at the outset, our knowledge is uniquely the work of nature, our instruction must follow its lessons, and the entire art of reasoning amounts to continuing as nature has made us begin.

Now, the first discovery that an infant makes is that of its body. It is thus not strictly speaking the child that makes the discovery it is nature that shows it to him ready-made.

But nature would never reveal his body to him if it made him perceive the sensations he experiences as modifications exclusively of his mind. The "I" of the infant, concentrated then in his mind, could never view the different parts of his body as several parts of himself.

Nature thus had only one means of leading him to know his body and this means was to lead him to perceive his sensations not as modifications of his mind but as modifications of sensory organs which are their occasional causes. In this way the "I," instead of being concentrated in the mind, must have spread out, extended, and repeated itself as it were in all the different parts of the body.

This device, by which we believe we find something of ourselves in organs which are not strictly ourselves, no doubt has its basis in the mechanism of the human body, and no doubt also this mechanism was chosen and arranged in relation to the nature of the mind. That is all we can know on the subject. When we know perfectly the nature of the mind and the mechanism of the human body, no doubt we will be able to explain readily how it is that the "I" which is only in the mind seems to be found in the body. As for us, it will be sufficient to observe this fact and to be quite sure of it.

Although the statue must have sensations that it perceives naturally as modifications of its sense organs, it will not, however, know its own body immediately as a consequence of undergoing such sensations. To discover its body, the statue needs to analyze, that is to say, it needs to observe its "I" successively in all the parts where it appears to be found. Now it is certain that the statue will not conduct this analysis all by itself: it is therefore the part of nature to lead it to conduct this analysis. Let us observe how.

5 How a Man Limited to Touch Discovers His Body and Learns That There Is Something External to Himself

1. *The statue moves*. I give to the statue the use of all its limbs: but what would lead it to move them? It cannot be the intention to make use of them for it does not yet know that it is composed of parts that can move one on top of the other or onto external objects. It is thus the part of nature to begin. It is her role to produce the first movements in the limbs of the statue.

2. If nature gives the statue a pleasant sensation, we imagine that the statue would be able to experience it while keeping all the parts of its body in the configuration that they were in at that moment, and such a sensation appears to tend to maintain the repose of the statue rather than to provoke it into movement.

But if it is natural for the statue to be taken up with a sensation that it finds pleasing and to experience it while at rest, it is equally natural for it to reject the sensation that hurts it. It is true that the statue does not know how it can reject such a sensation; but in the beginning, it has no need to know this, it is sufficient for it to obey nature. It follows from its makeup that its muscles, contracted by pain, incite its limbs and the statue moves without intending to do so, without knowing yet that it is moving.

It can even happen that the statue has pleasant sensations whose intensity does not allow it to remain in a state of perfect repose; at least it is certain that the alternation from pleasure to pain and from pain to pleasure must occasion movements in its body. If the statue were not structured so as to be moved when it experiences agreeable or disagreeable sensations, it would be condemned to perfect rest which would leave it no means to search out what can be useful to it and to avoid what can be noxious.

But as soon as movements occur in the statue as a result of its makeup, on the occasion of pleasure, pain, or the alternation from one to the other, it is

232

inevitable that among all these many movements some will eliminate or interrupt a sensation that hurts the statue, and others will procure a sensation that it finds pleasing. The statue will thus have an interest in studying these movements and as a result it will learn from them all that it can learn.

It is naturally, mechanically, by instinct and without being aware of it that the statue moves; and it remains for us to explain how it will discover, from these movements, that it has a body, and that beyond it there are other bodies.

If we consider the multitude and the variety of impressions that objects make on the statue, we will judge that its movements ought naturally to be repeated and to vary. Now as soon as these movements are repeated and vary, it necessarily will happen that the statue repeatedly places its hands on itself and on objects that come close to it.

In placing its hands on itself, the statue will only discover that it has a body when it distinguishes the different parts of that body and when it recognizes itself in each part to be the same sentient being; and it will discover that there are other bodies only because it does not find itself in those that it touches. touches.

3. *The sensation through which the mind discovers that it has a body.* Therefore the statue can only owe this discovery to one or another senstion of touch. Now what is the nature of this sensation?

Impenetrability is a property of all bodies; several bodies cannot occupy the same place: each one excludes all the others from the place that it occupies.

This impenetrability is not a sensation. Strictly speaking, we do not sense that bodies are impenetrable: rather we judge that they are so and this judgment is a consequence of the senstions that they incite in us.

Solidity is above all the sensation from which we draw this conclusion because, given two solid bodies pressing against each other, we perceive more perceptibly the resistance that they put up against each other to exclude each other mutually. If the bodies were able to penetrate each other, the two distinct bodies would become confounded into one: but as soon as they are impenetrable they are necessarily distinct and always two.

Thus it is not the same thing to have a sensation of solidity as to have sensations of sound, color, and odor that a mind, not knowing its body, perceives naturally as states in which it finds itself and only itself. Since the essence of this sensation of solidity is to represent at one and the same moment two things that exclude each other, the mind will not perceive solidity as one of those states in which it finds only itself; it will perceive it necessarily as a state in which it finds two things that are mutually exclusive and as a result it will perceive it in these two things.

There you have then a sensation with which the mind proceeds from itself to outside of itself and we begin to understand how it will discover objects.

Indeed, since the statue is structured to have movements when impressions are made on it, we can suppose that its hand will move naturally to some part of its body, onto the chest for example. Then its hand and its chest will be distinguishable by the sensation of solidity that they send mutually and that places them necessarily outside of each other. However, in distinguishing the chest from the hand, the statue will find its "I" anew in each of them because it senses itself in both of them. Whatever part of its body the statue touches, it will distinguish it in the same manner and likewise will discover itself there anew.

Although this discovery is due principally to the sensation of solidity, it will be made all the more easily if it is accompanied by other sensations; let the hand be cold for example and let the chest be warm and the statue will sense them as something solid and cold which touches something solid and warm: it will learn to associate the cold with the hand and the warm with the chest and it will distinguish the two all the better. Thus these two sensations, little suited in themselves to lead the statue to know that it has a body, will contribute nevertheless to giving it a more perceptible idea of its body when they are embraced within the sensation of solidity.

If up to now the hand of the statue, in moving from one part of its body to another, has always skipped over intermediary parts, the statue will find itself in each part as if in as many different bodies, and will not know yet that all of these bodies taken together form only a single body. This is because the sensations that the statue has experienced do not portray the parts of its body as contiguous nor, as a result, as forming a single continuum.

But if the statue happens to move its hand the length of its arm and, without skipping over any intermediate part, onto its chest, its head, etc. it will experience a continuity of self at its fingertips, so to speak; and this same hand that has brought together the formerly separated parts into a single continuum will thereby render extension more perceptible.

4. *How it recognizes itself.* The statue learns then to recognize its body and to recognize itself in all the different parts that make it up because as soon as it places its hand on one of these parts the same sentient being responds, as it were, from the one part to the other, "this is me." Let the statue continue to touch itself, and everywhere the sensation of solidity will represent two things that are mutually exclusive and at the same time contiguous, and everywhere also the same sentient being wll respond from one to the other: "this is me, this is me again." The statue senses itself in all the parts of its body. Thus it will no longer confuse itself with its states: it is no longer heat and cold but it senses heat in one part of its body and cold in another.

5. *How the statue discovers that there are other bodies.* As long as the statue places its hands only on itself, it is from its point of view as if it were the only thing that existed. But if it touches a foreign body, the "I" that feels a

modification in the hand does not feel itself modified in this foreign body. If the hand says "I" it does not receive the same response in turn. Thus the statue judges that the body's existence is entirely external to it. As it formed the concept of its own body it now forms that of all other objects. The sensation of solidity which gave them consistency in the one case gives it to them likewise in the other; with this difference that the "I" that responded previously ceases to respond.

6. *What its idea of bodies comes down to.* Thus the statue does not perceive bodies in themselves, it only perceives its own sensations. When touch circumscribes several distinct and coexisting sensations within limits where the "I" replies to itself, the statue takes cognizance of its body; when touch circumscribes several distinct and coexisting sensations within limits where the "I" does not respond to itself, the statue has the idea of a body different from its own. In the first case its sensations continue to be properties of itself; in the second case, they become properties of an entirely distinct object.

7. *Its surprise at not being all that it touches.* When the statue comes to learn that it is something solid, I imagine that it is quite astonished not to find itself in everything that it touches. It extends its arms, as if to look for itself outside of itself, and it cannot yet judge if it will not indeed find itself there anew; experience alone can instruct it.

8. *The effects of this astonishment.* From this astonishment is born the disquiet to know where it is and, if I may venture to express myself in this way, exactly up to what point it is. It thus takes in hand, releases, and picks up again everything that is around it: it grasps itself, it compares itself with the objects that it is touching; and as it forms ideas that are more exact, its body and the objects around it seem to it to take shape under its hands.

9. *With each thing that it touches it believes that it is touching everything.* But I conjecture that the statue will take a long time before imagining something beyond the bodies that its hand encounters. It seems to me that when it begins to touch it must believe that it touches everything. Only after moving from one place to another and having thoroughly manipulated various objects will it be able to suspect that there are bodies beyond those that it has grasped.

10. *How it learned to touch.* But how does the statue learn to touch? The answer is that since the movements nature has made it make yielded sensations that were sometimes pleasant, sometimes unpleasant, the statue wants to enjoy some and to avoid others. No doubt in the beginning it does not yet know how to guide its movements. It is ignorant of how it ought to move its hand to place it on one part of its body rather than another. It makes various tries, it makes false starts, it suceeds: it notices the movements that have tripped it up and it avoids them; it notices those that answered to its

desires and it repeats them. In a word, it engages in trial and error and it develops little by little a habit of movements that enable it to look after its own survival. Then it has bodily movements that correspond to its mind's desires; then it moves when it wishes.

6 Of Pleasure, Pain, and the Needs and Desires of a Man Limited to the Sense of Touch

1. *The statue has the pleasure of distinguishing the different parts of its body.* Let us give to our statue the use of all its limbs; and before inquiring into the knowledge that it acquires, let us see what are its needs.

The different kinds of pleasure and of pain are the source of these needs: for we must follow the same line of reasoning when discussing touch as we have done for the other senses.

First its pleasure as well as its existence appeared to it to be concentrated in a single point. But then it spread out little by little following the same progress as its basic sentience. For it has pleasure in noticing this sentience when it emerges in the various parts of its body, provided that it is not accompanied by any painful sensation.

2. *It enjoys moving.* The greatest happiness of an infant seems to consist in movement: even a fall does not seem to displease it. A mask over its eyes disturbs it less than a strap depriving it of the use of hands and feet. Indeed, the infant owes its keen awareness of its existence to movement. Vision, hearing, taste, smell seem to limit that awareness to an organ; but movement distributes awareness and leads the infant to enjoy its body in all of its extension.

If exercise is the pleasure that has the greatest attraction for the infant, it will have an even greater attraction for our statue: for not only does the statue know nothing that could distract it, but also it will discover that movement alone can obtain for it all the pleasures of which it is capable.

3. *It takes pleasure in manipulating objects.* The statue will especially like objects that do not hurt it: it will particularly appreciate objects whose surfaces are smooth and polished; it will take pleasure in finding them either cool or warm, depending on its needs.

Sometimes objects will give it greater pleasure the more easily it handles them; this is the case for those that, by their size and shape, lend themselves better to the extent and shape of its hand. At other times objects will please it by their astonishing size and the difficulty of manipulating them. The surprise that, for example, is evoked by the space it discovers around itself will contribute to its pleasure in going from one place to another.

Solidity and fluidity, hardness and softness, movement and rest, are agreeable feelings for the statue: for the more they contrast, the more they attract its attention and make themselves noticed.

4. *The statue takes pleasure in forming ideas.* But what will become for it a source of pleasure is the habit it will acquire of comparing and judging. Then it will not touch objects for the sole pleasure of handling them, it will want to know their relations and it will experience as many agreeable feelings as it forms new ideas. In a word, pleasures will be born in its hands and in its tracks. These pleasures will increase and multiply until its energy is exhausted. Then they will begin to be mixed with fatigue; little by little they will vanish; finally only lassitude will remain and rest will become the statue's greatest pleasure.

5. *The statue is more exposed to pain than with the other senses.* As for pain, the statue will be more frequently exposed to it with the sense of touch than with the other senses; indeed, sometimes it will find the intensity of pain considerably greater than that of the pleasures it knows. But the statue enjoys the advantage that pleasure is constantly available while pain makes itself felt only occasionally.

6. *What its desires consist of.* With the other senses, its desire consists principally in the mental effort to recall a pleasant idea as vividly as possible. This idea is the sole pleasure that it could obtain on its own because it was not within its power to give itself sensations. But the kind of desire of which it is capable with touch includes the effort of all the parts of its body that tend to move and that go forth, so to speak, in search of sensations on all palpable objects. We ourselves, when we desire something keenly, feel that our desires embrace this double tendency of mind and body. From that moment on, enjoyment is no longer limited to ideas represented by imagination, it extends beyond to all the objects that are within reach; and the statue's desires, instead of absorbing it in its own states as occurred with the other senses, lead it continually outside of itself.

7. *What is the purpose of this?* As a result, the statue's love, hate, will, hope, fear no longer have its own states as their sole object: rather it is palpable things that it loves, hates, hopes for, fears, wants.

Thus the statue is not limited to loving only itself but its love for objects follows from the love it has for itself. It has no other goal in loving them than the search for pleasure or the flight from pain and this will teach it how to behave in the space that it has begun to discover.

7 On the Manner in Which a Man Limited to a Sense of Touch Begins to Discover Space

1. *Pleasure rules the movements of the statue.* Since desire consists of an effort made by the parts of the body in concert with the mind, our statue cannot desire a sensation without in the same instant moving in order to seek out the object that can provide that sensation. It is thus foreordained to move every time that it remembers agreeable sensations that movement has enabled it to enjoy.

At first it will bestir itself without any particular goal and this agitation is itself a sensation that it experiences with pleasure; for it senses all the better its own existence. If next its hand encounters an object that yields a pleasant impression of warmth or coolness, all its movements are suspended immediately and it gives itself over entirely to this new feeling. The more agreeable the feeling, the more attention the statue devotes to it; it would even touch the object that occasions the sensation with all the different parts of its body: and this desire provokes movements that, instead of occurring without any particular goal, all tend to obtain the most complete enjoyment for the statue.

However this object loses its warmth or coolness; and the experience of it ceases to be pleasant. Then the statue remembers its first movements that pleased it, it desires them, and it bestirs itself a second time without any other goal than to bestir itself, and little by little it moves and touches new bodies.

One of the first things that surprises it is no doubt the space that it discovers surrounding it at every moment. It seems to it that the space must be drawn from its own being, that objects are extended beneath it hands at only the expense of its own body; and the more it compares itself with the space that surrounds it, the more it feels its outer limits constrict.

Each time that the statue discovers a new space, and touches new objects, it suspends its movements, or guides them in order to experience better the sensations that please it; and it begins again to move for the sole pleasure of moving as soon as it ceases to find these things agreeable.

When in this way the statue has discovered a certain space and has experienced a certain number of sensations, it recalls, at least confusedly, everything that gave it pleasure. Recalling on the one hand that it owes that pleasure to its movements, feeling on the other that its movements are under its control, it desires to explore this space again and to obtain the same sensations that it has learned to recognize. Thus it no longer moves solely for the pleasure of moving.

But as the statue does not always pass by the same places, from time to time it experiences sensations that were entirely unknown to it. The more it experiences them, the more it judges that its movements can obtain new pleasures for it and this hope becomes a driving force.

2. *The statue becomes capable of curiosity*. The statue begins then to judge that there are discoveries for it to make; it learns that the movements at its disposal give it a means of making them; and it becomes capable of curiosity.

Curiosity is in fact only the desire for something new; and this desire can arise only when we have made some discoveries and believe that we have a means for making more. It is true that we can be mistaken about the means. Having become curious by habit, we often get involved in investigations in which it is impossible to make any progress. But we would not have made this error if we had not had more success on other occasions.

3. *The statue was not curious with the other senses*. It is perhaps not impossible that, when our statue received the other senses one after the other, the habit of constantly experiencing different states led it to suspect yet others that it might enjoy: but not knowing how they might come to pass and not having any means to procure their enjoyment, the statue could not become involved in discovering new states in itself. It was much more natural for it to turn all its desires toward the pleasant sensations that it knew. This is why I did not attribute any curiosity at all to the statue.

4. *Curiosity is one of the principal motives for its actions*. We realize that curiosity is becoming a need for the statue which will lead it continually to go from one place to another. It will often be the unique motive for its actions. In this regard, it should be noted that I am not deviating at all from what I proved when I said that pleasure and pain are the only causes of the development of its faculties. For the statue is only curious in the hope of obtaining pleasant sensations or of avoiding those that are displeasing. Thus this new principle is a consequence of the first and confirms it.

5. *Pain suspends the desire to move*. In the beginning, the statue only drags itself about; then it moves on its hands and feet; finally coming across some elevation, it is curious to discover what lies above and it finds itself, as

by chance, on its feet. It totters, it walks, leaning against everything that can help it to stay up; it falls, it hurts itself, and feels pain anew. It does not dare get up, it scarcely dares move: the fear of pain offsets the hope of pleasure. If, however, the statue has not yet been hurt by objects it has touched, it will continue to extend its arms without fear. But, at the slightest scratch, it will lose confidence and remain immobile.

6. *This desire is reawakened accompanied by fear.* Little by little its pain will dissipate and the memory that remains, too feeble to resist its desire to move, is strong enough to cause it to move fearfully. Thus we have only to arrange the objects that surround our statue to give it its original feelings of security with pleasures that can even erase the memory of pain or to renew its mistrust with painful stimulation.

If we leave things to follow their natural course, accidents can occur so often that it never loses its misgivings.

7. *Circumstances in which fear would render the statue immobile.* If we had, right from the beginning, even put our statue in a place where it could not move without exposing itself to intense pain, movement would have ceased to be a pleasure for it and it would have remained immobile and would have never acquired any knowledge of external objects.

8. *Fear that occasions a kind of industry.* But if we watch over it and make sure that it experiences only very slight pain and that these pains are indeed even fairly rare, then it will wish to move; and this wish will only occasionally be accompanied by certain misgivings about movement. Thus the statue will no longer be consigned forever to immobility. Although it may fear a change of circumstances, it nevertheless desires one whenever it would be comforting and it obeys each of these two feelings in turn.

From this is born a kind of industry, that is to say, the art of directing its movements with caution and of using objects that it discovers can help it ward off the risks it runs. The very same chance that leads it to seize a stick will teach it little by little that the stick can help it to stand up, to judge objects it may encounter, and to spot the places where it can walk with assurance.

8 On the Ideas That a Man Limited to the Sense of Touch Can Acquire

1. *Pleasure and pain are equally necessary to the instruction of the statue.* Without pleasure our statue would never have the will to move: without pain it would move about with a sense of security and inevitably die. It is thus necessary that the statue is always exposed to pleasant or unpleasant sensations. And there you have the motive force and guiding principle of all its movements. Pleasure gives it an interest in objects, urges it to give them all the attention of which it is capable and to form more precise ideas about them. Pain removes it from everything that is harmful, makes it all the more sensitive to pleasure, leads it to understand how to enjoy pleasure without danger, and gives it lessons in industry. In a word, pleasure and pain are its only teachers.

2. *They alone determine the scope of its knowledge.* The number of ideas that can come from touch is infinite: for it embraces all the relations of size, that is to say, a body of knowledge which the greatest mathematicians will never exhaust. Thus we are not concerned with explaining the development of ideas that may be owed to the sense of touch: it is sufficient to discover those that our statue itself will acquire. The observations we have made provide us with the principle that should guide us in this investigation: it is that the statue will notice in its sensations only the ideas in which pleasure and pain lead it to take some interest. The extent of this interest will determine the extent of its knowledge.

3. *The order in which it will acquire ideas.* Two factors will determine the order in which the statue will acquire these ideas. One will be the chance encounter of objects, the other the simplicity of relations; for the statue will have exact notions of those things that require a certain number of comparisons only after having studied those that require fewer.

It is possible to follow the progress that the second of these causes will lead the statue to make; this is not at all the case for those that it owes to the first cause. But this is rather a useless undertaking and each person can suppose what he wishes on this topic.

4. *The first ideas that it acquires.* The statue's ideas on solidity, hardness, warmth, etc. are not at all absolute; that is to say, it judges that an object is solid, hard, warm, only in the measure that it compares it with others that do not have that attribute to the same degree or that have different attributes. If all objects were equally solid, hard, warm, etc., the statue would have sensations of solidity, hardness and warmth without noticing them; it would confuse all objects in this respect. But because it encounters in turn solidity and fluidity, hardness and softness, warmth and cold, it gives its attention to these differences, it compares them, it judges them, and from these ideas it learns to distinguish the objects. The more it applies its judgment to this topic, the more delicacy its touch acquires and it becomes increasingly capable of discerning the most subtle nuances in a single property. There you have the ideas that require the least in the way of comparisons and that are as a result the first ones that the statue will have occasion to notice.

5. *Its curiosity increases.* These bits of knowledge direct the statue's attention with a new keenness to the objects that it touches, and make it consider them from the various points of view that strike it. The more it discovers, the more it forms a habit of believing that it will discover yet more, and curiosity becomes a more pressing need for it.

6. *How intense its activity becomes.* This need will become the primary force behind the progress of its mind. However, I will not undertake to pursue all of its effects for I would fear to stray too far into conjecture. I will observe only that curiosity must be considerably more active for the statue than for the greater part of mankind. Education often snuffs out our curiosity because so little effort is expended in satisfying it; and, when we arrive at the age where we are left on our own, our many needs constrain our curiosity and do not allow us to follow all the interests that it inspires. But in the case of the statue, it seems that everything would only tend to increase it. The pleasant sensations that it often experiences, and the unpleasant sensations to which it it sometimes exposed[23] must interest it keenly in being able to recognize, down to the most subtle details, the objects that produce those sensations. The statue will then devote itself to the study of objects.

7. *The statue forms an idea of shape.* When the statue had only the sense of vision, we observe that its eye would perceive colors without being able to notice the totality of any shape, without having as a result a distinct idea of extension. The hand has, on the contrary, this advantage that it cannot

---

[23]I say "sometimes" because if these sensations recur too often they will entirely extinguish its curiosity.

handle an object without noticing the extent and the collection of parts that make it up: it embraces them all. It is sufficient, to this end, that it senses solidity. In squeezing a pebble, our statue gets the idea of an object different from a stick that it has touched along its whole length; it senses in a cube angles that it cannot find in a sphere; it does not perceive the same form in a bow and in a straight stick. In a word, the statue distinguishes solid things according to the shape that each imposes on its hand; and it considers that the parts of extension it cannot separate or that it separates with difficulty form a single whole. It acquires thus the ideas of a straight line, of a curved line and of various kinds of shapes.

8. *By comparing opposed qualities.* But if the first objects that the statue has occasion to touch all lead its hand to take the same shape, if it encounters for example only spheres of the same volume, the statue would be limited to noticing that one is rough, the other smooth, one warm, the other cold, and it would give no attention to the shape of its hand. Thus it would touch spheres without ever forming an idea of them. Let it handle, on the contrary, spheres, cubes, and other figures of various sizes, each in turn, and it will be struck by the differences among the shapes that its hand takes. In that case, the statue will begin to judge that all these shapes do not resemble each other. Its curiosity will lead it then to look for all the respects in which they differ and little by little it will form exact ideas of them. To acquire the idea of a shape, it is necessary then for the statue to notice several of them that, at first touch, perceptibly contrast in some respect: it is necessary that the first difference perceived inspires the desire to perceive others. The statue desires, for example, to know a cube only after having compared it with a sphere, and having found from one angle what it does not find from another. In short, the statue will look for new ideas in its sensations only to the extent that it is alerted by the first differences that strike it when it touches several objects in succession.

9. *How we can judge the ideas that the statue forms of objects.* The idea of an object is the more complex the larger the number of perceptions and relations distinguished by touch that it involves. In order to know which ideas ideas our statue will form of perceptible objects, we must therefore observe in what order it judges these perceptions and relations and how it arranges them in different groupings.

10. *Two kinds of sensations that it can compare.* Either the sensations that it will compare are simple with respect to it because they are uniform impressions in which the statue will not be able to distinguish several perceptions, as is the case with warmth and cold, or the sensations are composed of several others that it can sort out, as is the case with the impression of an object that has solidity, warmth, shape, etc. concurrently.

11. *Its judgments on simple sensations.* The simple sensations are of the same or of different kinds: for example, a sensation is of warmth and of

warmth, or it is of warmth and of cold. The judgments that the statue can make on these occasions are indeed highly limited.

If the sensations are of the same kind, the statue senses that they are distinct and similar; it senses moreover if the degrees are the same or different. However, it has no way to measure them and it only judges them with vague notions of more and of less. It senses that the warmth of its right hand is not the same as the warmth of its left hand; but it knows their relations only imperfectly.

If the sensations are of different kinds, the statue perceives only that the one is not the other. It judges that hot is not cold; but in the beginning it does not know that these are two contrary sensations and to discover this it must have occasion to notice that hot and cold cannot be found at the same time in the same object and that one always destroys the other. Thus, the judgment "hot and cold are contrary sensations" is not as natural for the statue as might appear; the statue owes that judgment to experience.

On all of these occasions it is obvious that the statue need only focus its attention on two sensations in order to make all the judgments it is capable of making.

12. *Its judgments on complex sensations.* When each of two objects yields a complex sensation, the statue perceives first that the one object is not the other; this is its first judgment.

But we have seen that attention diminishes the greater the number of perceptions among which it is distributed. It cannot embrace all those that two bodies produce without becoming attenuated with regard to each.

Consequently, the statue will form ideas of two objects only to the extent that pleasure limits its attention successively to the different perceptions that it receives from them and makes it notice each object in particular. The statue first judges their warmth considering them only in that regard; it judges next their size considering them only from that point of view; and in this fashion, working its way through all the ideas that it notices, it makes a series of judgments that it remembers. From this results its total judgment of each of the objects which unites in each the perceptions that it observed successively. The statue thus analyzes naturally: and this confirms what I have shown in my *Logic*, that we learn analysis from nature itself.

13. *The operation of the mind is the same for the two kinds of sensations.* The judgments that give the statue complex ideas of two objects are thus only a repetition of what it has done with the perceptions that it considers simple. It is a matter of paying attention first to two ideas, then to two others, and in this way successively to all those that it is capable of noticing. If any remain that it has not judged, it is because the statue has not yet given them any attention whatever; it has not noticed them.

As a result, when the statue compares two objects, when it judges them and forms complex ideas, it engages in no other operation whatever than when it judges two simple perceptions: for it never does anything other than give its attention.

14. *The statue becomes capable of reflection.* When the statue had only the sense of smell, it led its attention from one idea to the next, it noticed the difference, but it never organized them into groups with specified relations.

With vision, the statue could in truth distinguish several colors that it experienced together. But it did not notice that they formed structured wholes. It sensed only that it had several ways of being all in a single moment.

It is only when touch separates these states from its "I" and leads it to judge them as outside of itself, that it constructs variously structured wholes out of them in which it can distinguish innumerable relations.

The attention that it is capable of with touch therefore produces effects that are indeed different from those produced by the attention it was capable of with the other senses. Now this attention which combines sensations, which externalizes them and which, reflected as it were from one object to another, compares them in different respects, this is what I call "reflection." Thus we see why our statue, who was without reflection with the other senses, begins to reflect with touch.[24]

15. *The view it takes of an object.* An object that the statue touches is therefore only the perceptions of size, solidity, hardness, etc. that it considers reunited. Touch discovers all that for it and it has no need, to make this kind of judgment, to give these properties a subject, a support, or as philosophers put it, a "substrate." It is sufficient for it to sense them together.

16. *The properties from which it constitutes objects.* The statue distinguishes as many objects as it notices collections of this kind and it does not constitute them only of ideas of size, solidity, and hardness; it also takes account of warmth or cold, pleasure or pain, and in general all the sensations that touch teaches it to associate with external things. Its own sensations thus become the properties of objects. If they are keen, such as brutal heat, the statue thinks of them as being at the same time in its hand and in the object that it is touching. If they are weak, such as gentle heat, it thinks of them as only in the object. Thus it can sometimes cease to consider these properties as belonging to its sensations, but it will nevermore cease to attribute them to the objects that occasion the sensations. The other senses could not lead it into this error because it always perceived its sensations only as its "I" modified differently.

17. *It forms abstract ideas.* We have just seen that, to bring together in

---

[24] Since reflection was originally only attention itself, we could conceive of it so that it would occur with each sense. But agreement on questions of this kind requires only understanding. I have written this note to avoid disputes about words, a very common problem in metaphysics which we cannot guard against too carefully.

objects the properties that go with them, the statue was obliged to consider each of those properties separately. It has thus made some abstractions: for to abstract is to separate an idea from several others which enter with it in the composition of a whole.

In paying attention only to the solidity of an object, for example, the statue separates this property from the others which it has not considered at all. In the same way, it forms abstract ideas of shape, of movement, etc., and each of these ideas promptly generalizes, because the statue notices that each of them applies to several objects or appears in several collections.

From the preceding and from what we have said when discussing the other senses, we see that abstract ideas are necessarily the fruit of how we choose to use our sense organs; and that as a result they are not as remote from human intelligence as we seem to believe; and that, finally, their development is not so difficult to understand as to warrant supposing that we could have obtained them only from the author of all nature.

18. *There is no way to determine their number.* When the statue was limited to the other senses, it could only make abstractions based on its own states. It separated certain incidental properties that were common to several such states; it separated, for example, contentment or the lack of contentment accompanying them and in this way it formed general notions of pleasant and unpleasant states.

But now that it has become accustomed to considering its sensations as the attributes of perceptible objects, that is, as properties that exist outside of itself and, so to say, in groups, the statue can separate each of them from the collections to which they belong, consider them separately, and form innumerable abstractions. But as we have not defined the scope of its curiosity, we will not undertake to follow it here in all of these operations.

19. *The statue extends its ideas on numbers.* Its curiosity will not limit it to studying only the objects that surround it. It will touch itself and it will study above all the shape of this organ with which it handles bodies. It will examine its fingers when it spreads them and brings them together and bends them. Struck by the resemblance that it begins to discover between its hands, it will be curious to judge them better; it will observe its fingers one by one, two by two, etc.; in this way it will increase its abstract notions concerning the numbers, and will be able to learn that its right hand has as many fingers as its left hand.

If it then considers an object, it thinks of it as one, like one finger; if it examines two, it estimates that there are two, like two fingers. And thus it is that its fingers have become the signs of numbers. But we cannot affirm how far it will carry these kinds of ideas. It is sufficient for my purposes to prove by these details that all these ideas are embraced within touch and that our statue will notice them depending on its need to acquire them.

20. *Its other ideas become more distinct.* Having extended its ideas on the

numbers, it will be in a better position to take account of its abstract notions. It will be able, for example, to notice that it forms as many as five or six abstractions on a single object; in other words, that it can observe separately up to five or six of its different properties. Formerly, the statue perceived only a host of properties that it was unable to specify and this could not fail to be confusing. Its progress with numbers will contribute, therefore, to progress in all its other fields of knowledge.

21. *It does not go so far as to conceive abstract notions of being and substance.* But whatever the host of objects that the statue discovers, whatever combinations it makes of them, it will never attain the abstract notions of being, of substance, of essence, of nature, etc.; these sorts of phantoms are palpable only to the touch of philosophers. Given its habit of thinking of each object as a collection of several properties, the statue will find it entirely natural that these properties exist combined and it will not think of looking for an underlying support or connection. We often allow habit to take the place of reasoning and we must acknowledge that it is sometimes worth a good deal more than the reasoning of philosophers.

22. *Philosophers know no more about this subject than the statue.* But supposing that the statue was curious to discover how these properties exist in each collection, it would be led like us to imagine something that is the subject of these properties; and if it could give a name to this something it would have a ready response for the questions of philosophers. It would then know as much about it as they; that is to say, they do not know more about it than the statue. In truth, their definitions, clearly explained, inform even an infant only what his senses have already taught him.

23. *Its ideas of duration.* Among the abstract notions that it acquires there are two that merit particular consideration: those of duration and of space.

In truth, the statue only knows duration from the succession of its ideas. But it can frame for itself so perceptible an idea of duration by imagining the past as a space through which it has traveled and the future as a space through which it will travel that it conceives of time as a line along which it moves. This way of thinking of time will even appear so natural that it could easily fall into the error of believing that it knows duration only to the extent that it reflects on the movement of a body. When we have many ways of conceptualizing a thing we are often led to consider the most salient ones as the only one. This is a mistake that even philosophers themselves have difficulty avoiding. Thus Locke was the first to demonstrate that we know duration only by the succession of our ideas.

24. *On Space.* As the statue knows duration by the succession of its ideas, it knows space by the coexistence of its ideas. If touch had not conveyed together several sensations that the statue distinguishes, unites, and circumscribes within certain limits, and from which, in a word, it compares an object, then the statue would not have any idea of size. Thus it finds this

idea only in the coexistence of several sensations. Now as soon as it knows a size, it has what it needs to measure others; it has the wherewithal to measure the interval that separates them and the one they occupy; in short it has the idea of space. Thus, as it would have no idea of duration if it had not remembered having had several sensations successively, so it would have no idea of extent or of space if it had never had several sensations all at once.

Wherever the statue finds no resistance whatever, it judges that there is none and it forms the idea of an empty space. However, this is not a proof that there exists a space without matter: it has only to move swiftly to feel at least a fluid that resists.

25. *On immensity.* At first the statue imagines nothing beyond the space that it discovers around itself and, as a result, it does not believe that there are others. Subsequently, experience teaches it littly by little that space extends further. Then the idea of the space the statue wanders over becomes a model for imagining the space it has not yet explored; and when it has once imagined space where it has not roamed then it imagines several of them, outside each other. Finally, conceiving no limits beyond which it can stop imagining spaces, it is practically obliged to imagine further ones and it believes that it perceives immensity itself.

26. *Of eternity.* It is the same with duration. At the first moment of its existence, the statue imagines nothing before or after. But when it has become thoroughly accustomed to the changes to which it is subject, the memory of a succession of ideas is a model for imagining a prior duration and a subsequent duration. Now since the statue finds no instant in the past or in the future beyond which it can not imagine yet others, it seems to it that its thought embraces all eternity. The statue even believes itself eternal for it does not recall that it had begun and it does not suspect that it must end.

27. *Eternity and immensity are only illusions of its imagination.* However, in truth, the statue has neither the idea of eternity nor that of immensity. If it thinks it has, that is only because its imagination gives it the illusion by representing duration and an undefined space it cannot delimit as eternity and immensity themselves.

28. *Sensations are ideas for the statue.* With each discovery that it makes,it realizes that the essence of each sensation is to make it take cognizance either of some feeling that it thinks of as in itself or of some property that it thinks of as external; that is, the essence of each sensation is for the statue what we call "idea"; for every impression that gives some knowledge is an idea.

29. *How they differ from intellectual ideas.* If the statue considers its sensations as past, it no longer perceives them except in the memory it retains of them, and this memory is also an idea, for it presents anew or recalls a bit of knowledge. I will call these kinds of ideas "intellectual," or simply "ideas," to distinguish them from others which I will continue to call

"sensations." An intellectual idea is thus the memory of a sensation. The intellectual idea of solidity, for example, is the memory of having felt solidity in an object that one has touched; the intellectual idea of warmth is the memory of a certain sensation that one has had; and the intellectual idea of object is the memory of having noticed in a single collection extension, shape, hardness, and the like.

30. *The difference that the statue finds between its ideas and its sensations.* Now our statue feels a difference between currently experiencing sensations and remembering having had them. It distinguishes them from what I have called "intellectual ideas."

The statue notices that it has these kinds of ideas without touching anything and that it has sensations only to the extent that it touches things. Reason, which led it to think of its sensations as in objects cannot lead it to think about its intellectual ideas in the same way. These latter appear to the statue then as if it had them only in itself.

31. *If sensations are the source of its knowledge, ideas become the basis.* From sensations the statue knows only objects that are present to touch and it is from ideas that it knows those it has touched and no longer touches. Indeed, it only judges many objects that it touches insofar as it compares them with those that it has touched: and as current sensations are the source of its knowledge so the memory of past sensations or intellectual ideas are the whole basis: it is with their help that new sensations are sorted out and become more and more elaborated.

32. *Without ideas it would be a poor judge of the objects that it touches.* In fact, when the statue touches an object, it would not judge its size, nor its degree of hardness, or warmth, etc. if it had not remembered handling other sizes where it had found other degrees of hardness and of warmth. But as soon as the statue remembers all this, it judges the present object more or less hard, more or less warm by comparison. It is thus thanks to the memory of the intellectual idea it retains of certain sizes, certain degrees of hardness and of warmth that the statue judges new objects it may encounter: It is this memory which, leading it to make comparisons, leads it to notice the different ideas or bits of knowedge that current sensations are communicating.

33. *The statue does not notice that in their origin ideas and sensations are the same thing.* However, since as we have seen memory is only a manner of having sensations, it is a consequence that intellectual ideas do not differ essentially from sensations themselves. But probably our statue is not able to make this reflection. All that it can know is that it has ideas that serve to guide its judgments and that are not sensations. Supposing then that the statue had occasion to reflect on the origin of its knowledge, here is how, I think, it would reason.

34. *Faulty reasoning that the statue might commit.* "My ideas are quite different from my sensations since the former are in me and the latter, on the

contrary, are in objects. Now to know is to have ideas. My knowledge does not depend therefore on any sensation. Moreover, I judge the objects that make various impressions on me only by comparing them with ideas that I already have. Thus I have ideas before having sensations. But have I given myself these ideas? No doubt I have not: how would that be possible? To give oneself the idea of a triangle, would it not be necessary to already have the idea? Now if I had the idea, I do not give it to myself. I am thus a being which by myself naturally has ideas: they are born with me."

Since ideas are the basis of all our knowledge, they make up more particularly what we call the thinking being; and although sensations are the true source of thought and belong in truth only to the mind, they appear to stop in the body and to be entirely useless for the development of ideas. Thus our statue would surely fall into the error of innate ideas if it were capable, as we are, of becoming lost in vain speculation. But it is not worth the trouble to make a philosopher of the statue in order to teach it to reason so poorly.[25]

35. *Its knowledge is only practical and its guiding light is merely instinct.* Since I have not fixed the limits of its curiosity, the principal motive for its mental processes, I will not undertake here to go into greater detail concerning the knowledge that reflection can lead it to acquire. It is sufficient to obseve that since all the relations among magnitudes are included within the sensations of touch, the statue will notice them when it is concerned with knowing them. My goal is not to explain the development of all its ideas: I limit myself to showing that these ideas come to the statue through its senses and that its needs teach it to distinguish among them.

The statue's method for acquiring ideas is to observe the properties that it attributes to objects successively one after the other. It analyzes naturally but it has no language whatever. Now an analysis conducted without signs can only give very limited knowledge concerning only a few things; and because it was not possible to arrange this knowledge in some order, the collection must be very confused indeed. Therefore, when I discuss the ideas that the statue is acquiring, I do not contend that it would have practical knowledge. Its guiding light is essentially an instinct, that is to say a habit of behaving according to ideas that it cannot recognize, a habit that, once established,

---

[25] Following a similar line of reasoning, there are those who have accorded sensations to animals while refusing to accord them ideas, and who believe that our ideas do not come from our senses at all. Considering man when he had already acquired substantial knowledge and finding that he had ideas independent of ongoing sensations, philosophers have failed to see that these ideas were only the memory of prior sensations and concluded on the contrary that they had always preceded the sensations. Whence several philosophical systems, that of innate ideas, that of P. Malebranche, and that of some of the ancients, such as Plato, who believed that the mind was endowed with all sorts of knowledge before its union with the body and that as a result what we believe we are learning is only the memory of what we have known.

guides the statue surely without it needing to recall the judgments that led it to acquire the habit in the first place. In short, the statue has acquired ideas. But once its ideas have taught it how to behave, the statue no longer thinks about them and acts out of habit. A language is necessarily required to acquire theoretical knowledge, for ideas must be categorized and well specified and this presupposes signs used systematically. See the first part of my *Grammar* or my *Logic.*

9 Observations to Aid Understanding of What Will Be Said in the Discussion of Vision

1. *The goal of this chapter.* After the specifics that we have just gone into, this chapter will seem to be quite useless; and I acknowledge that it would be if it did not prepare the reader to be convinced by the observations that we will make concerning vision. The way in which the hands judge objects with the aid of a stick, or two, or an even greater number, resembles so greatly the way in which the eyes judge objects by means of rays that, ever since Descartes, it is common to explain one of these problems by the other. The former will be the goal of this chapter.

2. *How the statue can judge positions and distances with the aid of a stick.* The first time that the statue grasps a stick, it knows only the part that it is holding: and it attributes to that part all the sensations that the stick causes.

The statue thus does not know that the stick has extension; and as a result it cannot judge the distances of bodies that it touches with it.

The stick can be held at a different angle and thereupon it gives different impressions on the hand of the statue. But these impressions do not teach it that the stick is inclined as long as it does not know that the stick has extension. As yet then, these impressions cannot lead it to discover the different positions of objects.

To judge distances by means of a stick, the statue must have touched it throughout its length, and to judge position by the impression that it receives from the stick, the statue must, while holding the stick in one hand, study the direction of it with the other.

3. *With two sticks.* As long as the statue does not know how to judge the direction of two sticks of known length that it is holding in its hands, it will not be able to discover if they cross somewhere or even if their extremities diverge or converge. It will often believe that it has touched two objects when

in fact it has only touched one; it will believe that things are high up that in fact are low down and vice versa. But as soon as the statue is able to notice the different directions of the sticks according to the different impressions that they make, then it will know the arrangements of the sticks and thereby it will judge those of objects.

This judgment will be at first only the result of quite slow reasoning. The statue will say to itself as it were: these sticks can only cross if the extremity of the one in my left hand is on my right. As a result, the objects that they touch are in the opposite positions from those of my hands and I must judge what I sense with my left hand to be on the right and what I sense with my right hand to be on the left. Subsequently, this line of reasoning will become so familiar and will be executed so rapidly that the statue will judge the positions of objects without appearing to give the least attention to the positions of its hands.

4. *The statue attributes its sensations to the end opposite the one it is holding.* The statue no longer attributes the sensations caused by the stick to the end that is in its hand; it feels on the contrary that the hardness or softness of objects on which it places the stick are associated with the opposite end; and this habit will lead it to distinguish sensations that it did not distinguish previously.

Suppose the statue pressed its palm against three rods of equal length held together so that they seem to be only one; it would have a confused sensation in which it would be unable to distinguish the action of each rod. Let us separate these rods only at the bottom: immediately the statue will perceive distinctly three points of resistance and in this way it will discern the impression that each rod makes on it.

But we must notice that it makes this distinction only because it has learned to judge inclination from sensation. If the statue had not had the experiences necessary to make this judgment, it would feel in its hand a single point of resistance whether the three rods were joined at the bottom or whether they were separated.

This experiment confirms the point of view that I adopted on vision. For is it not possible that the eye, like the hand, confuses similar sensations when it judges them in itself and when it only begins to distinguish among them to the extent that it becomes accustomed to associate them with the external world? We need only consider that the rays have the effect on the eye that the rods have on the hand.

5. The statue invents a kind of geometry. In order to establish the distance between the ends of two crossed sticks, a geometer need only establish the magnitudes of the angles and the sides.

The statue cannot pursue a method with so much precision. But it knows roughly the size of the sticks, how much they are inclined, the point at which they are crossed; and it judges that the ends which touch various objects converge or diverge in the same proportion as the ends that it has in hand. Thus we readily imagine how as a result of various trials the statue will formulate a kind of geometry and will judge the size of objects with the aid of two sticks.

If the statue had four hands it could judge at once, following the same strategy, the height and width of an object; and if it had a greater number it could perceive the object in a greater number of respects. It would need only to acquire the habit of making these judgments based on the impressions that ten or more sticks would give to it.

So it is that without any knowledge of geometry the statue would behave, by trial and error, following the principles of that science; and, to go even further, it is thus that there are principles in the development of our mental faculties that we are unaware of even at the very moment that they are guiding us. We do not notice them and nevertheless we do nothing without their influence.

Thus a knowledge of the princples of geometry would be totally useless for our statue. It is only by trying things out that it can put the two sticks to use. Now as soon as it explores with the sticks, it necessarily makes the same judgments that it would make if it were reasoning according to the principles of geometry. It would be thus quite superfluous to conjecture that the statue has innate ideas about size and of position: it needs only hands.

10 On Rest, Sleep, and Awakening in a Man Limited to the Sense of Touch

1. *The statue at rest.* Movement seems such a natural state to our statue and it is so curious to go everywhere and handle everything that no doubt it does not anticipate the periods of inactivity into which it inevitably falls. But little by little its energy is depleted; it begins to feel a certain lethargy that it combats for a while because it still desires to move; finally rest becomes the most urgent of its needs and it senses that in spite of itself, its curiosity ebbs; it drops its arms and remains immobile.

2. *Its sleep.* However, its memory remains active and it seems to the statue that it is still alive only by virtue of the memory that it has of what it was. But memory takes its rest in turn; the ideas that it recalls become imperceptibly fainter, fade into the distance, and cast a feeble light that is soon extinguished. Finally, all its mental processes are dormant: the statue is asleep.

3. *Its awakening.* Several hours of rest begin to replenish its energy, and the statue's ideas come back slowly. It seems that they appear only to disappear; and its mind, suspended between sleep and waking, seems like a haze that dissipates in one moment and forms in the next. However, movement is gradually reborn in all parts of its body, the statue's ideas come into focus, its habits are renewed, its mind is entirely recovered and the statue believes that it is alive for the second time.

The statue finds this awakening delightful. It runs its hands over itself with astonishment; it touches everything around it. Delighted to discover itself anew and to rediscover familiar objects, its curiosity and all its desires are reawakened more intensely. It yields to them entirely and wanders about familiarizing itself anew with things that were already familiar and acquiring new knowledge. Thus the statue becomes tired for the second time and, giving in to its lethargy, it falls asleep once again.

4. *The statue anticipates that it will repeat these stages.* In passing repeatedly through the different states, the statue will acquire the habit of anticipating them, and they will become so natural for it that it will fall asleep and wake up without being surprised.

5. *How the statue distinguishes them.* The statue distinguishes these states by the memory it has of passing from one state to the other. It felt first that its energy was gradually slipping away. Then it felt that it was suddenly replenished. This abrupt passage from total inaction to the exercise of all of its faculties strikes it, surprises it, and for that reason appears to be a second life. Thus, all that is required for the statue to feel as if it had ceased to be is the contrast between the moment of debility that immediately precedes its sleep and the moment of vigor when it awakens. If it had regained the use of its mental processes by imperceptible degrees, it would not have noticed anything of the kind.

6. *The statue does not form the idea of a state of sleep.* However, the statue does not form a notion of what state it has come out of when it awakens. It does not judge what the duration was and it does not even know if it had a duration. For nothing can lead it to suspect that there was some succession in it or outside of it. Thus the statue has no idea of the state of sleep and it distinguishes it from the state of waking only by the shock that all its faculties give it at the moment that its forces are restored.

11 On Memory, Imagination and Dreams in a Man Limited to the Sense of Touch

1. *How ideas are linked in the memory of the statue.* The sensations that come from the sense of touch are of two kinds: The first are extension, shape, space, solidity, fluidity, hardness, softness, movement, rest; the others are warmth and cold, and different kinds of pleasures and pains. The relations among the latter are naturally indeterminate. They are retained in memory only because the sense organs have transmitted them repeatedly. But the former type have relations that can be known more exactly. Our statue measures the volume of objects with its hands; it measures space by going from one place to another; it determines shapes when it counts the sides of an object and follows its contour; it judges from resistance the properties of solidity or fluidity, hardness or softness; finally it grasps the perceptible difference between movement and rest when it considers whether an object changes or does not change its location in relation to others. And there you have the ideas that, among all others, are linked most strongly and most readily in its memory.

2. *All these ideas are linked to that of extension.* On the one hand, the statue has acquired the habit of relating all its sensations to extension since it regards them as properties of the objects that it touches. All its ideas are only warm extension or cold extension, solid or fluid, etc.; in this way all ideas, those whose relations are the most vague and those whose relations are the best specified, are linked to a single idea. In a word, all its sensations are from its point of view only modifications of extension.

3. *Memory is stronger and more durable as a result.* On the other hand, the sensation of extension is such that a statue can lose it only in deep sleep. When it is awake it always feels that it is extended; for it feels all the parts of its body that press on the spot where they rest and which they measure. As

long as the statue is awake then it cannot be deprived entirely of all kinds of sensations of touch, as it can with the other senses. One sensation always remains to which all others are linked and which I consider, for that reason, as the basis of all the ideas that the statue remembers. Everything indicates then that the recall of ideas coming from touch must be stronger and more long-lasting than that of ideas coming from the other senses.

4. *What the imagination of the statue consists of.* Ideas can be recalled more or less vividly. When they are awakened feebly, the statue recalls only having touched one object or another; but when they are awakened forcefully, it remembers objects as if it were still touching them. Now I called imagination this vivid memory which makes things appear to be present that are, in fact, absent.

5. *Reflection is joined to imagination.* If we add to this faculty that of reflection, the mental operation that combines ideas, we will see how the statue can attribute to one object the properties that it has noticed in others. Suppose it desires to experience all at once several properties that it has not yet encountered together; it will imagine them united and its imagination will provide it with an experience that it could not obtain by touch.

6. *The most extended sense in which we can take the word "imagination."* The most extended meaning that we can give to the word "imagination" is to consider it as the name of the mental process that combines the properties of various objects to create groupings for which there are no models in nature. In this way it provides experiences which in certain respects go beyond reality itself: for this process succeeds in endowing the things it leads us to enjoy with all the properties we wish to find.

7. *Experiences in which touch and imagination work together.* But pleasure from touch can be joined to that from imagination and this will be one of the greatest pleasures that the statue can know. When it touches an object nothing can hinder the imagination from sometimes portraying it with pleasant properties that it does not have, and from eliminating those properties that might displease. All that is needed is a keen desire to discover the former and not to find the latter.

8. *Excesses into which imagination leads the statue.* Imagination can offer the statue so many attractive qualities in objects that it often leads it to take pleasure in moving even when its limbs are tired and resist its bidding. Imagination may even evoke this pleasure so vividly that it distracts the statue from the lethargy of its organs. Then only excessive fatigue can make it enjoy rest. If the statue indulges itself immoderately in some desire, a state of pain and suffering will result; and when it has experienced this often, it will learn to be wary of the attractions of pleasure and will be more careful to judge its stamina.

9. *The state of dreaming.* Between waking and deep sleep we can distinguish two intermediate states: one in which memory recalls ideas only

quite faintly, the other in which imagination recalls them so vividly and combines them in so many perceptible ways that we believe we are even touching objects that in fact we are only imagining.

When the statue has gone to sleep in a place where it learned to move about without danger, it can imagine that the place is covered with thorns and with pebbles that it is walking, and that with each step it is lacerated, slips, falls to the ground, and experiences pain. Although astonished by these changes, the statue cannot doubt them and its state is the same for it as if it had been awake and this place was in fact exactly what it seemed to be.

10. *The cause of dreams and of the disorder in which they recall ideas.* In order to discover the cause of this dream we need only consider that before sleep the statue had the ideas of a place where it could walk without fear, those of thorns, of pebbles, of laceration, of falling, of pain; finally those of a place where it had experienced all these things. Now, what happens in sleep? What happens is that this last idea is not aroused at all. Those of thorns, of pebbles, of lacerations, of falling, of pain and of a place where it had formerly known nothing of the kind are recalled with the same vividness as if the objects were present; and as these ideas combine, the statue must believe that this place has become what its imagination represents it to be. If it had remembered the place where it was lacerated, where it had fallen down, it could not have made this error. Therefore, such bizarre and counterfactual associations occur in dreams only because the ideas that would reestablish order are intercepted.

It is not surprising that in sleep ideas proliferate in a disorder that brings together and unites those that are the most foreign to each other. Thus, just as sleep is rest for the body, it is also rest for memory, for imagination and for all mental processes; and this rest has different degrees. If these processes are competely deadened, sleep is profound. If they are so only to a point, memory and imagination are sufficiently awake to recall certain ideas but not sufficiently so to recall others. In this case those ideas that do appear come together in the most peculiar collections.

11. *Feelings of a statue when awake.* I strike the statue in the midst of its dream and I snatch it from sleep. Its first feeling is fear; scarcely daring to move, it extends its arms cautiously; quite astonished not to find the objects that it believed were hurting it, the statue gets up and tries to walk. Little by little it becomes reassured; it does not know if it is mistaken in this moment or if it was mistaken a moment earlier. Its confidence increases and it forgets the state that it was in when dreaming, experiencing only the one it is in on awakening.

12. *Its perplexity concerning the dream and the waking state.* However, sleep becomes necessary for the statue once again. It surrenders to sleep, it has new dreams, and on awakening it experiences the same astronishment.

In truth, these illusions must appear quite strange to the statue. It could not suspect that they occurred during the time that it was asleep because it has no idea of the duration of its sleep. On the contrary, it does not doubt that it was awake since to be awake is for it to touch and to reflect on what it has touched. Its dreams to not appear to be dreams and it must be all the more disquieted for that. It does not understand why it forms two very different opinions of the very same objects; it does not know where its error lies; and it passes in turn from the distrust inspired by these dreams to the confidence inspired by the state of waking.

13. *Why the statue has dreams that it remembers and others that it forgets.* It is not possible for the statue to remember all ideas that it has had while awake; it must be the same for those it has had when asleep. As for what causes it to remember some of its dreams, here are my conjectures.

If the impression made by a dream was vivid, and if it presented ideas in a disorderly way that sharply contradicts the statue's perception of them prior to falling asleep, then its astonishment will link these ideas to the rest of its knowledge. On awakening, the lingering astonishment causes the statue to make an effort to recall the details of the dream and it will recall them. On the contrary, it will have no recollection whatever if the time between dreaming and waking is long enough and filled with sleep sufficiently deep to efface all its astonishment. Finally, if only some slight surprise remains on awaking, sometimes the statue will recall only a part of its dream, other times it will recall only having had some extraordinary ideas.

The statue's dreams are thus etched in its memory only because they are linked to habitual judgments that they contradict; and its lingering surprise upon awakening obliges the statue to recall them.

12 On the Principal Organ of Touch

1. *The mobility and flexibility of the limbs are necessary for acquiring ideas from touch.* The details in the preceding chapters are sufficient demonstration that the hand is the principal organ of touch. It is in truth the one that lends itself best to touching all kinds of surfaces. Because of the ease with which we can open and close our hands, bend and separate them, and interlink their fingers, the hands take on many different shapes indeed. If this organ were not so mobile and so flexible, our statue would need much more time to acquire the ideas of shape: and how limited it would be in its knowledge if it were deprived of hands!

If its arms, for example, terminated at the wrist, the statue could discover that it has a body and that there are others external to it: it could, by putting its arms around objects, form some idea of their size and of their shape; but its judgment of the regularity or the irregularity of their shapes would be quite imperfect.

The statue would be even more limited if we left it no articulation whatever in its limbs. Reduced to basic sentience, if that sentience were uniform it would experience itself as if at a point and if the sentience were heterogeneous it would only feel itself in several states at once.

2. *But greater mobility and flexibility than we have would be useless for the statue or even deleterious.* Since the organs of touch are less perfect and less suited to transmitting ideas the less they are mobile and flexibile, can we not conclude that the hand would be an even greater aid if it was composed of twenty fingers each of which had a great number of joints? And if the hand

was divided into an infinity of parts all equally mobile and flexible, would not such an organ be a kind of universal geometry?[26]

It is not enough for the parts of the hand to be flexible and mobile, it is also necessary that the statue can notice these parts one after the other and can form exact ideas of them. What knowledge would it have of objects thanks to touch if it had only an imperfect knowledge of the organ with which it touches things? And what idea would it form of that organ if the number of its parts was infinite? It would apply its hand to an infinity of little surfaces. But what would result? A sensation so complex that the statue could not discern any part of it. The study of its hands would be too extensive for it; it would use them without being able to know them well and it would acquire only vague notions.

I will go even further: twenty fingers would perhaps not be as useful for the statue as five. The organ that would give the statue a knowledge of the most complex shapes had to be not too complex itself; without this it would have been difficult for the statue to form a distinct notion of its shape and as a result the complexity of the hand would have been an obstacle to the growth of knowledge. In such a case, the statue would have needed a simpler organ that, since it was more readily understood, would have allowed it to form an idea of the more complex one.

3. *Thus the statue has all that it needs in this respect.* I believe therefore that the statue leaves nothing to be desired in this respect. In truth, what do its hands lack? If there are ideas that they do not give to the statue immediately, in any event they put it on the right track to acquire them. If we were to suppose the impossible, that having numerous slender and sensitive fingers the statue would discern all the concurrent impressions that they transmitted to it, still the statue would not know sizes any the better, which are the subject of mathematics. All it would gain is that it would notice irregularities on the surfaces of objects which now escape its attention; but these will no longer escape its attention once it enjoys the sense of vision.

---

[26]"If the hand." says M. de Buffon, "had a greater number of parts, if it were, for example, subdivided into twenty fingers each with a greater number of joints and movements, no doubt the sensory experience of touch would be infinitely more perfect in such an arrangement than it is at present; a hand so structured could be applied more closely and more exactly to the various surfaces of objects; and if we suppose a hand divided into an infinity of parts, all mobile and flexible, and all of which can be applied at the same time to all points of the surface of an object, then such an organ would be a kind of universal geometry (if I may so express myself), from which we could derive, at the very moment of touching, exact and precise ideas of the shapes of all objects and of the differences, even infinitely small, among their shapes." *Natural history*, vol. 3, p. 359.

PART THREE:
HOW TOUCH TEACHES
THE OTHER SENSES TO
JUDGE EXTERNAL OBJECTS

1 On Touch With Smell

1. *Judgment of the statue on odors.* Let us unite the sense of smell with that of touch and, giving our statue memory for the judgments it made when it was limited to the first of these senses, let us lead it into a garden full of flowers; all its habits return and it will believe itself to be all the odors that it smells.

2. *The statue does not suspect the cause of these sensations.* Astonished to find itself what it has ceased to be for so long a time, it could not yet suspect the cause. It does not know that it has just received a new sense organ and if touch has taught it that there are palpable objects, it has not taught it yet that none of these objects is the cause of the sensations we have just given it.

On the contrary, the statue judges those sensations according to habit, considering them as its own states. It appears to it entirely natural that it is a certain odor at one moment and a different odor at another. It does not imagine that objects can contribute to this; all it knows about them are the properties that touch alone has led it to discover.

3. *The statue is two different beings.* And there you have the statue two different beings at once: one that it cannot take hold of and that seems to evade it at every moment; the other that it touches and that it can always find anew.

4. *The statue begins to suspect that odors come from bodies.* Putting its hand, by chance, on the objects that it encounters, the statue grasps a flower which remains in its hand. It moves its arm aimlessly, now towards its face, now away: the statue experiences itself in a certain state with more or less vividness.

Astonished, it repeats this experiment by design. It takes and releases this flower several times. The statue confirms that it is in, or ceases to be in, a certain state, depending on whether it brings the flower close or holds it at a distance. Finally it begins to suspect that the change in state is due to the flower.

5. *It discovers the organ of smell.* The statue gives all of its attention to this sensation, it observes how vividly it increases, it follows it in all its degrees, compares them with the differing distances of the flower from its face; and since its organ of smell was more affected when it was touched by the fragrant body, the statue discovers that it has a new sense.

6. *It judges that odors are in objects.* It starts its experiments over again: it brings the flower close to this new sense organ, and it moves it away; it compares the present flower with the sensation produced and the absent flower with the sensation extinguished: it confirms that the sensation comes from the flower and judges that it is in the flower.

7. *It experiences odors as in the bodies from which they emanate.* As a result of repeating this judgment, it becomes so much a matter of habit that the statue makes it at the very instant that it smells something. Thereafter it confounds the judgment so thoroughly with the sensation that it could no longer tell the difference. The statue does not confine itself any longer to judging the odor as being in the flower, it senses it to be there.

8. *Odors become properties of objects.* The statue habitually makes these judgments whenever it encounters objects that give it sensations of this kind, and odors are then no longer its own states: they are impressions that odorous bodies make on the organ of smell or rather they are the properties themselves of these objects.

9. *How much trouble the statue has in becoming familiar with these judgments.* It is not without a certain surprise that the statue observes itself led to make judgments that are so different from those that it formerly found so natural; and it is only after repeated experiments that touch destroys the habits that were acquired with smell. The statue has as much trouble placing odors among the various properties of objects as we have ourselves in considering them as states of our own being.

10. *It distinguishes two kinds of objects.* But finally familiarized little by little with these kinds of judgments, the statue distinguishes objects to which it judges odors belong from those to which it judges odors do not belong. Thus the union of smell with touch leads the statue to discover a new class of palpable objects.

11. *And several kinds of odorous objects.* Noticing next the same smell in several flowers, the statue no longer regards it as a particular idea; it regards it on the contrary as a property that is common to several objects. As a result it distinguishes as many classes of odorous objects as it discovers different odors; and it forms a greater number of abstract or general notions than when it was limited to the sense of smell alone.

12. *Discernment that the sense of smell acquires.* Curious to study these

new ideas more and more, sometimes the statue smells flowers one by one, sometimes several together. It notices that the sensation that they engender separately, and that which they engender when they are brought together. It distinguishes several odors in a bouquet and its sense of smell acquires a discernment that it had never had before without the aid of touch.

But this discernment will have its limits if the odors emanate from a certain distance, if they are numerous, and if, above all, none predominates in the mixture; they will be confounded in their joint impression and it will be impossible for the statue to recognize any one odor. However, there is reason to conjecture that its discernment will be more extensive in this respect than our own: since odors have more attraction for it than for us who enjoy all the other senses, the statue will devote itself more than we to distinguishing the differences among the odors.

Because each of the two senses leads to the exercise of the other, they will yield knowledge and pleasures now that they are united that they did not provide when separate.

13. *Judgments that are confounded with sensations.* In order to make quite clear how judgments are distinct from the sensations with which they are often confounded, let us scent some objects whose relatively simple shapes are familiar to our statue and let us present them at the first moment that we give it the sense of smell. Let a certain odor be, for example, always in a triangle, and another always in a square, each will be linked with its own particular shape and thereafter the statue cannot be struck by one or the other without immediately thinking of a triangle or a square: it will believe that it smells a shape in an odor and touches an odor in a shape.

It will notice that although there are shapes that have no odor at all, all odors are associated with a certain shape; and it will attribute to smell ideas that belong only to touch. To further confuse all its ideas we would only have to put different scents on objects of the same shape and to put the same scent on objects of different shapes.

14. *Judgments that are not confounded with sensations.* The judgment that links a triangular shape to an odor can be repeated rapidly whenever the occasion presents itself because it has as its only object ideas that are not particularly complex. That is why this judgment is suited to being confused with sensation. But if the shape were complicated, it would take a greater number of judgments to link it to the odor. The statue would no longer conceptualize it with the same ease; it would no longer think that the same sense conveys knowledge of shape and of odor.

When the statue studies a rose, for example, with its sense of touch, it links the scent with the cluster of leaves, with their texture, and with all the tactual properties that distinguish the rose from other flowers it knows. In this way the statue forms a complex notion which entails as many judgments as there are identifying properties that it notices. In truth, it sometimes makes this judgment right from the first impression that it has when placing its hand on the flower. But it will be mistaken so often it will soon realize that it is obliged, in order to avoid all error, to recall the clearest idea of the flower that tact has given it, and to say to itself, "The rose differs from the carnation because it has such a shape and such a texture," and so on. Now, since these judgments are quite numerous, it is no longer possible for the statue to repeat them all at the moment that it smells the flower. Instead then of experiencing the palpable properties in the odor, it realizes that they are coming little by little from memory and it no longer makes the mistake of attributing to smell ideas that it owes only to touch. Its misapprehensions are quite evident when it smells an odor and repeats some habitual judgment without realizing it. It will make other errors which are much less evident when we give it the sense of vision.

2 Of Hearing, of Smell and of Touch United

1. *The state of the statue at the moment we give it hearing.* As in the preceding chapter, our statue will be astonished to find itself in the state it had once been in if at the moment that we add hearing to smell and touch, it obeys all the habits that it had acquired with the first of these senses. Here the statue is the song of birds, there the noise of a waterfall, further on that of trees in the wind, a moment later the noise of thunder of a terrible storm.

Completely absorbed in these sensations, its touch and smell are no longer in use. If a total silence should suddenly arise, it will seem to the statue that it is snatched from itself. It will go for some time without being able to resume the use of its initial senses. Finally, coming back to its senses little by little, it is again concerned with objects it can touch and smell.

2. *It discovers it has a sense of hearing.* The statue finds what it was not looking for. Having grasped an object that makes noise, it shakes it without intending to; and if by change it brings this object close to its ear and removes it in turn, then this will be sufficient to decide it to bring it close and remove it several times. Guided by the different degrees of impression, the statue applies the object to the organ of hearing; and having repeated this experiment several times, it judges that sounds are in this part of its body as it judged that odors were in another.

3. *It judges that sounds are in objects.* However, it observes that its hearing is altered only on the occasion of this object; it hears sounds when it shakes the object and it no longer hears anything when it stops. It judges, therefore, that these sounds come from the object.

4. *It hears them there.* The statue repeats this judgment and finally makes it with such promptness that it no longer notices an interval between the moment when the sounds strike its ear and the moment that it judges that they

are in the object. Hearing these sounds and judging them as external to itself are two operations that it no longer distinguishes. Instead of perceiving them as its own states, it perceives them as states of the sonorous object. In short it hears them in the object.

5. *The statue forms a habit of this manner of hearing.* If we make the statue repeat the same experiment with other sounds, it will again make the same judgments and it will confuse them with sensation. In what follows, this way of perceiving will become so familiar that its ear will no longer need the lessons of touch. All sounds will appear to come from outside, even on the occasions when it cannot touch the objects that are transmitting them. This is because once a judgment has been confounded by habit with a sensation, it must be confounded with all sensations of the same kind.

6. *Discernment of its ear.* If several sounds that the statue has studied occur together, it will distinguish them not only because its ear is capable of perceiving the difference up to a point but above all because it has just acquired the habit of considering them in objects that it distinguishes. Thus it is that touch contributes to enhancing the discrimination of the ear.

As a result, the more the statue is aided by touch in distinguishing among sounds, the more it learns to distinguish them. But it will confuse them whenever the objects that are producing them are no longer distinguishable by touch.

Discernment by hearing thus has limits because there are cases where touch itself will not be able to sort everything out. I will not speak of limits that are the result of an impairment in the organ of hearing.

7. *The statue judges distances and locations from hearing.* The statue begins to conduct experiments with objects that are within reach. As a result it has the impression initially that, for each noise that strikes its ear, it has only to extend its arm to grasp the object producing the sound, for it has not yet learned to judge that it can be further away. But as it is mistaken with objects at a distance, it takes a step and then a second and as it comes closer it notices that the noise increases right up to the moment at which the object producing the noise is as close to the statue as it can be.

These experiments teach it little by little to judge differing distances of this object; and these judgments, once familiar, are repeated so rapidly that they are confounded with sensation itself and in the end the statue recognizes distances by ear. It will learn if an object is on its left or on its right in the same way. In a word the statue will perceive distance and location of an object by ear, whenever they are the same as under the conditions in which it has made many experiments. Having only this means of making these judgments, in the absence of touch, the statue will use it so often that it will sometimes make judgments as confidently as we ourselves judge with our eyes.

But the statue will run a risk of misapprehension whenever it hears objects whose locations and distances it has not yet studied. It must thus become accustomed to making as many different judgments as there are kinds of sonorous objects and circumstances in which they are audible.

8. *Errors into which the statue can be led.* If the statue had never heard the same sound without touching the same shape, and reciprocally, it would believe that shapes include with them the ideas of sounds and that sounds include with them the ideas of shapes; and it would not know how to assign to touch and to hearing the ideas that belong to each of these senses. Likewise if each sound had constantly been accompanied by a certain odor and if each odor had been accompanied by a certain sound, it would not be possible for the statue to distinguish the ideas that are due to smell and those that are due to hearing. These errors are similar to those that we led it to make in the preceding chapter; and they prepare us for the observations that we are going to make on vision.

3

How the Eye Learns to See Distance, Location, Shape, Size, and the Movement of Objects

1. *State of the statue when it receives vision.* The astonishment of our statue is once again the first thing to notice at the moment that we give it vision. But probably the experiments that it had conducted on the sensations of smell, hearing and touch will soon lead it to suspect that what appears once again to be its own state can be properties that a new sense will lead it to discover in objects.

2. *Why the eye can be instructed only by touch.* We have seen that, limited to touch, the statue could not judge sizes, locations, and distances with two sticks whose length and direction were unknown. Now rays are to its eyes what these sticks were to its hands; and the eye can be considered as an organ that in some sense has an infinity of hands for holding an infinity of sticks. If the eye was capable of knowing on its own the length and direction of rays, it could, like the hand, attribute to one extreme what it senses at the other and judge sizes, distances and locations. But far from teaching the eye the length and direction of rays, the sensation that it experiences does not even teach it that there are such rays. The eye receives the impression only the way the hand receives the impression of the first stick that it touched at one of its ends.

Even if we were to give our statue a perfect knowledge of optics, it would be no further advanced. It would know that in general rays have greater or lesser angles in proportion to the size and distance of objects. But it would not be able to measure these angles. If, as is the case, the principles of optics are insufficient to explain vision, they are all the more insufficient to teach us to see.

Moreover, this science does not instruct us at all on the way in which we must move our eyes. It supposes only that the eyes are capable of different movements and that they must change shape according to the circumstances.

The eye thus has need of the aid of touch in order to form the habit of movements suited to vision; to become accustomed to attributing sensations to the extremities of rays or approximately so; and to judge in this way distances, sizes, locations and shapes. We are concerned here with discovering the experiments that are the most suitable for instructing it.

3. *It senses colors in contact with its eyes.* Either by chance or because of the pain caused by a light that is too bright, the statue puts its hand on its eyes: in that instant, colors disappear. It removes its hand and the colors are renewed. Thereafter, it ceases to consider colors to be its own states. It seems to the statue that color is something intangible that it senses in contact with its eyes, as it senses at its fingertips the objects that it touches.

But, as we have seen, each color is a simple change in state that in itself gives no distinct idea of extension: for a distinct idea of extension would be shaped or circumscribed and this would be an idea that the statue, limited to the sense of vision, was completely deprived of. Therefore, a color will not represent dimensions to eyes that have not learned to attribute it to all the parts of a surface: the eyes will only sense that they are modified within themselves and they will not yet see anything beyond that.

But although the sensations of hot and cold do not carry with them any idea of extension, they are, however, spread over all the dimensions of objects to which we have learned to attribute them. In the same way, colors will become extended over objects: touch will lead the eyes to form the habit of judging colors on a surface as it judges hot or cold there itself.

4. *It sees that they form a surface.* Because colors are blotted out when the statue places its hand on the exterior surface of its visual organ, and because they reappear whenever it removes its hand, the statue must necessarily see them appear or disappear as if they were on this very surface, and it is there that it begins to give them extension.

When objects are removed or brought closer then, the statue does not yet judge either their distance nor their movement. It perceives only colors that appear more or less or that disappear entirely.

5. *This surface appears enormous to the statue.* This luminous surface is equal to the exterior surface of the eye and that is all that the statue sees; its eyes see nothing beyond that, therefore it sees no limits to this surface and it sees it as immense.

6. *The statue has no need to learn to see but it needs to learn to look.* If we let the statue see a large part of the horizon, the surface that it will see on its eyes could represent a vast landscape, varied by the colors and shapes of innumerable objects. The statue then sees all these things: it sees them, I say, but it has no idea of them whatever and it cannot even have such an idea.

This proposition will appear no doubt a paradox to those who contend that "vision alone, independent of touch, gives us the idea of extension since extension is the necessary object of vision"; and that "differences among colors will lead us necessarily to notice the boundaries or limits that separate two colors and as a result will give us an idea of shape."

Certainly, we notice all that ourselves, and I agree that the statue sees all that we notice and indeed more. But as long as it has not learned from touch to direct its eyes, is it capable of noticing these things as we are? And has it ideas of them if it does not notice them?

It is not sufficient to reaffirm, following Locke, that all our knowledge comes from the senses: if I do not know how it comes from the senses, I must believe that as soon as objects make an impression on us we have all the ideas that our sensations can contain, and I would be mistaken. This is indeed what happened to me and what is still happening to all those who write on this topic. It seems we do not know that there is a difference between seeing and looking; and yet we do not form ideas as soon as we see; we form ideas only insofar as we look in an orderly way, with method. In a word, our eyes must analyze: for they will not grasp the configuration of the least complex figure if they have not observed all the parts separately, one after the other and in the order that exists among them. Now do the eyes of the statue know how to analyze when as yet they only see colors within themselves or at the most on their pupils? There you have, strictly speaking, what the question comes down to. I am persuaded that if we were to put the problem to a mathematician, using the word "analyze" as I have, he would answer without equivocating that the eyes of the statue do not analyze; for he remembers how much trouble he went to to learn analysis. But if we put the question with the word "look," which basically leaves it unchanged, I believe that he would respond, equally without equivocation, that his eyes look, because they see.

He would certainly give this response if he thinks that the eyes alone, *independent of touch*, give us ideas of shape as soon as they see colors. But how would eyes whose vision does not extend beyond the pupil know how to look? For in the end, in order to look, they must know how to aim at one of several objects that they are seeing; and to have an idea of the shape of that object, however uncomplicated it might me, they must know how to direct themselves toward each of its parts, successively and in the order that they have among themselves. But how could the eyes direct themselves following an order that they do not know? How indeed can they aim at anything? Does not this action on their part imply a space in which they would take in objects that are at different distances from their pupils and at different distances among themselves, a space that the eyes do not yet know? Thus I will not say, as everyone else does and as I myself have formerly said rather imprecisely, that our eyes need to learn to see; for they see necessarily all that makes an impression on us; but because it is not sufficient to see in order to form ideas, I will say that they need to learn to look.

Progress in this matter has hinged on the difference between these two words. Now why does this difference, which a schoolboy grasps, elude philosophers? See how we reason. We set forth the question poorly, we do not even know how to set it forth, and yet we claim to have resolved it.[27] I just caught myself in this practice and I acknowledge that I have often caught myself in the past; but I catch others more often.

Finally, whatever it may have cost us, here we have the question reduced to a simple question indeed and it is demonstrated that the eyes of the statue need to learn to look. Let us see how touch will instruct them.

7. *The statue judges the surface to be far from it.* Through curiosity or restlessness the statue places its hand in front of its eyes; it removes its hand and it places it there again; and the surface that it sees is, as a result, more brightly lit or less so. From this it judges that the movement of its hand is the cause of these changes and, as it knows that it moves it at a certain distance, it suspects that this surface is not as close as it had thought.

8. *It sees colors on bodies.* Let it then touch an object in front of its eyes and it will substitute one color for another if it covers the object with his hand; and if it removes its hand, the first color reappears. It seems to the statue then that its hand causes these two colors to succeed each other at a certain distance.

Once more the statue moves its hand on a surface and, seeing one color moving over another whose parts appear and disappear in turn, it judges that the stationary color is on the object and the moving color is on its hand. This judgment becomes familiar and it sees colors retreat from its eyes and move onto its hand and the objects that it touches.

9. *Experiments that complete the acquisition of this habit.* Astonished by this discovery, the statue looks around itself considering touching everything that it sees. Its hand encounters an object of a new color, its eye then perceives another surface, and the same experiences lead it to make the same judgments.

Curious to discover if the same thing applies to all sensations of this kind, it puts its hand on everything around it and, touching a multicolored object, its eye acquires the habit of discerning the colors on the surface that it judges to be at some distance.

No doubt the statue has a series of quite agreeable sensory expriences as it guides its eyes in this confusion of light and color. In pursuit of pleasure, the statue never tires of repeating the same experiments and of conducting new ones. The statue accustoms its eyes little by little to fixate on the objects that it touches; they form the habit of certain movements; and soon they penetrate, as through a cloud, to see in the distance the objects that its hand grasps and seems to paint with light and color.

---

[27]I have shown in my *Logic* that we owe all our ideas to analysis, and that every question that is well-formulated solves itself in some sense on its own.

10. *It sees objects at the distance where it touches them.* In leading its hand succesively from its eyes to the objects and conversely, the statue measures distances. Next it brings these same objects close and withdraws them in turn. It studies the different impressions that its eye receives each time and, accustomed to linking these impressions with the distances made known by touch, it sees the objects sometimes as closer, sometimes as further, because it sees them where it touches them.

11. *It learns to see a sphere.* The first time that it casts its gaze on a sphere, the impression that it receives represents only a flat circle mixed with shade and light. Thus it does not yet see a sphere, for its eye has not learned to judge relief on a surface where light and shade are distributed in a certain proportion. But it touches and because it learns to make the same judgments with vision that it made with touch, the object takes on in its eyes the relief that it has in its hands.

The statue repeats this experiment and repeats the same conclusion. In this way it links ideas of roundness and of convexity to the impression that a certain mixture of light and shade makes on it. It tries next to judge a sphere that it has not yet touched. In the beginning no doubt it finds itself in some difficulty but touch removes the uncertainty. As a result of the habit that it acquires of judging spheres by sight, so rapidly and confidently does it make this judgment and so thoroughly does it link the idea of this shape to a surface where light and shade are in a certain proportion, that finally it only sees each time what it said to itself so often it ought to see.

12. *The statue distinguishes a sphere and a cube.* The statue will also learn to see a cube when its eyes study the impressions they receive at the moment that its hand senses the angles and the faces of this shape, and it acquires the habit of noticing in the different degrees of light the same angles and faces; and it is only then that it will distinguish a sphere from a cube.

13. *How its eyes are guided by touch.* Thus the eye only comes to see a shape distinctly because the hand teaches it to grasp the configuration. The hand must lead the eye over the different parts of an object and cause it to give its attention first to one, then to two, and little by little to a greater number of parts and, at the same time, to the different impressions of light. If the eye did not study each part separately, it would never see the entire shape; and if it did not examine the various effects of light on it, it would only see flat surfaces. Thus the statue only comes to see so many things all at once because, having noticed them separately, it recalls in an instant all the judgments that it has made one after the other.

14. *The aid that it finds in memory.* Our own experience can convince us how thoroughly memory is necessary in order to come to the point where we can grasp the whole of a complexly structured object. At the first glance that we give to a painting we see it quite imperfectly but we look from one shape to the next and may not even look at one in its entirety. The more we fixate on

the painting, the more our attention limits itself to one of the parts: we perceive only, for example, the mouth.

In this way we acquire the habit of rapidly scanning all the details of the painting; and we see it in its entirety because all the judgments that we have made succesively are presented by memory at the same time.

But all that is still highly limited for us. If, for example, I enter a crowd I have only a vague idea at first of the throng. I do not know that I am in the midst of ten or twelve people until I have counted them; that is to say, until I have scanned them one by one so slowly that I am led to notice the sequence of my judgments. If there had only been three in the crowd, I would not have scanned them any the less; but it would have been with such a speed that I would have not been able to realize it.

If our eyes encompass a multitude of objects only with the help of memory, those of our statue will need the same aid in order to grasp the totality of the simplest shape. For since its eyes are untrained, the simplest shape is still too complicated for them. Thus the statue will have an idea of a triangle only after having analyzed it.

15. *It judges position.* It is the hand that, guiding vision successively over the different parts of a shape, etches all these parts in memory; it is the hand that, so to say, guides the engraving tool when the eyes begin to attribute to the exterior the light and colors that they first experienced as in themselves. They perceive these properties where touch teaches them that they must be: they see as up what touch teaches them to judge as up and they see as down what it leads them to judge as down; in a word, they see objects in the same positions as the sense of touch represents them to be.

Reversing the image does not create any obstacle whatever because as long as the eyes have not been instructed, there is strictly speaking neither an up nor a down for them. It is only touch that can discover these sorts of relations and it is only touch that can teach the eyes to judge them.

Moreover, since the eyes see things as external only because they associate colors with the objects that the hand touches, the eyes must necessarily conform in their judgment of position with the sense of touch.

16. *They do not see double at all.* Each eye fixes on the object that the hand has grasped, each attributes the colors to the same place, at the same distance, and as the reversal of the image does not prevent them from seeing an object in its true location, so the same image, although double, does not prevent them from seeing it as simple. The hand forces them to judge according to what it senses in itself. In forcing them to attribute to the exterior sensations that they experience in themselves, the hand makes each of them refer their sensations to the single object it is touching and to the very same spot where it touches it. Thus it is natural for the eyes not to see double.

17. *They judge size.* For the same reason, the hand teaches the eyes at the same instant to judge size. As soon as it teaches them to see the colors on

what it is touching, it teaches them to associate each color with the parts of the object that display it; it sketches a surface in front of the eyes and marks its contours.

Thus whether the hand moves an object closer or further away, it seems to the eyes to have the same size although the image grows or diminishes as a result, as it seems to them simple and upright although the image is doubled and reversed.

18. *They judge movement.* Finally, the hand makes them see the movement of objects because it accustoms them to following objects that it displaces from one point in space to another.

19. *They do not yet see beyond arm's length.* Up until now, the statue has studied with the aid of vision only those objects that are within reach; for it is in this way that it must necessarily begin. Therefore it has not yet learned to see beyond that scope, and it perceives itself as enclosed within a small space. In truth, going from one place to another has taught it that space must be much larger but it does not yet imagine how it would appear by eye. In vain it would say to itself, there is extension beyond what I see; such a judgment could not render that space visible. Thus the statue sees only as far as it can reach because it has repeatedly touched and seen the objects in this space at the same time and it has so strongly linked tactual judgments with sensations of light that seeing and judging occur together and are confused: the statue will not see further until new experiences lead it to confound the same sensations with judgments it will make about other distances.

Thus the statue perceives a space that extends roughly two feet around it. Its eye, instructed by touch, measures the parts of this space, fixes the shape and the size of objects that are included within it, places them at different distances, judges their locations, their movement and their rest.

20. *How objects that are further away become visible for the statue.* As for those objects that are farther away, the statue sees them all at the extremity of this ring that bounds its visual field. It perceives them as if they were on a concave, immobile and luminous surface. They appear to have shape because the experiments that the statue has conducted on those within its reach are adequate for that purpose. If the objects move horizontally, it sees them go from one part of the surface to another; if they come closer or withdraw, it sees them only become larger and smaller in a highly perceptible way. But it does not judge their true size at all; for it has learned to recognize objects within its limited visual field only because touch has led it to link different ideas of size to different impressions made on its eyes. Now these impressions vary proportiontely with distance since the images grow or decrease in the same proportions. Not having conducted any experiment to link these impressions with the sizes that are several feet away, the statue can judge distant objects only in accord with the habits it has formed perviously. The impression caused by small images ought conse-

quently to make them appear small and the impression caused by large images ought to make them appear large; for it is thus that the statue judges those that touch has brought into view. The associations that the statue has learned in order to judge visually sizes that are one or two feet away are thus not sufficient to enable it to judge those that are further away. They can only in this circumstance lead it into error.

This surface bounding its vision is precisely the same phenomenon as the vault of the heavens to which all the stars seem to be attached and which appears to extend on all sides to the furthest points on the earth that the eye can see. The statue sees this surface as immobile as long as it remains immobile itself: it sees it recede before it or follow it when it changes place. It is thus that the sky on the horizon appears to us to move.

21. *The eyes learn to see beyond arm's length.* However, the statue extends its arms to grasp what it sees. Surprised at touching nothing, it moves forward. Finally it encounters an object: immediately the judgments of vision confirm those of touch. A moment later the statue withdraws. At first, the object does not appear to be further away as a result but when the statue tries to reach it and fails, it approaches it again; and approaching and withdrawing repeatedly, the statue becomes accustomed little by little to see the object beyond arm's reach.

The movement away from the object gives the statue a rough idea of the space that it left between itself and the object; it knows what the size of the object was when it was touching it; and if touch has taught the statue to see the object at two feet with a certain size, the memory that remains of the size leads the statue to still attribute it at a greater distance.

Thus the statue can judge by eye if the object is moving closer or away or in some other direction; for it sees its movements in the changes that occur in the impressions made on its eyes. Now it is true that these changes are the same whether the statue approaches the object or vice versa, whether it passes in front of it in a certain direction or conversely; however the feeling that it has of its own movement or of its own rest will not let it make a mistake.

Thus the statue becomes accustomed to linking different ideas of distance, of size and of movement to different impressions of light. It does not know in truth that the images that appear on the retina diminish in proportion to distance. It does not even know that there are such images. But it experiences different sensations, and since the judgments that have become habitual according to the circumstances are confounded with these sensations, the statue no longer senses the lights and the colors in its eyes; it senses them to be at the other end of the rays, as it senses solidity, fluidity etc. at the other end of a stick with which it touches objects.

Thus the more its eyes guide their judgments according to the lessons of touch, the more space appears to them to take on depth. The statue perceives light and color which distributed over objects allow it to deduce then size and shape and to follow their movements in space; in a word the statue sees them where it judges they must be.

22. *Why receding objects appear to diminish gradually.* However, whatever memory the statue has of the size of an object, it cannot stop the object from diminishing in its eyes in proportion as it moves away. Here is the reason for this phenomenon.

An object is only visible insofar as the angle that determines the extent of its image on the retina has a certain value. I suppose that it ought to be at least one minute: but I say this only to anchor our discussion, for the angle must vary according to the eyes.

With this supposition we can readily understand that an object seen distinctly at a certain distance cannot move away without the angles that made the smallest parts visible becoming smaller and without several ending up less than one minute. It must even be that in some objects the sides come together and merge into a single line. Thus several angles will be merged into one and the sides will be further confounded if the object continues to move away. Thus there will be parts that cease to be represented on the retina. These parts will come together, interpenetrate, and become confused with those that are still depicted; and the boundaries of the object will move toward each other. The image—for example, the head of a man—will lose its distinctive features.

Now touch teaches the eyes to see objects in their true size only because it teaches them to discern their parts and to perceive them one outside of the other. It can do this only insofar as the parts are distinctly drawn on the retina. For the eyes would be unable to notice in their sensations what is not there. They must, therefore, judge an object more compact and smaller when it is at such a distance that many of the features of its image are confounded. As a result, whatever the distance of an object, it continues to appear the same size as long as the reduction in the angles does not perceptibly alter the image painted on the retina, and it is because this alteration takes place by imperceptible degrees that a receding object gradually appears to diminish.

23. *How the eyes learn to dispense with the aid of touch.* Not only do the eyes of the statue distinguish the objects that it no longer touches, they also distinguish those that it has not touched provided that it receives similar sensations from them or roughly so. For once touch has linked different judgments to different impressions of light, these impressions cannot recur without the judgments recurring and becoming confused with them. Thus it is that the statue becomes accustomed little by little to see without the aid of touch.

24. *Why the eyes will make errors.* However, the experiments that taught the statue to see the distance, size, and shape of an object will not always be

adequate to teach it to see the distance, size and shape of every other object. The statue must make as many observations as there are objects that reflect light differently; it must even multiply its observations on each object according to the varying degrees of distance; and further, despite all these precautions, it will often be mistaken with regard to size, distance, and shape.

It is only, as a result, after much study that the statue will begin to be more certain of its visual judgments; but it will be impossible for it to avoid absolutely all errors. Often it will be misled by the very experiments it believes it should rely on more completely. Accustomed, for example, to link the idea of proximity to the brightness of light, and the idea of distance to dimness, sometimes brightly lit bodies will appear to it to be closer than they are, and, on the contrary, poorly lit bodies will appear too far away.

25. *Vision will contradict touch.* It can even happen that its vision will be in contradiction with touch to such a degree that it can no longer conform with touch in making the same judgments. For example, its eyes see convexity in a painted relief where its hand perceives only a flat surface. No doubt astonished by this new phenomenon, the statue does not know which of its two senses to believe: touch detects the error in vain, since the eyes are accustomed to judging by themselves and no longer consult their teacher. Having learned from touch to see in one way, they can no longer learn to see differently.

Indeed, the eyes have acquired a habit that cannot be taken away from them because the judgments that lead them to see convexity in a certain impression of light and shade have become natural. Because they have been made many times over, they are repeated rapidly, and they are confused with sensation whenever the same impression of light and shade occurs.

If one arranged things so that among the objects that our statue would have occasion to touch, there were as many painted reliefs on flat surfaces as truly convex objects, the statue would have considerable difficulty in distinguishing by sight those that have convexity from those that do not. It would be mistaken so often that it would not dare to rely on its eyes; it would only believe touch thereafter.

A mirror would also put the two senses in contradiction. The statue would not doubt that there was a great space beyond the mirror. It would be quite astonished to be stopped by a solid body and it would still be just as much astonished when it began to recognize the objects that the mirror reflects. The statue does not conceive how they are reproduced visually and does not know if they also can be reproduced tactually.

26. *And even itself.* Not only will vision be in contradiction with touch but it will even contradict itself. The statue judges, for example, that a tower is round and very small when it is at a certain distance. It approaches the tower and it sees angles emerge, it sees the tower grow before its eyes. Is it mistaken now or was it mistaken before? That is what it will not know until the tower is

within reach. Thus touch, the eyes' only teacher, is also the only aid to identifying when they can be relied on.

27. *Distance is judged by size.* But if the statue is deprived of this aid, it will draw on all the knowledge that it has acquired. Sometimes it will judge distance by size. An object that appears as large by sight as by touch it will see as close; one that appears smaller it will see as far away. For it has noticed that the appearances of size vary according to distance.

28. *And by the sharpness of images.* On other occasions the statue will establish distances by the distinctness of shapes that it can see. Having often noticed that distant objects are less distinct and closer ones more so, the statue links the idea of distance to the indistinct perception of a shape and the idea of proximity to distinct perception. It thus acquires the habit of seeing an object as quite far when it sees it indistinctly and close when it distinguishes the various parts better.

29. *The eyes judge size by distance.* Then judging size by distance, as it has on other occasions judged distance by size, it sees as larger what it believes to be farther away. Two trees, for example, that provide it with images of the same extension will not appear at all equal nor at the same distance if the image of one is more indistinct than the other: the statue will see as larger and farther the one in which it discerns fewer things. Further, a fly will seem to be a bird in the distance if, as it passes rapidly before the statue's eyes, it allows the perception of only a vague image similar to that of a distant bird.

These principles are known to everyone and painting confirms them. A horse that occupies the same space on the canvas as a sheep will appear larger and in the background provided that it is not painted as distinctly as the sheep.

Thus it is that ideas of distance, of size and of shape, first learned from touch, then cooperate to make visual judgments more certain.

30. *They judge distances and sizes by intermediate objects.* Since our statue sees space take on depth before its eyes, it has yet another means for knowing distances and therefore sizes; namely, to look at the things that are between it and the object it is examining. The statue will see the object as farther and larger if the two are separated by fields, woods, rivers. Since it knows the extent of the fields, woods and rivers that can serve as a measure to establish how far away the object is. But if some elevation hides the intermediate objects, the statue would be able to judge the object's distance only to the extent that some circumstance recalls its size. A stationary horse, for example, can appear rather small and rather close. It moves: and by its movements the statue recognizes it; immediately it judges it to have the usual size and it perceives the horse in the distance.

The statue first believes the horse to be rather small and close because no intermediate object leads it to see its distance and no circumstance indicates what that distance could be. But as soon as the movement makes the statue recognize the horse, it sees it with roughly the size that it knows belongs to this animal; and it sees it as far from itself because it judges that distance is the only cause that could have made it appear so indistinct.

31. *A case where the eyes no longer judge size or distance.* With these aids, the statue discerns distances fairly well by eye but it is no longer successful as soon as these aids are lacking; and its vision is limited at that point where it ceased to see intermediate objects and only sees objects whose size it has not learned from touch. The heavens seem to the statue to form a vault that does not rise higher than the mountains nor extend beyond the land that its eye encompasses. Let the statue see other objects above these mountains and beyond these lands and this vault will become higher and more extended. But it would be less so if we had supposed mountains that were less elevated and lands that were more circumscribed. The top of a tree would have appeared to touch the sky.

This phenomenon is then, as we have stated, the same as that which limited its vision to a distance of two feet. Since its eyes have no way to judge the distance of the stars, they all appear at the same distance. This is a proof that all objects must have appeared to the statue to be within arm's reach under the conditions we hypothesized earlier.

32. *Effects that result from comparing sizes.* However, since the statue is familiar with sizes, it compares them and this comparison influences the judgments that it makes. In the beginning, the statue does not judge an object as absolutely large or absolutely small but rather in relation to sizes that are more familiar and are therefore the measure of all others. It sees as large, for example, everything that is taller than it is, and small everything that is shorter. These comparisons become so rapid that it no longer notices them; and thereafter largeness and smallness become absolute ideas for the statue. It will find a pyramid of twenty feet absolutely large alongside of one of ten feet but absolutely small alongside of one of forty feet; and it will not suspect that it is the same pyramid in the two cases.

Moreover, it is not necessary for these experiments that the objects be of the same kind: the eye needs only some occasion to compare one size with another. That is why the same objects always appear smaller on a very broad plain than in a landscape broken up by hills.

This way of comparing sizes is yet another cause that contributes to making them appear smaller the more they are farther away and especially higher. For the eye cannot follow something rushing away from it or rising into the air without comparing it with a space proportional to its distance.

33. *The exclusive use of vision impairs the sophistication of the other senses.* Such are the means by which the statue will learn to judge space, distances, locations, shapes, sizes, and movement by eye. The more it uses its eyes the more it finds it convenient to do so. They enrich memory with the

most beautiful ideas, make up for the weaknesses of the other senses, judge objects that are inaccessible to those senses, and encompass a space that only imagination can amplify. Thus it is that their ideas are linked so strongly with all others that it almost becomes impossible for the statue to think about odorous, sonorous or palpable objects without immediately clothing them in light and color. From their acquired habit of apprehending a whole, and even several such ensembles, and of judging their relations, the eyes acquire a level of discernment so superior that the statue consults them preferentially. Thus it makes less of an effort to recognize positions and distances by sound, to distinguish objects by the nuances of odors they give off, or by the differences that the hand can discover on their surfaces. Hearing, smell and touch are less exercised as a result. They gradually become more lazy and they cease to notice all the differences in objects that they were able to distinguish formerly; and they lose their fineness of discrimination the more vision becomes sophisticated.

4

Why We Tend to Attribute to Vision Ideas that are Due Only to Touch. By What Series of Reflections We Come to Discard This Preconception

1. *Why we have trouble persuading ourselves that the eye needs to learn.* It has become so natural for us to judge sizes, shapes, distances, and locations by eye that the reader perhaps still has considerable difficulty convincing himself that this is only a habit resulting from experience. All of these ideas seem so intimately bound up with the sensations of color that we cannot imagine that they were ever separated from them. And there you have, I think, the sole cause that can maintain the preconception. In order to destroy it entirely, we need only make some suppositions similar to those we have already made.

2. *Suppositions that finish off this preconception.* Our statue would believe unfailingly that odors and sounds come from its eyes if, having given it vision, smell and hearing all at once, we were to suppose that these three senses were always engaged together in such a way that with each color the statue saw, it would smell a certain odor and hear a certain sound and that it would cease to smell and hear as soon as it saw nothing.

Thus, it is because odors and sounds are transmitted without intermingling with colors that the statue distinguishes so well what belongs to smell and what to hearing. But since the senses of sight and touch work at the same time, the one giving us ideas of light and color, the other those of size, shape, distance and location, we have difficulty in distinguishing what belongs to each of these senses and we attribute to one of them alone what we ought to divide between them.

Thus vision is enriched at the expense of touch because it acts only along with touch or as a result of its lessons, and hence visual sensations are mixed with those ideas it owes to touch. Touch, on the contrary, often acts alone

287

and does not allow us to imagine that sensations of light and color belong to it.

But if the statue never saw any objects other than those it touched, and if it never touched any other than those it saw, it would be impossible for it to distinguish the sensations of sight from those of touch. The statue would not even suspect that it had eyes. Its hands would appear to see and touch at the same time.

Thus it is habitual judgments that lead us to attribute to vision the ideas that we owe only touch.

3. *Suspicions and reflections that have led to this discovery.* It seems to me that when a discovery is made it is interesting to know the first hints of it that philosophers had and above all the reflections of those who were on the point of grasping the truth.

On Malebranche. Malebranche is, I believe, the first who said that judgments are mixed in with our sensations. He states that many readers will be shocked by this point of view. But they will be especially shocked when they see the explanation this philosopher gives. For he avoids a preconception only to make another mistake. Not able to understand how we would make these judgments ourselves, he attributes them to God: a very convenient way of reasoning indeed and one almost always the resort of philosophers.

"I believe I should warn the reader," he says, "that it is not at all our mind that makes these judgments of distance, size, etc. of objects; . . . it is rather God, as a result of the laws that unite the mind and the body. It is for this reason that I call these kinds of judgments 'natural' to indicate that they are made within us but without our participation and despite us . . . God alone can instruct us in an instant concerning the size, the shape, the movement and the colors of objects that surround us."[28]

He goes on to explain at greater length in an appendix on optics how he imagines that God makes these judgments for us.

On Locke. Locke could not make up systems like that. He recognized that we see convex figures only by virtue of a judgment that we make ourselves and which has become habitual for us. But the reason that he gives for this is not satisfying.

"But we having, by use, been accustomed to perceive what kind of appearance convex bodies are wont to make in us; what alterations are made in the reflections of light by the difference of the sensible figures of bodies;— the judgment presently, by an habitual custom, alters the appearances into their causes. So that from that which is truly variety of shadow or colour,

---

[28]*Recherches de la vérité*, book 1, ch. 9.

collecting the figure, it makes it pass for a mark of figure, and frames to itself the perception of a convex figure . . ."[29]

Can we suppose that men know the images that convex objects produce in them and the changes that occur in the reflection of light according to differences in the perceptible shapes of these objects?

On Molineux. Molineux, in posing a problem that was the occasion for discussing all that concerns vision, seems to have grasped only a part of the truth.

"Suppose," Locke has him say, "someone born blind, now an adult, whom we had taught to distinguish a sphere and a cube of the same metal and of about the same size by touch . . . We ask whether if, in seeing them, he could distinguish them?"

The conditions that the two objects are of the same metal and the same size are superfluous; and the latter seems to suppose that vision can, without the aid of touch, give different ideas of size. That being the case, we do not see why Locke and Molineux deny that vision alone can distinguish shapes.

On Berkeley. Moreover, they should have considered distances, locations, and sizes as they did shapes and concluded that at the moment the person born blind opened his eyes to light he would not judge any of these things. For all of these properties are found on a small scale in the perception of the different parts of a sphere and a cube. It is self-contradictory to suppose that an eye able to discern location, size and distance would be unable to discern shapes. Dr. Berkeley is the first who thought that vision by itself could judge none of these things.

Another consequence that should not have escaped Locke is that eyes without experience would only see light and color as in themselves; and that touch alone can teach them to see them as external.

Finally, Locke should have noticed that judgments are mixed in with our sensations whatever the sensory organ by which they are transmitted to the mind. But he says exactly the opposite.[30] It only shows that it takes a good deal of time, many mistakes, and many half-truths to arrive at the truth. Often it is right at hand and yet we do not know how to grasp it.

---

[29]*Essay Concerning Human Understanding*, book 2, ch. 9, sec. 8.

[30]Book 2, ch. 9, sec. 9.

5 Of a Man Born Blind Whose Cataracts Were Removed

1. *The blind man did not want the operation.* Cheselden, a famous London surgeon, had occasion several times to observe people born blind whose cataracts he removed. As he noticed that all of them told him roughly the same thing he restricted himself to giving an account of the patient from whom he obtained the most details.[31]

This patient was a young man of thirteen to fourteen years of age. It was difficult for him to agree to the operation; he did not imagine what he might be lacking. Would I know my garden better, he asked? Will I walk there more freely? For that matter, do I not have an advantage over others in moving about at night with greater confidence? Thus it was that the compensations he found in his present state led him to think that he was as well constituted as we. In truth, he could not long for an advantage that he did not know.

Invited to allow his cataracts to be removed in order to have the pleasure of varying his walks, it seemed to him to be more convenient to stay with those places he knew perfectly; for he could not see how it would ever be as easy for him, with the aid of sight, to stroll in those places where he had never been. Thus he would have never agreed to the operation if he had not wanted to know how to read and write. This sole motive decided him. And they began by removing the cataract in one of his eyes.

2. *The state of his eyes after the operation.* We must point out that he was not so blind that he could not distinguish day from night. He even distinguished white, black, and red in very bright light. But these sensations were

---

[31] *Transactions of the Philosophical Society*, No. 402, 1728.

so different from those that he had subsequently that he was not able to recognize them.

3. *After the operation objects appeared to him to be at the border of his eye.* When he began to see, objects appeared to touch the exterior surface of his eye. The reason for this is clear enough.

Before his cataracts were removed, he had often noticed that he stopped seeing light as soon as he put his hand on his eyes. Thus he acquired the habit of judging it as external. But because it was a dim and indistinct glimmer he did not discriminate colors sufficiently to discover the objects that displayed them. He did not consider them then to have a certain distance and it was not possible for him to distinguish depth; as a result, the colors must have seemed to him to be immediately touching his eyes. Now the operation could produce no other effect than to make light more intense and more distinct. This young man must then have continued to see light where he had judged it to be until then, that is to say, against his eye.

As a result, he only perceived a surface equal to the size of this sense organ.

4. *And very large.* But he proved the truth of the observations we have made: for all that he saw seemed to him to be of astonishing size.[32] Since his eye had not yet compared one size with another, it could not have relative ideas on this topic. As yet it did not know at all how to distinguish the limits of objects, and the surface that touched it must have appeared immense, as it did for the statue. We are assured that some time passed before he imagined that there was something beyond what he saw.

5. *He does not distinguish objects by shape or by size.* He perceived all objects tossed together in the greatest confusion and he did not distinguish them at all no matter how different they were in shape and size. This is because he had not yet learned to grasp several configurations all at once using vision. How could he have learned it? His eyes had never analyzed anything, they did not know how to look nor as a result how to notice different objects and to form a distinct idea of each.

But as he became accustomed to giving depth to light and to creating, as it were, a space in front of his eyes, he placed each object at different distances, assigned to each the location it must occupy and began to judge by eye their shapes and relative sizes.

6. *He does not imagine how one can appear smaller than another.* As long as he had not yet become familiar with these ideas, he had difficulty comparing them and he was far from imagining how his eyes could judge relations of size. This is why, before ever leaving his room, he said that although he knew it to be smaller than the house, he did not understand how it

---

[32]Part 3, ch. 3, sec. 5.

could appear so by sight. Indeed, his eye had never made any comparisons of this kind at all until then. And it is also for this reason that a one-inch object placed in front of his eye seemed to him to be as big as the house.

7. *He learns to see only as a result of study.* Sensations as novel as these, in which he made discoveries at every moment, could not fail to make him curious to see everything and to study everything by eye. Thus when he was shown objects that he recognized by touch, he observed them carefully in order to recognize them on another occasion by sight. He devoted all the more attention to them as he had not recognized them at first by their shape nor by their size. But he had so many things to remember that he forgot the way in which he saw some objects as he learned to see others. I am learning, he said, a thousand things in a day and I am forgetting exactly as many.

8. *Objects he saw with particular pleasure.* Under these conditions, objects that reflected light the best and whose configuration was grasped more easily, must have pleased him more than the others. Glossy and regular objects are examples. We are assured that these appeared to him more pleasing but he could not explain why. They had even pleased him more at the time when he could not yet say what their shapes were at all.[33]

9. *His astonishment at seeing a painted relief.* As the relief of objects is not as perceptible in painting as in reality, this young man was for some time in the habit of considering paintings as only differently colored planes. It was only after two months that they appeared to him to represent solid bodies; and this was a discovery he seemed to make all at once. Surprised by the phenomenon, he examined the paintings, he touched them and he asked which of his senses was misleading him, was it vision or was it touch?

10. *The sight of a miniature portrait.* But he marvelled at a miniature of his father. That seemed as extraordinary to him as "putting a hogshead into a pint." That was his expression. What caused his astonishment was the habit his eye had acquired of linking the shape of an object to its size. He was not yet accustomed to judging that these two things can be separated.

11. *His bias.* We have a tendency to prejudge matters and we readily assume that everything is good in something that pleases us in one respect or another. Thus this young man seemed to be surprised that the people he liked

---

[33]I believe I should warn the reader that this is not exactly what Cheselden reports. For at the same time that he says that this young man could not distinguish objects, however different were their shapes and sizes, he also says that he found regular objects much more pleasing. As far as I am concerned this seems completely contradictory and Cheselden did not explain matters carefully enough. It was natural that this young man did not distinguish shape or size at the first moment that he saw light but it would not have been possible for him to find more pleasure in seeing regular objects if his vision had remained so indiscriminate. Thus he could not judge them more pleasing until he began to sort out shapes and sizes. No doubt he had trouble explaining to his observers the differences he then noticed and that is perhaps what led them to judge that those differences had eluded him up until then.

the best were not the most beautiful and that the foods for which he had a preference were not the most attractive to his eye.

12. *He had several ways of seeing things.* The more he used his vision, the more he was pleased to have had his cataracts removed and he said that each new object was a new delight for him. He seemed especially delighted when he was taken to Epsom where the view is very beautiful and extended. He called this vista a new way of seeing. He was not wrong for there are in truth as many manners of seeing as there are different judgments that play a role in vision: and how many must be involved in viewing a vast and variegated landscape. He sensed this better than we because he made these judgments less easily.

13. *He found black unpleasant.* We note that he found black unpleasant and that he was even horrified the first time that he saw a black man. It is perhaps because this color reminded him of his original state.

14. *How he saw when the operation was completed on both eyes.* Finally, more than a year later, an operation was performed on the other eye and it was also successful. He now saw everything large with this eye but less so than he had with the first. I think I can discern the reason for this difference. It is that the young man, expecting that he ought to see with this eye in the same way as he did with the first, mixed in with the transmitted sensations judgments that had become habitual through the use of the first eye. But as he could not make these judgments with the same precision right from the start, he saw objects as too large with the recently operated eye. The same provision could also lead him to see these objects less vaguely than he had with the first eye to be operated. But nothing is said about that.

When he began to see objects with both eyes, he believed that he saw them with twice their normal size. This is because it was more natural for the eye that saw things smaller to add to the sizes it perceived than it was natural for the eye that saw things larger to reduce them.

But his eyes did not see double because touch, in teaching the just-operated eye to distinguish objects, led it to see them where it had led the first eye to see them.

15. *The difficulty he had in directing his gaze.* Moreover, Cheselden remarks that patients blind from birth whose cataracts he had removed had considerable difficulty in directing their gaze on objects that they wanted to look at. That had to be the case: having had no need to move their eyes until that moment, they had not been able to acquire the habit of such behavior and this confirms what I have demonstrated earlier.

It is impossible not to leave something to be desired in observations that are made for the first time on such phenomena where a thousand details are involved that are difficult to grasp. But these observations serve at least to provide some guidelines for making further observations with more success. I will venture my own in the following chapter.

6 How We Could Study a Person Born Blind Whose Cataracts Had Been Removed

1. *Necessary precautions.* A precaution to take before the operation to remove the cataracts is to lead the patient to reflect on the ideas that he has received from touch so that when he is in a position to say, he can tell if vision is giving him ideas and he can report what he sees without our being almost obliged to put questions to him.

2. *Observations to be made.* With the cataracts removed, it would be necessary to prohibit his using his hands until we had recognized those ideas that do not depend on touch. We would note if the light that he perceives seems to him to be quite extended; if he is able to determine its limits; if it is so vague that he is unable to distinguish several changes in it.

After having shown him two colors separately, we will show them to him together and ask if he recognizes something he had seen before. On some occasions we would expose a greater number of colors successively, on some occasions we would present them at the same time, and we would be interested in discovering how many he can distinguish at the same time; we would determine, above all, if he distinguishes sizes, shape, locations, distances and movement. But we must question him skillfully and avoid all questions that can indicate their answers. To ask him if he sees a triangle or a square would be to tell him how he ought to see and to give lessons in seeing.

3. *Means to employ.* One sure way to conduct experiments that can allay all out doubts would be to place the blind man whose cataracts had been removed in a glass chamber. For either he will see objects that are outside of it and judge their shape and size or he will only perceive the space that is bounded by the sides of the chamber and will take all those objects to be only variously colored surfaces that appear to spread out, the closer he brings his hand.

In the first case, this would be a proof that the eye judges without having relied on touch; and in the second that it does so only after consulting touch.

If, as I presume, this man would not see beyond the boundaries of his chamber, it follows that space that he discovers by eye will be smaller the smaller the size of his chamber: it will be one foot, or half a foot, or even smaller. In this way we will be convinced that he could not have seen colors outside of his eyes if touch had not taught him to see them on the sides of his enclosure.

7 The Idea of Duration Given by Vision Joined with Touch

1. *The statue's amazement the first time that it notices a change from day to night and night to day.* When our statue begins to experience light, it does not yet know that the sun is the basic source. To realize this, the statue must have noticed that day ends almost as soon as that star has disappeared. This event will no doubt surprise it a great deal the first time that it happens. The statue believes the sun lost forever. Surrounded by impenetrable darkness, the statue fears that the objects lit by the sun have been lost with it. It scarcely dares to move, it fears that the earth has fallen from beneath its feet. But at the moment it seeks to confirm this by touch, the sky becomes clear, the moon resumes its light and myriad of stars shine in the firmament. Struck by this spectacle, the statue does not know if it should believe its eyes.

Soon the silence of all nature invites it to rest; a delicious calm stills its senses; its eyelids become heavy, its ideas slip away and escape; it falls asleep.

Imagine its surprise on awakening to discover anew the star that it had believed extinguished forever. It will now doubt its disappearance and will wonder what to make of the spectacle that had followed.

2. *Soon the sun's revolutions appear natural to the statue.* However, these revolutions are too frequent not to allay its doubts in the end. It judges that the sun will appear and disappear again because it has noticed that it has appeared and disappeared several times; and it makes this judgment all the more confidently as it has always been confirmed by events. The succession of days and nights thus becomes for the statue an entirely natural thing. Given its ignorance, the statue's ideas of possibility only have habitual judgments as a basis. We have already mentioned this and it cannot fail to lead the statue into many errors. For example, something that is impossible

today for lack of the conjunction of circumstances that alone can produce it will appear to the statue to be possible because it happened yesterday.

3. *The course of the sun becomes the measure of its duration.* The revolutions of the sun attract its attention more and more. The statue observes it when it rises, when it falls, and follows it in its course; and it judges from the succession of its ideas that there is an interval between the rise of this star and its fall and another interval between its fall and its rise.

Thus the sun in its course becomes a measure of time for the statue and marks the duration of all the states through which the statue passes. Formerly, a single idea, a single sensation that did not vary at all, persisted in vain for it was only an indivisible instant for the statue; and however the instants of that idea varied in duration, they were all equal for the statue: they made up a succession in which it could notice neither speed nor slowness. Now judging the duration of the idea by the distance that the sun has traveled, it appears slower or more rapid to the statue. Thus having judged the revolutions of the sun by the duration of all the state, that it experienced, the statue now judges the durations of these states by the revolutions of the sun; and this judgment becomes so natural for it that it no longer suspects that it came to know duration by the succession of its ideas.

4. *As a result the statue has a more distinct idea of duration.* The more the statue relates those events it recalls and those it is accustomed to anticipating to the revolutions of the sun, the more it grasps their succession. It will see more clearly then in the past and in the future.

In truth, if all our measures of time were taken away from us, if we no longer had any idea of a year, month, day, hour, if we had forgotten their very names, then duration would appear to us quite confused since it would be limited to the succession of our ideas. Thus we owe the most sharply defined ideas of duration to these measures.

In the study of history, for example, the sequence of events reconstructs the time only vaguely; the division of duration into centuries, years, months, gives us a clearer idea; finally the linkage of each event with its century, with its year, with its month, allows us to scan them in their order. The device here consists above all in creating epochs; we imagine that our statue could do likewise.

Moreover, it is not necessary that the revolutions of the sun have equal duration in order to serve as a measure; it is only necessary that the statue supposes they do. We do not consider them otherwise ourselves.

5. *Three things contribute jointly to the idea of duration.* Three things thus contribute jointly to the way in which we think of duration; first, the succession of our ideas; second, our knowledge of solar revolutions; finally, the connection of events with these revolutions.

6. *From which come the appearance of long days and short years, and of*

short days and long years. It is for this reason that, for most men, there are days that seem long and years that seem short while, for others, there are days that seem short and years long.

If the statue is for some time in a state of boring uniformity, it will be more aware of the time that the sun spends above the horizon and it will find each day intolerably long. If it spends an entire year in that way, it will see that all its days were the same, and since its memory cannot reckon them by noting various events, they will seem to have rushed by at astonishing speed.

If, on the contrary, its days are spent in a pleasurable state and each of them could be the occasion of a noteworthy event, the statue would scarcely notice the time that the sun is above the horizon and it would find the days surprisingly short. But a year will appear long to it because it will recall the year as a succession of numerous days distinguished by a succession of events.

This is why, when we are idle, we complain about both the slowness of the days and the speed of the years. Activity, on the contrary, makes the days appear short and the years long: the days are short because we do not pay attention to the time marked by solar revolutions; the years are long because we recall them by a series of things that presupposes a considerable duration.

8

How Vision Added to Touch Gives the Statue Some Knowledge of the Duration of Sleep and Teaches it to Distinguish Dreaming from Waking

1. *How vision leads it to know the duration of sleep.* If our statue fell asleep when the sun was in the east and wakes up when it descends toward the west, it will judge that its sleep had a certain duration; and if it does not remember any dreams it will believe that it has existed for a time without thinking. But this could be an error for perhaps its sleep was not profound enough to suspend its mental processes entirely.

2. *And leads it to know the illusion of dreams.* If, on the contrary, the statue recalls having had some dreams, it has a further way to confirm the duration of its sleep. But how will it recognize the illusion of dreams? By the striking way that a dream contradicts the knowledge the statue had before falling asleep, knowledge that is confirmed upon awakening.

Suppose, for example, that while asleep the statue believed it saw some extraordinary things and that at the moment before awakening it seemed it was in a place where it had never been before. No doubt it would be astonished not to find itself there on awakening; to recognize, on the contrary, the place where it lay down, to open its eyes as if they had been closed to light for a long time; and to regain the use of its limbs as if they had been perfectly rested. It does not yet know if it was mistaken or if it is mistaken. It seems that it is equally justified in thinking that it has not changed places and that it has. But finally, having had dreams repeatedly, the statue notices their jumble in which its ideas are always in contradiction with the waking state that follows as well as that preceding, and the statue judges that dreams are only illusions. This is because it is accustomed to attributing its sensations to something outside of itself and thinks of them as real only insofar as it can discover objects to which it can still refer them.

9 On the Chain of Knowledge, Abstractions, and Desires When Sight is Added to Touch, Hearing and Smell

1. *The principal idea to which visual sensations are linked.* We have proven that judgments link ideas of space, size, and shape to sensations of light and color. At first these judgments are occasioned by objects that act at the same time on vision and on touch; subsequently, they become so familiar that the statue repeats them even when the object makes an impression only on the eyes; and it forms the same ideas as if vision and touch continued to judge these objects together.

In this way, light and color become the properties of objects; and they are linked to the notion of extension, basis of all the ideas that memory comprises.

The chain of knowledge is more extended as a result, bits of knowledge are interconnected more fully, and ideas that are intercepted in sleep cause a thousand different associations. Although in darkness, the statue will see objects in its dream with the same light and color as they have in broad daylight.

2. *Since vision was joined to touch the idea of sensation has become more general.* The statue will have a more general notion of what we call "sensation." For knowing that light and color come to it from a particular sensory organ, it will consider them from that point of view and distinguish four kinds of sensations.

3. *Each color becomes an abstract idea.* When the statue was limited to vision, a color was only a particular mental state. Now each color becomes an abstract and general idea, for the statue notices it on several objects. This is a further way for it to distribute objects into various classes.

4. *Sight becomes active.* When sight was the statue's only sense, it was almost passive; now it is more active since it is joined to touch. For the statue

has learned to use its ability to demarcate objects. It does not wait until they act on it, it anticipates their action. In a word, it has learned to look.

5. *Sight becomes the seat of desire.* Since the activity of vision is increased, it becomes a more important source of desire. We have seen that the lack of some pleasure causes dissatisfaction which stimulates mental processes comprising desire.

6. *Imagination is less concerned with recalling colors.* Thus imagination ceases to recall colors with the same vividness because the easier it is to obtain the sensations themselves, the less we apply ourselves to imagining them.

7. *Power of the senses over one another.* Finally, since the statue is capable of attending with vision as well as with the three other senses, it can distract itself from sounds and odors by applying itself to considering a colored object intently. It is thus that the senses have the same power over one another that imagination has over all of them.

10 Of Taste United with Touch

1. *This sense has almost no need of learning.* The sense of taste develops so rapidly that we scarcely realize it needs some instruction. This is as it should be since it is necessary for our preservation from the very moment of our birth.

2. *Hunger felt for the first time has no definite object.* Hunger cannot yet have any well-specified goal when the statue experiences this feeling for the first time: for the means suited to alleviating it are entirely unknown. Thus the statue does not desire any sort of nourishment, it only wishes to leave a state which it finds displeasing. With this goal in mind, it indulges itself in all the pleasant sensations that it knows. This is the only remedy that it can use and it distracts the statue a little from its discomfort.

3. *Hunger makes it seize indifferently whatever is offered.* However the discomfort redoubles, spreads to all the parts of its body and appears more particularly on its lips, in its mouth. Then the statue tries to bite everything at hand; it bites stones, eats earth, nibbles grass, and its first choice is to nourish itself on those things that are most readily available. Satisfied with the nourishment that has relieved its hunger, the statue does not think about looking for better. As yet, it knows no other pleasure in eating than that of alleviating its hunger.

4. *The statue discovers suitable nourishment.* But on another occasion it finds some fruit whose color and fragrance charm its senses, and picks it up. The dissatisfaction it feels whenever its hunger returns leads it naturally to take in hand all the objects that can please it. This fruit is in its hand: it looks at it, it smells it with keen attention. Its hunger increases, it bites the fruit without expecting any other benefit than a reduction in its discomfort. But imagine its surprise! And what pleasure it will take in savoring this delicious

juice! Can it resist the attraction of eating the piece of fruit and of eating yet more?

5. *Food becomes the object of its desires.* Having had this experience[34] several times, the statue comes to know a new need, discovers with which organ it can satisfy it, and learns what things are suited to it. Then hunger is no longer, as it was before, a feeling that has no specific object: The statue uses all its faculties to obtain the enjoyment of whatever can alleviate it.

---

[34]This is nature's device for leading us to meet our needs with remedies whose effects we are not yet able to know. It is admirably clear in a newborn infant. Dissatisfaction spreads from the stomach to the cheeks and mouth and leads him to take the nipple as he would have any other thing; it makes him move his lips in every way until they secure the nourishing milk. Then the pleasure leads the infant to repeat the same movements and he does all that is necessary for his preservation.

11 General Observations on the Union of the Five Senses

Now that it needs nourishment our statue will become the subject of many observations. But before going into the details of all the circumstances that give rise to this need, let us consider common properties of each sense joined to touch.

1. *General ideas the statue develops about its sensations.* When the statue has touch and smell at the same time, it notices the properties of objects by their relation to these two senses and it forms general ideas of two kinds of sensations: sensations of touch, and sensations of smell; for it would not knowhow to confound in a single class impressions that are made on such different sensory organs.

The same thing is true when we add hearing, vision and taste to these two senses. Therefore, in general, the statue knows about five kinds of sensations.

So if we suppose that when it reflects on objects it considers their properties without regard to the five different ways in which they act on its sensory organs, then the statue will have the general notion of sensations; that is to say, it will form only one class of all the impressions that these objects make on it. And this idea is more general when it has three senses rather than two, and when it has four rather than three, and so on.

2. *How its imagination loses activity.* Deprived of touch, the statue was unable to use any of the other senses on its own and it could experience an odor, a sound, a color and a taste only insofar as its imagination acted with sufficient vividness to render them present. But now the knowledge of odorous, sonorous, palpable, and savory objects, and the ability to obtain them readily provide it with such a convenient way of getting what it desires that its imagination has no need to make the same effort as before. The more these objects are within reach therefore, the less its imagination will work on

304

the sensations that they provoked. Thus it will lose some of its activity: but because smell, hearing, vision and taste are more exercised as a result, their discrimination becomes finer and more extensive. Thus what these senses gain by their union with touch more than offsets what the statue has lost in imagination.

3. *Linkages of all kinds of sensations in memory.* Since these sensations have become the very properties of objects, the statue cannot recall, imagine, or experience them without thinking of objects. In this way, they all enter into one or another of the collections that touch has led the statue to make. They became properties of extension, they are linked up closely with the chain of knowledge by the same basic idea that links the sensations of touch; and memory as well as imagination became richer than when the statue did not yet have the use of all its senses.

4. *Activity that the statue acquires through the union of touch with the other senses.* We mentioned when we separately considered smell, hearing, vision, and taste, that our statue was entirely passive with respect to the impressions they made. But now it can be active in this respect on many occasions: for it has the means to seek the impressions that objects make on it or to avoid them.

5. *How its desires embrace all mental processes.* We have also mentioned that desire simply consisted of mental processes focused on the memory of an odor. But now that smell is joined to touch, desire can further involve the action of all faculties that can help it obtain some fragrant object. Thus, when the statue desires a flower, the excitation spreads from the organ of smell into all parts of its body and its desire mobilizes all its capacities.

We must make the same observation when it comes to the other senses. For once touch has instructed them, it continues to act with them whenever it can give them some aid. It takes part in all that concerns them, it teaches them to help each other, and all our sense-organs, all our mental processes are indebted to touch for the habit of focusing on the objects needed for survival.

PART FOUR:
ON THE NEEDS, SKILLS AND IDEAS OF AN ISOLATED MAN WHO ENJOYS ALL HIS SENSES

If the reader recalls that I have demonstrated how necessary signs are to develop distinct ideas of all kinds, he will be inclined to believe that I often suppose the statue to have more knowledge than it could acquire.

But we must distinguish theoretical knowledge and practical knowledge as I have done above. We need language for the former because theory consists of a series of distinct ideas and as a result we need signs to arrange them and to characterize them distinctly.

Practical knowledge is made up on the contrary of vague ideas that guide our actions without our being able to perceive how they lead us to act. This is because it is comprised of the habits that result from our judgments rather than the judgments themselves. For, once we have acquired these habits, we act without being able to observe the judgments that accompany them and this is why we are unaware of them. Then although we may be doing something properly, we do not know how we are doing it; we obey an impulse, an instinct unknown to us: for these words "impulse" and "instinct" signify, strictly speaking, the same thing.

We have long been forced to recognize that judgments are involved necessarily in our use of our senses. So even if I have not clearly explained how the statue learns to use its senses, it is true nonetheless that it makes such judgments. Now these judgments, which it does not perceive, are the instinct that guides it; and the habits of action that it has acquired following these judgments are what I understand by "practical knowledge." In order to acquaint us with these judgments, I am obliged to expand on them, but I do not contend that the statue explores them itself. It cannot because, having no language, it has no means to conduct the analysis. But to acquire habits, it is sufficient for the statue to make these judgments and it has no need to perceive them. Do we think that a child makes judgments only after he has learned to speak? Certainly, he would not feel the need to acquire language if he did not feel the need to express judgments. Thus he has already made them when he begins to speak, that is to say, when he begins to conduct the analysis of his thought with words. He now says what before he did but could not say.

1 How This Man Learns to Satisfy His Needs with Choice

1. *The statue without needs.* If we imagine that nature arranges things so as to anticipate all the needs of our statue and that, wanting to take all the precautions of a mother who is concerned with the welfare of her child, nature protects the statue from even the mildest discomforts and safeguards its survival, then this state will seem perhaps worthy of envy. Nevertheless what will a man of this kind be like? An animal immobilized in a trance. He is, but he stays as he is; he scarcely feels. Unable to notice the objects that surround him, unable to notice what goes on within himself; his mind is divided indiscriminately among all perceptions to which his senses open a passage. Similar to a mirror in a way, he constantly receives new images and never preserves any of them.

In truth, what occasion would this man have to take in interest in himself or in what goes on around him? Nature has taken all responsibility and she has so thoroughly anticipated his needs that she leaves him nothing to wish for. She wanted to protect him from all dissatisfaction, all pain; but fearful of making him unhappy she limited him to sensations whose value he cannot know and which pass like a shadow.

2. *With needs easy to satisfy.* I require then that nature appear less concerned with anticipating the dangers that can threaten him, that she leaves some precautions to the man and that she is satisfied with placing within reach all that is necessary for his needs.

In this abundance, the statue has desires but it has on the spot all that it needs to satisfy them. All of nature still seems to watch over it: no sooner does it allow the statue's rest to be interrupted by some slight uneasiness than it appears to regret its decision and is devoted to avoiding any further

309

discomfort. By this vigilance, it protects the statue from many ills but it also hinders it from many pleasures. The uneasiness is minor, the desire that follows it is not great, prompt satisfaction does not allow any need to become very strong, and pleasure, which pays the price for all this, is as slight as the need.

With our statue's rest so little disturbed, calm reigns almost always and equally in all the parts of its body and its mood suffers scarcely any change. The statue must live a long time as a result but it is hardly alive and its level of existence is barely above the minimum.

3. *And difficult to satisfy.* Let us change the scene and suppose that the statue has some obstacles to overcome in order to obtain what it desires. Then needs subsist for some time before being alleviated. An uneasiness that starts out minor becomes imperceptibly stronger; it is changed into discomfort and sometimes ends in pain.

As long as the discomfort is slight, the desire has little force; the statue is not in a rush to enjoy what it desires: a strong sensation can distract it and hold its dissatisfaction in abeyance. But desire grows along with the dissatisfaction and the moment comes when it is so forceful that nothing can alleviate it except the desired object: it becomes a passion.

4. *The statue is still improvident.* The first time that the statue satisfied a desire, it does not suspect that it will experience that desire again. Once the need is satisfied, it returns to its initial tranquility.

Thus, without concern for the future, the statue thinks only of the present and of eliminating the discomfort caused by some need, as soon as it is uncomfortable.

5. *How the statue becomes capable of foresight.* The statue remains in about this state as long as its needs are mild and few and it finds few obstacles to alleviating them. It is accustomed to regulating its desires with a view to the contrast between pleasure and pain; only the experience of suffering from ills it could have foreseen can lead it to look beyond its immediate situation. Only the past can teach the statue to learn to read the future.

Thus the statue has only to notice the recurrence of its needs and the anguish that it suffered whenever it did not have some remedy soon enough, in order for it to form a habit of anticipating its needs and of taking precautions to ward them off or to alleviate them promptly. Even at the moment when the statue does not have any dissatisfaction whatever, imagination recalls all the pains to which it was exposed and represents them as liable to overwhelm it agin. Then as soon as it feels something like the yearning that need can induce, it suffers in advance something similar to what it would suffer if the need were present.

Imagination would make our statue unhappy indeed if its effects stopped there. But it soon reminds the statue of the objects that have served several times to comfort it and thereafter it provides almost the same pleasures as they do. It appears that it troubled the statue about a remote discomfort just so that it could give it pleasure beforehand.

Thus when fear threatens the statue with pains like those it has already suffered, hope deludes it that it will head them off or alleviate them: the hope and the fear compete to distract it from the feelings of the moment and concern it with a time that has not yet come or indeed will never come; from these two passions is born the need of precautions and the skill to take them. Thus the statue goes in turn from the one emotion to the other depending on whether the dangers are repeated and are more or less difficult to avoid: and these passions acquire new force with each passing day. The statue will be frightened or confident at every turn. When hopeful, imagination removes all the obstacles in its path, presents it with objects in the best light and shows it that it will enjoy them: an illusion that often makes us more happy than the enjoyment itself. When fearful, the statue is beset by dangers on all sides, is threatened by them, comes close to the moment when it will be overwhelmed, knows no way of avoiding them, and might even be less unhappy to actually experience them.

Thus it is that imagination presents the statue with all the objects that have some relation to hope or to fear. Sometimes the former of these passions dominates, sometimes the latter; and sometimes they are so well balanced that we could not say which of the two had the upper hand. They make the statue more diligent in taking measures for its survival and these passions seem to ensure that it will be neither too happy nor too unhappy.

6. *Stages in its reasoning in this matter.* Instructed by experience on how to alleviate or anticipate its needs, the statue reflects on the choices that it has. It examines the advantages and disadvantages of objects that it has sought or avoided until then. It recalls the mistakes it has made in deciding things too often in haste, blindly obeying the first urgings of its passions. It regrets that it did not behave more appropriately. It feels that hereafter it must rely on itself to act according to the knowledge it has acquired and, becoming accustomed to using that knowledge, it gradually learns to resist its desires and even to subjugate them. Thus, because it is concerned with avoiding pain, it reduces the dominion of the passions to extend the sway that reason must have over its will and to become free.[35]

7. *The order of its studies is determined by its need.* Under these circumstances, the statue studies the objects that can contribute to its pleasures or its pains all the more as it knows that it has suffered for not having studied them sufficiently and as experience shows it that it is within its power to know them better. Thus it is that the order of its studies is

---

[35]See the Dissertation [on liberty] at the end of this work.

determined by its needs. The most urgent and the most frequent are therefore those that engage it in its first investigations.

8. *And particularly by the need of nourishment.* Nourishment is one of these since it is so necessary for survival. In alleviating its hunger the statue restores its strength and it feels that it is important for it to do so in order to enjoy the use of all its faculties. All of its other needs cede to this one. Sight, touch, hearing and smell seem to exist only for discovering and obtaining what pleases the sense of taste. Thus the statue takes a new interest in what nature offers it. Its curiosity is no longer restricted to distinguishing the color of objects, their smells, their shape, etc. If it studies them in terms of these properties, it is above all to learn to recognize those that are suitable nourishment. Thus the statue never fails to see some fruit it has eaten, or to touch it, or to smell it without judging whether it is bad or good to the taste. This judgment increases the pleasure that it has in seeing it, in touching it, in smelling it; and this sense contributes to making the others more valuable. It has above all a considerable analogy to smell. The aroma of fruit interested it much less before it had the sense of taste; and taste would lose much of its discrimination if the statue were deprived of smell. But as soon as the statue has these two senses, their sensations become intermingled and all the more delicious for that.

The statue gives its ideas a very different order than they had before because this need that regulates its faculties is itself quite different from those that motivated it previously. It takes an interest in objects that it had never paid attention to in the past and those that are suited for its nourishment are also those that it distinguishes into more classes. The statue forms complex ideas of them by considering them as having a certain color, a certain smell, a certain shape and a certain taste all at once; and it forms abstract and general ideas on their occasion by considering their common properties.

9. *Judgments that give more scope to this need.* The statue compares these objects with one another and desires first to take nourishment from some fruit that it recalls had a particularly pleasing taste. In what follows it gradually becomes accustomed to this nourishment and makes so great a habit of it that this governs its choice as much as the pleasure of tasting it.

Thus the statue soon mixes judgments with the pleasure it finds in its foods. If it did not mix these it would only eat for nourishment. But the judgment "It is good, it is excellent, it is better than any other," gives it a need for the sensation that fruit can produce. What then suffices to nourish it does not suffice for its pleasure. It has two needs, one caused by the deprivation of nourishment, the other by the deprivation of a taste that has earned its preference; and the latter is a hunger that misleads it sometimes and causes it to eat more than is necessary.

10. *The excess into which the statue falls.* However, the taste of certain fruits may cloy; then either it takes a dislike to them or, if it still wishes to eat

some, it is only out of habit. In the latter case, the statue eats the fruit always hoping to savor it as it had in the past. It has become so accustomed to this experience that it still thinks it will rediscover a pleasure for which it is no longer suited; and this idea contributes to sustaining its desire.

Frustrated in its hopes, its desire only becomes more keen. It tries again and contines to try until it is no longer possible for it to go on. Thus it is that the excesses into which it has fallen are often caused by habits that it acquired and the shadow of a pleasure that is continually recalled in imagination but is always just out of reach.

11. *The statue is punished as a result.* Pain soon warns it that the goal of pleasure is not only to make it happy on the moment but also to contribute to its survival; or rather to restore its strength, allowing it to use its faculties: for the statue does not know what self-preservation means.

12. *How necessary it was to warn it by pain.* If out of affection for the statue nature had involved only pleasant feelings in these matters, it would have misled it and would have been mistaken itself: the statue would only have contributed to its own undoing while believing it was searching for happiness.

But these warnings cannot be repeated without the statue finally learning that it must rein in its desires. For nothing is more natural than to view one thing as the effect of another if it comes constantly in its wake.

From then on, the statue will never experience such desires without imagination immediately recalling all the painful consequences it had suffered. This perspective makes it fear even those objects that particularly please it and it is caught between two opposing yearnings.

Now if the idea of pain is only faintly reawakened, the statue's fear will be mild and will put up little resistance. If the idea of pain is vivid, however, the fear will be strong and will keep it from acting for a longer time. Finally, this idea can reach such intensity that it extinguishes desire entirely and inspires disgust for an object which the statue had once wanted ardently.

Thus, finding both pleasure and danger in selecting the fruit it prefers, the statue learns to nourish itself with a wider selection; and finding more obstacles to satisfying its desires, it will be exposed to greater needs. For it is not enough that the statue alleviate the distress caused by the need for nourishment; it must also alleviate the distress caused by the privation of a pleasure and it must do so without danger.

2 On the State of a Man Left to Himself and How the Accidents to which He Is Exposed Contribute to His Instruction

1. *Circumstances in which the statue is not limited to the study of objects for its nourishment.* Once instructed on the things suitable for nourishing it, the statue will be occupied by concern for its nourishment to a greater or lesser degree depending on the obstacles it will have to overcome. Thus we can imagine it during a period of time when it is completely absorbed by this need and acquires no other knowledge.

If we reduce the obstacles, the statue will promptly hear the call of the pleasures available to each of its senses. It will take an interest in everything that strikes them. As a result, everything will sustain its curiosity, excite it, and augment it; and the statue will pass in turn from the study of objects suited for its nourishment to the study of everything that surrounds it.

2. *It studies itself.* Soon curiosity leads it to study itself. It observes its senses, and the impressions that they transmit; it observes its pleasures, it pains, its needs, and the means for satisfying them; and it makes a kind of sketch for itself of what it must flee or seek.

3. *It studies objects.* On other occasions, the statue studies more particularly the objects that attract its attention. It groups them into different classes according to the differences among them that it perceives, and the number of its abstract notions increases in proportion as its curiosity is excited by the pleasure of seeing, feeling, tasting, hearing, touching.

Curiosity leads the statue to cast its eyes on animals; it sees that they move about and nourish themselves as it does; that they have organs for grasping what suits them, eyes to guide their movements, weapons to attack or defend themselves, agility or cunning to escape danger, industry to set traps: and the statue distinguishes them by shape, color, and above all by the properties that surprise it even more.

314

Astounded by the fights they engage in, the statue is even more surprised when it notices that the weakest, lacerated by the strongest, spill their blood and become immobile. This scene depicts the passage from life to death concretely but the statue does not think that it can be destined to end in the same way. Life appears to it to be something so natural that it cannot imagine how it could be deprived of it. It knows only that it is exposed to pain, that there are bodies that can harm it, wound it. But experience has taught it to recognize and avoid them.

The statue thus lives in great security amidst animals that are at war. The universe is a theatre where the statue is only a spectator and it does not foresee that it must ever bloody the scene.

4. *Accidents to which it is exposed.* However, an enemy comes forth. Unaware of the danger that threatens, the statue does not think of avoiding it and as a result it has a cruel experience. It defends itself. Fortunately it is strong enough to ward off some of the blows directed at it and it escapes; it has only received some wounds that are not dangerous. But the idea of this animal is still present in memory; it becomes linked to all the circumstances in which the statue was assailed by it. Was it in some woods? Then the sight of a tree, the noise of the leaves will place the image of danger before its eyes. The statue is intensely fearful because it is weak; it feels that fear reinforced because it does not yet know the precautions its situation demands; everything becomes an object of terror because the idea of peril is so strongly linked to everything it encounters that finally it no longer knows how to identify what it ought to fear. A sheep terrifies it and to dare stand fast the statue needs more courage than it can yet have.

Recovering from its fright, it is almost astonished to see animals flee from it. It sees them flee a second time, it sees them always flee and it takes confidence in the end that it has nothing to fear.

Scarcely does it begin to assuage its concern, than its first enemy reappears or it was even attacked by a second. It escapes from this new danger but not without having received some blows.

5. *How it learns to protect itself.* These kinds of accidents disturb it and worry it the more they recur and the more serious their consequences. It fears them so much that it trembles all over violently. The dangers pass but the trembling persists or recurs repeatedly and recalls the image of the attacker. Since the statue cannot distinguish among the circumstances on which it is more or less likely to be safe from such events, it is as apprehensive about a remote danger as one that threatens close at hand; often it is even more fearful in the first case. The statue flees both dangers alike because it senses how very vulnerable it was when it waited too long to protect itself. Thus, its fear becomes more active than its hope, it follows its urgings all the more closely, and it takes many more precautions against the dangers to which it is exposed than measures to obtain the good things it can

enjoy. It applied itself then to learning which animals are ready to fight it; it flees those places where they appear to live; it judges what it has to fear from them by the blows that it sees them give to others as weak as itself. The fears of these victims redouble its own; their flight, their cries warn it of its own danger. Sometimes the statue undertakes to avoid the attack by cunning. Sometimes it seizes whatever chance may provide it for its defense; it compensates by its own labor, but quite slowly, for the arms that nature has refused it; it learns gradually to defend itself; it is the victor in some combat; pleased with its success, it begins to feel a certain courage that sometimes places it out of danger's reach or even emboldens it. Then the statue sees everything in a new light; it has a new vision of things, new interests; its curiosity focuses on new objects; it is more often occupied with its defense than with the need of nourishment, and it is all the better at fighting.

6. *Other accidents*. The statue is soon exposed to new ills. The season changes almost all at once, the plants dry out, the country becomes arid and the air it breathes assails it on all sides; the statue learns to wear whatever can keep it warm and to take refuge in places where it is less exposed to the weather.

However, it is often exposed to long suffering because it is deprived of all sorts of nourishment. Now the statue uses the superiority that cunning or strength gives it over some animals: it attacks them, seizes them, devours them. Having no other means of obtaining nourishment, it invents ruses and weapons: and it succeeds all the more in this art as combat becomes as essential for it as nourishment. And there it is then at war with all the animals either to attack them or to defend itself against them.

It is thus that experience gives it lessons that it must often pay for in blood. But could the statue be instructed at a lower cost?

7. *Conclusion*. To take nourishment, to take precautions against all accidents, or to defend itself against them, and to satisfy its curiosity: there you have all the natural needs of our statue. They govern its faculties in turn and they are the basic source of the knowledge that it acquires. Sometimes it is in control of the circumstances and the statue gives free rein to its desires; other times, it is dominated by them and it weaves its own unhappiness. If successes encounter reverses, reverses are also balanced by successes; and these objects seem by turns to conspire for its suffering and for its pleasure. The statue thus floats between confidence and uncertainty; trailing its hopes and its fears, it grazes against happiness in one moment and ruin in the next. Experience alone places it just barely beyond danger, leads it to attain the knowledge necessary for its survival and makes it acquire all the habits that must govern it. But just as without experience there is no knowledge, so there would be no experience without needs and there would be no needs without

the alternatives of pleasure and pain. Everything then is the fruit of the principle that we have established from the very beginning of this work.

We are going to discuss the judgments that the statue makes about objects according to the part that they play in its pleasure or its pain.

3 Of the Judgments That a Man Left to Himself Can Make About the Goodness and Beauty of Things

1. *Definition of the words "goodness" and "beauty."* The words "goodness" and "beauty" express the properties through which things contribute to our pleasure. As a result, every sentient being has ideas of goodness and of beauty relative to himself.

In truth, we call "good" everything that pleases smell or taste and we call "beautiful" everything that is pleasing for vision, hearing, or touch.

The good and the beautiful are furthermore relative to the passions and to the mind. Whatever pleases the passions is good; what the mind has a taste for is beautiful; and what is pleasing at the same time to the passions and to the mind is good and beautiful together.

2. *The statue has ideas of the good and the beautiful.* Our statue knows agreeable smells and tastes and objects that are pleasing to its passions: it thus has ideas of the good. The statue also knows objects that it sees, that it hears, that it touches and that its mind thinks of with pleasure: it thus also has ideas of the beautiful.

3. *The good and the beautiful are not absolutes.* One consequence is that the good and the beautiful are not at all absolute: they are relative to the nature of the man who judges them and to his makeup.[36]

4. *The good and the beautiful aid each other.* The good and the beautiful assist each other. A peach that the statue sees pleases him by the vividness of

---

[36]We must not lose sight of the title of this chapter. We are considering a man who lives alone and we are not inquiring about the goodness and beauty of things but only the judgments he may make of them. Not everything that he judges good will be morally good as not everything he judges beautiful will be really beautiful.

its colors: it is beautiful in its eyes. Thereupon the flavor is recalled in imagination and the peach is seen with a greater pleasure; it is for that more beautiful.

The statue eats this peach; then the pleasure of seeing it is mingled with that of tasting it and the peach is even better.

5. *Usefulness contributes to both.* Utility contributes to the goodness and the beauty of things. Fruits that are good and beautiful solely by virtue of the pleasure of seeing them and tasting them are better and more beautiful when we think that they are suitable for restoring our strength.

6. *Novelty and rareness also contribute.* Novelty and rareness also contribute to these judgments: the surprise caused by an object already good and beautiful within itself when joined to the difficulty of possessing it increases the pleasure of having it.

7. *Two kinds of goodness and beauty.* The goodness and the beauty of things consists in a single idea or in a multitude of ideas that have certain relations among them. A single taste, a single odor can be good: Light is beautiful, a sound considered alone can be beautiful.

But when there is a multitude of ideas, an object is better or more beautiful to the degree that the ideas are better discriminated and their relations better perceived, for then we experience the objects with more pleasure. A fruit in which we recognize many tastes that are equally agreeable is better than a single one of these tastes; an object whose colors are mutually enhancing is more beautiful than light alone.

The sensory organs can grasp only a certain number of sensations distinctly; the mind can compare all at once only a certain number of ideas; too large a number leads to confusion. This in turn detracts from pleasure and as a result from the goodness and the beauty of things.

A small quantity of sensations or ideas can become confused if one dominates too much over the others. Thus it is necessary for the greatest goodness and the greatest beauty that the mixture be constituted in certain proportions.

8. *How the statue becomes aware of goodness and beauty.* It is through using its organs and its mind that our statue gains the advantage of encompassing more ideas and more relations. The good and the beautiful are thus relative to the use that it has learned to make of its faculties. A certain thing that at one time was very good or very beautiful may cease to be so whereas another to which the statue gave no attention whatever becomes of the greatest goodness or beauty.

In that, as in every other thing, the statue will judge only in relation to itself. At first, it takes as its models the objects that contribute most directly to its happiness; thereafter, it judges other objects by these models; and they appear to it the more beautiful when they resemble their models more. For after this comparison, the statue finds a pleasure in seeing them that it had never tasted before. For example, a tree laden with fruit pleases it and makes it happy to see another that has none at all but bears some resemblance to it.

9. *Why the statue has less ideas on this topic than we do.* It is not possible to imagine all the different judgments that the statue will make under the various circumstances: that would in any case be a rather useless investigation. It is sufficient to observe that there is for it as for us a real goodness and beauty and that if it has fewer ideas on this topic than we, that is because it also has fewer needs, less knowledge, and fewer passions.

4 On the Judgments that A Man Left to Himself can Make about the Objects He Requires

1. *The statue believes that everything acting on it does so by design.* The statue feels at every instant how dependent it is on everything that surrounds it. If objects often respond to its wishes, they also controvert its projects almost as often: they make it unhappy or give it only a portion of the happiness that it desires.

Persuaded that it does nothing without having the intention to do it, the statue believes that it sees a plan wherever it discovers some action. In truth, it can only judge such things according to what it perceives in itself; and it would require many observations indeed to guide its judgments better. The statue thinks then that what is pleasing to it has its pleasure as a goal and what is offensive has as a goal to offend it. As a result, its love and its hate become passions that are all the more violent as the intention of contributing to its happiness or its unhappiness is the more evident in everything that acts on it.

2. *Superstitions that this belief induces.* Then the statue no longer limits itself to seeking the enjoyment of pleasures that objects can obtain for it and the avoidance of pains that they threaten: it desires that they have the intention of lavishing favors on it and of deflecting all sorts of evils: in short,it desires that they are well disposed toward it and this desire is a kind of prayer.

It supplicates the sun; and because it judges that, if the sun lights its way and warms it, it must have the intention of lighting its way and warming it, the statue prays to the sun to continue to light the way and to keep it warm. It turns to the trees and asks them for fruit, not doubting that it is up to them whether to bear fruit or not. In a word, the statue supplicates all the things that it believes it depends on.

Does it suffer without discovering the cause in what strikes its senses? Then it will address pain, as an invisible enemy that it is important for it to appease. Thus it is that the universe fills up with visible and invisible beings that it implores to work for its own happiness.

These are its first ideas when it begins to reflect on its dependence. Other circumstances will give rise to other judgments and will multiply its errors. I have shown elsewhere the ways in which it can be led astray by superstition[37]; but I refer the reader to the works of enlightened philosophers to inform himself on the discoveries that reason properly conducted can make on this topic.

---

[37] *Treatise on systems.* Chapter on Divination.

5 On the Uncertainty of Judgments that We Make about the Existence of Sensory Properties

1. *Our judgments on the existence of sensory properties can be absolutely false.* Our statue, I presume, remembers that it was itself sound, taste, smell, color: It knows how much trouble it had to become accustomed to externalizing these sensations. Are there, therefore, sounds, tastes, odors, colors in objects? What can assure it of that? Certainly not hearing, nor smell, nor taste, nor vision: these senses by themselves can only inform it about the changes it experiences. The statue first felt only its own being in the impressions to which these senses were susceptible; and if they lead him to feel them now in bodies it is because they have acquired the habit of judging according to the testimony of touch. Is there then at least extension? But when the statue has the feeling of touching what does it perceive if it is not still its own modifications? Touch is therefore no more believable than the other senses: and since we recognize that sounds, tastes, odors, and colors do not exist in objects, it could be that extension does not exist there any the more so.[38]

---

[38]Perhaps it will be objected that if there is no extension then there are no bodies. I do not say that there is no extension, I merely say that we perceive it only in our own sensations. From which it follows that we do not see bodies in themselves. Perhaps they are extended and even savorous, sonorous, colored, odorous; perhaps they are nothing of the sort. I support neither position; and I await a proof that they are what they seem to be or that they are something else entirely.

Were there not extension, there would not then be a reason to deny the existence of objects. All that we could and should reasonably infer is that objects are existences that occasion sensations in us and have properties about which we can have no certain knowledge.

But, one might insist, it is decided in the scripture that bodies are extended and at least you are casting doubt on that.

2. *Greater certainty on this topic would be useless.* The statue will probably not pause over these doubts. Perhaps the judgments that have become habitual for it will prevent it from having such doubts. It will be more capable of doubting than we are, however, because it knows better how it learned to see, to hear, to smell, to taste, and to touch. Be that as it may, it is useless for it to have more certainty in this regard. The appearance of sensory properties is sufficient to give it desires, to guide its conduct, and to make it happy or unhappy; and its dependence on objects to which it is obliged to attribute sensory properties does not allow it to doubt that there are existences outside of itself. But what is the nature of these existences? The statue does not know, and we do not know ourselves. All that we know is that we call them "bodies."

If so, then faith makes certain what is doubtful in philosophy and there is no contradiction there. In such a case, the philosopher must doubt when he consults reason, as he must believe when revelation enlightens him. But scripture in fact decides nothing on this topic. It supposes that bodies are extended as it supposes them colored, sonorous, etc. and certainly we have there one of the issues that God wanted to leave to disputes among philosophers.

6 Considerations on Abstract and General Ideas that can be Acquired by a Man Living Outside Society

The account that we have just given of the knowledge of our statue shows clearly how it distributes existences into different classes according to their relations with its needs; and, as a result, how it forms abstract and general notions. But to understand better the nature of its ideas, it is important to go into some new details.

1. *The statue has no general idea that was not particular.* It has no general idea that was not at first a particular one. The general idea of orange, for example, is only in its origin the idea of a particular orange.

2. *What its idea of a present object consists of.* The particular idea, when an object is present to the senses, is a collection of several properties that appear together. The idea of a certain orange is the color, the shape, the taste, the smell, the solidity, the weight, and so forth.

3. *Of an absent object.* This particular idea, when the object no longer acts on the senses, is the memory that remains of what one had known by vision, taste, smell, etc. Close your eyes and the idea of the light is the memory of an impression that you have experienced; touch nothing: the idea of solidity is the memory of the resistance that you have encountered in handling objects; and so on for the rest.

4. *How, from particular ideas, its ideas become general.* Let us substitute successively, one for one, several oranges for the first one, all of which are similar; our statue will believe that it is always seeing the same orange and it will have only a particular idea on this topic.

Does the statue see two at the same time? In that moment it will recognize in each the same particular idea. And this idea becomes a model to which it compares them and sees that each matches. The statue will discover in the same way that this idea is common to three, four oranges and it will make the idea as general as it can be for it.

The particular idea of a horse and that of a bird will become likewise general when circumstances will lead the statue to compare several horses and several birds; and so forth for all perceptible objects.

As the statue does not have the use of any sign, it cannot organize its ideas with order nor, as a result, have ideas as general as we do. But it also cannot have absolutely no general ideas at all. If an infant who does not yet speak were not to have ideas general enough to be common to at least two or three instances, we could never teach him to speak; for one can begin to speak a language only because, before speaking, one has something to say, and because one has general ideas: every proposition necessarily includes such ideas.

Having the general notions of orange, horse, bird, our statue will distinguish them for the same reason that it distinguishes an orange from a bird and a bird from a horse. It thus will relate each of these individuals to the general model of which it has formed an idea, that is to say, to the class, to the species to which it belongs.

Now just as a model that applies to several individuals is a general idea, in the same way two or three models, to which we assign very different instances are different classes or, to speak the language of philosophers, different species of general notions.

5. *How the statue goes from a general idea to less general ones.* When the statue glances at a landscape, it perceives many trees that it does not yet notice the differences among; it sees only what they have in common; it sees that each of them has branches and leaves and that they are fixed to the spot where they grow. And there you have the model of the general idea of tree.

The statue will next look from one to the other: it observes the difference in their fruit, it makes several models with which to distinguish as many kinds of trees as it notices kinds of fruit; and these are ideas that are less general than the first.

The statue will form the general idea of animal in the same way if it sees several animals in the distance whose differences escape it; and it will sort them into several kinds when it is close enough to see the ways in which they differ.

6. *The statue generalizes the more confusedly it sees.* It generalizes further the more it sees things in a confused way and it forms less general notions the more it distinguishes differences among these things. We see from this how easy it is for it to form general ideas.[39]

---

[39] The distribution of existences into different kinds has only our imperfect way of seeing things as its basis. It is then not founded in the nature of things and the philosophers were wrong to want to determine the essence of each kind of thing. This was nevertheless always the object

First, all apples, for example, appear to it to conform to the same model. But subsequently it does not find that each has an equally agreeable taste. Thereafter the desire for pleasure and the fear of distaste leads the statue to compare them in those respects that it can discover: it learns to distinguish them sight, by smell, by touch; it forms different models to guide its choice; and it distributes the apples into as many classes as it notices differences among them.

7. *Objects that it does not become acquainted with at all.* As for the objects that do not interest it, which give it neither pleasure nor pain, they remain confused in the mass and the statue acquires no familiarity with them.

We have only to reflect on ourselves to become convinced of this truth. All men have the same sensations; but the masses occupied in hard labor, the cosmopolite devoted entirely to frivolous objects, and the philosopher who finds a need to study nature, are not sensitive either to the same pleasures or the same pains. Thus they draw from the same sensations very different knowledge.

8. *In what order the statue forms ideas of species.* Here you have then the order in which our statue forms ideas of species. First it takes account of only the differences that are the most perceptible and it has ideas that are very general and few.

If it is color that particularly strikes it, the statue will only make one class of several kinds of flowers: if it is mass, a hare and a cat will compromise for it only one species of animal.

Because its needs will subsequently give it occasion to consider these things in the light of other properties that they have, the statue will compose species subordinate to the first. From a general notion it will form several that are less so.

The statue thus passes in a single stroke from particular ideas to general ones; from which it descends to less general ones, in the measure that it notices the differences among things. Thus it is in an infant, after having called "gold" everything that is yellow, acquires next ideas of copper and of brass; and from a general idea forms several that are less so.

9. *Its ignorance on the nature of things.* From the development of these ideas it is evident that they will present our statue only with properties in various combinations. It sees, for example, solidity, extension, divisibility, shape, mobility, etc. united in everything that it touches; and it has, as a result, the idea of objects. But if we ask it what an object is and if it were able to answer, it would point out one and say, "It is that"; that is to say, that where you find concurrently solidity, extension, divisibility, shape, etc.

10. *Shared by philosophers.* A philosopher would answer, "It is something

---

of their investigations. The error arose because they were persuaded that our ideas had been etched in our minds by the hand of a God who before giving them to us undoubtedly referred to the nature of things.

that exists, an extended substance, solid" etc. Let us compare these two responses and we will see that the philosopher knows the nature of bodies no better than the statue. His sole advantage, if it is one, is to have constructed a language which appears sophisticated only because it is not the language of everyone. For in truth, the words "something that exists" and "substance" signify nothing more than the word "that."

11. *Its ideas of objects are confused.* From this we must conclude that the ideas that the statue has of perceptible object are confused; for I call confused every idea that does not represent all the properties of its object in a distinct way. Now the statue does not have such perfect knowleged of any object; it only notices the properties that its needs give it occasion to notice. With more wisdom, the statue will discern a larger number and if it were able to penetrate into the nature of things it would not find two that were perfectly similar. Thus the statue supposes that several objects do not differ at all among themselves only because it fails to see them distinctly.

12. *Its abstract ideas are of two kinds.* As for its abstract notions the statue has those that are vague and those that are distinct.

For example, it knows a sound sufficiently well to distinguish it from a smell, from a taste, and from every other sound; but it appears to the statue to be simple although it is multiple.[40] Several colors, mixed together, produce for the statue the appearance of a single color. It is the same with all the impressions of the senses. The statue thus does not distinguish all that they include and it is still far from discovering all the causes that work together to produce each sensation. It thus has only rather vague notions on this topic.

But these same sensations give it ideas of size and of shape; and if it cannot determine exactly what is the size and the shape of some objects, nor determine exactly what the relations are among them, it still knows how a size can be the double or the half of another, and it knows very well what a line is, a triangle, a square. Thus it has, in such cases, distinct ideas. For this suffices that the statue considers sizes while abstracting from objects.

13. *It knows two kinds of truths.* From these two kinds of ideas are born two kinds of truths. When the statue notices that an object is triangular, it makes a judgment that can become false, for this object can change shape. But when it notices that a triangle has three sides, its judgment is true and will always be so since three sides specify the idea of triangle. Therefore, the statue perceives truths that change or that can change whenever it wants to judge what things are in themselves; it perceives truths that, on the contrary,

---

[40]That is evident when it comes to noise and is no less true of harmonic sounds; for we have observed that there is none that is not triple.

cannot change at all whenever it limits itself to judging abstract and distinct ideas that it has of magnitudes.

The statue has, as a result, solely through the aid of senses, knowledge of all kinds.

7 Of a Man Found in the Forests of Lithuania

1. *Circumstances in which the need of nourishment benumbs all mental faculties.* Our statue, as we have mentioned, could be so occupied with a concern for its nourishment that it would not have a moment to give to the study of objects about which it was curious before it had the organ of taste. Living only to satisfy this pressing need, the pleasures of the other senses would no longer have any attraction for it: it would no longer notice the objects that could produce those pleasures. Without astonishment, without curiosity, the statue would cease to reflect on what it knew and it would soon forget a part of that; it would forget how it learned what it still knows; and it would think that it had always felt, heard, seen, and touched what it feels, hears,sees, and touches. Totally absorbed in the search for nourishment, which I suppose to be very hard to obtain, the statue would live a life that was purely animal. Does it have hunger? It moves, it goes wherever it recalls having found nourishment. It its hunger satisfied? Then rest becomes its most urgent need and it rests where it is and it goes to sleep.

Under such circumstances, the need of nourishment benumbs its mental faculties in certain respects as it turns all of their activity toward itself. It is even probable that in place of behaving according to its own reflection it would take lessons from the animals with which it would live more familiarly. The statue would walk as they do, imitate their cries, feed with them on grass, or devour those that it would have the strength to overcome. We are so strongly inclined to imitation that in its place a Descartes would not learn to walk on two feet: everything that he would see would be enough to lead him to do otherwise.

2. *An infant found in the forests of Lithuania.* Such apparently was the fate of a child of some ten years who lived among bears and who was found in

1694 in the forests that separate Lithuania from Russia. He gave no sign of reason, walked on his hands and feet, had no language, and uttered sounds that it no way resembled human sounds. It was a long time before he could utter a few words and even then he did it in quite a primitive way. As soon as he could speak, he was interrogated concerning his original state; but he remembered no more of that than we remember of what happened to us in the crib.

3. *Why we say that he gave no sign of reason.* When we say that this child gave no sign of reason, we do not mean that he did not reason sufficiently to take care of his survival but rather that his reflection, which up to the present had necessarily been applied to this sole end, had not had occasion to concern itself with those things that concern us. He had none of the ideas that our statue had acquired when it knew other needs than those of looking for food; he lacked all the knowledge that men owe to their interactions. In a word, the child appeared to be without reason not because he absolutely had none but because he had less than we do.

4. *Why the child forgot its initial state.* Sometimes our consciousness, that is to say, the awareness of what is happening within us, is distributed over such a large number of perceptions that act on us with roughly equal force, and is so weak, that it retains no memory whatever of what we have experienced. Then we are scarcely aware of our existence: days go by in a moment without our marking the difference; and we experience the very same perception thousands of times without noticing that we have already had it. A man who has acquired many ideas and has made them familiar cannot go on living for a long time in this kind of lethargy. The greater the supply of his ideas, the more reason we have to believe that one will find some occasion to awaken and to capture his attention in a particular way and to draw him out of this trance-like state. The child did not receive any aid of this kind. His deadened faculties could only be provoked by the need to look for nourishment and his life resembled sleep disturbed only by dreams. It was thus natural that he forgot his initial state.

However it does not seem probable that he forgot it all at once. If, after severl days, he had been led back into the woods where he had been captured, he no doubt would have recognized the places where he had lived; he would have remembered the foods with which he nourished himself and the means that he had employed to obtain them. He would not have needed to instruct himelf a second time in all these matters but the memory of them was effaced by new ideas and above all by the long interval that passed until he was able to answer the questions that were put to him. Nevertheless, to be more certain of all this, it would have been necessary to lead him back into the forest where he had been found. Although he did not remember these places when they were spoken of, perhaps he would have been able to recognize them when he had seen them.

8 Of a Man Who Remembers Having Received the Use of His Senses One After the Other

Supposing that our statue recalls the order in which the senses were given to him, we would only need to make it reflect on itself to demonstrate the principal truths that we have established.

1. *The statue compares its present state with that when it knew nothing outside of itself.* What am I, it would say, and what have I been? What are these sounds, these smells, these tastes, these colors, which I took one after the other for my own states and which objects seem now to take from me? What is this limitless extension that I discover in myself and beyond? Are these only different ways of experiencing myself? Before vision was given me, the space of the skies was unknown to me; before I had the use of my limbs, I was ignorant of the fact that there were things outside of me. What am I saying? I did not know that I had extension: I was only a point when I was reduced to uniform feeling. What then is this series of sensory experiences which has made me what I am and which perhaps has made for me everything around me?

I sense only myself and what I see externally is in what I sense in myself; or rather I do not see externally but I have formed the habit of certain judgments which refer my sensations where they are not.

At the first moment of my existence I did not know at all what was taking place in me; I distinguished nothing there as yet; I had no consciousness of myself; I existed but without desires, without fear, I scarcely experienced myself; and if I had continued to exist in that way, I would never have suspected that my existence could include two instants.

But I experience several sensations in a row: they occupy my capacity to feel, in proportion to the extent of the pains or pleasures that accompany them. In this way they remain present in my memory when they are no longer so in my sensory organ. My attention is distributed among them, I compare them, I judge their relations, I form abstract ideas, I learn general truths.

Then all the activity I am capable of is concerned with those states that pleased me the most; I have needs, I form desires, I love, I hate, I hope, I fear, I have passions; and my memory serves me so vividly at times that I imagine I am experiencing sensations that in fact I am only recalling.

Astonished by what is taking place in myself, I observe myself with even more attention. At each instant I feel that I am no longer what I was. It seems that I stop being myself in order to become another me. Enjoyment and suffering make up my existence in turn; and I come to recognize that I endure by the succession of my states. Thus my "I" had to vary constantly, often to be replaced by another in which it was painful to find myself.

The more I compare my states, the more enjoyment or suffering become perceptible for me. Pleasure and pain continue to vie for my attention, the one and the other develop all my faculties: I form habits only because I obey them and I now live only to desire or to fear.

2. *The statue remembers how it discovered its body and other objects.* But soon I am in several states at once. Accustomed to noticing them when they follow one another, I notice them still when I experience them together; and my existence seems to me to proliferate in a single moment.

However I place my hands on myself, I place them on what is around me. In that moment a new sensation seems to give substance to all my states. Everything takes on solidity at my fingertips. Astonished by this new experience, I am all the more amazed as I do not rediscover myself in everything that I touch. I look for myself where I am not: it seems to me that I alone had the right to exist and that everything that I encounter, since it is formed at the expense of my own being, becomes known to me only to confine me to smaller and smaller limits. What will I become indeed when I compare the point where I am with the space that is filled by this multitude of objects that I am discovering?

From this moment it seems to me that my states no longer belong to me. I make collections of them outside of myself; I create from them all the objects that I come to know. From those ideas that require fewer comparisons, I proceed to those that I can acquire only to the extent that I make combinations. I lead my attention from one object to the next; I join the ideas and the relations that I notice in the concept that I develop of each; and I reflect on them.

If at first I moved only for the pleasure of moving, soon I moved in the hope of encountering new pleasures; and becoming capable of curiosity, I went continually from fear to hope, from movement to rest: sometimes I forget what I have suffered, other times I take precautions against the dangers that threaten me. Finally pleasure and pain, the sole sources of my desires, teach me to how to behave in space and how to form new ideas on every occasion.

3. *The statue recalls how touch instructed its other senses.* Could I have faculties other then those of moving about and of manipulating bodies? I did not imagine it for I had totally lost all memory of what I had been. What then was my surprise when I rediscovered sound, taste, smell, light, and color! Soon it seems to me that I let myself be seduced by an illusion that touch made disappear. I judge that all these states came to me from objects and I form such a habit of experiencing them as if they were in objects, that I have difficulty in believing they do not belong to those objects.

What is more simple than the way in which I learned to make use of my senses!

I open my eyes to light and I only see at first a luminous and colored cloud. I touch, I advance, I touch again: a fog gradually clears before my eyes. Touch decomposes the light, as it were; it separates the colors, distributes them on objects, distinguishes a lit space, and in this space sizes and shapes, guides my eyes up to a certain distance, opens the path for them to look at great distances on the earth and to raise themselves up to the heavens: in a word, it spreads out the universe before them. Then they seem to revel in the immense space; they deal with objects that touch cannot reach; they measure them and they scan them with astonishing speed, they seem to give and remove existence from all of nature at my command. With the mere movement of my eyelids I create or I annihilate everything around me.

When I did not have the use of this sense could I ever have been able to understand how, without changing location, it was possible to know what was beyond arm's reach? What idea would I have formed for myself of an organ that grasped shapes and sizes at such a great distance? Is it a kind of arm that stretches out in some extraordinary way to reach them or do they come toward it? Why does it reach beyond certain objects while it is stopped by others? How does it touch objects on the surface of the water while it touches them on land? Is this an illusion or does all of nature exist in double?

It seems to me that with each object that I study I create a new way of seeing and obtain a new pleasure. Here we have a vast uniform plane, where my vision passes beyond everything close to me, fixes at an indeterminate distance, and loses itself in a space that astonishes me. There we have a more rugged and a more limited terrain where my eyes, having rested on each object, take in a scene that is more sharply defined and more variegated. Green lawns, clumps of flowers, woods where the sun scarcely penetrates, waters that flow gently or that rush headlong with violence, ornament this countryside which seems to trigger a light that spreads a thousand different colors over it. I stand frozen at this sight, everything calls my attention. Scarcely do I move my eyes than I do not know if I ought to fix them on the objects that I have just discovered or to cast my glance anew on those that I have just lost. I gaze with disquiet from one to the next and the better I distinguish all the sensations that I am experiencing, the more I am aware of the pleasure of seeing.

Curious, I eagerly survey the places that intrigued me at first glance and I like to recognize by hearing, by smell, by taste and touch the objects that strike my eyes from every quarter. Each of my sensations seems to fear being overwhelmed by another. The variety and the vividness of colors competes with the perfume of the flowers; the birds seem more admirable by their shape, movement and plumage than by their song. And what is the murmur of the waters compared to their course, their waterfalls and their dazzling crystal!

Such is the sense of vision: no sooner has it been instructed by touch than it dispenses the treasures in nature; it lavishes them everywhere to decorate the places that its guide has led it to discover and it makes an enchanting spectacle of the heavens and the earth which is magnificent only because it distributes there its own sensations.

4. *The statue remembers how pleasures and pains were the first motives for its faculties.* What would I be if, always turned in on myself, I had never known how to refer my states outside of myself? But as soon as touch instructs my other senses, I see external objects that attract my attention by the pleasure or pain that they caused me. I compare them, I judge them, I feel the need to seek them or avoid them; I desire them, I like them, I hate them, I fear them: each day I acquire new knowledge and everything around me becomes the instrument of my memory, of my imagination and of all the operations of my mind.

Why must it be that I find obstacles to my desires? Why must it be that my happiness is mingled with pain? But what am I saying! Would I enjoy the good things given me if I never had to gain some through conquest? Would I appreciate them if the evils that I bemoan did not lead me to know their value? My unhappiness itself contributes to my happiness and the deepest enjoyment of my blessings arises from the vivid idea of the evils to which I compare them. It is to the recurrence of the one and the other that I owe all my knowledge and all that I am.

From all of this follow my needs, my desires and the different interests that are the motives for my actions; so that I study things only to the degree that I believe there are pleasures to be found there or pains to avoid. And there you have the light in which I view objects in their relation to me: it illuminates them in different ways enabling me to distribute them in various classes; and those that its rays do not reach are condemned to darkness where I cannot discover them.

I study fruit and everything that is suitable for my nourishment; I look for ways to obtain their enjoyment. I study animals, I observe those that are dangerous, I learn to protect myself against their blows. Finally I study everything which strikes my curiosity: I construct rules, according to my passions, to judge the goodness and the beauty of things. Sometimes I take precautions that I believe necessary for my happiness, sometimes I let objects follow their natural course; and it seems to me that I am surrounded only by friends or enemies.

Instructed by experience, I examine, I deliberate before acting. I no longer obey my passions blindly, I resist them and I behave according to my lights, I am free; and I make better use of my liberty the more knowledge I have acquired.

5. *The statue reflects on the judgments that have become habitual.* But how certain am I of this knowledge? Strictly speaking I see only myself, I only experience myself, for I see only my own states, they are my only experience. Although my habitual judgments lead my strongly to believe that sensory properties exist outside of myself, they nevertheless do not prove it. I could thus be what I am, have the same needs, the same desires, the same passions even though the objects that I seek or that I avoid had none of these properties. In truth, without touch I would always have thought of smells, tastes, colors and sounds as my own; never would I have judged that there are odorous, sonorous, colored, and savory bodies. How then could I be certain that I am not in error when I judge that there is extension?

But it is really not important for me to know with certainty if these things exist or do not exist. I have agreeable sensations or disagreeable ones: they affect me as much as if they express the very properties of the objects to which I tend to attribute them and that is sufficient to safeguard my survival. In truth, the ideas that I form of perceptible things are vague and I only register their relations imperfectly. But I only have to make a few abstractions to have distinct ideas and to perceive relations that are more exact. From that moment on I notice two kinds of truths, some that can cease to be and others that have been, are, and will always be.

6. *The statue reflects on its ignorance of itself.* However, if I know external objects imperfectly, I do not know myself any better. I see myself made up of organs suited to receiving different impressions; I see myself surrounded by objects that act on me, each in its own way; finally, in the pleasure and pain that constantly accompany the sensations I experience, I believe I see the fundamental motive of my life and of all my faculties.

But this "I" which takes on color in my eyes, solidity beneath my hands, does it know itself any the better for now considering as its own all the parts of this body that it finds interesting and in which it believes it exists? I know that these parts are mine without being able to understand it: I see myself, I touch myself, in a word I experience myself but I do not know what I am; and if I believed that I was sound, taste, color, smell, now I no longer know what I ought to believe myself to be.

9 Conclusion

1. *In the natural order everything comes from sensations.* We do not know how to apply to ourselves all of the suppositions that I have put forth but they prove, at least, that all our knowledge comes from the senses and particularly from touch because it is this sense which instructs the others. If in supposing only sensations in our statue it has acquired general and particular ideas and becomes capable of all intellectual operations; if it has formed desires and passions that it obeys or resists; if, finally, pleasure and pain are the only motives for the development of its faculties, then it is reasonable to conclude that we had at first only sensations and that our knowledge and our passions are the effects of pleasures and pains that accompany sensory impressions.

In truth, the more we reflect, the more convinced we become that there we have the sole source of our enlightenment and of our sentiment. Consider enlightenment. As soon as we receive it we experience a new life and one that is indeed different from that which raw sensations, as it were, obtained for us in the past. Consider sentiment, observe it especially when it is increased by all the judgments we are accustomed to confusing with sensory impressions. Thereupon, these sensations, which presented at first only a few gross pleasures, will give birth to delicate pleasures which will succeed each other in astonishing variety. Thus the further we get from what our sensations were in the beginning, the more the life of our being develops and becomes variegated: it will come to embrace so many things that we will have difficulty in understanding how all our faculties could have a common principle in sensation.

2. *This source is not equally abundant for all men.* As long as men notice

in their sensory impressions only those sensations that they do not know how to combine with more than a few judgments, the life of one is roughly similar to that of another: there is scarcely any difference save in the degree of vividness with which they have sensations. Experience and reflection will be for them what the chisel is in the hands of a sculptor who discovers a perfect statue in a formless stone. Depending on the art with which men handle this chisel, they will see emerge from their sensations new enlightenment and new pleasures.

If we observe them, we will see how these materials remain unformed in some cases or are put to work in others. If we examine the differences between one man and another, we will be astonished to see how, in the same period of time, some live so much more than others do; for to live is essentially to experience and life is longer for the man who is better at increasing the range of his experience.

We have seen that enjoyment can begin with the first agreeable sensation. At the first moment, for example, that we gave vision to our statue it enjoyed; even if its eyes were merely struck by a dark color. For we must not judge its pleasures by our own. Many sensations are indifferent for us, or even disagreeable either because they have nothing new to offer us or because we know more vivid ones of the same kind. But the statue's situation is quite different and it can be thoroughly delighted when it experiences sensations that we do not deign to notice or that we notice only with distaste.

Let us look at the enlightenment that comes when touch teaches the eye to spread colors throughout all of nature: There you have as many new feelings and, as a result, new pleasures as there are new things to enjoy.

We must reason in the same way for all the other senses and all the operations of the mind. For we enjoy things not only by sight, hearing, taste, smell, touch; we enjoy them further through memory, imagination, reflection, the passions, hopes; in short by all our faculties. But these basic sources are not all equally active in all men.

3. *Man is only what he has acquired.* It is pleasures and pains compared, that is to say, our needs which exercise our faculties. As a result, it is to them that we owe the happiness that is ours to enjoy. We have as many needs as different kinds of enjoyment; as many degrees of need as degrees of enjoyment. And there you have the germ of everything that we are, the source of our unhappiness or of our happiness. To observe the influence of this principle is thus the sole means to study ourselves.

The history of the faculties of our statue makes clear the development of all these things. When it was limited to basic sentience, a uniform sensation was all its being, all its knowledge, all its pleasure. By giving it successively new states and new senses, we have seen it form desires, learn from experience to regulate or satisfy them, and pass from need to need, from one bit of knowledge to the next, from one pleasure to the next. Thus the statue is nothing other than what it has acquired. Why would the same not be true of man?

End of the Treatise on Sensations.

BOOK III:

LOGIC, OR THE FIRST DEVELOPMENTS OF THE ART OF THINKING

PURPOSE OF THIS WORK

It was natural for men to make up for the weakness of their arms by the means nature put within their reach. Thus, they were mechanics before they studied the subject of mechanics. They were logicians in the same way—they thought before they inquired how they thought. Centuries had to pass before men suspected that thought could be subject to laws. Even today, most men still think without suspecting anything of the kind.

However, a happy instinct called *talent*, that is, a more certain and sensitive manner of seeing, guided the better minds without their knowing it. Their writings became models, and in them people tried to discover by what strategy—unknown even to the writers themselves—they produced pleasure and enlightenment. The more astonishing their talent, the more people imagined that these writers possessed some extraordinary technique and they tried to discover these extraordinary techniques when they should have looked only for simple ones. People soon believed they had figured out these men of genius. But it is not easy to figure them out. Their secret is all the more protected as it is not always within their power to reveal it.

People thus looked for the laws of the art of thinking where they were not. And that is probably where we would look for them ourselves if we had to begin this search. But by seeking them where they are not, people have shown us where they are, and we can be sure of finding them if we know how to observe better than those who came before us.

Now, just as the art of moving large masses has its laws in the faculties of the body and in the levers that our arms have learned to use[1], the art of thinking has its laws in the faculties of the mind, and in the levers that our mind has likewise learned to use. [a]Thus we must observe these faculties and levers.

Certainly, if a man wanted, for the first time, to make some use of the faculties of his body, he would not dream of establishing definitions, axioms, or principles. He cannot. He is forced to begin by using his arms. It is natural for him to use them. It is likewise natural for him to get help from anything that he thinks can be of some assistance, and he soon converts a stick into a lever. This use increases his powers. Experience, which shows him why he has done something badly and how he can do better, gradually develops all his bodily faculties and thus he educates himself.

This is how nature forces us to begin when we first make some use of the faculties of our mind. Nature alone controls them, as it first controlled the

---

[1]The comparison is due to Bacon.

[a]Cf. for example, Bacon, *Novum Organum*, Book 1, Sec. 2.

faculties of the body. And if in what follows we are capable of guiding them ourselves, it is only insofar as we continue in the way nature made up begin, and we owe our progress to the first lessons that it gave us. Thus, we shall not begin this *Logic* with definitions, axioms, or principles. We shall begin by observing the lessons that nature gives us.

In the first part, we shall see that analysis is a method that we have learned from nature itself. And we shall use this method to explain the origin and generation both of ideas and of the faculties of the mind. In the second part, we shall consider the means and the effects of analysis and we shall reduce the art of reasoning to a well-formed language.

This *Logic* resembles no other written up to the present time. But the new way in which it is treated ought not to be its only advantage, it must furthermore be the simplest, the easiest, and the most illuminating.

PART ONE:

HOW NATURE ITSELF TEACHES US TO ANALYZE; AND HOW WITH THIS METHOD WE EXPLAIN THE ORIGIN AND DEVELOPMENT OF EITHER IDEAS OR THE FACULTIES OF THE MIND

1 How Nature Gives Us Our First Lessons in the Art of Thinking

The first faculties we notice are our senses. It is through them alone that impressions of objects reach our mind. If we had been deprived of sight, we would know neither light nor colors. If we had been deprived of hearing, we would have no knowledge of sounds. In short, if we had never had any senses, we would know none of the objects of nature.

But to know these objects is it enough to have senses? Doubtlessly not, for the same senses are common to us all, and nevertheless we do not all have the same knowledge. This inequality can only arise from the fact that we do not all know equally how to put our senses to the use for which they were given us. If I do not learn to control them, I acquire less knowledge than someone else, for the same reason that I dance well only to the extent that I have learned to control my steps. Everything can be learned, and there is an art for directing the faculties of the mind, just as there is one for directing those of the body. But we learn to direct the latter only because we know them; therefore we must know the former in order to learn how to direct them.

The senses are only the occasional cause of the impressions that objects make on us. It is the mind that has sensations; it is to the mind alone that sensations belong; and sentience is the first faculty that we notice in it. This faculty can be separated into five parts because we have five kinds of sensations. The mind has sensations because of the action of sight, hearing, smell, taste, and chiefly touch.

Since the mind has sensations only through the action of the organs of the body, it is obvious that we will learn to direct systematically this faculty of having sensation, if we learn to direct our organs systematically toward the objects we want to study. But how is the proper control of the senses learned? By doing what we did when we controlled them properly. Everyone has chanced to control them well, at least sometimes. It is a matter in which needs and experience promptly instruct us, as infants prove. They acquire knowledge without our help. They acquire it in spite of the obstacles we put in the way of the development of their faculties. Thus they have an art for acquiring knowledge. It is true that they follow the rules without knowing them, but they still follow them. Therefore, we have only to make them notice what they sometimes do in order to teach them how to do it always. And it will turn out that we have taught them only what they already knew how to do. Since they began by themselves to develop their faculties, they will realize that they can develop them still further if, to complete this development, they do what they did to begin it. They will realize it all the more since, having begun at a point where they had learned nothing previously, they began properly because nature began for them.

Such is nature, that is, our faculties determined by our needs: for needs and faculties are properly what we call the nature of each animal. By that we only mean that an animal is born with certain needs and certain faculties. But, because these needs and faculties depend on the animal's constitution and vary with it, consequently, by nature we understand the structure of our organs, and indeed therein lies its principles.

Animals that rise up in the air, those that stay on the ground, those that live in water, are just so may species that, having been formed differently, have needs and faculties that belong uniquely to each or—which is the same thing—each has its own nature.

It is thus nature that begins, and it always begins well because it begins alone. The Intelligence that created it willed it so and He gave it everything with which to begin well. Early on, each animal had to be able to look out for its own survival. It could not therefore instruct itself too promptly; and nature's lessons must be as prompt as they are certain.

A baby learns only because he feels the need to instruct himself. He has an interest in knowing, for example, his wet-nurse, and he soon gets to know her. He distinguishes her from other people, and confuses her with no one, and that is what knowing is. Indeed, we acquire knowledge only insofar as we distinguish more and more things, and take better notice of their distinguishing characteristics. Our knowledge begins with the first object we learn to distinguish.

The knowledge a baby has of his wet-nurse or of anything else only amounts so far to a knowledge of sensory qualities. Thus he acquired it only because of the way in which he controlled his senses. An urgent need may lead him to make a false judgment because it leads him to make it in haste; but the error can be only momentary. Misled by his expectations, he soon feels the need to judge a second time, and he judges better; experience, which watches over him, corrects his mistakes. Does he believe he sees his wet-nurse because he perceives someone who looks like her in the distance? His error does not last long. If a first glance deceived him, a second glance disabuses him, and he searches about for her with his eyes.

Thus the senses themselves often clear up the errors they led us into. If a first observation does not meet the need for which it was made, we are thus warned that we have observed badly, and we feel the necessity to observe again. This warning is never lacking when the things we are mistaken about are absolutely necessary to us; for in experience, pain comes in the wake of a false judgment as pleasure follows from a true one. Thus pleasure and pain are our first teachers. They enlighten us because they inform us whether we are judging badly or well. That is why as children we make, without any help, progress that seems as rapid as it is astonishing.

An art of reasoning would thus be completely useless to us if all we ever had to judge were things related to the needs of first necessity. We would reason well naturally because we would regulate our judgments according to the warnings of nature. But hardly do we begin to emerge from childhood than we have already formed a multitude of judgments about which nature no longer informs us. On the contrary, it seems that pleasure accompanies false judgments as much as it does true ones, and we confidently make mistakes. On these occasions, curiosity is our only need and ignorant curiosity is satisfied with anything. Curiosity indulges itself in its errors with a kind of pleasure. It often becomes obstinately attached to them, taking a word that means nothing for an answer, incapable of recognizing that this answer is only a word. Then our errors last. If, as happens only all to often, we have judged things beyond our reach, experience does not disabuse us. And if we have judged other things with undue haste, it also does not disabuse us because our prejudices do not permit us to consult it.

Thus errors begin when nature ceases to alert us to our mistakes; that is, in judging things that bear little relation to our primary needs, we do not know how to test our judgments in order to recognize whether they ar true or false. (*Course of Study, Ancient History*, Book 3, Ch. 3)[2]

---

[2]To learn a mechanical skill, it is not sufficient to conceptualize the theory, you must acquire practical experience; for theory is only a knowledge of rules, and no one is a mechanic by virtue of this knowledge alone; it requires the habit of performance. Once this habit is acquired, the rules are useless; there is no need to think about the task and it is done well, as it were naturally.

It is thus that we must learn the art of reasoning. It will not be sufficient to conceptualize this Logic: if we do not make a habit of the method it teaches, and if this habit is not such as to allow us to reason well without needing to think about rules, we will not have practical mastery of the art of reasoning, we will only have the theory.

This habit, like all others, can be acquired only through long exercise. We must practice on many objects. I indicate here the readings that are necessary to this end, and I will indicate them elsewhere in the same way. But because the practice of an art is acquired more easily the more the theory has been grasped, it would be best not to read the selection I cite until the reader has grasped the spirit of this Logic: and this requires that it be read at least once through.

Once you have grasped the spirit of this Logic, you can begin it anew; and, as you go along, you can read the selections I cite. I venture to promise to those who study it in this way, that they will acquire from all their studies a facility which will surprise them: I know it from experience.

But finally, since there are things we judge well, even from childhood on, we have only to observe how we led ourselves to judge them, and we shall know how we ought to conduct ourselves to judge other things. It is enough to continue as nature had us begin, that is, to observe and to submit our judgments to the test of observation and experience.

That is what we all did in our first infancy, and if we could recall that age, our first studies would put us on the right road to conducting others successfully. Each of us then made discoveries that he owed only to his own observations and experiences. And we would make yet more today if we knew how to follow the path that nature had cleared for us.

Thus it is not a matter of devising on our own a system for knowing how we ought to acquire knowledge. Let there be no doubt about it. Nature itself contrived this system. Only nature could do so. It did it well, and all we have to do is to observe what it teaches us.

It seems that, to study nature, it would be necessary to observe in children the first developments of our faculties, or to remember what happened to us. Both are difficult. We would often be reduced to the necessity of making suppositions. But such suppositions would have the drawback of sometimes seeming gratuitous, and at other times requiring that we should put ourselves in situations where not everyone could follow. It is enough to have noticed that children acquire true knowledge only because, by observing just those things related to their most urgent needs, they do not make mistakes; or, that if they do make mistakes, they are immediately alerted to them. Let us confine ourselves to inquiring how we conduct ourselves now in acquiring knowledge. If we can assure ourselves of some knowledge, and of the manner in which we have acquired it, we shall know how we can acquire further knowledge.

2 Analysis is the Only Method for Acquiring Knowledge. How We Learn it from Nature Itself

I imagine a chateau overlooking some wide, luxuriant open landscape where nature has pleased to lavish variety, and where art has profited from the site to vary and embellish it still further. We arrive at the chateau during the night. The next day, the windows open at the moment when the sun begins to gild the horizon, and then immediately close.

Although this landscape was shown to us only for an instant, it is certain that we saw everything included within it. In a second instant, we would only have received the same impressions that the objects made on us in the first. A third opening would produce the same effect. Consequently, if the windows had not been reclosed, we would have continued seeing what we saw at first.

But this first instant is not sufficient for us to know the landscape, that is, for us to distinguish the objects that it contains. That is why, when the windows are reclosed, none of us could give an account of what he had seen. This is how it happens that we can see many things and yet learn nothing.

Finally, the windows are thrown open, and are not closed as long as the sun remains above the horizon, and we see again at length everything that we saw at first. But if, like men in a trance, we continue as in the first instance to see this multitude of different objects all at once, we shall know no more when the night comes upon us that we knew when the windows that had just been opened were suddenly closed.

To know this landscape, it is thus not sufficient to see all of it at once. We must see each part one after another. And, instead of taking everything in at a glance, we must fix our attention on one subject after another. This is what nature teaches us all. If nature gave us the faculty of seeing many things at once, it also gave us the faculty of looking at one thing only, that is, of directing our eyes to a single object. It is to this faculty, which is a consequence of our make-up, that we owe all the knowledge that we acquire through the sense of sight.

This faculty is common to everyone. If, however, we later wish to talk about this landscape, it will be noticed that we do not all know it equally well. Some of us will give more or less true descriptions, in which many things will be found as they in fact are, while others of us will mix everything up and give descriptions in which nothing is recognizable. Still, we have all seen the same objects, but some of us directed our gaze haphazardly while others looked at things with a certain orderliness.

Now what is this order? Nature itself points it out. It is the order in which it presents the objects. Some objects particularly attract our gaze; they are more striking, more dominant, and all the other objects seem to arrange themselves around them. These are the ones we observe first. When we have noticed their respective positions, the others arrange themselves in the intervals, each in its place.

We therefore begin with the main objects. We observe them successively, and compare them in order to judge the relations among them. When, by this means, we have their respective locations, we observe in turn all those that fill in the intervals. We compare each one with the nearest major object, and determine its location.

Then we sort out all the objects whose form and location we have grasped and we take them in in a single glaze. Their order in our minds is thus no longer successive but simultaneous. This is the order in which they actually exist, and we see them distinctly all at once.

The knowledge we have thus acquired we owe uniquely to the skill with which we have directed our gaze. We acquired the knowledge in successive stages; but, once acquired, it is all present in the mind at the same time, as the objects that it recalls are all present to the eye that sees them.

It is thus with the mind as with the eye. It sees a multitude of things all at once, and we must not be surprised by that, since all visual sensations belong to the mind.

This seeing with the mind is extended as in seeing with the body. If you have a good constitution, both require only practice, and we cannot set limits on the range of either one. Indeed, the practiced mind sees in a subject on which it is reflecting a multitude of relations that we do not perceive, just as the practiced eyes of a great painter instantaneously distinguish in a landscape a multitude of things we see with him, but which escape our notice.

By going from chateau to chateau, we may study new landscapes, and sketch them in our mind's eye as we did the first. Then we may either prefer one to the others, or find that each has its own charms. But we judge them only because we compare them. We compare them only because we recall them at the same time. The mind sees more than does the eye.

If we now reflect on how sight yields knowledge, we will notice that a

known; it is even fought against, though it is simple, obvious, and fundamental.

Indeed, if I want to know a machine, I decompose it in order to study each part separately. When I have an exact idea of each of the parts and can put them back in their original order, I then have a perfect conception of this machine beause I have decomposed and recomposed it.

What then is it to understand this machine? It is to have a thought made up of as many ideas as there are parts of the machine itself, ideas that represent each part exactly, and that are arranged in the same order. When I have studied the machine with this method, which is the only one, then my thought has only distinct ideas to offer; and the analysis falls out by itself should I wish to understand the machine or give an account of it to others.

Anyone can convince himself of this truth by his own experience. Even the humblest seamstresses are convinced of it, for if you give them a dress of unusual form as a model and ask them to make another like it, they will naturally imagine taking the model apart and putting it back together again in order to learn how to make the dress that you have asked for. They therefore know analysis as well as philosophers do, and they know its utility much better than those who obstinately maintain that there is another method for instructing oneself.

Let us believe with the seamstresses that no other method can stand in for analysis. None other can shed the same light; we have the proof of this every time we want to study a fairly complex object. We have not invented this method, we have only found it, and we should not fear that it will lead us astray. Like philosophers, we could have invented others and put our ideas into any order whatever; but this nonanalytical order would have put the same confusion in our thoughts that it has put in their writings: for it seems that the more they make a show of order, the more muddled they get and the less they are understood. They do not know that only analysis can instruct us—a practical truth known to the plainest workman.

There are men of sound minds who seem to have studied nothing, because they do not seem to have reflected in order to instruct themselves. They have studied, however, and they have studied well. As they did it without prior plan, it never occurred to them to take lessons from some teacher, but they had the best teacher of all, nature. Nature made them analyze the things they studied; and the little that they know, they know well. Instinct, which is so sure a guide; taste, which judges so well while nonetheless judging at the very moment of perception; talent, which is only taste producing what it judges— all these faculties are the work of nature, which by making us analyze without knowing it, seems to want to hide from us everything that we owe to it. It is nature that inspires the man of genius; it is the muse that he invokes when he does not know where his ideas come from.

There are muddle-headed men who have studied a great deal. They pride themselves on much method, but they only reason the worse for it. When a method is not good, the more we follow it, the further astray we go. We take vague notions, words devoid of sense for principles; we invent a scientific jargon in which we think we see certain truths, and yet we do not really know what we see, think, or say. We are capable of analyzing our thoughts only insofar as they themselves are the product of analysis.

Thus, once again, it is through analysis and analysis alone that we must instruct ourselves. It is the simplest way because it is the most natural; and we shall see that it is also the shortest. Analysis is responsible for all discoveries; it is by means of analysis that we shall rediscover everything that has been found, and what is called the *method of invention* is none other than analysis. (*Course of Study, Art of Thinking*, Part 2, Ch. 4)[c]

---

[c]The conception of analysis developed by Condillac should be compared with certain ideas of Leibniz, although we cannot however speak of Leibniz' influence on Condillac. Cf., for example, Leibz *Meditationem - Cognitione Veritate et Ideis*, Gerhardt ed., Vol. 4, p. 422–426.

4 How Nature Causes Us to Observe Sensible Objects in Order to Give us Ideas of Different Kinds

We can proceed only from the known to the unknown is a commonplace principle in theory, and almost unknown in practice. It seems that only men who have had no education are conscious of it. When they want to make you understand a thing you are not familiar with, they compare it with something else that you do know. If they are not always happy in their choice of comparisons, they reveal at least that they sense what they must do to make themselves understood.

It is not so with learned men. Although they undertake to instruct, they readily forget to proceed from the known to the unknown. If you want me to conceive ideas that I do not have, however, you must begin with ideas that I do have. What I know is the beginning of everything that I do not know, and of everything that it is possible to learn. If there is a method for giving me new knowledge, it can only be the same method that has already yielded me some.

Indeed, all our knowledge comes from the senses, that which I lack as well as that which I have. Those more learned than I have been as ignorant as I am today. Now if they have instructed themselves by proceeding from the known to the unknown, why do not I instruct myself by proceeding like them from the known to the unknown? If some knowledge that I have acquired prepares me for new knowledge, why cannot I proceed, through a series of analyses, from knowledge to knowledge? In short, why should I not find what I am ignorant of in the sensations where they have found it, and which are common to us all?

Learned men undoubtedly would easily cause me to discover everything that they have discovered, if they themselves always knew how they instructed themselves. But they are ignorant of it because it is something which they have observed poorly or which most of them have not even thought of. Certainly they instructed themselves only insofar as they analyzed and did it well. But they did not notice it; nature made these analyses, as it were, within them but without their aid; and they liked to believe that the ability to acquire knowledge is a gift, a talent that is not easily communicated. We must not be surprised if we have trouble understanding them. As soon as a man prides himself on his unique talents, he is ill-suited for placing himself within the compass of others.

Be that as it may, everyone is forced to recognize that we can proceed only from the known to the unknown. Let us see what use we can make of this truth.

As children, we acquired knowledge through a series of observations and analyses. It is therefore with this knowledge that we ought to begin again in order to continue our studies. We must observe and analyze it and, if possible, discover everything it includes.

This knowledge is a collection of ideas: this collection is a well-ordered system, that is, a series of precise ideas, which analysis has arranged in the same order as that of the things themselves. If the ideas were imprecise and without order, we would have only imperfect knowledge, which properly speaking would not even be knowledge at all. But each of us has some system of precise, well-ordered ideas if not on speculative matters, then at least on ordinary things that bear some relation to our needs. This is all we require: It is with these ideas that we must begin with the people we want to instruct and, clearly, we must make them take note of the origin and development of these ideas if we want to lead them for these to others.

Now, if we observe the origin and development of ideas, we see them arise successively one from another. If this succession follows the order in which we acquired them, we will have analyzed them well. The order of analysis here has therefore the same order as the development of ideas. We have said that ideas of sensible objects are, in their origin, only the sensations that represent these objects. But in nature there exist only individual things. Thus our first ideas are only individual ideas, ideas of one or another object.

We did not dream up names for each individual; we only distributed them into different classes, which we distinguish by particular names. These classes are called *genera* and *species*. We have, for example, placed in the class *tree* the plant whose stem rises to a certain height to divide into a multitude of branches, and forms all its boughs into a more or less large cluster. There you have an example of the kind of general class called *genus*. When we later observed that trees differ in height, structure, fruit, and the like, we distinguished other classes subordinate to the first, which includes them all. These subordinate classes are called *species*.

Thus we distribute into different classes all the things that may come within the purview of our knowledge. By this means, we give them each an unmistakable place, and we always know where to find them again. Let us forget these classes for a moment, and imagine that each individual thing has been given a different name. We immediately feel that the multitude of names would tire our memory, mix everything up, and that we would find it impossible to study the objects that multiply under our eyes and to have distinct ideas of them.

Nothing is more reasonable than this distribution. When we consider how useful or even necessary it is to us, we might be led to believe that we have done it by design. But we would be mistaken. This design belongs uniquely to nature. Nature began it without our participation.

Following our example, a child will call *tree* the first tree that we show him, and this name will be for him the name of an individual thing. Nevertheless, if we show him another tree, he will not think to ask for the name. He will call it a tree, and he will give this common name to two individual things. He will in the same way make it common to three, four, and finally all plants that seem to him to bear some resemblance to the first trees that he saw. This name will even become so general that he will call *tree* everything that we call *plant*. He is naturally led to generalize because it is more convenient for him to use a name he knows rather than learn a new one. He thus generalizes without having planned to and without even noticing that he is generalizing. It is thus that an individual idea suddenly becomes general. Often, the idea even becomes too general. That happens every time we confound things it would be useful to distinguish.

The child will soon perceive this himself. He will not say, "I have generalized too much: I must distinguish different species of trees." Without a plan and without noticing it, he will form subordinate classes just as he formed—without a plan and without noticing it—a general class. He will do nothing but obey his needs. That is why I say he will make these distributions naturally and without knowing it. Indeed, if we lead him into a garden and get him to pick and eat different sorts of fruit, we shall see that he will soon learn the names, "cherry tree," "peach tree," "pear tree," "apple tree," and that he will distinguish different species of trees.

Our ideas thus begin by being individual in order to become suddenly as general as possible. Only later do we distribute them into different classes according as we feel the need to distinguish them. There you have the order of their development.

Since our needs are the motive for this distribution, we do this for their sake. These classes, which proliferate, more or less, thus make up a system whose parts are naturally bound together because all our needs go hand in hand. This more or less extended system is consistent with the use we want to put things to. The need that instructs us gives us little by little the discernment that reveals differences we had not seen before. If we extend and perfect this system, it is because we continue as nature made us begin.

Philosophers therefore have not just dreamt up this system. They found it by observing nature. If they had observed it better, they would have explained it far better than they have done. But they believed it was their own property, and they treated it as if it were indeed their own. they put it in the arbitrary and the absurd, and they went to strange excesses in their use of general ideas.

Unfortunately, we believed we were learning this system from them, while in fact we had learned it from a better master. But because nature did not make us notice that it was our teacher, we thought we owed the knowledge to those who did. We thus confounded the philosophers' lessons with the lessons of nature, and we reasoned badly.

According to everything we have said, to form a class of certain objects is nothing other than to give the same name to all of them we judge similar. When we take this class and make two or more other classes out of it, we do nothing but choose new names in order to distinguish objects that we judge different. It is only by this device that we put order in our ideas. But this device does only that. We must notice that it can do nothing more. Indeed, we would be making a big mistake if we imagined that species and genera actually exist in nature because there are species and genera in our conception of it. Strictly speaking, general names are not the names of anything that actually exists. They express only the perspective of the mind, as we consider things from the point of view of their resemblances or differences. There is no tree in general, or apple tree in general, or pear tree in general. There are only individuals. Thus in nature there are neither genera nor species. This fact is so simple that we might think it pointless to notice it. But often the simplest things escape us precisely because they are simple: we do not deign to observe them and this is one of the main causes of our bad reasoning and of our errors.

We distinguish classes, not according to the nature of things, but according to our manner of conceiving. At first, we are struck by resemblances, and we are like a child who takes all plants for trees. In what follows, the need to observe develops our discernment; and because we then notice differences, we form new classes.

The better our discernment becomes, the more classes proliferate. Because there are no two individual entities that do not differ in some respect, it is obvious that there would be as many classes as individuals if, for each difference, we wanted to make a new class. Then our ideas would contain no more order, and confusion would replace the light shed on them when we generalized methodically.

Thus there is a point at which we must stop. Because if it is important to make distinctions, it is even more important not to make too many. When we do not make enough of them, if there are things that we do not distinguish and that we ought to, there at least remains those that we do distinguish. When we make too many distinctions we mix everything up because the mind is led astray by a great number of distinctions that it feels no need for: It may be asked up to what point we can multiply genera and species. I reply, or rather nature replies, up to the point where we have enough classes to guide us in the use of things relative to our needs. The correctness of this reply is palpable since it is only our needs that lead us to distinguish classes, since we do not bother giving names to things we do not want to do anything with. It is thus, at least, that men behave naturally. When they stray from nature to become bad philosophers, they believe that by dint of distinctions as subtle as they are useless, they will explain everything, and they get everything mixed up.

Everything in nature is distinct, but our minds are too limited to see it all distinctly in detail. We analyze in vain. Things always remain that we cannot analyze and that for this reason we see only confusedly. The art of forming classes—so necessary for having precise ideas—illuminates only the chief points; the intervals remain obscure, and in these intervals the middle classes are confounded. A tree and a shrub, for example, are two very distinct species. But a tree can be smaller, a shrub can be larger, and we arrive at a plant that is neither a tree nor a shrub, or which is both at the same time, that is, we do not know which species to relate it to.

There is no disadvantage to this; for to ask whether this plant is a tree or a shrub is not to ask in truth what it is; it is only to ask if we ought to give it the name of a tree or that of a shrub. It is unimportant whether we give it the one name rather than the other. If the plant is useful, we can make use of it and we will call it *plant*. We would never raise such questions if we did not suppose that genera and species existed in nature as in our minds. This is the abuse that we have made of classes: it was necessary to know it. It remains for us to observe how far our knowledge extends when we class the things we study.

Since our sensations are the only ideas that we have of sensible objects, we see in them only what they represent. Beyond that, we perceive nothing and, consequently, can know nothing.

Therefore, no answer can be given to those who ask, "What is the subject of the properties of bodies? What is its nature? What is its essence?" We do not see these subjects, these natures, these essences. In vain would someone try to show them to us. It would be like undertaking to show colors to the blind. These are words for which we have no ideas at all. Such words mean only that underlying the properties there is something that we do not know.

Analysis gives us exact ideas only insofar as it shows us in things only what we see there. We must accustom ourselves to seeing only what we see. That is not easy for most men, not even for most philosophers. The more ignorant we are, the more impatient we are to judge. We believe we know everthing before we have observed anything, as if a knowledge of nature is a kind of divination with words.

Precise ideas acquired by analysis are not always complete. They can never be so as long as we are occupied with sensible objects. Then we discover only some properties and we can have only partial knowledge.

We will study each object in the same way that we studied the countryside we saw from the windows of our chateau; for like the countryside, each object contains primary things to which all the others must be related. We must take them in this order if we want to have distinct and well-ordered ideas. For example, all the phenomena of nature presuppose extent and movement. Thus, every time we would like to study some phenomenon, we will regard extent and movement as the principal properties of bodies.

We have seen how analysis acquaints us with sensible objects and how the idas that analysis yields are distinct and consistent with the order of things. We must remember that this method is the only one, and that it must be absolutely the same in all our studies. For to study different sciences is not to change methods, it is only to apply the same method to different objects, it is to do something again we have already done; and the main point is to do it well once in order to make it known forever. This is, in truth, where we were when we began. From childhood on, we have all acquired knowledge. Thus, without knowing it, we have followed a good method. It only remains for us to notice it; that is what we have done and we can henceforth apply this method to new objects. (*Course of Study*, preliminary lessons, Art. 1: *The Art of Thinking*, Part 1, Ch. 8[d]; *Treatise on Sensations*, Part 4, Ch. 6)

---

[d]Also see, *Essay on the Origin of Human Knowledge*, Part 1, Sec 5, which was reworked for this chapter of the *Art of Thinking*.

5 Ideas of Things that do not Excite the Senses

Through observing sensible objects, we naturally work our way up to objects that do not excite the senses because, from the effects that we see, we infer causes that we do not see. The movement of a body is an effect, therefore it has a cause. It is beyond doubt that this cause exists, although none of my senses allows me to perceive it, and I call it *force*. This name does not make me know it better; I know only what I knew before—the movement has a cause that I do not know. But I can speak of it; I judge it greater or weaker according as the movement itself is greater or weaker. I measure it, in some sense, by measuring the movement.

Movement takes place in space and in time. I perceive space by seeing sensible objects that occupy it; I perceive duration in the succession of my ideas or my sensations. But I see nothing absolute either in space or in time. The senses cannot unveil what things are in themselves: They show me only some of the relations things have among themselves and some they have to me. If I measure space, time, movement, and the force that produces movement, the results of my measurements are only relations; for to look for relations or to measure is the same thing.

Because we give names to things we have an idea of, it might be supposed that we have an idea of everything to which we give names. This is an error we must keep clear of. It may happen that we give a name to a thing only because we are persuaded of its existence. The word *force* is a proof of it.

Movement, which I considered as an effect, becomes a cause in my eyes as soon as I observe that it is everywhere and that it produces, or participates in the production of, all phenomena of nature. Then, by observing the laws of movement, I can study the universe as I study the countryside from a window; the method is the same.

But although everything in the universe is sensible, we do not see everything; and although art comes to the aid of the senses, they are still too weak. Nevertheless if we observe well, we will discover phenomena. We see them, as a chain of cause and effect, form different systems; and we develop precise ideas of some parts of the whole. Thus it is that modern philosophers have made discoveries that would not have been judged possible several centuries before, and that lead us to presume we can make others. (*Course of Studies*, Art of Reasoning, Modern History, Last Book, Ch. 5 ff.)

But, as we have judged that movement has a cause because it is an effect, we judge that the universe also has a cause, because it is itself an effect; and this cause we call *God*.

This expression is not like that of *force* of which we have no idea. God, it is true, does not excite the senses; but he has printed his character on sensible things; we see him there and the senses raise us up toward him.

Indeed when I notice phenomena giving birth one to another, as a chain of effects and causes, I necessarily see a first cause; and with the idea of first cause begins the idea that I have of God.

Since this cause is a first one, it is independent and necessary; it is everlasting and in its immensity and eternity it embraces everything that exists.

I see order in the universe. Above all, I observe this order in the parts I know best. If I myself have intelligence, I acquired it only to the extent that ideas in my mind conform to the order of things outside me. My intelligence is only a copy—and quite a feeble one—of the intelligence that arranged the things that I conceive, and those that I do not conceive. The first cause is thus intelligent: it has arranged everything everywhere and forever; and its intelligence, like its immensity and its eternity, embraces all times and all places.

Since the first cause is independent, it can do what it wants. Because it is intelligent, it wills with knowledge and consequently with choice. It is free.

Because it is intelligent, it appraises everything. Since it is free, it acts accordingly. Thus, from the ideas that we have formed of its intelligence and of its liberty, we form an idea of its goodness, its justness, its mercy, in short, of its providence. This is an imperfect idea of the Divinity. This idea comes and can only come from the senses; but it will develop more fully, the more we go deeply into the order that God has put in his works. (*Course of Study*, Preliminary Lesson, Art. 5; *Treatise on Animals*, Part 2, Ch. 6)

6 Continuation of the Same Subject

Movement considered as the cause of some effect is called *action*. A moving body acts on the air it divides, and on the bodies it strikes. But that is only the action of an inanimate body. The action of an animate body is likewise found in movement. Capable of different movements following the difference in the organs it was endowed with, an animate body has different ways of acting; and in its action as in its make-up each species has something peculiar to it.

All these actions come within the purview of the senses, and to form an idea of them, it is sufficient to observe them. It is no more difficult to notice how the body acquires or loses habits, for everyone knows from his own experience what has often been said, that one does it without needing to think about it; and on the other hand, we no longer do with the same ease what we ceased to do for some time. To acquire a habit, we must do something and do it over again several times; and to lose it, we need only to do it no longer. (*Course of Study*, Preliminary Lesson, Art. 3; *Treatise on Aminals*, Part 2, Ch. 1)

These are the actions of the mind that determine those of the body. And from the latter, which we see, we judge the former, which we do not see. It is sufficient to have noticed what we do when we desire or we fear, to perceive in the movements of others their desires or their fears. Thus, the actions of bodies represent the actions of the mind and sometimes reveal the most secret thoughts. This language is that of nature. It is the first, most expressive, and the truest. We will see that it is according to this model that we have learned to create languages.

Moral ideas seem to escape the senses. At least they escape those of the philosophers who deny that our knowledge comes from sensation. They would gladly ask what color virtue is, or what color vice. I reply that virtue

365

consists of the habit of good actions, as vice consists of the habit of bad ones. Now these habits and these actions are visible. But is the morality of actions something that falls under the senses? Why then does it not so fall? This morality consists uniquely in the conformity of our actions with laws. Now these actions are visible and the laws are equally so because they are conventions that men have made.

If laws are conventions, it will be argued that they are arbitrary. There may be some arbitrary laws. There may even be too many. But those that determine whether our actions are good or bad are not arbitrary and cannot be so. They are our works because they are conventions that we have made. Nevertheless, we did not make them alone. Nature made them with us. It dictated them to us, and it was not in our power to make others. Given the needs and the faculties of man, the laws are themselves given.

Although we make laws, God, who created us with certain needs and certain faculties, is in truth our only legislator. By following these laws consistent with our nature, it is thus him that we obey. And there you have the culmination of the morality of our actions.

If, from man's being free, we conclude that there often is some arbitrariness in what he does, we will be correct. But if we think that there is only arbitrariness we will be mistaken. As it does not rest with us not to have the needs that are a consequence of our make-up, so it does not rest with us not to be led to do what we are determined to do by these needs. If we do not do it, we are punished for it. (*Treatise on Animals*, Part 2, Ch. 7)

7 Analysis of the Faculties of the Mind

We have seen how nature teaches us to analyze sensible objects and, by this method, gives us ideas of all kinds. Thus we cannot doubt that all our knowledge comes from our senses.

But we are concerned with enlarging the sphere of our knowledge. Now if to enlarge it, we need to know how to conduct our mind, we realize that, to learn to conduct our mind, we need to know it perfectly. Thus we are concerned with sorting out all the faculties that are bound up in the faculty of thought. To accomplish this purpose—and still others, too, whatever they may be—we will not have to look for a new method for each new study, as some have done up to now. Analysis is sufficient to answer on all occasions if we know how to use it. It is the mind alone that knows because it is the mind alone that has sensations; and it is only for the mind to conduct the analysis of everything it knows from sensation. However, how will the mind learn to conduct itself if it does not know itself, if it is ignorant of its faculties? Thus, as we have just remarked, the mind must study itself. We must discover all the faculties of which it is capable. But where will we discover them if not in the faculty of having sensation? Certainly this faculty includes all those that we can come to know. It if is only because the mind has sensations that we know the objects outside of it, will we know what happens inside of it by some means other than because it has sensations? Everything thus invites us to analyze the faculty of having sensations; let us try.

A single reflection makes this analysis very easy. To decompose the faculty of having sensations, it is sufficient to observe successively everything that happens when we acquire any bit of knowledge whatever. I say *any bit of knowledge whatever* because what happens in acquiring several bits of knowledge can only be a repetition of what happens in acquiring any one alone.

When a countryside presents itself to my sight, I see everything in the first glance, and I discern nothing as yet. To distinguish different objects and to form a distinct idea of the shape and their position, I must rest my gaze on each of them in turn; this is what we have already observed. But when I look at one, the others, although I still see them, are nevertheless, in their relation to me, as if I no longer saw them. And among the many sensations that happen all at once, it seems that I experience only one, that of the object on which I fix my gaze.

This gaze is an action by which my eye tends toward some object to which it is directed. For this reason, I give it the name *attention*. And it is obvious to me that this direction of the organ is the entire part that the body can play in attention. What then is the role of the mind? The sensation that we experience is as if it were alone, because all the others are as if we did not have them.

Thus, the attention that we give to an object is only, on the part of the mind, the sensation that that object engenders in us—sensation that becomes in some sense exclusive. And this faculty is the first one that we notice in the faculty of having sensations.

Just as we give our attention to one object, we can give it to two at the same time. Then, in place of a single exclusive sensation, we have two; and we say that we compare them, because we only experience them exclusively in order to observe them one next to the other, without being distracted by other sensations. Now that is what the word *compare* strictly means.

Comparison is thus only a twofold attention; it consists of two sensations that we experience as if we had them only and that exclude all others.

An object is either present or absent. If it is present, attention is the sensation that it currently engenders in us; if it is absent, attention is the memory of the sensation that it made. It is to this memory that we owe the power of exercising the faculty of comparing absent objects like present objects. We shall discuss memory shortly.

We can compare two objects, or experience side by side the two sensations that they produce exclusively in us, only by perceiving that they resemble each other or that they differ. Now to perceive resemblances or differences, is to judge. Judgment is thus nothing more than sensations. (*Grammar*, Part 1, Ch. 4)

If by a first judgment I know a relation, to know another, I need a second judgment. If I want to know, for example, how two trees differ, I successively observe the form, the trunk, the branches, the leaves, the fruit, and so forth. I successively compare all these things. I form a series of judgments. And because my attention reflects, as it were, from one object to another, I say that I reflected. Reflection is thus only a series of judgments made through a series of comparisons; and since these comparisons and judgments contain only sensations, thus there are only sensations in reflection.

When reflection causes us to notice the properties by which objects differ, we can, by the same reflection, gather together in a single object the properties that are separated among several. It is thus that a poet, for example, forms the idea of a hero who never existed. Then the ideas formed are images that are real only in the mind. And reflection which makes these images takes the name *imagination*.

A judgment that I express can implicitly include another one that I do not express. If I say that a body is heavy, I implicitly say that if it is unsupported, it will fall. Now when a second judgment is thus enclosed in another, we can express it as following from the first and for this reason we say it is the consequence. We say, for example, "This vault is very heavy. Thus if it is not well enough supported, it will fall." This is what we understand by pursuing a line of argument. It is nothing other than expressing two judgments of this kind. Thus there are only sensations in our reasoning as in our judgments.

The second judgment in the line of argument that we have just given is perceptibly enclosed in the first, and it is a consequence that we do not need to look for. We would, on the contrary, have to look for it if the second judgment was not to appear in the first; that is, in going from the known to the unknown, we would have to pass through a series of intermediary judgments, from the first to the last, and to see them all successively included one in another. This judgment, for example, "Mercury is suspended at a certain height in the tube of a barometer," is implicitly included in this one: "Air has weight." But because we do not see this all at once, we must, in going from the known to the unknown, discover by a series of intermediary judgments that the first is a consequence of the second. We have already done such reasoning. We will be doing still more. When we have gotten in the habit of doing so, it will no longer seem difficult to get to the bottom of the art, for it is the skills we have mastered that we can explain. So, let us begin to reason.[3]

You see that all the faculties we have just observed are included in the faculty of having sensations. Through them the mind acquires all it knowledge. Through them it understands [*elle entend*] the things that it studies, as it were, as with the ear, it hears [*elle entend*] sound. That is why the uniting

---

[3]I remember that I was taught in school that the art of reasoning consists of comparing two ideas by means of a third: To judge, we were told, if idea A includes or excludes idea B, take a third idea C, and compare A and B with it in turn. If idea A is included within C, and idea C is in idea B, conclude that idea A is in idea B. If idea A is in idea C and idea C excludes B, conclude that idea A excludes B. We will make no use of all that.

of all the faculties is call *understanding [entendement]*. Understanding thus includes attention, comparison, judgment, reflection, imagination, and reasoning. There is no way to arrive at a more precise idea of it. (*Course of Study*, Preliminary Lessons, Art. 2; *Treatise on Animals*, Part 2, Ch. 5).[e]

---

[e]Also see, *Essay on the Origin of Human Knowledge*, Part 1, Sec. 2, Ch. 1–18; *Treatise on Sensations*, Part 1, Ch. 2; and *Preamble to the Treatise* on the *Sensations*, Part 1.

8 Continuation of the Same Subject

In considering our sensations as representative, we have seen all our ideas arise from them, and all the operations of the understanding. If we consider our sensations as agreeable or disagreeable, we shall see all the operations that relate to the will arise from them.

Although, by suffering, we strictly understand experiencing a disagreeable sensation, it is certain that deprivation of an agreeable sensation is suffering to a greater or lesser degree. But we must notice that to be deprived of and to lack do not mean the same thing. We may never have had possession of the things we lack. We may, in fact, never have known them. It is quite otherwise with things we are deprived of. Not only do we know them, but we are even in the habit of having them or at least of imagining the pleasure that having them promises. Now such deprivation is suffering that we more particularly call *need*. To need a thing is to suffer because one is deprived of it. In its weakest degree, this suffering is less a pain than a state in which we do not feel well or are not at ease—I call this state *uneasiness*.

Uneasiness leads us to make movements to obtain the thing we need. Thus we cannot remain in a state of perfect quiescence, and for this reason uneasiness takes the name *disquiet*. The more we find obstacles to enjoyment, the more our disquiet increases. This state can become tormenting.

Need disturbs our rest or produces disquiet only because it directs the faculties of the body and of the mind toward the object whose deprivation makes us suffer. We recall the pleasure that they gave us. Reflection makes us realize what pleasure they can still give us; imagination exaggerates it, and to get pleasure, we make all the movements of which we are capable. All our faculties therefore are directed toward objects we feel need of. And this direction is strictly what we understand by *desire*.

As it is natural for us to get into the habit of enjoying agreeable things, it is also natural to get into the habit of desiring them. Desires transformed into habits are called *passions*. Such desires are in some sense permanent; or at least if they hold themselves in abeyance from time to time, they are renewed at the slightest occasion. The livelier they are, the more violent the passions. If, when we desire something, we judge that we shall get it, then this judgment joined to desire produces hope. Another judgment produces the will: It is the one we make when experience has given us the habit of believing that we should find no obstacle to our desires. "I want" means "I desire and nothing can oppose my desire; everything must concur in it."

Such is strictly speaking the accepted sense of the word *will*. But we usually give it a more extended meaning. We understand by *will* a faculty that includes all the habits born of need, desire, passion, hope, despair, fear, confidence, presumption, and several others it is easy to imagine.[f] Finally, the meaning of the word thought, an even more general term, includes in its accepted sense all the faculties of understanding and will. For to think is to have sensations, to pay attention, compare, judge, reflect, imagine, reason, desire, have passions, hope, fear, and so forth. (*Treatise on Animals*, Part 2, Ch. 8, 9, and 10).

We have explained how the faculties of the mind successively arise from sensation. We see that they are nothing but the faculty of sensation transformed to become each of them.

In the second part of this work, we propose to discover the whole strategy of reasoning. We must therefore prepare ourselves for this investigation. We do so by trying to reason on some matter that is simple and easy, although we are inclined to judge it otherwise when we think of the efforts that have hitherto been made to explain it, always very badly. This is the subject of the following chapter.

---

[f]Cf. *Treatise on the Sensations*, Part 1, Ch. 3, and *Preamble to the Treatise on Sensations*, Part 1.

9 Of the Causes of Sensibility and Memory

It is impossible to explain in detail all the physical causes of sensibility and memory. But instead of reasoning from false hypotheses, we can consult experience and analogy. Let us explain what can be explained, and not pretend to give an account of everything.

Some people[g] represent nerves as stretched cords, capable of perturbation and vibration, and believe they have discovered the cause of sensation and memory. It is obvious that this supposition is completely imaginary.

Others[h] say that the brain is a pliant substance in which animal spirits leave traces. These traces are preserved: the animal spirits pass over and over again; the animal is endowed with sentience and memory. These people do not realize that if the substance of the brain is soft enough to receive traces, it would not have enough consistency to preserve them; and they have not considered how impossible it is that an infinity of traces should remain in a substance where there is continual circulation.

It is by considering the nerves to be like the strings of an instrument that the first hypothesis was imagined. The second came from describing the impressions formed on the brain as imprints on a surface all parts of which are at rest. Certainly this is not to reason according to observation, nor according to analogy. It is to compare things that bear no relation to each other.

[g]Cf. Buffon, *Discourse on the Nature of Animals*, in *Natural History*, Vol. 4, p. 3–168. See the critical review by Condillac in *Treatise on Animals*, Part 1, Ch. 3.

[h]Cf. *Descartes, Treatise on Man, Refraction*, Discourse 4, *Principles*, Book 4, Sec. 189ff.; Malenbranche, *On the Search for Truth*, Book 1, Ch. 10 and Book 2, Part 1, Ch. 2–8.

I do not know whether there are animal spirits. I do not even know whether nerves are the organ of sensory experience. I know neither the texture of the fibers, nor the nature of the solids, nor that of the fluids. In short, I have only a very imperfect and vague idea of this whole mechanism. I know only that there is a movement that is the principle of vegetation and of sensibility; that the animal lives as long as the movement subsists, and that it dies when this movement ceases.

Experience teaches me that an animal can be reduced to a state of vegetation. It is in that state naturally during a deep sleep. It is in that state accidentally in a fit of apoplexy.

I form no conjectures on the movement that then occurs in it. All we know is that the blood circulates, that the viscera and glands perform the functions necessary to maintain and repair the life function. But we are ignorant of the laws by which this movement achieves all these effects. Nevertheless, these laws do exist, and they impose on the movement the pattern that makes the animal vegetate.[i]

But when the animal leaves the vegetative state to become sentient, the movement obeys other laws, and follows new patterns. If the eye, for example, opens to the light, the rays striking it impose on the movement that made it vegetate, the pattern that makes it sentient. It is the same with the other senses. Each kind of sensibility thus has as a cause a particular kind of pattern in the movement that is the principle of life.

Thus we see that the movement that makes the animal sentient can only be a modification of the movement that makes it vegetate, a modification occasioned by the action of objects on the senses.

But the movement responsible for sentience occurs not only in the organ exposed to the action of external objects; it is also transmitted to the brain, that is, to the organ that observation shows to be the first and the chief motive force of sentience. The cause of sensibility is thus the communication between the organs and the brain.

Indeed, let the brain, blocked by some cause, be unable to obey the impressions sent by the organs, and the animal immediateloy becomes insensible. Let this motive force be unconstrained again and the organs act on it, it acts on them in turn, and sentience returns.

Although unconstrained, the brain could happen to have little or no communication with some other part. An obstruction, for example, or a strong ligature around the arm would diminish or suspend communication

---

[h]Cf. Descartes, *Treatise on Man, Refraction*, Discourse 4, *Principles*, Book 4, sec. 189 ff.; Malebranche, *On the Search for Truth*, Book 1, Ch. 10 and Book 2, Part 1, Ch. 2–6.

[i]This mistrust of hypotheses that go beyond the data of observation and this search for laws that express relations among facts, reflect once again the influence of the ideal defined by Newton.

between the brain and the hand. Feeling in the hand would therefore be weakened or would cease entirely.

All these propositions are confirmed by observation. I have done nothing but free them from all arbitrary hypotheses. This was the only means of putting them in their true light.

Since the different patterns given to the movement that causes vegetation are the only physical and occasional cause of sensibility, it follows that we have sensations only insofar as our organs touch or are touched. And it is by contact that objects, acting on our organs, communicate to the vegetative movement the patterns that make us sentient. Thus, we can consider smell, hearing, sight, and taste as extensions of touch. The eye will see nothing if bodies of a certain shape do not collide with the retina. The ear will not hear if other bodies of a different shape do not strike the eardrum. In short, the principle of the variety of sensations lies in the different patterns that objects produce in the movement, following the structure of the parts exposed to their action.

But how does the contact of certain particles bring about the sensations of sound, light, and color? Perhaps we could give an account of this if we knew the essence of the mind, the mechanism of the eye, the ear, and the brain, the nature of the rays that spread out over the retina, and of the air that strikes the eardrum. But that is what we do not know. We can leave the explanation of these phenomena to those who like to make hypotheses about things where experience is no help.

If God were to fashion a new bodily organ suited for making the movement take on new forms, we would experience sensations different from those we have had up to now. This organ would lead us to discover in objects properties that at present we have no idea of. It would be a source of new pleasure, new pain, and consequently, new needs.

We would have to say the same of a seventh sense, of an eighth, and of all those we could suppose, whatever their number. It is certain that a new organ in our body would render the movement that makes it vegetate capable of many modifications that we cannot imagine.

These new senses would be excited by particles of a certain shape. Like the other senses, they would learn by touch, and from it they would learn to report their sensations of objects.

But the senses that we have are sufficient for our survival. They are even a storehouse of knowledge for those who know how to make use of them. And if other people do not draw the same riches from this storehouse, they do not suspect their own impoverishment. How could they conceive that we see in sensations which they also have what they do not see there themselves?

The senses' action on the brain thus makes the animal sentient. But that does not suffice to give the body all the movements of which it is capable: In addition, the brain must act on all the muscles and all the interior parts whose observation. Consequently, when this principal motive force receives certain observaton. Consequently, when this principal motive force receives certain patterns from the senses, it communicates others to some of the parts of the body, and the animal stirs.

The animal would move only uncertainly if the action of the senses on the brain, and that of the brain on the limbs, had been accompanied by no feeling whatever. Moved without feeling pain and pleasure, the animal would take no interest in the movements of its body. It thus would not have observed them, and it would not have learned to control them itself.

But as soon as pain or pleasure invites it to make or to avoid certain movements, it consequently studies how to make or avoid them. It compares its feelings. It notices the movements that precede these feelings and those that accompany them. In short, it feels its way along. After much such exploration, it finally acquires the habit of moving at will. Then, its movements are controlled. Such is the principle of all the habits of the body.

These habits are controlled movements that happen within us without our seeming to direct them ourselves; because by dint of having repeated them we make them without having to think about them. These are the habits that we call *natural movements*, *mechanical actions*, *instinct*, and that we wrongly suppose to be inborn. We will avoid this prejudice if we judge these habits by others that have become as natural, although we remember having acquired them.

The first time that I put my fingers on a harpischord, for example, they can move only uncertainly. But as I learn to play this instrument, I imperceptibly develop the habit of moving my fingers on the keys. First, they have difficulty in executing the patterns I want them to follow. Little by little, they overcome the obstacles. Finally, they move according to my wish, they even anticipate it, and they execute a piece of music while my reflection dwells on some completely different matter.

Thus my fingers acquire the habit of moving according to a certain number of patterns. As there is no key on which a song cannot begin, there is no pattern that cannot be the first of a certain series. Exercise every day combines these patterns differently; the fingers acquire greater facility every day. Finally, they obey, as if by themselves, a series of specified movements, and they obey without effort, without my needing to pay attention to them. It is thus that the sensory organs having acquired different habits, move on their own, and the mind no longer needs to watch over them continually in order to control their movements.

But the chief organ is the brain. It is the common center where everything is united, and from which everything seems to arise. Thus, judging the brain by the other senses, it would be correct to conclude that all the habits of the body reach it, and that, consequently, its constituent fibers, suited by their flexibility to movements of all kinds, acquire, like the fingers, the habit of obeying different series of specific movements. That being so, my brain's power to recall an obejct can only be the facility it has acquired of moving in the same way as it was moved when this object struck my senses.

The physical and occasional cause that preserves or recalls ideas thus lies in the patterns made habitual by the brain—the chief organ of sentience—and that continue to exist, or are reconstituted when the senses even cease to contribute. For we would not recall objects that we have seen, heard, or touched if some movement did not take the same patterns as when we see, hear or touch. In short, the mechanical action follows the same laws whether we feel sensation or only remember having felt it, and memory is only a manner of feeling.

I have often heard asked, "What becomes of ideas that we have stopped thinking of? Where are they preserved? Where do they come from when they present themselves to us anew? Do they exist in the mind during those long intervals when we are not thinking of them at all? Do they exist in the body?"

From these questions, and from the answers given by metaphysicians, one would think that ideas are like everything we lay in stock, and that memory is only a huge warehouse. It would be just as reasonable to give existence to different forms that a body had taken successively and to ask, "What happens to a body's roundness when it takes another form? Where is it preserved? And when the body becomes round again, where does the roundness come from?"

Like sensations, ideas are ways of being of the mind. They exist as long as they modify it. They no longer exist as soon as they cease modifying it. To look in the mind for those I am not thinking about is to look where they no longer are. To look in the body is to look where they never were. Where then are they? Nowhere. Would it not be absurd to ask where are the sounds of a harpsichord when the instrument has stopped resonating? And would we not reply, "They are nowhere. But if the fingers strike the keyboard, and move as they had moved, they will reproduce the same sounds."

I shall therefore answer that my ideas are nowhere when my mind stops thinking about them, but that they will come back to me as soon as the movements appropriate for reproducing them are renewed.

Although I do not know the mechanism of the brain, I can judge that its different parts have acquired the capacity to move on their own in the same way that the action of the senses moved them; that the habits of this organ are stored; and that every time it follows them, it regenerates the same ideas because the same movements recur in it. In short, we have ideas in memory as we have harpsichord pieces in the fingers: that is, the brain has, like all the other senses, the capacity to move according to the patterns it has made habitual. We experience sensations in somewhat the same way a harpsichord gives forth sounds. The external organs of the human body are like the keys, the objects that strike the organs are like the fingers on the keyboard, the internal organs are like the body of the harpsichord, sensations or ideas are like the sounds; and memory takes place when the ideas produced by the action of objects on the senses are reproduced by the movements that have become habitual for the brain.

If memory—whether slow or quick—recalls things somewhat with order and sometimes with confusion, it is because our multitude of ideas required such numerous and variegated movements in the brain that it is not possible always to reproduce them with the same facility and accuracy.

All the phenomena of memory depend on habits acquired by the movable and flexible parts of the brain and all the movements of which these parts are capable are interconnected, just as all the ideas that they recall are interconnected.

Thus, the movements of the fingers on the keyboard are interconnected like the sounds of a melody that is played. The air is too slow if the fingers move too slowly. And it is jumbled up if the movements of the fingers are jumbled up. Now, just as the numerous pieces that we learn on the harpsichord do not always allow the fingers to preserve the habits required for executing them with ease and clarity, so the multitude of things that we wish to recollect does not always allow the brain to preserve the habits required for recalling ideas with ease and precision.

When a skillful organist places his hands on the keyboard without plan, the first sounds he produces set the pattern for his fingers to continue to move and follow a series of movements that produce a series of sounds whose melody and harmony sometimes surprise him. Nevertheless, he directs his fingers effortlessly and without seeming to pay attention.

It is in this way that a first movement—occasioned in the brain by the action of an object on our senses—determines a series of movements that recall a series of ideas. While we are awake, our senses are always exposed to the impressions of objects; because they do not stop acting on the brain, it turns out that our memory is always active. The brain, continually excited by the sense organs, responds not only to the impressions that it receives from them immediately, but also to all the movements that this first impression must regenerate. Through habit, it proceeds from one movement to another; it anticpates the action of the senses; it recalls long series of ideas: it does still more, it acts on the senses in turn vigorously and sends back to them sensations that they have previously sent to it, and it persuades us that we are seeing what we do not see.

Thus, as the fingers keep the habit of a series of movements, and can, at the slightest occasion, move as they had moved, likewise the brain keeps its habits. Once excited by the action of the sense, the brain goes through the movements familiar to it, and it recalls ideas.

But how are these movements carried out? How do they follow different patterns? It is impossible to go more deeply into this matter. Even if these questions were asked about the habits acquired by the fingers, I could not answer. Thus I shall not be tempted to get lost in conjectures on this subject. It is enough for me to judge the habits of the brain by the habits of each sense. We must be satisfied with knowing that the same mechanism, whatever it is, gives, preserves, and reproduces ideas.

We have just seen that memory has its seat chiefly in the brain. It seems to me that it also exists in all the organs of our sensations. For memory must be found wherever we find the occasional cause of ideas that we remember.Now if, in order to give us an idea for the first time, the senses had to act on the brain, it seems that the memory of this idea would never by more distinct than when in turn the brain acts on the senses. This reciprocal action is thus necessary to evoke the idea of a prior sensation, as it is necessary to produce a current one. Indeed, we never recall a shape, for instance, better than when our hands take the same form that touch had made them take before. In such a case, memory speaks to us, in some sense, in a language of action.

The memory of a song played on a musical instrument has its seat in the fingers, in the ear, and in the brain. In the fingers, which have developed the habit of a series of movements; in the ear, which monitors the fingers and, in case of need, directs them only because it has developed for its part, the habit of another series of movements; and in the brain, which has developed the habit of passing through the forms that correspond exactly to the habits of the fingers and the ears.

We easily notice the habits that the fingers have acquired. We cannot observe those of the ears as well, still less those of the brain, but analogy proves that they exist.

Could we know a language if the brain did not acquire the habits that correspond to those of the ears for hearing it, to those of the mouth for speaking it, and to those of the eyes for reading it? The memory of a language thus does not lie uniquely in the habits of the brain. It also lies in the habits of the organs of hearing, of speech, and of sight.

From the principles that I have just established, it would be easy to explain dreams. For the ideas that we have in sleep possibly resemble what an organist does when, distracted for a moment, he lets his fingers wander as if randomly. Certainly his fingers do only what they have learned to do, but they do not do it in the same order. They combine various passages drawn from various pieces that they have studied.

Let us thus judge by analogy what happens in the brain according to what we observe in the habits of a hand that has practiced on an instrument. We conclude that dreams are the effect of the action of this chief organ on the senses when with all parts of the body at rest, it keeps active enough to follow a few of its habits. Now as soon as it moves in the way it was itself moved when we had sensations, it acts on the senses, and we immediately hear and see. Thus it is that a one-armed man believes that he feels the hand that he no longer has. But in such a case, the brain normally recalls things in a very disordered way, because the habits whose action is stopped by sleep block a great many ideas.

Since we have explained how the habits responsible for memory are acquired, it will be easy to understand how they are lost. First, if they are not continually maintained, or at least frequently revived; that will be the lot of all the habits that the senses have ceased to occasion. Second, it they proliferate to a certain point; for then there will be some that we will neglect. Therefore, some knowledge escapes us in proportion as we acquire other knowledge. Third, an illness of the brain will weaken or disturb memory, if there be things that we would have no memory of at all. No memories whatever would remain if the illness impeded all the habits of the brain.

Fourth, a paralysis in the organs would produce the same effect. The brain's habits would gradually disappear when they are no longer maintained by the actions of the senses.

Finally, old age attacks memory. Then, the parts of the brain are like fingers that are too inflexible to move according to all the patterns familiar to them. Little by little, habits are lost. There remain only weak sensations that are soon going to be lost: the movement that seems to maintain them is itself on the point of stopping.

The physical and occasional principle of sensibility thus lies uniquely in certain patterns that may be imposed on the movement that makes the animal vegetate. The principle of memory lies in these patterns when they become habits. Analogy allows us to suppose that, in the organs we cannot observe, something takes place that is similar to what we observe in the others. I do not know by what mechanism my hand has enough flexibility and mobility to acquire the habit of certain patterns of movement, but I do know that it has flexibility, mobility, exercise and habits. And I suppose that all these are also found in my brain and in the organs that with it are the seat of memory.

From all of this, I have no doubt only a very imperfect idea of the physical and occasional causes of sensibility and memory. I am completely ignorant of first principles. I know that there is a movement in us, and I cannot understand what force produces it. I know that this movement is capable of different patterns, but I cannot discover the mechanism that controls them. Thus my only gain is to have rid from every arbitrary hypothesis this bit of knowledge that we have about this most obscure matter. It is this, I think, that physical scientists must restrict themselves to when they want to construct systems about things whose first causes it is not possible to observe.[j]

---

[j]Cf. on the occasionalism of Condillac, *Essay on the Origin of Human Knowledge*, Part 1, Sec. 1, Ch. 1.

PART TWO:

ANALYSIS CONSIDERED IN ITS MEANS AND EFFECTS, OR THE ART OF REASONING REDUCED TO A WELL-FORMED LANGUAGE

LANGUAGE

We know the origin and the development of all our ideas. Similarly, we know the origin and development of all the faculties of the mind. And we know that analysis, which led us to this knowledge, is the only method that can lead us to other knowledge. It is quite simply the lever of the mind. We must study it, and we are going to consider it in terms of its means and its effects.

1

How the Knowledge We Get from Nature Forms a System in Which Everything is Perfectly United; and How We Go Astray When We Forget its Lessons

We have seen that by the word *desire* we can understand only the orientation of our faculties toward the things we need. Thus, we have desires only because we have needs to be satisfied. Thus, needs and desires are the originators of all our investigations.

Our needs, and the means of satisfying them, have their guiding principle in the structure of our organs, and in the relations of things to this structure. For example, the way in which I am constituted determines the kinds of food I need; and the way in which various products are themselves constituted determines which ones I can use for food.

Of these different structures I can have only very imperfect knowledge. I am properly ignorant of them. But experience teaches me the use of things that are absolutely necessary for me. I am instructed about them by pleasure or pain, and promptly so. It would be useless for me to know more about them, and there nature limits its lessons.

In nature's lessons we see a system whose parts are all perfectly well ordered. If there are in me needs and desires, there are outisde of me objects appropriate for satisfying them, and I have the faculty of knowing and making use of them.

This system naturally restricts my knowledge to the sphere of a few needs and a few things for my use. But if my knowledge is not extensive, it is well ordered because I have acquired it in the same order as my needs and in that of the relations that things bear to me.

Thus, I see a system in the domain of my knowledge that corresponds to the system the author of my nature followed in making me. And that is not surprising, for given my needs and faculties, my explorations and my knowledge are themselves given.

Everything is equally united in both systems. My organs, the sensations I experience, the judgments I make, the experience that confirms or corrects them, form both systems for my survival, and it seems that he who made me has disposed everything with so much order only to watch over me himself. That is the system we must study in order to learn to reason.

We cannot too much observe the faculties that our structure gives us, or the use it causes us to make of them. In short, we cannot too much observe what we do solely by it. Its lessons, if we know how to profit from them, would be the best of all logics.

What, indeed, does this structure teach us? To avoid what is harmful to us, and to seek out what can be useful to us. But does that mean that we must juldge the essence of beings? The author of our nature does not require it. He knows that he has not put these essences within our reach. He only wants us to judge the relations things have to us and those that they have among ourselves, when knowledge of the latter can be of some use to us.[k]

We have one means for judging these relations, and it is peerless. It is to observe the sensations that objects cause in us. As far as those sensations can be extended, so far our sphere of knowledge can itself be extended. Beyond that, all discovery is forbidden us.

In the order that our nature or structure puts among our needs and things, it shows us the order in which we ought to study the relations that it is essential for us to know. Since the more pressing our needs, the more readily we learn its lessons, we do what is shows us to do, and we observe with order. It thus causes us to analyze very early on.

Since our study is restricted to the means of satisfying the small number of needs that it has given us, if our observations were well made in the first place, the use we put things to immediately confirms them. If we have observed poorly, this same use just as promptly cancels them, and shows us other observations to be made. Thus we may fall into error because errors lie in our path. But this path is the way of truth, and truth leads us along it.

To observe relations, to confirm judgments by new observations, or to correct them by observing anew—this is what nature causes us to do. And all we do is do it and do it over again for each new bit of knowledge that we acquire. Such is the art of reasoning; it is as simple as nature which teaches it to us.[l]

It thus seems that we already know this art insofar as it is possible to know it. This would indeed by true if we were always capable of noticing that it is nature and nature alone that teaches it, for then we would have continued as it caused us to begin.

---

[k]This is a Cartesian theme previously developed by Malebranche.

[l]This is a Newtonian theme previously developed by Condillac.

But we have made this observation too late. Let us say more; we make it today for the first time. For the first time, we see in the lessons of nature all the art of this analysis, which has given to men of genius the power to create the sciences, or to expand their scope.

We have thus forgotten these lessons. That is why, instead of observing things that we wanted to know, we have tried to imagine them. From false supposition to false supposition, we have strayed into a host of errors. These errors having become preconceptions, we have, for this reason, taken them for principles; thus we have strayed even farther. Then we knew how to reason only by following the bad habits we had acquired. The art of reasoning was for us the art of abusing words: arbitrary, frivolous, ridiculous, absurd— it had all the failings of imagination gone wild.

To learn to reason, we must correct all these bad habits. That is what makes this art—which would be easy by itself—so difficult today. For we yeild to these habits much more readily than we follow nature. We call them second nature in order to excuse our weakness or our blindness. But this nature is spoiled and corrupt.

We have remarked that to acquire a habit, we have only to do it; and that, to lose it, we have only to stop doing it. It thus seems that the one is as easy as the other, but that is not so. When we want to acquire a habit, we think before acting. When we want to lose it, we act before thinking. Indeed, when habits have become what we call second nature, it is almost impossible for us to notice that they are bad. Discoveries of this sort are the most difficult, and therefore escape most of us.

I refer only to the habits of the mind. When those of the body are involved, everyone knows how to judge them. Experience is sufficient to teach us whether they are beneficial or harmful. When they are neither, common practice makes of them what it will, and we judge them according to it.

Unfortunately, the mind's habits are also subject to the caprices of custom which seems to permit neither doubt nor examination. These habits are all the more contagious as the mind is as reluctant to see its defects as it is lazy to reflect on itself. Some people are ashamed not to think like everybody else; others find it too tiring to do only that. And if some people are ambitious to distinguish themselves, it turns out often only to allow even more careless thought. Contradicting themselves, they do not want to think like others, and yet they will not tolerate anyone thinking differently from them.

If you want to know the bad habits of the human mind, observe people's different opinions. Observe the ideas—false, contradictory, absurd—that superstition has spread everywhere, and judge the force of habits by the passion that leads us to respect error much more than truth.

Consider nations from their beginning to their decline, and you will see the prejudices proliferate with the disorder they create. You will be astonished at how little light you will find even in the centuries called enlightened. In general, what legislation, what governments, what jurisprudence! How few people have good laws! And how short a time good laws last!

Finally, if you observe the philosophic spirit of Greeks, of the Romans, and of the people who followed them, you will see in the opinions transmitted from age to age, how the art of governing thought was so little known in all centuries, and you will be surprised at the ignorance that still surrounds us when you consider that we are descended from men of genius who have enlarged the boundaries of our knowledge. Such in general is the character of sects—ambitious to rule exclusively, they rarely seek only truth. They want above all to distinguish themselves. They raise frivolous questions, speak an unintelligible jargon, observe little, and offer their dreams as interpretations of nature. Finally, concerned with oppressing each other, they use all sorts of means to gain new partisans, and sacrifice everything to the opinions that they want to popularize.

The truth is very difficult to recognize among so many monstrous systems, which are maintained by the causes that produced them, that is, by superstition, government, and bad philosophy. Errors too closely intertwined mutually defend each other. In vain would we combat only some of them. We would have to destroy them all at once; that is, we would suddenly have to change all the habits of the human mind. But these habits are too deeply rooted. And they are kept alive by the passions that blind us. If by chance some men are capable of opening their eyes, they are too weak to correct anything; those in power want the abuses and prejudices to continue.

All these errors seem to presuppose in us as many bad habits as false judgments taken for true. Nevertheless, all the errors come from the same source, and arise equally from the habit of using words before determining their meanings, and even without feeling the need to determine them. We observe nothing; we do not know how important it is to observe. We judge in haste, without realizing the judgments that we make, and we think we have acquired knowledge by learning words that are only words. Because, in childhood, we get our thoughts from others, we adopt all their prejudices. When we reach an age where we believe we think for ourselves, we still continue thinking second hand, because we think according to the prejudices they have bequeathed us. Under these conditions, the more progress the mind seems to make, the further afield it strays, and errors pile up from generation to generation. When matters reach this point, there is only one means of restoring order to the faculty of thought—to forget everything that we have learned, to takeup our ideas again at their origin, and to follow their elaboration and to reconstitute, as Bacon put it, human understanding.

This way of proceeding is all the more difficult to put into practice the more we think we are educated. Thus it is that works in which the sciences would be treated with great clarity, precision and order would not be equally within everyone's reach. Those who have studied nothing would understand them better than those who have studied a great deal and, above all, than those who have written a great deal on the sciences. It would even be nearly impossible that the latter should read such works as they demand to be read. Good logic would produce a very slow revolution in their minds, and time alone would one day be able to make them understand its utility.

These, then, are the effects of a bad education. This education is bad only because it runs counter to nature. Children are determined by their needs to be observers and analyzers. With their emerging faculties, they have what it takes to be both. They are even forced, as it were, to be observers insofar as nature alone guides them. But, as soon as we begin to guide them ourselves, we prohibit any observation or analysis. We suppose they do not reason, because we do not know how to reason with them. By waiting until an age of reason, which begins without us and which we put off with all our might, we condemn them to judge only according to our opinions, our prejudices, and our errors. They must therefore be mindless or mentally confused. If some of them distinguish themselves, their structure has enough energy to overcome, sooner or later, the obstacles that we have put in the way of the unfolding of their talents. The others are plants that we have lopped off down to their roots, and that die sterile.

2 How the Language of Gesture Analyzes Thought

We can reason only with the means given or indicated to us by nature. Therefore, we must observe these means, and try to discover how they are sometimes reliable and sometimes not.

We have just seen that the cause of our errors lies in the habit of judging according to words whose meaning we have not determined. In the first part, we have seen that words are absolutely necessary for us to formulate ideas of any kind. We will soon see that abstract and general ideas are nothing but names. Everything thus goes to confirm that we think only with the help of words. This is sufficient to make it clear that the art of reasoning began with languages, that it could progress only insofar as languages themselves did, and that, consequently, they must contain all the means that we can have to analyze well or badly. Therefore, we must observe languages. If we want to know what they were at their birth, we must even observe the language of gesture that they were modelled after. This is where we are going to begin.[m]

The elements of the language of gesture are born with man. These elements are the organs given us by the author of our nature. Thus, there is an innate language, although there are no innate ideas. Indeed, the elements of any language whatever, prepared beforehand, necessarily came before our ideas, because, without some kind of signs, we could not analyze our thoughts in order to realize what we are thinking, that is, to see it distinctly.

As a matter of fact, our outward appearance is fated to represent everything that happens in the mind. It is the expression of our feelings and judgments. When it speaks, nothing can be hidden.

---

[m]Cf. for what follows, *Essay on the Origin of Human Knowledge*, Part 1, Sec. 1, Ch. 1.

The essentials of gesture do not lie in analysis. Since gesture represents feelings only because it is an effect of them, it represents at the same time all those that we feel at the same instant, and the simultaneous ideas in our thought are naturally simultaneous in this language.

But a crowd of simultaneous ideas can be distinct only insofar as we make a habit of observing them successively. To this habit we owe our capacity to disentangle them with a promptness and facility that astonishes those who have not acquired the habit. For example, why does a musician listening to some harmony distinguish all the individual parts that he hears all at the same time? Because he has a practiced ear for listening to sounds and evaluating them.

Men begin to speak the language of gesture as soon as they feel, and then they speak it without intending to communicate their thoughts. They will not undertake to speak it in order to be understood until they will have noticed that they have been understood. In the beginning, however, they do not yet contemplate anything because they have observed nothing. Therefore, everything is then confused for them in their language. They will distinguish nothing as long as they have not learned to analyze their thoughts.

But although everything in their language is confused, it still contains everything they feel. It includes everything that they will distinguish when they know how to analyze their thoughts, that is, their desires, fears, judgments, reasoning—in short, all the operations the mind is capable of. For, finally, if all these were not there, analysis could not find them. Let us see how these men learn from nature to analyze all these things.

They need to help each other. Thus, each of them needs to make himself understood, and consequently to understand himself.

First, they obey nature. And without a plan, as we have just remarked, they say at the same time everything that they feel, because it is natural to their movements to do so. However, he who listens with his eyes will not hear if he does not decompose these gestures in order to observe the successive movements. But it is natural for him to decompose it, and consequently he does so before having planned to. For if he sees all the movements at once still, at a first glance, he looks only at those that strike him the most forcibly; in a second glance, he looks at others; in a third, still others. He thus observes them successively, and analysis is performed.

Thus, each of these men will sooner or later notice that he never understands others better than when he had decomposed their gestures. Consequently, he can notice that, to make himself understood, he needs to decompose his own gestures. Then he will gradually develop the habit of repeating, one after another, the movements that nature causes him to make all at once. For him, the language of gesture naturally becomes an analytic method. I say *method* because the succession of movements will not be made arbitrarily and without rules. For since gesture is the effect of one's needs and circumstances, it is natural to decompose it in the order given by these needs and circumstances. Although this order can and does vary, it can never be arbitrary. Thus it is that in a picture, the position of each person, his expression, and his character are determined when the subject is specified with all of its particulars.

By decomposing his expressive movements, this man decomposes his thoughts for himself as well as others. He analyzes it, and he makes himself understood because he understands himself.

Since the whole pattern of gesture is the picture of the whole thought, partial gestures are so many pictures of ideas that make up a part of this whole. Thus, if this man decomposes these partial gestures, he will likewise decompose the partial ideas they are signs of, and he will continually construct new and distinct ideas.

This means for analyzing his thought, the only one he has, he can elaborate it down to the smallest details. For, given the first signs of a language, we have only to consult analogy, which will give us all the others.

There will be thus no ideas that the language of gesture cannot express. And it will express them with all the more clarity and precision as analogy appears more perceptibly in the series of signs chosen. Perfectly arbitrary signs will not be understood because, since they are not analogous, the meaning of a known sign would not lead to the meaning of an unknown sign. It is analogy that makes up the whole art of languages. They are easy, clear, and precise in proportion as the role of analogy is more evident.

I have just said that there is an innate language, although there are no innate ideas. This truth, which may not have been self-evident, is shown by the observations that follow from it and that explain it.

The language I call innate is a language that we have not learned, for it is the natural and immediate effect of our make-up. It says all at the same time everything that we feel. Thus it is not an analytic method. It does not decompose our sensations. Thus, it does not lead us to observe what they contain. Thus it yields no ideas.

When this innate language becomes an analytic method, it then decomposes sensations and it yields ideas. But, as a method, it is learnable, and thus from this point of view, it is not innate.

On the contrary, from whatever point of view we consider ideas, none can be innate. If it is true that they are all in our sensations, it is no less true that they were not there yet when we did not know how to observe them. And this is what causes the educated and the uneducated to differ from each other in their ideas, although both of them have the same constitution. They resemble each other in their manner of having sensations. Both are born with the same sensations as with the same ignorance. But one of them has analyzed more than the other. Now if it is analysis that yields ideas, they must be acquired, since analysis itself is learned. Thus there are no innate ideas.

Thus we are reasoning badly when we say, "This idea is in our sensations. Thus we have this idea." Nevertheless, some seem never to tire of this kind of reasoning. Because nobody had yet noticed that our languages are just so many analytical methods, it was not noticed that we analyze only with their aid, and it was not known that we owe all our knowledge to them. Therefore the metaphysics of many writers is only an unintelligible jargon, for themselves as well as for others.

3 How Languages are Analytical Methods. The Inadequacy of These Methods

We can easily conceive how languages are so many analytical methods if we conceive how the language of gesture is itself such a method; and if we understand that without it men would have been powerless to analyze their thoughts had they substituted for the language of gesture the language of articulate sounds. Analysis is performed, and can only be performed, with signs.

We must even notice that if analysis had not first been performed with the signs of the language of gesture, it would never have been done with the articulate sounds of our languages. Indeed, how would a word become the sign of an idea, if this idea could not be shown in the language of gesture? And how would this language have shown that idea, if it had not caused it to be observed separately from every other one?

Men are ignorant of their capabilities, so long as experience does not make them notice what they are doing by nature alone. That is why they have only done by design the things that they had already done without having planned to. I believe that had it not escaped us, we would reason better than we have done until now.

Men did not think of making analyses until they observed that they had made some. They did not think of speaking the language of gesture in order to make themselves understood until they had observed that they had been understood. Similarly, they will not have thought of speaking with articulate sounds until after observing that they had spoken with such sounds; and languages began before men undertook to create them. Thus men were poets and orators before they dreamt of being so. In short, everything they became, they first were by nature alone. And they did not study to become these things until they had observed what nature had made them do. Nature began everything, and always began well. That is a truth that we cannot too often repeat.

Languages were precise methods as long as men spoke only of things related to their primary needs. For if it happened that analysis caused them to suppose what could not be the case, experience could not fail to make them perceive it. They thus corrected their errors and spoke better.

In truth, languages were then very limited. But we must not believe that they were any the worse constructed for that. It could be that ours were less well constructed. Indeed languages are precise not because they speak of many things with much confusion, but because they speak clearly, although of a small number of things.

If, in wanting to improve them, men could have continued as they began, they would have looked for new words in analogy only when a well-done analysis would have yielded new ideas; and languages, always precise, would have been more extensive.

But that could not be. Since men analyzed without knowing it, they did not notice that, if they had precise ideas, they owed them uniquely to analysis. Thus, they did not grasp the importance of this method and they analyzed less, as they felt less need to analyze.

Now, when men had made sure of satisfying their primary needs, they created less necessary ones. From these, they went on to those less necessary still, and by degrees they went on to create needs out of pure curiosity, needs of opinion, and finally useless needs, each more frivolous than the other.

Then men felt less and less the need to analyze. Soon, they felt only the desire to speak, and they spoke before having any idea what they wanted to say. Judgment was no longer naturally put to the test of experience. They did not have the same stake in making sure that the things they judged were as they had supposed. They wanted to believe them without examination. Judgments that had become habitual became opinions that were not questioned. These mistakes must have been the more frequent, as the things judged had not been observed, and often could not be.

So one first false judgment brought on a second, and soon men made innumerable ones. Analogy led from error to error because people made inferences.

This is what happened, even to philosophers. It was only a short time ago that they learned analysis. And even then, they know how to make use of it only in mathematics, physics, and chemistry. At least I am unacquainted with any who know how to apply it to ideas of all kinds. Thus, none of them have thought of considering languages as so many analytic methods.

Languages thus became very defective methods. However, commerce brought together people who exchanged, as it were, their opinions and their prejudices, as well as the products of their land and their industry. Languages were confounded, and analogy could no longer guide the mind in the meanings of words. The art of reasoning thus appeared to be unknown, and one would have said that it was no longer possible to learn it.

Nevertheless, if men had first been placed by their nature on the path of discoveries, they could by chance sometimes still find themselves on it. But they found themselves there without recognizing it because they had never studied it, and they strayed anew.

Thus, for centuries men made vain efforts to discover the rules of the art of reasoning. They did not know where to find them, and they looked for them in discourse—a mechanism that admits of all the vices of languages.

There was only one way to have found these rules. That was to observe our manner of conceiving things, and to study it in the faculties with which nature has endowed us. It should have been noticed that languages are in truth only analytic methods—highly defective methods today, though they were once precise and could still be. We did not not see this because, not having noticed how necessary words are for us to formulate ideas of all kinds, we believed that their only advantage was as a means of communicating our thoughts. Moreover, since in many respects languages seemed arbitrary to grammarians and philosophers, they ended by supposing that languages had only the vagaries of usage for rules; that is, that they often had none. Now every method always has rules, and ought to have them. Therefore, we should not be surprised if up to now no one has suspected that languages are so many analytical methods. (*Course of Study*, *Grammar*, the first eight chapters of Part 1).

4 On the Influence of Languages

Since languages, which take form in proportion as we analyze them, became so many analytical methods, it is understandable that we find it natural to think according to the habits that they caused us to acquire. We think with them. Rulers of our judgment, they determine our knowledge, opinions, and prejudices. In short, they do in this domain everything good or bad. Such is their influence, and it could not have happened differently.

Because they are imperfect methods, they lead us astray. But since they are methods, they cannot be imperfect in every respect, and they sometimes lead us well. There is no one who cannot, solely with the help of habits acquired in his language, do some good reasoning. We have all begun in this way, and we often see uneducated men reason better than highly educated men.

Some people wish that philosophers had presided over the formation of languages, and believe that they would have done it better. If so, they would have to have been other philosophers than the ones we know. It is true that in mathematics we speak with precision because algebra, a work of genius, is a language that could not be badly constructed. It is also true that a small number of excellent minds fit for observing well have treated some parts of physics and chemistry with the same precision. Otherwise, I do not see that the languages of the sciences have any advantage. They have the same defects as the others and even greater ones. We speak them just as often without saying anything: or again, we often speak them only to say things that are absurd. In general, it does not seem that we speak them with the aim of making ourselves understood.

In conjecture, the first ordinary languages were the most appropriate for reasoning. For nature, which was in charge of their construction, had at least made a good beginning. The development of ideas and of the faculties of the

395

mind had to be perceptible in these languages where the original meaning of a word was understood and where analogy provided all the others. In the names of ideas that eluded the senses one found the names of the sensible ideas they came from. And, instead of being seen as the proper names of these ideas, they were seen as figurative expressions that revealed their origin. Then, for example, it was not asked if the word *substance* meant anything other than *what lies beneath*. If the word *thought* meant anything other than *to weigh, balanlce, compare*. In short, no one imagined formulating the questions that metaphysicians pose today. Languages, which answered all questions beforehand, did not allow them to be posed and bad metaphysics had not yet begun.

Good metaphysics began before languages, and they owe to it the better part of their nature. But this metaphysics was then less a science than an instinct. Nature guided men without their knowing it. And metaphysics became a science only when it ceased to be good.

A language would be indeed superior if the people who made it cultivated the art and sciences without borrowing from any other community, for in this language, analogy would perceptibly show the progress of knowledge, and we would not need to look elsewhere for its history. This would be a truly learned language, and it would be unique. But when a language is a collection of several unrelated languages, everything is confounded: Analogy can no longer make clear in the different meanings of words, the origin and the development of knowledge: we no longer know how to make our speech precise. We do not dream of doing so. We ask questions at random, and answer them the same way. We continually abuse words and no opinion is so extravagant that it has no advocates.

It is philosophers who have brought things to this point of disorder. Their writings were all the worse since they tried to write about everything. Their writings were all the worse since each of them, when it happened that he thought like everyone else, wanted to appear to have his own unique way of speaking. Hairsplitting, peculiar, visionary, unintelligible, often they seemed to fear being insufficiently obscure, and they make a show of covering up their real or claimed knowledge with a veil. Thus, for several centuries the language of philosophy was only jargon.

Finally, this jargon was banished from the sciences. I say it was banished, but it did not banish itself. It is still looking for some refuge there by disguising itself behind new forms, and the best minds have great difficulty in closing it off from all access. But finally, the sciences did make progress, because philosophers observed better, and because they put into their language the precision and the exactitude that they had put in their observations. They thus corrected the language in many respects, and so reasoned better. Thus, the art of reasoning has followed all the variations of language, and that is what had to happen. (*Course of Study, Ancient History*, Book 3, Ch. 26; *Modern History*, Books 8 and 9, Ch. 8 and 9 and ff., last book).

5 Considerations on Abstract and General Ideas; or How the Art of Reasoning Reduces to a Well-Formed Language

General ideas, whose formation we have explained, are a part of the total idea of each individual to which they apply. For this reason, we consider them to be so many partial ideas. That of *man*, for example, is part of the total ideas of Peter and of Paul, since we find it equally in Peter and in Paul.

There is no man in general. This partial idea thus has no reality outside of us. But it does have reality in our minds, where it exists separately from the complete or individual ideas to which it belongs.

It has some reality in our minds only because we consider it as separated from each individual idea. For this reason, we call it *abstract*, for *abstract* means nothing other than *separate*. Thus all general ideas are just so many abstract ideas, and you see that we formulate them only by taking from each individual idea what is common to all of them.

But what, at bottom, is the reality that a general and abstract idea has in our mind? It is only a name, or if it is something else, it necessarily ceases to be abstract and general[n]. When, for example, I think of *man*, I can consider this word only a common denomination, in which case it is obvious that my idea is, as it were, circumscribed in this name, that it extends to nothing beyond that, and that consequently it is only this very name.

If, on the contrary, in thinking of *man*, I consider that there is in this word something other than a denomination, it is because in effect I depict a man to myself, and a man, in my mind as in nature, cannot be the abstract and general man.

---

[n]Cf. *Essay on the Origin of Human Knowledge,* Part 1, Sec. 5, which takes its inspiration from Locke's *Essay*, Book 2, Ch. 11, Sec 9–11, and Book 3, Ch. 3.

Abstract ideas are thus only denominations. If we wanted absolutely to suppose them to be something else, we would be like a painter who obstinately wanted to paint man-in-general, and who nevertheless never painted anything but individuals.

This observation confirms what we have already shown, how necessary words are. For if we had no denominations, we would have no abstract ideas. If we had no abstract ideas, we would have neither genera nor species. And if we had neither genera nor species, we could not reason about anything. Now if we reason only with the help of these denominations, this is a new proof that we reason well or badly only with the help of these denominations. It is a new proof that we reason well or badly only because our langauge is well or badly formed. Analysis thus teaches us to reason only insofar as, by teaching us to specify abstract and general ideas, it teaches us to construct our language well, and all the art of reasoning reduces to the art of speaking well.

To speak, to reason, to formulate general or abstract ideas, are thus fundamentally the same thing: This truth, simple as it is, could pass for a discovery. Certainly it was not suspected. Yet it can be seen in the manner in which we speak and reason. It can be seen in the abuse made of general ideas. Finally, it can be seen in the difficulties in conceiving abstract ideas reportedly found by those who have so little difficulty in speaking.

The art of reasoning reduces to a well-formed language only because the order of our ideas is itself only the subordination among names given to genera and species. Since we have new ideas only because we form new classes themselves. Then we will reason well because analogy guides us in forming judgments as well as in understanding words.

Convinced that classes are only denominations we will not imagine that genera and species exist in nature, and we will see in these words *genera* and *species* only a manner of classifying things according to their relations to us and to each other. We will recognize that we can discover only these relations, and not believe that we can say what genera and species are. Consequently, we will avoid many errors.

If we notice that all these classes are necessary only because, in order to formulate distinct ideas, we need to decompose the objects we want to study, we will recognize not only the limitations of our mind, we will see moreover where its boundaries are, and we will not contemplate crossing them. We will not get lost in idle questions. Instead of seeking what we cannot find, we shall find what is within our reach. All we have to do is formulate precise ideas—which we always can do when we know how to use words.

Now we shall know how to use words when, instead of looking for essences that we could not put in them, we look only for what we have put there—the relations of things to us and to each other.

We will know how to make use of them when, considering them relative to the limitations of our mind, we regard them only as a means we require for thinking. Then we would sense that the most powerful analogy ought to determine the choice of words, that it ought to determine all the meanings; and we would necessarily restrict the number of words to the number we need. We would no longer stray among frivolous distinctions, divisions, endless subdivisions, and foreign words that become barbarous in our language.

Finally, we shall know how to use words when analysis has enabled us to acquire the habit of looking for the chief meaning in their first use, and all the others in analogy.

It is to this analysis alone that we owe the power of abstracting and generalizing. It thus creates languages and gives us precise ideas of all kinds. In short, analysis makes us capable of creating the arts and the sciences, or rather, let us say that it is analysis itself that created them. It has made all discoveries, and we have had only to follow it. Imagination, which is credited with all kinds of abilities, would be nothing without analysis.

It would be nothing! I am mistaken! Imagination would be a source of opinions, prejudices, and errors. We would be making up nothing but foolish dreams if analysis did not sometimes control it. Indeed, do writers who have only imagination do anything else?

The route that analysis lays out for us is marked by a series of well-made observations. We walk along it with confident steps because we always know where we are and always see where we are going. In fact, analysis helps us in everything that can be of some use. Our mind, so weak by itself, finds in analysis levers of all kinds. It observes phenomena of nature, with the same ease, in some sense, as if it controlled them itself.

But to judge correctly what we owe to analysis, we must know it well. Otherwise its works will seem to us merely those of imagination. Because the ideas that we call abstract no longer come within the purview of the senses, we will believe that they do not come from the senses at all. Because we will not see what they can have in common with our sensations, we will fancy that they are something else. Preoccupied by this error, we will be blind to their origin and their development. It will be impossible for us to see what they are, and yet we will believe we see it. We will have only visions. Sometimes ideas will be beings that exist separately in the mind—innate beings, or ones successively added to the mind; at other times, they will exist only in God and that we see only in Him. Such dreams necessarily will lead us away from the path of discoveries, and we will advance only from error to error. There you have, however, the systems that imagination creates. Once we have adopted them, we can no longer have a well-formed language. We are doomed to reason almost always badly, because we reason badly about the faculties of our mind.

As we have remarked, men did not behave this way when they left the hands of the creator of nature. Although they looked without knowing what they were looking for, they looked properly. They often found what they sought without realizing that they had been searching. This is because the needs given them by the author of nature, and the circumstances he placed them in, forced them to observe, and often warned them not to imagine. Analysis, which created language, created it well because it always determined the sense of words. And the language, which was not extensive but was well formed, led to the most needed discoveries. Unfortunately, men did not know how to observe the way in which they went about learning. You might say that they are able to do well only what they do without knowing it. And philosophers, who ought to have searched with more discernment, often looked only to find nothing or to go astray. (*Course of Study, The Art of Thinking*, Part 2, Ch. 5).

6

How Those who Regard Definitions as the Only Means of Remedying the Abuses of Language are Mistaken

The defects of languages are readily perceptible, especially in words whose meaning is not well specified or that have no sense. People have wanted to remedy this defect and because we can define some words, they said that we must define them all. Consequently, definitions were regarded as the basis of the art of reasoning.

A triangle is a surface bounded by three lines. This is a definition. If it gives an image of a triangle without which we could not determine its properties, it is because to discover the properties of a thing, we must analyze it; and to analyze it, we must see it. Such definitions thus show the things we propose to analyze, and that is all that they do. Our senses likewise show us sensible objects, and we analyze them, although we cannot define them. The necessity of defining is thus only the necessity of seeing things about which we want to reason and if we can see without defining, definitions become useless. That is the commonest case.

No doubt, to study a thing, I must see it. But when I see it, I have only to analyze it. Thus, when I discover the properties of a surface bounded by three lines, the basic source of my discovery, if we insist on principles, is only analysis. This definition only shows me the triangle that is the object of my inquiry just as my senses show me sensible objects. What, then, does this language mean: *definitions are principles*? It means that we must begin by seeing things in order to study them, and that we must see them as they are. That is all it means, although some people believe it says something more.

Principle is *synonymous* with beginning, and it was in this meaning that it was first used. But later, by dint of using it repeatedly, people employed it out of habit—mechanically and without attaching ideas to it—and they had principles that are not the beginning of anything.

I will say that our senses are the principle of our knowledge because it originates with them, and I am saying something intelligible. It will not be the same if I say that *a surface bounded by three lines is the principle of all the properties of a triangle, because all the properties of a triangle begin with a surface bounded by three lines*; for I would be about as willing to say that *all the properties of a surface bounded by three lines begin with a surface bounded by three lines*. In short, this definition teaches me nothing. It only shows me something I already knew and whose properties can be discovered only by analysis.

Thus definitions are limited to showing things. But they do not always shed the same amount of light on them. *The mind is something that has sensations*. Conscious is a definition that gives an imperfect picture of the mind to everyone to whom analysis has not taught that all its faculties are, in principle or in the first place, only the faculty of having sensations. Thus it is not with such a definition that we must begin to discuss the mind. For, although all its faculties are in principle nothing but ways of having sensations, this truth is not a principle or a beginning for us if, instead of coming first, it comes last. Now, it does come last because it is a result obtained by analysis.

Disposed to everything, geometers often make vain efforts to do so, and look for definitions that they do not find. An example is that of a straight line. For to agree with geometers that is is the shortest distance between two points is not to lead us to know it, but to assume that we already know it. Now since a definition is a principle in their language, it should not assume that the thing defined is already known. This is a trap into which all the axiomatizers fall, to the indignation of some geometers who complain that we still do not have a good definition of a straight line and who seem to be unaware that we ought not to define what is undefinable. But if definitions are limited to showing us things, what does it matter whether we are shown them before we know them or only afterward? It seems to me that the essential point is to know them.

Now we would be convinced that the only means of knowing them is to analyze them if we had noticed that the best definitions are only analyses. That of a triangle, for example, is one: for certainly, to say that it is a surface bounded by three lines, the sides of this figure, one after another, had to be observed and counted. To be sure, this analysis is, as it were, performed all at once, because we count up to three quite quickly. But a child would not count so quickly, and still he would analyze the triangle as well as we do. He would analyse it slowly, as we ourselves after having slowly counted, would define or analyze a many-sided figure.

Let us not say that in our investigation we must have definitions for principles. Let us say more simply that we must begin well, that is, see things as they are, and let us add that, in order to see them this way, we must always begin with analyses.

By expressing ourselves this way, we will speak more precisely, and we shall not trouble ourselves to look for definitions that are not to be found. We will realize, for example, that to know what a straight line is, there is no need to define it the way geometers do, and all we have to do is observe how we have acquired the idea.

Because geometry is called an exact science, some people believed that to treat all the other sciences adequately, they had only to emulate the geometers, and the rage to define everything as they do became the craze of all philosophers, or of those who set themselves up as such. Open up a dictionary and you will see that it tries to give definitions for each entry and they have little success. The best defintions, like that of a straight line, assume that the meanings of the words are already known; otherwise, if they assume nothing, we do not understand them.

Ideas are either simple or compound. If they are simple, we do not define them; it would be useless for a geometer to try it—he would fail, as he did in the case of the straight line. But, although ideas cannot be defined, analysis will always show us how we have acquired them, because it will show where they come from and how they come to us.

If an idea is compound, it is still analysis alone that must lead us to know it, because only analysis can, by decomposing the idea, show us all the partial ideas in it. Thus, whatever our ideas, only analysis can characterize them clearly and precisely.

Nevertheless, there will always remain ideas that cannot be specified or at least that cannot be specified to everyone's satisfaction. This is because men could not agree on their composition, and so these ideas are necessarily indeterminate. The idea we designate by the word *mind* is an example. But, although analysis cannot specify what we understand by a word that we do not all understand in the same way, it does nevertheless spell out everything that it is possible to understand by this word, however, preventing anyone from understanding what he pleases. That is, it is easier for analysis to correct our language than ourselves.

But, finally, only analysis will correct everything that can be corrected, because it alone can make known the development of all our ideas. Therefore, philosophers got themselves far off the track when the abandoned analysis, and when they believed they had supplanted it with definitions. They strayed all the more so as they did not yet know how to give a good definition of analysis itself. To go by their efforts in explaining this method, one would think that there is a great mystery in decomposing a whole into its parts and recombining it. Yet all that needs to be done is to observe successively and with order. See the word *Analysis* in the *Encyclopedia*.

It is synthesis that has brought about this craze for definitions—this murky method that always begins where it should end, and that is nonetheless called *the method of doctrine*.

I will not attempt to give a more precise notion of it, either because I do not understand it or because it is impossible to understand. It is all the more elusive because it takes on the attributes of whatever school of thought seeks to use it, and above all those of wrong thinkers. This is how one famous writer explains the matter. "Finally," he says, "these two methods (analysis and synthesis) differ only as the path that we take to climb up from a valley to a mountain differs from the one we take to go down from a mountain to the valley."[4] This language shows me only that these methods are mutually exclusive, and that if the one is good, the other is bad. In fact, we can proceed only from the known to the unknown. Now if the unknown is on the mountain, we will not reach it by going down; if it is in the valley, we will not reach it by climbing up. Thus, there cannot be two contrary paths for getting there. Such opinions do not merit more serious criticism. (*Course of Study, The Art of Thinking*, Part 1, Ch. 9)[0]

Some thinkers assume that the essence of synthesis is to combine our ideas, and that the essence of analysis is to decompose them. This is why the author of this *Logic* believes he is explaining them when he says the one path leads from the valley to the mountain, and the other path from the mountain to the valley. But, whether we reason well or badly, it is necessarily the case that the mind climbs up and goes down by turns. Or to put it more simply, it is as essential for it to compose as it is for it to decompose, because a chain of reasoning is and can be only a series of compositions and decompositions. Thus synthesis includes decomposition as well as composition, and analysis includes composition as well as decomposition. It would be absurd to suppose that these two procedures are mutually exclusive, and that we could reason while repudiating as we chose the use of all composition or all decomposition How then do these two methods differ? In that analysis always begins well and synthesis always begins badly. The former, without pretending to order, has order naturally because it is the method of nature; the latter, which is unacquainted with the natural order, because it is the method of philosophers, pretends to much order only to weary the mind without enlightening it. In short, true analysis—that which we ought to prefer—begins at the beginning and uses analogy to show the structure of language and, in the structure of the language, the progress of science.

---

[0]Also see *Essay on the Origin of Human Knowledge*, Part 1, Sec. 2, Ch. 7 which was reworked for this chapter of the *Art of Thinking*.

7 How Reasoning is Simple When Language Itself is Simple

Although analysis is the only true method, mathematicians—who are always ready to abandon it—seem to use it only as much as they are forced to. They prefer synthesis, which they believe is shorter and simpler, and their writings are all the longer and more perplexing for it.[5]

We have just seen that synthesis is the exact opposite of analysis. It puts us off the track of discoveries. Nevertheless, most mathematicians delude themselves that synthesis is the most appropriate method for informing ourselves. They believe it so strongly that they will not have us follow any other method in their basic texts.

Clairaut thought otherwise[P]. I do not know whether Euler and LaGrange have pronounced themselves on this topic[8] but they acted as if they had, for in their elements of algebra, they followed only the analytic method.[6]

---

[5]This generally well-founded criticism is not without exceptions. MM. Euler and La Grange, for example, led by their genius to the greatest clarity and elegance, preferred analysis, which they have perfected. In their highly creative writings, this method finds new life, and they are great mathematicians because they are great analysts. They do algebra superlatively well, of all languages, the one in which good writers are the rarest because it is the best constructed. best constructed.

[P]Cf. Clairaut, *Elements of Algebra*, Paris 1746.

[q]Cf. Euler, *Elements of Algebra*, translated from the German with notes and additions, 2 vol., Lyon, 1774.

---

[6]The *Elements* of M. Euler bears no resemblance to any previous work of algebra. In the first part, definite analysis is treated with a simple and clear method that is entirely the

The approbation of these mathematicians counts for something. Thus the others must be singularly prejudiced in favor of synthesis, to get it into their heads that analysis, which is the method of invention, is still not the method of doctrine, and that there is a better means for learning the discoveries of others than the one we would have them engage in.

Not only has analysis been largely banished from mathematics whenever synthesis was an alternate possibility, but also it seems to have been shut out of all the other sciences and only slips in when the author is unaware of it. That is why of so many works of early and modern philosophers, there are so few that are enlightening. The truth is seldom recognizable when analysis does not reveal it, and on the contrary synthesis covers it over with a heap of vague notions, opinions, and errors, and creates a jargon taken for the language of the arts and sciences.

However little we reflect on analysis, we recognize that it spreads more light in proportion as it is simpler and more precise. If we recall that the art of reasoning reduces to a well-formed language, we will conclude that the greatest simplicity and precision of analysis can be only the result of the greatest simplicity and precision of language. Thus, we must get some idea of this simplicity and precision in order to come as close as possible to it in all our studies.

We label *exact sciences* those in which we give rigorous proofs. Why then are not all sciences exact? And if there are some that do not give rigorous proofs what kind of proofs do they give? Do we know what we mean when we speak of proofs that are not strictly proofs?

A proof is not a proof unless it is rigorous. But it must be acknowledged that if a proof does not speak the language that it ought to speak, it will not appear to be what it is. Thus it is not the fault of the sciences if they do not give rigorous proofs. It is the fault of the scientists who speak badly.

Algebra, the language of mathematics, is the simplist of all languages. Are there thus proofs only in mathematics? And because the other sciences cannot achieve the same simplicity, are they doomed to lack sufficient simplicity to convince us that they prove what they prove?

It is analysis that gives proofs in all the sciences and it gives them rigorously whenever it speaks the language that it ought to speak. I know very

---

author's own. Only the theory of equations is sometimes too summarily discussed. No doubt M. Euler was loath to enter into the details which were so thoroughly discussed by others, but the reader who wishes to be better informed will regret this.

Indeterminate analysis, so little known in France, and to which MM. Euler and La Grange have contributed so much, is the topic of the second part, a masterpiece that includes the additional material of M. La Grange. The excellence of this work derives from the analytical method which these two great geometers know perfectly. Those who do not know it will endeavor futilely to write on the elementary principles of the sciences.

well that different kinds of analysis are distinguished—logical, metaphysical, and mathematical—but there is really only one, and it is the same in all the sciences because in all of them it leads from the known to the unknown by reasoning, that is, by a series of judgments that are embodied one in another. We will get an idea of this language analysis ought to speak if we try to solve one of the problems that we usually solve only with the help of algebra. We will choose one of the easiest, because it will be more within our reach. Moreover, it will be sufficient to elaborate the whole art of reasoning.

Having some tokens in my two hands, if I move one from the right hand to the left, I will have as many in one as in the other; and if I move one from the left to the right, I will have twice as many in the latter. I ask you how many tokens I have in each hand.

It is not a matter of guessing the number or making suppositions. The answer must be found by reasoning and proceeding from the known to the unknown by a series of judgments.

There are two conditions given, or, to speak like mathematicians, there are two givens: one, that if I move a token from the right hand to the left, I will have the same number in each hand; the other, that if I move the token from the left to the right, I will have twice as many in the latter. Now you see that, if it is possible to find the number that I ask you to look for, it could only be by observing the relations these two givens have to each other; and you will readily understand that these relations will be more or less apprehensible insofar as you express the givens in a more or less simple manner.

If you were to say, "The number that you have in the right hand when a token is taken away is equal to the number you have in the left hand when one is added to the latter," you express the first given with many words. Let us say it more succinctly, "The number in your right hand minus one unit is equal to the number in your left hand plus one unit;" or, "The number in your right minus one unit is equal to the number in your left plus one unit;" or still more succinctly, "The right minus one equals the left plus one."

Thus from translation to translation we arrive at the simplest expression of the first given. Now the more you shorten your discourse, the more your ideas approach each other; the more they come closer together, the easier it will be for you to grasp them in all their relations. It thus remains for us to treat the second given like the first—it must be translated into the simplest expression.

By the second condition of the problem, if I move a token from the left hand to the right, I would have twice as many in the latter. Thus the number in my left hand, minus one, is half of that in my right hand, plus one. Consequently, you express the second given by saying, "The number in your right hand, plus one, is equal to two times that in your left, minus one."

You will translate this expression into a simpler one if you say, "The right plus one is equal to two lefts, each minus one." You will arrive at the simplest expression of all, "The right plus one equals two lefts minus two." Thus, here are the expressions into which we have translated the givens:

The right minus one equals the left plus one;

The right plus one equals two lefts minus two.

In mathematics, these sorts of expressions are called *equations*. They consist of two equal numbers: *The right minus one*, is the first member of the first equation; *The left plus one*, is the second. In each of these members the unknown quantities are mixed in with the known quantities. The known are *minus one, plus one, minus two*. The unknowns are *the right* and *the left*, by which you express the two numbers that you are trying to find out.

As long as the knowns and the unknowns are thus mixed up in each member of the equations, it is not possible to solve a problem. It does not require a great deal of reflection to notice that, if there is a means of transferring the quantities from one member to the other without changing the equality between them, we can, by leaving only one of the two unknowns in one member, separate it out from the known quantities with which it is intermingled.

This means comes to mind very naturally, for if the right minus one is equal to the left plus one, the entire right hand will be equal to the left plus two; and if the right plus one is equal to two lefts minus two, then the right alone will be equal to two lefts minus three. For the two first equations you thus substitute the two following ones:

The right equals the left plus two.

The right equals two lefts minus three.

The first member of these two equations is the same quantity, *the right;* and you see that you will know what this quantity is when you know the value of the second member of one or the other equation. But the second member of the first equation is equal to the second number of the second equation, since they are both equal to the same quantity expressed by *the right*. Consequently, you can make this third equation:

The left plus two equals two lefts minus three.

There thus remains only one unknown, *the left*; and you will determine its value when you have separated it out, that is, when you have moved all the knowns to the same side. Thus you say:

Two plus three equals two lefts minus a left.

Two plus three equals a left.

Five equals a left.

The problem is solved. You have discovered that the number of tokens I have in my left hand is five. In the equations, *the right equals the left plus two* and *the right equals two lefts minus three*, you find that the number of tokens I have in my right hand is seven. These two numbers, five and seven, satisfy the conditions of the problem.

This example clearly shows how the simplicity of expressions facilitates reasoning; and you can understand that if analysis requires such clear language when a problem is as easy as the one we have just solved, it needs it even more when the problems become more complicated. The advantage of analysis in mathematics stems only from the fact that it speaks the simplest language. A slight acquaintance with algebra is enough to make it understood.

We do not need words in this language. We express *plus* by +, *minus* by —, *equals* by =, and we designate the quantities by letters and figures. x, for example, will be the number of tokens I have in my right hand, y the number I have in my left hand. Thus $x - 1 = y + 1$ means that the number of tokens I have in my right hand minus one is equal to the number I have in my left hand plus one. $x + 1 = 2y - 2$ means that the number in my right hand plus one is equal to twice the number in my left hand minus two. Thus, the two givens in our problem are contained in these two equations:

$$x - 1 = y + 1$$
$$x + 1 = 2y - 2$$

which becomes, by isolating the unknown in the first member,

$$x = y + 2$$
$$x = 2y - 3$$

which successively becomes

$$2 = 2y - y - 3$$
$$2 + 3 = 2y - y$$
$$2 + 3 = y$$
$$5 = y$$

Finally, from $x = y + 2$ it follows that $x = 5 + 2 = 7$; and from $x = 2y - 3$ we similarly conclude $x = 10 - 3 = 7$

This algebraic language shows clearly how judgments are interrelated in reasoning. We see that the last one is contained in the penultimate, the penultimate one in the one preceding it, and so on, going back to the first one, because the last one is identical with the penultimate, the penultimate with the one that precedes it, and so forth, and we recognize that this identity carries the weight of the argument.

When some reasoning is performed with words, the evidence similarly consists in the identity that is perceptible in going from one judgment to another. Indeed, the series of judgments remains the same, and only their expression changes. We need only remark that we perceive identity more easily when it is expressed in algebraic signs.

But whether the identity is perceived more easily or less easily, it is enough that it is there to ensure that some line of reasoning constitutes rigorous proof. We should not suppose that the sciences are exact—or that we prove rigorously—only when we use x's, a's, and b's. If some sciences do not seem to lend themselves to proofs, that is because we are accustomed to speaking about them before we have formulated their language, and without even suspecting that it is necessary to do so. For every science would have the same precision if we spoke them all with well-formed languages. That is the way we treated metaphysics in the first part of this work. For example, we explained the development of the faculties of the mind only because we recognized that they are all identical with the faculty of having sensation. And our reasoning with words can be proven as rigorously as reasoning done with letters.

Thus, if there are inexact sciences, it is not because we do not express them algebraically, but because their languages are ill-formed, because we do not perceive this, or because if we do suspect it, we mend them for the worse. Should we be surprised that we do not know how to reason when the language of the sciences is only a jargon made up of too many words, of which some are vulgar words that have no determinate sense, and others are foreign or barbarous words that are poorly understood? All the sciences would be exact if we knew how to speak the language of each.

Everything thus confirms what we have already proven, that languages are so many analytical methods; that reasoning can be improved only as they themselves are improved; and that the art of reasoning, reduced to its simplest form, can only be a well-formed language. I do not agree with mathematicians who claim that algebra is a kind of language. I say that it is a language and cannot be anything else. In the problem that we have just solved, you see that it is a language into which we translated the reasoning we did with words. Now if letters and words express the same reasoning, it is obvious that, since with words we do nothing other than speak a language, we do nothing other than speak a language with letters.

We can make the same observation about the most complicated problems. For all algebraic solutions offer the same language; that is, reasoning, or successively identical judgments expressed in letters. But because algebra is the most methodical language, and because it develops lines of argument that cannot be translated into any other language, we suppose that it is not, strictly speaking, a language; that it is a language only in certain respects; and that it must be something else again.

Algebra is indeed an analytic method. But it is no less a language for that if all languages are analytic methods. Now that is, I repeat; what they are. But algebra provides striking proof that scientific progress depends solely on the progress of languages, and that only well-formed languages could provide analysis with the degree of simplicity and precision it is capable of, depending on the kind of studies we are doing.

I say that well-formed lanaguages could do this, because in the art of reasoning, as in the art of calculating, everything comes down to composition and decomposition. And we should not think that these are two different arts.

8 What the Whole Technique of Reasoning Consists of

The rule for the method we followed in the preceding chapter is that we can discover a truth we do not know only insofar as we find it in truths that we do know, and that, consequently, every issue to be resolved presupposes some givens in which the known and the unknown are intermingled, as they indeed are in the givens of the problem we resolved above.

If the givens do not include all the knowns needed to discover the truth, the problem is insoluble. This is the first thing to think of and we almost never do. Thus, we reason poorly because we do not realize that we have too few knowns to reason well.

However, if we noticed that when we have all the knowns, we are led by clear and precise language to the solution we are looking for, we would suspect that we do not have all the knowns when we adhere to an obscure and confused language that leads nowhere. We would therefore try to speak better inorder to reason better, and we would learn how greatly two things depend on each other.

Nothing is simpler than reasoning when the givens include all the knowns needed for the discovery of the truth. We have just seen this and it must not be said that the problem we tackled is easy to settle. For the manner of reasoning is one: It does not change, cannot change, and its subject changes only with each new question asked. With the most difficult questions, as with the easiest ones, we must proceed from the known to the unknown. Thus the givens must include all the knowns needed for the solution. And when they include them, there remains only to express these givens simply enough to separate out the unknowns with the greatest possible ease.

Thus there are two things in a question: the statement of the givens and the isolation of the unknowns.

The specification of the givens is properly what we understood by the statement of the problem, and isolating the unknowns is the reasoning that solves it.

When I proposed that you discover the number of tokens that I had in each hand, I specified all the givens you needed, and it consequently appears that I myself set forth the statement of the question. But my language did not anticipate the solution of the problem. That is why, instead of confining yourself to repeating my statement word for word, you ran it through different translations until you arrived at the simplest expression. Then the reasoning does itself, as it were, because the unknowns are separated out, as if by themselves. Thus to set forth the statement of a problem is, properly, to translate the givens into their simplest expressions, because the simplest expression facilitates reasoning by facilitating the separating out of the unknowns.

But it will be said, that is the way we reason in mathematics, where reasoning is carried out with equations. Will it be the same in other sciences, where reasoning is carried out with propositions? I reply that *equations, propositions,* and *judgments* are at bottom the same thing, and that consequently we reason the same way in all the sciences.

In mathematics, he who poses a problem usually states it with all its givens, and its solution is only a matter of translating it into algebra. In the other sciences, on the other hand, it appears that a question is never posed with all its givens. You will be asked, for example, what is the origin and development of the faculties of human understanding, and you will be left to look for the givens because the person who asked the question does not know them himself.

But although we have to look for the givens, we should not conclude that they are not embodied, at least implicitly, in the question posed. If they were not there, we would not find them. However, they ought to be found in any question we can solve. We need only remark that the question does not always include them in a manner we can easily recognize. Consequently, to find them, we have to disentangle them from some expression in which they occur only implicitly. And to solve the question, we must translate this expression into another one that shows all the givens explicitly and distinctly.

Now to ask what is the origin and development of the faculties of human understanding is to ask what is the origin and development of the faculties by which sentient man conceives of things when framing ideas about them. We see immediately that attention, comparison, judgment, reflection, imagination, and reasoning are, along with sensation, the knowns of the problem to be solved, and that the origin and development are the unknowns. There you have all the givens, with the knowns intermingled with the unknowns.

But how can we separate out the origin and the development that are the unknowns here? Nothing is simpler. By *origin* we understand the known that is the principle or beginning of all the others. By *development* we understand the manner in which all the knowns come from a first one. This first one, which I know as a faculty, is not yet known to me as first. Thus it is properly an unknown that is intermingled with all the knowns and that is to be separated out from them. Now even the most casual observation shows me that the faculty of having sensation is mixed in with all the other faculties. Thus sensation is the unknown we have to disentangle in order to discover how it becomes in turn attention, comparison, judgment, and so forth. That is what we have done. We have seen that, like the equations $x - 1 = y + 1 = 2y - 2$, go through different transformations to become $y = 5$ and $x = 7$, sensation likewise goes through different transformations to become understanding.

Thus, the technique of reasoning is thus the same in all the sciences. As, in mathematics, we state the problem by translating it into algebra; so in the other sciences, we state it by translating it into the simplest expression possible. Once we have stated the problem, the reasoning that solves it is still only a series of translations in which a proposition translating the preceding one is itself translated by the one that follows it. It is thus that the facts move with identity from the statement of the question to the conclusion of the reasoning.

9 Of Different Degrees of Certainty; or of Fact, Conjectures, and Analogy

I shall only indicate the different degrees of certainty, and refer the reader for the rest to the art of reasoning which is properly the topic of this whole chapter.

The evidence we have just spoken about and which I call the *evidence of reason*[r] consists uniquely in identity; that is what we have proven. This truth must be very simple to have eluded all philosophers, although it was greatly in their interest to get clear about evidence, a word they had continually on their lips. I know that a triangle is obviously a surface bounded by three lines because, for whoever understands the import of the terms, *surface bounded by three lines* is the same thing as *triangle*. Now, as soon as I obviously know what a triangle is, I know its essence, and in this essence I can discover all the properties of this figure.

Similarly, I should see all the properties of gold in its essence, if I knew it. Its weight, ductility, malleability, and so forth, would only be its essence transformed, and which in these transformations would present me with different phenomena; and I could discover all its properties by a line of reasoning that would only be a series of identical propositions. But that is not how I know it. In truth, every proposition that I make about this metal if it is true is identical. Such a one is the following, gold is malleable; for it means *A body that I have observed to be malleable and that I call gold, is malleable*—a proposition in which an idea is affirmed of itself.

When I state several equally true propositions about a body, I thus affirm

---

[r]Cf. *The Art of Reasoning*, Book 1, Ch. 1–3.

in each of them the same thing. But I perceive no identity of one proposition with another. Although the weight, ductility, and malleability are to all appearances the same thing differently transformed, I do not see it. Thus I cannot get at knowledge of these phenomena through the evidence of reasoning. I know them only after having observed them, and I call the certainty I have of them *evidence of fact*[S]

I could also call evidence of fact the certain knowledge of phenomena that I observe in myself. But I call it *evidence of feeling* because it is feeling that makes these sorts of facts known to me.[t]

Since the absolute qualities of bodies are beyond the reach of our senses, and we can know only their relative qualities, it follows that every fact we discover is nothing other than a known relation. Nevertheless, to say that bodies have relative qualities is to say that they are something in relation to each other. And to say that they are something in relation to each other is to say that they are each something, independently of every relation, something absolute. The evidence of reason thus teaches us that there are absolute qualities, and consequently, bodies. But it teaches us only their existence.

By *phenomena* we strictly understand the facts that are a consequence of the laws of nature. And these laws are themselves just so many facts. The object of physics is to know these phenomena, these laws, and if possible, to grasp their system.

To this end, we pay particular attention to phenomena. We consider them in all their relations, we let no detail escape us, and, when we have made sure of them through careful observations, we give them the name *observations*.

But to discover them, it is not always enough to observe. We also must, by various means, sort them out from everything that hides them, bring them closer to us, and put them within view. This is what we call experiments. These are the distinctions we must make among *phenomena, observations,* and *experiments*.

We seldom arrive at evidence all at once. In all the arts and sciences, we begin with a kind of groping.

From known truths, we suspect others we are not yet certain of. These inferences are based on circumstances that show less the true than the probable, but they often set us on the road to discoveries because they teach us what we have to observe. That is what we understand as conjecture[u].

Conjectures are weakest when we assume something only because we do not see why it should not be so. If we indulge in conjectures of this kind, it

---

[S]Cf. *The Art of Reasoning*, Book 1, Ch. 7–8.

[t]Cf. *The Art of Reasoning,* Book 1, Ch. 4–6.

[u]Cf. *The Art of Reasoning*, Book 4, Ch. 2.

ought to be only as suppositions that need to be confirmed. Thus it remains for us to make observations or experiments.

We seem to be on solid ground in believing that nature acts by the simplest ways. Consequently, philosophers tend to believe that, among the many ways something can come about, nature must have chosen those that they imagine to be the simplest. It is obvious that such a conjecture will have force only insofar as we are capable of knowing all the means, and of judging their simplicity. This can happen only very rarely[7].

Conjectures hold a place somewhere between evidence and analogy, which itself is often only a weak conjecture[v]. Thus we must distinguish different degrees of analogy, depending on whether it is based on relations of resemblance, means to end, cause to effect, or effects to causes.

The earth is inhabited; therefore the other planets are. This is the weakest of analogies, because it is founded only on the relation of resemblance.

But if we notice that the planets go through diurnal and annual revolutions, and that consequently parts of them are in turn lighted and heated, do these measures not seem to have been taken for the preservation of some kind of inhabitants? This analogy, which is founded on the relation of means to end, thus has more force than the first one. If it proves, however, that the earth is not alone in being inhabited, it does not prove that all the planets are; for what the author of nature repeats in several corners of the universe toward the same end, he may sometimes permit only as a consequence of the general system; it could still happen that a revolution reduces an inhabited planet to a desert.

The analogy founded on the relation of effects to cause, or of cause to effects, is the one that has the most force. It even becomes a proof, when it is confirmed by all of the circumstances in concert.

It is an evidence of fact that the earth goes through diurnal and annual revolutions. It is an evidence of reason that these revolutions can be produced by the movement of the earth, by that of the sun, or by both.

But we observe that the planets describe orbits around the sun, and we are similarly assured by evidence of fact that some of them rotate on their more or less inclined axis. Now it is evidence of reason that this twofold revolution ought necessarily to produce days, seasons, and years; thus the earth has a twofold revolution, since it has days, seasons, and years.

This analogy presupposes that the same effects have the same causes, a presupposition that, confirmed by new analogies and new observations, can

---

[7]Regarding the role of conjectures in the Study of History, see *Course of Study, Ancient History*, book 1, Ch. 3–8.

[v]Cf. *The Art of Reasoning*, Book 4, Ch. 3.

no longer be called into question. Thus it is that good philosophers have reasoned. If we want to learn to reason like them, the best means is to study the discoveries made from Galileo down to Newton. (*Course of Study, Art of Reasoning, Modern History*, last book, Ch. 5 ff.).

We have tried to reason this way in this work. We have observed nature, and learned analysis from it. With this method we have studied ourselves, and having discovered, through a series of identical propositions, that our ideas and faculties are just different forms of sensation, we ascertained the origin and development of both.

We have remarked that the development of our ideas and faculties unfolds only by means of signs, and cannot occur without them; that, consequently, we can improve our reasoning only by correcting language; and that this whole art reduces to making the language of each science well formed.

Finally, we have proven that the first languages were originally well formed, because the metaphysics that presided over their formation was not the science it is today, but an instinct given by nature.

It is thus from nature that we must learn true logic. This was my aim, and because of it this work has become newer, simpler, and shorter. Nature will never fail to instruct whoever knows how to study it. It instructs all the better as it always speaks the most precise language. We would be clever indeed if we knew how to speak with the same precision, but we use too much verbiage to always reason well.

I think it my duty here to add some advice to young people who want to study this logic. Since the whole art of reasoning reduces to doing well the language of each science, it is obvious that the study of a well-treated science reduces to the study of a well-formed language.

But to learn a language is to make it familiar, and that can only come from long use. You must, therefore, read with reflection several times over, talk about what you have read and reread further in order to make sure that you have spoken well.

You will easily understand the first chapters of this logic. But if, because you understand them, you think you can immediately proceed to others, you are going too fast. You ought to go on to a new chapter only after you have appropriated both the ideas and language of the preceding ones. If you follow some other approach, you will no longer understand with the same ease and sometimes you will not understand at all.

A greater danger is that you will misunderstand because you take your language of which you will keep something, and mine, which you endeavor to adopt, and make up an unintelligible gibberish. This will happen particularly to those who think they are well educated either because they have studied what is often preposterously called philosophy, or because they taught it. In whatever manner they read me, they will find it difficult to forget what they have learned in order to learn only what I have taught. They will decline to begin again with me. They will set little value on my work, if they perceive that they do not understand it. And if they fancy they do understand it, they will set even less value on it because they will understand it in their own fashion and believe they have learned nothing. Men who deem themselves learned very commonly see in the best books only what they already know, and consequently read them without learning anything new. They see nothing new in a work in which everything is new for them.

Therefore I write only for the uninstructed. Since they do not speak any scientific language they will find it easier to learn mine. It lies closer to hand than any other because I have learned it from nature, which will speak to them as it does to me.

If they find passages that trouble their understanding, they should guard against appealing to learned men such as I have just spoken of. They would do better to question uninstructed people who have read me with intelligence.

They should say to themselves, *In this work, the author proceeds from the known to the unknown; thus, the difficulty in understanding a chapter is due only to the fact that the preceding chapters are not sufficiently familiar to me.* They will then judge that they ought to retrace their steps, and if they have the patience to do so, they will understand me without needing to consult anyone. We never understand better than when we understand without outside help.

This logic is short, and hence it is not daunting. To read it with the reflection it requires will oblige you to take only the time that you would waste in reading some other logic.

Once you understand this logic—and by understand, I mean that you can recount it easily and if necessary expound it—when you understand it, I say, you can read a little less slowly those books in which the sciences are properly discussed, and sometimes you will even learn by rapid reading. For, to proceed rapidly from one bit of knowledge to another, it is sufficient to have adopted the method that is the one good one, and that is hence the same in all the sciences.

You can also acquire the facility provided by this logic by studying the preliminary lessons of my *Course of Study* if you add on the first part of the *Grammar*. Having studied these well, you will easily understand all my other works.

But I also want to warn young people against a prejudice natural to beginners. Because a method of reasoning ought to teach us to reason, we are apt to believe that, for each line of reasoning, the first thing we ought to do is to think about the rules for pursuing it, and here we are mistaken. It is not up to us to think of rules, it is up to them to guide us without our thinking about them. We would not speak if, before beginning each sentence, we had to concern ourselves with grammar. Now, like all languages, the art of reasoning, can be spoken well only insofar as it is spoken naturally. Reflect on this method, and reflect on it a lot. But do not think about it any longer when you want to think about something else. Some day it will become familiar to you. Then you will always have it, it will observe your thoughts that progress on their own, and it will watch over them in order to keep them from straying: that is all you ought to expect from this method. Fences are not placed along precipices to make the traveler walk, but to prevent him from tumbling down.

If, at the beginning, you have any trouble familiarizing yourself with this method, it is not because it is difficult: it cannot be, since it is natural. But it has become difficult for you whose nature has been corrupted by bad habits. Get rid of these habits and you will reason well naturally.

It may seem that I ought to have given this advice before the beginning of this logic, but it would not have been understood. Moverover, for those who knew how to read it from the first, this advice comes just as well at the end, as it does for others who will appreciate better the need they have of it.

CLARIFICATIONS REQUESTED BY MONSIEUR POTÉ DE LA DOCTRINE PROFESSOR AT PÉRIGUEUX

God can act only where he is; and God is simple. How can we reconcile these two assertions?

First let us establish that since all our knowledge comes from the senses, it extends only as far as our sensations do, and that beyond that, we can discover nothing. We stand in the same relation to truths to which our senses do not lead us, as the blind stand in relation to colors.

I think I have shown that any being who compares two ideas is necessarily simple, not compound. See the more reason then for God to be simple since he apprehends all relations and all possible truths.

On the other hand, it is obvious that he can act only where he is. Thus he is in all his works or rather, all his works are in him. *In ipso movemur et sumus.*

These are two truths. If I cannot reconcile them, it is because in this regard I am a blind man who cannot judge colors.

Are bodies really extended? Or do they seem to be extended without really being so? It is useless to question my senses. They cannot answer me. They were not given to me in order to judge what things are in themselves, but only to judge their real or apparent relations to me, and those that they have to each other, when it is useful for me to know them.

If bodies are really extended, there will be extension in God—extension in a nonextended being. If bodies are not extended, extension is like colors, that is, it is only a phenomenon, an appearance. Leibniz said this. But whatever side we take, difficulties ensue that my ignorance does not allow me to clear up. For this reason, it forbids me to decide anything.

It would be more impudent of me to judge duration and eternity. You say that *an instant is the sojourn that an idea makes in our mind.* I would not use the word *sojourn* which assumes what is in question, namely, that an instant is made up of several others. For *sojourn* brings in the idea of succession.

Now, if an instant is made up of several others, also made up of yet others, and so on without end, we would have to say that an instant contains an infinite succession. But let us consider our idea of duration, and let us see what we can conclude from it.

I know duration only through the succession of my ideas. If there is some duration other than this succession, I do not know it, I cannot know it, and I cannot judge it.

As soon as I know duration is only the succession of my ideas, then an instant is for me only the presence, without succession, of an idea in my mind. Presence, I repeat, and not *sojourn.*

Now an instant for me, or the presence of an idea in my mind, can coexist with several successive ideas in your mind, and which are as many instants for you. That is why I say that an instant in duration for one being can coexist with several instants in duration for another being.

I judge my duration without being able to judge yours, because I have no means of perceiving the succession of your ideas, I perceive only the succession of mine.

In the same way, we each judge our own duration without either of us able to judge the duration of any other thing; because it is not in themselves that we perceive the successions that the objects surrounding us undergo, it is uniquely in the succession happening within us.

The succession that produces duration in an external object is a series of changes that modify it in some way; the succession that produces it in us in a series of sensations or ideas. These two series would correspond to each other, instant for instant, if each change caused a sensation, which is not the case.

Why, for example, does the sun seem to be motionless to the eye? Because each successive change that it appears to describe in its orbits does not provoke a new sensation in the eye.

But is duration something other than the successive changes that occur in each creature? Is there some absolute duration with which the duration of each creature coexists instant for instant? Locke affirms this and believes he has proven it. As for me, I think that if there were such a duration, we could not judge it, for we can judge only insofar as we can see. And for us this duration would be what colors are for blind men.

I am not in the least afraid to say that such duration would be real only in our imagination which is only too ready to fantasize chimeras. Indeed, if this duration existed, it would be an attribute of some being. Now, what being? Of

God no doubt, since he has always been and will always be. But if God has duration, there would thus be succession in him. Consequently, he acquires, loses, changes, and is not immutable.

There can be succession only in what changes. There is change only in the things in which there is progress and decline. And the things in which there is progress or decline are necessarily imperfect: such are creatures.

In making creatures, God thus created the things in which there are necessarily progress, decline, change, succession, and hence duration. In creating these things, he thus created duration. Duration is thus not an attribute of God it is an attribute only of creatures. It is their manner of existing.

Now, as duration is the manner of creatures' existence, eternity is the manner of God's existence. This eternity is an instant that coexists with all the successive changes in created things—successive changes that do not correspond to each other instant for instant, just as the succession of my ideas does not correspond instant for instant to the succession of yours.

For each change there is in each creature an instant, and as a change in one creature coexists with several changes in another, it is a consequence that an instant coexists with several instants; in each creature, every change or instant is indivisible, because in every creature every change or instant is without succession.

Consequently, if we are led to suppose that there is a common duration, instant for instant, in each being, it is not that there is indeed such a duration; it is that our imagination generalizes the idea of our own duration, and attributes this duration—the only one we perceive—to everything that exists.